Artificial Intelligence and Sustainable Development

Series Editor

Tshilidzi Marwala, United Nations University
Shibuya-ku, Tokyo, Japan

Artificial Intelligence (AI) and Sustainable Development closes the divide between technology advancements and sustainable practices. The series investigates, clarifies, and promotes the incorporation of AI technology in tackling worldwide sustainability issues. The series accommodates a wide range of individuals, such as scholars, professionals, policymakers, and students, by offering them a thorough and all-encompassing source of information. The book series has the following specific objectives:

- AI Knowledge: Providing detailed insights on AI applications in sustainable development, trends, and successful implementations.
- Interdisciplinary Collaboration: Promoting cooperation among experts in AI, environmental science, economics, and social sciences.
- Innovation and Best Practices: Showcasing AI applications in agriculture, energy, water management, and waste management for global adoption.
- Ethical Use of AI: Addressing ethical considerations, risks, and governance challenges, promoting transparent and accountable AI systems.
- Policy Influence: Guiding policymakers with evidence-based insights for ethical AI use in sustainability.
- Global Awareness and Knowledge Transfer: Enhancing awareness and transferring advanced technology to less developed regions.

Opeoluwa Israel Akinradewo •
Clinton Ohis Aigbavboa •
Ayodeji Emmanuel Oke

Blockchain Technology for Information Management: A New Era for Sustainable Construction Practices

Springer

Opeoluwa Israel Akinradewo
Department of Quantity Surveying and Construction Management, Faculty of Natural and Agricultural Sciences
University of the Free State
Bloemfontein, South Africa

Ayodeji Emmanuel Oke
SARChI in Sustainable Construction Management and Leadership in the Built Environment, Faculty of Engineering and the Built Environment
University of Johannesburg
Johannesburg, South Africa

Clinton Ohis Aigbavboa
SARChI in Sustainable Construction Management and Leadership in the Built Environment, Faculty of Engineering and the Built Environment
University of Johannesburg
Johannesburg, Gauteng, South Africa

ISSN 3059-2984 ISSN 3059-2992 (electronic)
Artificial Intelligence and Sustainable Development
ISBN 978-981-95-2663-5 ISBN 978-981-95-2664-2 (eBook)
https://doi.org/10.1007/978-981-95-2664-2

This Springer imprint is published by the registered company Springer Nature Singapore Pte Ltd.
The registered company address is: 152 Beach Road, #21-01/04 Gateway East, Singapore 189721, Singapore

This book is dedicated to God Almighty, the giver of knowledge.

Preface

In today's digital age, the construction industry is on the brink of a technological revolution, and blockchain technology plays a central role. Blockchain is crucial for construction because the industry is becoming more complex, and there's a growing need for reliable data, efficient project management, and better collaboration among stakeholders. Traditional information systems are struggling to keep up with these demands, making a book like this important and necessary. This book bridges the theoretical potential of blockchain and its practical application in the real world of construction. It offers a unique chance to reshape how construction projects are managed and to tackle issues like isolated information systems, fragmentation of information, and inefficiencies. Researchers and practitioners in the construction industry face the challenge of understanding the technical aspects of blockchain and how it can benefit construction specifically. This book aims to guide all construction stakeholders on this path, highlighting the exciting possibilities and manageable challenges ahead.

The book offers a comprehensive guide on embedding blockchain technology into construction information management, emphasising sustainable practices and the broader socio-economic impacts. It moves beyond mere technical integration, presenting a practical blueprint that aligns with environmental stewardship and sustainable development goals. This guide equips readers with the tools to implement blockchain effectively and encourages a holistic view of construction processes, considering technological adoption's social and ethical dimensions. In exploring the technical facets of blockchain and its application to the construction industry, the book tailors its approach to address the unique challenges and opportunities in this field, strongly focusing on promoting sustainability practices. It also delves into the human and cultural aspects, examining how blockchain technology can enhance transparency, accountability, and stakeholder engagement in construction projects.

Furthermore, the book provides a forward-looking analysis, preparing readers for future trends and ensuring the adaptability of the developed framework to evolving sustainability standards and societal expectations. Additionally, it offers detailed insights into the legal and regulatory attributes governing blockchain use, with a particular emphasis on compliance, ethical considerations, and social responsibility.

This comprehensive approach ensures that readers can navigate the complex landscape of blockchain adoption in construction, making informed decisions that benefit the industry and the broader community.

Bloemfontein, South Africa Opeoluwa I. Akinradewo
Johannesburg, South Africa Clinton O. Aigbavboa
Johannesburg, South Africa Ayodeji E. Oke

Competing Interests The authors have no competing interests to declare that are relevant to the content of this manuscript.

Contents

About the Authors

Opeoluwa Israel Akinradewo is an academic and professional in Quantity Surveying and Construction Management. He is currently a Senior Lecturer at the University of the Free State, Bloemfontein, South Africa. His extensive education includes a PhD in Construction Management from the University of Johannesburg, an M.Tech in Quantity Surveying from the University of Johannesburg, a Diploma in Blockchain from the University of Zurich, and a B.Tech in Quantity Surveying at the Federal University of Technology, Akure. Dr. Akinradewo has published extensively, contributing to over 150 peer-reviewed journal articles and conference papers, with research interests in blockchain technology, construction automation, and sustainable construction practices.

Clinton Ohis Aigbavboa is a distinguished scholar with over 18 years of experience in the Built Environment and Construction sectors. He is a Professor of Sustainable Construction Digitalisation and Construction Industry Research at the University of Johannesburg. He holds a PhD in Engineering Management, a Master's in Construction Management, and certifications in Good Governance and Artificial Intelligence from MIT. He has authored over 30 research books, co-authored six edited books, and published over 1000 accredited journal articles and conference papers. His research interests include Construction 4.0, smart cities, sustainable human development, and digitalisation in construction.

Ayodeji Emmanuel Oke is an Associate Professor at the Department of Quantity Surveying, Federal University of Technology Akure, Nigeria. He won the Best Researcher award during the 2023 Excellence and Productivity Award ceremony at the Federal University of Technology Akure, achieving the runner-up of the same award in 2022. Prof. Oke is an author and a lecturer with several years of teaching and research involvement in higher learning institutions worldwide. He founded the Research Group on Sustainable Infrastructure Management Plus (RG-SIM+) at the Federal University of Technology, Akure, and he is currently the team leader. Prof. Oke's research interest is in sustainable infrastructure management (SIM), emphasising sustainable construction, value management, quantity surveying, and construction in the digital era.

Chapter 1
Introduction to Sustainable Construction Information Management

Abstract The construction industry is experiencing a paradigm shift driven by the increasing need for efficiency, sustainability, and technological integration. This chapter explores the concept of sustainable construction information management by establishing a foundational understanding of information, management, and their intersection as a strategic tool for project success. Information is recognized not merely as data but as contextually interpreted knowledge essential for decision-making, communication, and coordination. Management, on the other hand, involves planning, organizing, and utilizing resources to achieve defined objectives. The convergence of these concepts has evolved into the practice of information management, which plays a critical role in enhancing performance across construction projects. The chapter delves into how the construction industry, despite its traditional reliance on paper-based systems, is adopting digital technologies to improve collaboration and streamline operations. It reviews various information management systems and tools used to facilitate sustainable practices such as project management information systems (PMIS), computer-aided design (CAD), and cost estimation software. By leveraging these tools, construction professionals can enhance data accuracy, reduce project inefficiencies, and support environmentally responsible development. The chapter concludes by emphasizing the importance of digital transformation in achieving sustainable construction outcomes through effective information management.

Keywords Information management · Construction industry · Sustainability · Digital transformation · Project efficiency

1.1 Introduction

In the evolving landscape of the construction industry, the importance of information management has become increasingly evident. As construction projects grow in complexity and demand greater collaboration among stakeholders, the need for

O. I. Akinradewo et al., *Blockchain Technology for Information Management: A New Era for Sustainable Construction Practices*, Artificial Intelligence and Sustainable Development, https://doi.org/10.1007/978-981-95-2664-2_1

efficient, accurate, and timely information handling is critical. Information, which is multidisciplinary in nature, serves as a central resource for communication and decision-making. In the construction context, the ability to interpret, disseminate, and manage information effectively can significantly influence project success, cost control, quality assurance, and time management. Information is not simply data; it encompasses knowledge, interpretation, context, and meaning (Davenport and Marchand 2000; Sheriff et al. 2012). In construction, this distinction is vital because decisions rely on contextualized data interpreted by professionals across various disciplines. Capurro and Hjørland (2003) emphasized that nearly every scientific and technical discipline utilizes information within its own contextual framework, which is particularly relevant in construction where architectural, engineering, and management functions intersect. As a result, understanding and managing information is crucial for effective communication, collaboration, and operational excellence.

In today's global construction environment, the pressure to deliver sustainable, efficient, and cost-effective projects has never been higher. The digitalization of information processes offers a pathway to address these pressures while fostering innovation and competitiveness. Thus, understanding the foundations and practical applications of sustainable construction information management is essential for stakeholders aiming to thrive in a digitally driven construction ecosystem. This chapter introduces the core concepts of information, management, and their intersection as information management within the construction industry. It explores the evolution of information management practices, the tools that facilitate them, and the implications of digital transformation for sustainable project delivery. Through this, the chapter aims to provide a foundational understanding of how information can be strategically managed to enhance the performance and sustainability of construction projects.

1.2 The Concept of Information

The concept of information is multidisciplinary in nature and perceived differently by various authors. The concept has been defined by various authors based on their knowledge of what it entails. According to Ellis (1998), information was coined from a layman's view as an item of intelligence; a fact or circumstance of which one is told. In the work of McCreadie and Rice (1999), the concept of information was reviewed over the past five decades. The following summary of the concepts was put forward as follows: Information as a representation of knowledge (information is stored knowledge); Information as data in the environment (information can be derived from a variety of environmental stimuli and phenomena, not all of which are meant to communicate a message but can be informative when understood correctly); and information is part of the communication process (meanings are found in people, not words or data). In the processing and interpretation of information, timing and social factors play a key role. Therefore, information is a resource or commodity (information is sent from sender to recipient in the form of a message). The communication is interpreted by the receiver in the same way that it was intended by the sender. As the knowledge is distributed or exchanged, there may be added value.

Information is derived from the interpretation and understanding of data contextually (Capurro 1996). Decisions, emotions, expertise, judgement and knowledge are expressed through information by individuals (Davenport and Marchand 2000; Sheriff et al. 2012). Radović-Marković and Vučeković (2015) further expressed information as converted data that users find usable owing to its value. Information, as used in everyday English, has been adjudged to be important in any contemporary society (Capurro and Hjørland 2003). This is because IT is gaining more ground globally even though knowledge and its communication are the basic characteristics that improve every human society. Capurro (1996) stated further that information can be considered the basic requirement to achieve economic growth in a society coupled with labour, capital and raw material availability. However, what makes information stand out is its digital nature. Based on the foregoing, Capurro and Hjørland (2003) opined that "*almost every scientific discipline uses the concept of information within its own context and with regard to specific phenomena*". However, Machlup (1983) sees information as a human phenomenon that is characterised by messages being transmitted and received by individuals for possible actions. In support of this view, Capurro (1996) established that information is "*an anthropological category concerning the phenomenon of human messages, whose vertical and horizontal structures are related to the Greek concept of message (angelia) as well as to philosophical discourse (logos).*" From these presentations, it can be concluded that information serves as an entity for communication to be achieved among individuals to ensure action is taken by the receiver.

The term 'information' has been widely used side by side with IT and information systems (Hollander et al. 1999). For example, in the view of Laudon and Laudon (2000), technology includes a computer-based system of information and also refers to a group of system computers that are being controlled by a human (Laudon and Laudon 2000; Turban et al. 2004). To give a more detailed explanation and clarification on the concept of IT, according to Lin (2007), it is the study, development support or management, design, and implementation of computer-based information systems especially for computer hardware and software applications. The Information Technology Association of America (ITAA) (2010) further asserted that IT involved the use of computer software and electronic computers in the conversion, protection, storage, retrieving, transmitting and processing of information. Also, Bjork (1999) maintained that the definition of IT deals with the use of programs and electronic machines in transferring, presenting, processing and storing information. Turban et al. (2007) noted that an information system, which is also referred to as IT, is the collection of components that process, analyse, store and distribute information for various reasons. From the foregoing regarding the meaning of IT, it could be conceptualised as any form of technology that is used by companies in collecting, processing and disseminating data in any form (Laudon and Laudon 1995). This includes the use of IT hardware (such as scanners, mouse, monitors, printers, and computers, among others), software applications (such as office applications, programming language, operating systems, among others), and telecommunication equipment. IT includes components such as people, database, procedure, hardware, purpose, social context, documents and software (Capurro 1996; Turban et al. 2009).

1.3 The Concept of Management

Management has been conceptualised by several scholars (Stoner et al. 1995; Naylor 2004; Robbins and Coulter 2005; Schermerhorn 2005; Jones and George 2018; Boddy 2017; Griffin 2013; Cole and Kelly 2015). The concept of management, according to Griffin (2013), involves various activities which are directed at the resources of an organisation (such as people, information, finance and physical) to attain the goals of an organisation efficiently and effectively. Griffin (2013) further opined that management is about organising, leading, controlling, planning and making decisions. Hitt et al. (2012) viewed the concept of management as the method of gathering and using groupings of resources towards a goal-directed manager in completing the task within an organisation. Williams (2018) observed it as the process of getting work done through others. The concept of management was perceived in the view of Certo and Certo (2016) as ways of achieving the goal and objectives of an organisation by collaborating with the people and through the people and their resources.

The definition of management was further observed by Jones and George (2018) as the way of organizing, planning, leading and regulating people and other projects that are research based to meet the goals of an organisation effectively and efficiently. Other definitions of management were collated from various authors. For example, Taylor (1911) asserted that management is about having the exact understating on what is expected that men to do and ensuring that they do it to the best of their capacity and most cheaply. Drucker (1954) defined the meaning of management as a multipurpose organ that manages businesses, managers, workers and work. Koontz (1961), Montana and Charnov (2008), and Boddy (2017) postulated management as the art of getting things done through people in a formal group that is organised. Koontz (1961) further contended that it is the art of creating an organised environment where people can perform a cooperatively or as individuals toward the attainment of their goals. Dunham and Pierce (1989), Aldag and Steams (1991), Stoner et al. (1995) and Schermerhorn (2005) refer to management as the process of planning, directing, controlling, staffing, and directing organisational resources in achieving organisational goals. According to Bovee et al. (1993), management is the process of leading, organizing, planning, and controlling human, financial, physical and information resources of the organisation in achieving organisational goals. Bedeian (1993) and Malik (2000) noted that it is the process of attaining desired results through the effective and efficient usage of human and material resources. Naylor (2004) added to the concept of management as the ways of attaining organisational goals in a changing environment by balancing equity, effectiveness and efficiency, achieving the most from limited resources and working with other people. In the view of Robbins and Coulter (2005), management deals with the coordination of work activities with and through the people so that they can be effective and efficient. Mintzberg (2009) observed management as the process of helping organizations and units to get work done while Robbins and Coulter (2016) defined it as the way of coordinating and monitoring the activities of an organisation by assembling and using sets of resources in a goal-directed manner to complete the task in an organisation. It is also the act of working through and with a group of people to attaining an expected goal or objective effectively and efficiently (Gulati et al. 2017; Bateman et al. 2018; Williams 2018). Kinichi and Williams (2018) combined different elements of other definitions and defined it as the pursuit of goals of an organisation by integrating people's work through the organisation, leading, planning, and directing the resources of an organisation.

From the above definitions, it can be seen that various management scholars have viewed the concept of management from different perceptives. Furthermore, different management thinkers emphasized different aspects. For example, Henry Fayol (1916) referred to management as the art or activities of planning, organizing, commanding, coordinating, and regulating (in recent definitions, 'commanding' has been replaced with 'leading'). The second component is to use people or, in a less constricted situation, resources in general. According to a popular quote often attributed to Das and Mishra (2019), management is "the art of getting things done through people". This is one of the major definitions on which most of the earlier definitions built. The third aspect is that management seeks to achieve sets of goals and objectives which the other definitions do not articulate very well in their explanations. Having examined the concept of information and management, the next section discusses information in the construction industry.

1.3.1 Attributes of Management

The review of various concepts of management shows that management has certain attributes. This subsection outlines the major attributes of management as follows:

1. **Management is seen as a factor of production:** One of the targets of the managers of any organisation is to ensure that the performance of production is secured through planning, directing, and controlling. The expectation of management is to achieve desired outcomes (D4H 2021).
2. **Management is observed to infer experience and skill in ensuring that things are done through and with the people.** Most works that are done under management involves people. The ability to earn profit return from a job done cannot be completed without including the cooperation of and securing better responses from people (Detlor 2010).

3. **Management is perceived as a process:** Functions or processes are an attribute of management. The process continues from one stage to the next until the objectives that have been set by the organisation are achieved through the coordination of human and material resources by organising, leading, staffing and controlling to attain the stated objectives (Campos 2016).
4. **Management is opined as a form of activities:** Management does not only apply to a business that is an undertaking; it also deals with the social, religious, and political institutions (Mabope 2018).
5. **Management is noted as the combination of activity:** The existence of management is seen when there is a combination of activity toward the achievement of desired goals and objectives (Goodman 2009).
6. **Management is observed to be goal-oriented**: Management is a group of activities with a pre-determined target to be achieved (Hitt et al. 2012).
7. **Management deals with decision-making:** It could be inferred from the definitions that management involves the act or process of making organisational and business decisions although in different dimensions (Williams 2018).

1.3.2 Scope of Management

The scope of management includes different aspects, according to Das and Mishra (2019), such as matters of management (i.e., planning, staffing, controlling, directing, and organising), functional areas of management (i.e., financial, human resource, marketing, production, material, purchasing and maintenance management), essentials of management (i.e., scientific method, human relation and quantitative techniques) among others. In addition to these core functions, the scope of management also includes other important areas such as decision-making, innovation, and ethics (Derenskaya 2018). Effective management requires a combination of knowledge, skills, and abilities in all of these areas to ensure the success of an organisation (Das and Mishra 2019).

1.4 The Concept of Information Management

The term 'information management' (IM) has been bandied about for a while; however, no single definition has emerged from the academic literature or professional practice to gain widespread acceptance (Vodáček and Vodáčková 1996). This is owing to the different phases in which scholars had attempted to provide a definition for it; nevertheless, the definitions extend beyond the initial opinion (Estélyiová 2012). During the first phase, which lasted until the middle of the 1960s, IM was seen as primarily responsible for ensuring 'engineering efficiency' in the solution of technical and technological tasks through the careful selection and application of data, methods, and approaches (Taylor 1966). In the latter part of the 1970s, the term 'information management' (IM) became commonly used for certain data processing tasks, such as organising information resources in technical documentation, libraries, and the likes (Estélyiová 2012; Vodáček and Vodáčková 1996).

The second phase of IM's history covers the decade between the late 1970s and early 1980s, when the term was most commonly applied to the practices and procedures used by informatics experts in their daily work (Estélyiová and Koráb 2011). Focus had been placed on managerial strategies and methods for the effective management of information resources, especially with regard to the creation, distribution, and consumption of information systems (ISs) (Earl 1989). Earl saw IM as managerial support for handling information because planning, organisation, and control are central to most conceptualizations of sequential managerial functions (Estélyiová and Koráb 2011; Vodáček and Vodáčková 1996).

Since the early 1990s, the third phase has seen the concept of IM evolve to better reflect the importance placed on IS/IT by managers (Říhová 2015). The focus is on how IS/IT is ultimately put to use, specifically in the creative resolution of managerial tasks and, most importantly, the efficient realisation of the organization's mission and goals. It is clear that people are starting to care more about whether their data processing is efficient ("doing the right things") (Best 1996; Estélyiová 2012).

1.5 Information Management in the Construction Industry

Given the increased focus on information resources, improved management of these resources may become important to project success (Dikbas et al. 1999). Information technologies (IT) are useful in the creation of new opportunities (such as coordination, collaboration and information sharing among related construction organisations) in the construction industry (Craig and Sommerville 2007). However, the unique characteristics of IT often affect the progress of IT implementation in the construction industry. This makes it different from other industries such as industry fragmentation, one-off projects, low awareness of the technology and training, ongoing maintenance cost, required up-front investment and resistance to change (Feng 2006; Sommerville et al. 2010). In all elements of project planning, organization, operation, and control, IT tends to be more useful. However, within the construction industry, IT is not as effective as it is in other industries (Sun and Howard 2003).

The construction industry maintains a vast amount of information flow on a project. According to Chalmers (2010), the term 'information technology' refers to the information systems that is used to process project data. The engineering information management system (EIMS), and the enterprise resource management system (ERMS) are the two main types of information systems adopted in the built environment as noted by Winch (2010). The EIMS is more concerned about the project's information while the ERMS deals with the information that is being processed. The confluence of both systems is referred to as a project management information system (PMIS) (Maritz 2003).

1.5.1 Exchange of Information in the Construction Industry

According to Shafique and Mahmood (2010), the IT revolution has established a platform for the global free movement of information, ideas, and expertise. The revolution has the potential to bring about significant improvements in the construction industry's utilization of data and information (Datti 2017). The customers, their team of professional advisers (consultants), the main contractor, subcontractors, and suppliers are all directly involved in the construction industry. Architects, engineers, and quantity surveyors make up the consultant team. The consultants create the documents and information (drawings, bills of quantities, specifications, and equipment schedules) that all project participants will need at some time during the project's construction (Shafique and Mahmood 2010). As observed by Luiten et al. (1998), paper documents (i.e., engineering and architectural drawings, material schedules, and specification bills of quantities) have traditionally been used to convey information among project stakeholders (Datti 2017). From architecture and design to building and operation and maintenance, the process requires a wide range of skills, expertise, and disciplines. Clients who commission work, planners, regulators, future occupants and users, and society as a whole all have an impact on the process (Shafique and Mahmood 2010). Each of these stakeholders must have access, create, share and interpret different sorts of information: visualisations, specifications, architectural plans and models, structural calculations, plans of work, bills of quantities, and quality assessments, among others. Duyshart (1997) added that duplication, information loss, continuous transcription and interpretation from one form to another, are the factors that are involved. As a result, satisfaction is far from the practice, as more than two-thirds of most building problems are attributed to a lack of communication and data exchange. (Cornick 1990). IT usage does not only help to minimize such issues, but it also helps to improve the process (Oladapo 2007; Datti 2017). This explains the present construction sector's shift in paradigm from the old ways of practice, which is paper based, to a modern way of sharing information that is digitally based. According to Rivard et al. (2004), the digitally based method of sharing information has been adopted in other industries such as finance and aircraft manufacture.

Microelectronics, in combination with computing and telecommunications, is transforming IM and storage (Smith 2003; Datti 2017). Large volumes of data can now be stored, retrieved, rearranged, and disseminated almost instantaneously thanks to microelectronics. Computing and telecommunications have combined to allow/enable people to communicate over long distances and with large groups of people (Fryer 1990). A sketch, for example, can be changed on a computer in a country and accurately duplicated on paper in another country in a matter of seconds. Software and databases will need to grow in a compatible manner as information flows progressively become electronic quantity surveying computer tools (Serpell et al. 2005). Documentation and data will inevitably become more automated to the level at which measurement and other technical operations will only require minimal human interaction (Smith 2003; Datti 2017).

1.5.2 Available Information Management Tools in the Construction Industry

Extant studies have shown that successes recorded in the building industry are projected to bring about more investment in technology, especially in the IT field (Gaith et al. 2012). In recent years, IT has become an intrinsic aspect of many fundamental business activities as a result of the technology revolution (Shafique and Mahmood 2010). Gaith et al. (2012) further noted that the majority of the functions of management, particularly planning and organizing activities are contributed by modern information technology. With the level of modernization and civilization, the usage of IT in the construction industry is expected to increase (Maskuriy et al. 2019). Most of the stakeholders within the built environment have now understood the potency of IT in enhancing activities of the construction industry, especially in obtaining and maintaining a competitive advantage (Li et al. 2000).

As a result, the increasing demand on the design and construction industry or firms has brought about the need for new technology (Ahmed et al. 1995). In spite of the increasing demand, the level of success recorded in the implementation is still low. The introduction of IT into a company is a test of its efficiency. Information and communication technology provide forward-thinking construction firms with new ways to cooperate, communicate, and achieve information flow more efficiently and effectively (Bowden et al. 2006; Maskuriy et al. 2019). According to the findings of the study by Li et al. (2000), in addition to building, architecture appears to profit greatly from the usage of IT. As the industry grows more technologically oriented, IT investment is expected to rise in the near future. Miyatake and Kangari (1993) stated that IT should be seen as a significant resource in today's professional practice and that the automatic flow of relevant information throughout a corporation is critical. Akinsola et al. (2000) asserted that business integration and other strategies have developed from the industrial sector in the past 30 years or more.

Previous studies have shown their successful application and strategies in the manufacturing industry. Others have supplied researchers with the motivation to adopt the idea in the construction business (Demian and Walters 2014; Maskuriy et al. 2019). Implementing IT is regarded as one of the most effective and strategic management tools for increasing competitiveness and productivity. One of the focuses of IT is to increase communication and information transmission among a company's employees or team personnel, which explains the process of design in control and management (Luiten and Tolman 1997; Maskuriy et al. 2019). When properly implemented, strategic systems have a favourable impact on the business of a company's survival and growth (Cleveland 1997). Akinsola et al. (2000) added that one aspect of this strategy adopted from the manufacturing operation is based on the concept of a 'single point of responsibility' in that one organization is responsible for the design and construction of structures. As a result, there has been a significant cultural shift, as well as an increase in the development of new alternatives and variations on old methods (Demian and Walters 2014). The early involvement of contractors in pre-construction activities as a means of bridging the gap between design and building is one of the most important aspects of development (Maskuriy et al. 2019). Unfortunately, without the backing of integrated IT, this method has proven insufficient in tackling the increasing complexity of construction projects (Serpell et al. 2005). A major shift in the prominence of IT has occurred during the past 30 years. Amenity design, delivery process design, and organization design are all simulated, analyzed, and assessed using IT by building specialists (Shafique and Mahmood 2010).

According to Michel et al. (2000), implementation of IT programs in some core areas (i.e., encouragement of technological innovation, creation of sustainable economy and environment, emphasizing global business opportunities, and supporting a well-informed market) has strong international consensus to improve the reform agenda of the construction industry (Maskuriy et al. 2019). As a result of the emergence of new communication technologies, companies are now able to better compete in the marketplace (Serpell et al. 2005). As IT helps companies automate many of their manual processes, it also creates enormous volumes of data, most of which is kept in elaborate databases and knowledge repositories (Michel et al. 2000; Maskuriy et al. 2019). Tuman (1998) found that information overload eventually leads to problems with data communication in and among teams. Nevertheless, when IT is combined with sufficient network connectivity, there is the possibility of managing projects through the teams of project management which are made of up different stakeholders or personnel within the built environment, states and nations (Demian and Walters 2014).

Virtual project management teams have demonstrated improved control over the design process and design revisions as a consequence of leveraging IT services. Project managers in the construction industry rely heavily on reliable computer networking systems to make virtual teams successful (Anumba et al. 2008). Traditional project management methods have adopted computer technologies for tracking and reporting on projects. Instead, virtual project management teams are totally dependent on technology and would cease to exist without it (Michel et al. 2000; Maskuriy et al. 2019). Every sector need information, and it is a significant investment for a firm to prosper. Information is more important than ever before. The evolution of IT has considerably aided the way a company conducts business (Demian and Walters 2014). The majority of sectors have transitioned from a paper-based to digital-based information exchange (Rivard et al. 2004; Maskuriy et al. 2019). Many domains of activities, such as stages of construction particularly in planning, designing, procurement, and operations on the site; digital sites, as well as adding IT and automation in operations on site, could enjoy technological-based predicted gains and impacts (Mahadevan and Vijayakumar 2012). In addition, corporate operations, project management, and contractual and legal issues can be attended to using IT (Amusan et al. 2018). Building and construction life cycle performance; monitoring and performance measurements; quick, efficient, and cost-effective construction; building product customisation and differentiation; supply chain management; and costing and accounting activities are all examples of where ICT is used (Rudden 2019).

Most components of a building project can be supported by IT (Sun and Howard 2004). These technologies were primarily designed to address specific problems. The software applications or information technology could be grouped into the following, namely building engineering applications; business and information management; computer-aided cost estimation; computer aided design and visualization; computer aided facilities management; integration; planning, scheduling, and site management (Maskuriy et al. 2019).

1.5.2.1 Computer-Aided Facilities Management (CAFM) Tools

There are administrative and scheduling functions in CAFM software that help project managers schedule and keep track of facility operations. This job is more closely related to administrative duties than with technical ones (Subramani et al. 2014). By using CAFM systems, for example, it is possible to record information on departments and employees, access permissions and security levels for leased spaces, and information on tenant chargebacks. With the use of the database of a CAFM system, a 4-D simulation may be generated that can be used to schedule and optimize changes and eventually evolve into the field of change management (Shahrubudin et al. 2019). It is possible to incorporate other parameters such as cost and performance when modelling facilities and their circumstances. This new technology is known as n-D. With the passage of time, all facilities will eventually be digitally modelled. Because the model will change as the project progresses, standard methods of disclosing information will become superfluous (Atkins and Brooks 2009).

1.5.2.2 Building Engineering Applications

Nowadays, customers in the construction business have high expectations. They want their buildings to look attractive, to be secure, to be comfortable for their occupants, and to consume less energy when they are in use (Serpell et al. 2005). Building engineering design has had to adopt a new technique based on computer software owing to the growing complexity of the process. Correcting a building's architectural problems after construction has begun is prohibitively expensive. In order that faults may be discovered and fixed, it is vital that the building's efficiency be simulated accurately throughout the design process (Subramani et al. 2014). To predict a building's thermal, lighting, acoustic, and structural performance, several algorithms and methodologies have been created throughout the years. Atan and Climasoft's CARGASW are two examples of this type of application. Other examples are Calculux for lighting and building services design, CYPE INGENIEROS S.A for structural design, COSMOS for finite element analysis, and Elite Software's DUCTSIZE for electrical nets and water nets design (Shahrubudin et al. 2019).

1.5.2.3 Computer-Aided Design and Visualization Tools

According to Narayan (2008), computer-aided design (CAD) refers to the use of computer systems in the development, modification, analysis or optimization of a design. Computer technology is used in the design and documentation stages of CAD. CAD software, a type of computer program that replaces labour-intensive manual drafting with a speedy digital procedure, is used for this function. Idea research, concept visualization through animations and photorealistic renderings, and design simulation are all made easier with CAD software. According to Charles et al. (2004), visualization is essentially the creation of a mental picture of an idea or object. According to Langerdorf (1992), such a picture can be graphically translated using CAD or computer-generated imagery (CGI). To convey a message, the technique generates images, diagrams, or animations. Since the dawn of time, visual imagery has been an effective means of communicating both abstract and concrete ideas. Such images can now be represented in 3-D as virtual reality images thanks to recent advances in computer technology. Bourdakis (1997) defined virtual reality as an artificial environment created with an application and addressed to the user in such a way that the client willingly suspend disbelief and acknowledges it as a real environment. The most basic form of virtual reality is a 3-D image that can be an ionic interaction on a desktop computer by trying to manipulate keys or the computer keyboard so that the image's content moves in some direction or zooms in or out (Shahrubudin et al. 2019).

1.5.2.4 Planning, Scheduling, Site Management and Construction Tools

Projects requiring construction involve precise planning and skilful management of both human and physical resources to be successful (Mahalingam et al. 2010). Planning ahead, evaluating choices and selecting the most effective building operation may all be done with the aid of computer systems (Shahrubudin et al. 2019). JobMaster, ICON, GEST, and Presto Control are just some of the applications that may be used to track and monitor internal operations and project construction in addition to the frequently used planning packages such as Microsoft Project, Primavera, Power Project, and others (Subramani et al. 2014). It is possible to use a site operation simulation program to model what happens on an actual construction site by attempting to represent personnel, machinery, and supplies and computing the cycle to each step while taking into consideration various unpredictable elements (Paulson 1995).

1.5.2.5 Computer-Aided Cost Estimation Tools

The ability to control the cost of project during project construction is regarded as the requirement that is very important (Hu et al. 2016). For there to be any form of accomplishment, contractors as well as subcontracting clients must first estimate costs accurately. To control spending, a rigorous estimation of a project would have to be adopted. In the recent times, complex packages of system software packages, such as Soft's Esti-Mate, Manifest, FBS-Estimator, and PRESTOR, Star's GO, and AM2's ITEC and ARQ, enable project managers to develop estimates and maintain track of project spending (Akinradewo et al. 2020).

1.5.2.6 Business and Information Management Tools

One of the very intensive aspects in the process of construction is how to manage information, with a large amount of created as well as absorbed information that includes all the professionals in the built environment (Zhu et al. 2017). Site surveys, cost analyses, design drawings, documents, correspondence, faxes, computer files, and emails are all examples of common types of information. A system that involves the management of electronic documents could be of help in the creation of a better environment where various types of information could attached together in the purview of projects or organizations for easy control as well as accessibility (Morgan 2019). The entire formal cost estimating, planning, as well as scheduling tools and system applications would be developed at a specific project or construction level. At any moment during the project, the information can be revised, altered, or contacted. As a result, the system of managing document is a tool that consist of whichever information is required through the entire project's phases, from the conceptualisation of such a requirement to reach the level of servicing (Luiten and Tolman 1997; Shibeika and Harty 2015).

1.6 Summary

This chapter provided an in-depth exploration of sustainable construction information management, beginning with the foundational concepts of information and management. Information was examined as a multidimensional concept involving knowledge, data interpretation, and communication, while management was reviewed as the process of organizing and coordinating resources to achieve specific goals efficiently and effectively. The convergence of these two concepts forms the basis of information management, which has evolved over time from basic data handling to a strategic organizational function. The chapter further discussed the significance of information management within the construction industry, highlighting its role in enhancing communication, coordination, and decision-making across project phases. Despite challenges such as project fragmentation and resistance to change, the construction sector is increasingly adopting information technologies to improve performance. Various information management tools and systems—such as project management information systems, computer-aided design, cost estimation software, and planning applications—were reviewed for their contributions to efficient project delivery. The chapter emphasized the transformative impact of digital technologies in construction, particularly in fostering sustainable practices. By leveraging modern information systems, stakeholders can manage data more effectively, reduce inefficiencies, and enhance collaboration. Overall, the chapter establishes a foundational understanding of how information management underpins sustainable construction practice in the modern era.

References

Ahmed, S. M., R. L. Tucker, and D. R. Smith. 1995. Transformation issues in the construction industry. *Journal of Construction Engineering and Management* 121 (2): 177–188.

Akinradewo, O., A. E. Oke, and C. O. Aigbavboa. 2020. *Cost estimation practice of construction professionals in Nigeria*. Springer.

Akinsola, A. O., K. F. Potts, I. Ndekugri, and F. C. Harris. 2000. Project delivery and procurement systems: A primer for owners and developers. *Construction Management and Economics* 18 (2): 143–153.

Aldag, R. J., and T. M. Stearns. 1991. *Management*. 2nd ed. Cincinnati: South-Western.

Amusan, L. M., J. A. Awotinde, and S. E. Ajiboye. 2018. ICT utilization trends and barriers in construction project delivery in Nigeria. *International Journal of Civil Engineering and Technology* 9 (3): 944–954.

Anumba, C. J., D. Bouchlaghem, J. Whyte, and A. Duke. 2008. Perspectives on an integrated IT infrastructure for collaborative design, construction and operation of buildings. *Automation in Construction* 17 (2): 111–121.

Atkins, P. W., and J. H. Brooks. 2009. *Total facilities management*. 3rd ed. Wiley-Blackwell.

Bateman, T. S., S. A. Snell, and R. Konopaske. 2018. *Management: Leading & collaborating in a competitive world*. 13th ed. McGraw-Hill Education.

Bedeian, A. 1993. *Management*. 3rd ed. Orlando: The Dryden Press.

Best, D. 1996. The role of information systems in strategic planning. *Journal of Strategic Information Systems* 5 (4): 255–271.

Bjork, B. C. 1999. Information technology in construction: Domain definition and research issues. *International Journal of Computer Integrated Design and Construction* 1 (1): 3–16.

Boddy, D. 2017. *Management: An introduction*. 7th ed. Pearson Education.

Bourdakis, V. 1997. Virtual reality: A communication tool for urban planning. In *Proceedings of the 2nd UK VR-SIG conference*, 17–24.

Bovee, C. L., J. V. Thill, and M. H. Mescon. 1993. *Excellence in business*. McGraw-Hill.

Bowden, S., A. Dorr, A. Thorpe, and C. Anumba. 2006. Mobile ICT support for construction process improvement. *Automation in Construction* 15 (5): 664–676.

Campos, M. L. 2016. Management process as a factor of production. *International Journal of Advanced Studies in Economics and Public Sector Management* 4 (2): 77–85.

Capurro, R. 1996. Information and digital technology. In *The philosophy of information*, ed. I. Cornelius and M. Featherston, 25–42. Queensland University of Technology.

Capurro, R., and B. Hjørland. 2003. The concept of information. *Annual Review of Information Science and Technology* 37 (1): 343–411. https://doi.org/10.1002/aris.1440370109.

Certo, S. C., and S. T. Certo. 2016. *Modern management: Concepts and skills*. 14th ed. Pearson.

Chalmers, M. 2010. *Information systems and project data: A conceptual exploration*. Routledge.

Charles, S., M. C. Ang, and M. Munro. 2004. Visualization and simulation: A review. *ITcon* 9:83–96.

Cleveland, A. D. 1997. Information and knowledge resources: The impact of technology. *Annual Review of Information Science and Technology* 32:3–35.

Cole, G. A., and P. Kelly. 2015. *Management theory and practice*. 8th ed. Cengage Learning EMEA.

Cornick, T. 1990. *Quality management for building design*. Butterworth-Heinemann.

Craig, R., and J. Sommerville. 2007. *Information management systems on construction projects*. Spon Press.

D4H. 2021. Information management: Challenges in an emergency response. D4H Technologies. www.d4htechnologies.com/blog/6-informationmanagement-challenges-in-an-emergency-response. Accessed 6 Sept 2021.

Das, S., and S. Mishra. 2019. *Principles of management*. New Age International.

Datti, Y. Y. 2017. Information exchange practices in the Nigerian construction industry. Doctoral dissertation, University of Salford.

Davenport, T. H., and D. A. Marchand. 2000. Is knowledge management just good information management? *Business Strategy Review* 11 (1): 3–7. https://doi.org/10.1111/1467-8616.00155.

Demian, P., and D. Walters. 2014. The advantages of information and communication technologies in the construction industry. *Engineering, Construction and Architectural Management* 21 (1): 92–107.

Derenskaya, Y. 2018. Project scope management process. *Baltic Journal of Economic Studies* 4 (1): 118–125.

Detlor, B. 2010. Information management. *International Journal of Information Management* 30 (2): 103–108.

Dikbas, A., E. Ergen, and D. Arditi. 1999. Improving construction project management with IT. In *Proceedings of the 7th international conference on construction applications of virtual reality*, 47–60.

Drucker, P. F. 1954. *The practice of management*. Harper & Row.

Dunham, R. B., and J. L. Pierce. 1989. *Management*. Scott Foresman.

Duyshart, B. 1997. *The digital document revolution*. UNSW Press.

Earl, M. J. 1989. *Management strategies for information technology*. Prentice Hall.

Ellis, D. 1998. The concept of information. *Annual Review of Information Science and Technology* 34:343–411.

Estélyiová, K. 2012. The concept and evolution of information management. *Acta Informatica Pragensia* 1 (2): 57–69.

Estélyiová, K., and V. Koráb. 2011. The development of information management: From data processing to strategic management. *Acta Informatica Pragensia* 2 (1): 39–49.

Fayol, H. 1916. *Administration industrielle et générale; Prévoyance, organisation, commandement, coordination, controle*. Paris: H. Dunod & E. Pinat.

Feng, J. 2006. Barriers to IT implementation in construction. In *Proceedings of the International Conference on Construction Information Technology*, 83–90.

Fryer, B. 1990. *Information technology in construction*. Longman Scientific & Technical.

Gaith, M. A., A. M. Rasli, and M. Zain. 2012. The impact of ICT adoption on the performance of construction companies. *International Journal of Academic Research* 4 (2): 140–147.

Goodman, J. 2009. Thomson financial's comms resources for managers. *Strategic Communication Management* 13 (4): 12.

Griffin, R. W. 2013. *Management*. 11th ed. Cengage Learning.

Gulati, R., A. J. Mayo, and N. Nohria. 2017. *Management: An integrated approach*. Cengage Learning.

Hitt, M. A., J. S. Black, and L. W. Porter. 2012. *Management*. 3rd ed. Pearson Education.

Hollander, R., E. Denna, and J. Cherrington. 1999. *Accounting, information technology, and business solutions*. 2nd ed. McGraw-Hill Education.

Hu, Y., S. Zhang, and M. J. Skibniewski. 2016. Development of a decision support system for cost estimation of building projects. *Automation in Construction* 72:178–186.

ITAA (Information Technology Association of America). 2010. What is information technology? https://www.itaa.org

Jones, G. R., and J. M. George. 2018. *Essentials of contemporary management*. 8th ed. McGraw-Hill Education.

Kinicki, A., and B. K. Williams. 2018. *Management: A practical introduction*. 8th ed. McGraw-Hill Education.

Koontz, H. 1961. The management theory jungle. *Academy of Management Journal* 4 (3): 174–188.
Langerdorf, H. 1992. Computer-generated visualization in construction. *Automation in Construction* 1 (2): 123–132.
Laudon, K. C., and J. P. Laudon. 1995. *Management information systems: Organization and technology*. Prentice Hall.
Laudon, K. C., and J. P. Laudon. 2000. *Management information systems: Organization and technology in the networked enterprise*. 6th ed. Prentice Hall.
Li, H., Z. Irani, and P. E. D. Love. 2000. The IT implications of construction process reengineering. *Construction Management and Economics* 18 (2): 183–194.
Lin, B. W. 2007. Information technology capability and value creation: Evidence from the US banking industry. *Technology in Society* 29 (1): 93–106.
Luiten, G. T., and F. P. Tolman. 1997. Design management in the building industry: The role of computer-integrated information. *Construction Management and Economics* 15 (3): 345–353.
Luiten, G. T., M. A. N. Hendriks, and F. P. Tolman. 1998. Traditional information exchange in building construction. *Automation in Construction* 7 (4): 345–355.
Mabope, N. 2018. Strategies and practices for effective talent management in the Mangaung metropolitan municipality. Master's dissertation, University of the Free State.
Machlup, F. 1983. Semantic quirks in studies of information. In *The study of information: Interdisciplinary messages*, ed. F. Machlup and U. Mansfield, 641–671. Wiley.
Mahadevan, B., and P. Vijayakumar. 2012. *Information technology for construction productivity*. McGraw-Hill.
Mahalingam, A., R. Kashyap, and C. Mahajan. 2010. An evaluation of the applicability of 4D CAD on construction projects. *Automation in Construction* 19 (2): 148–159.
Malik, F. 2000. *Managing performing living: Effective management for a new era*. English ed. 2006 ed. Frankfurt am Main: Campus.
Maritz, M. J. 2003. Project management information systems in construction: A south African perspective. *Acta Structilia* 10 (2): 1–20.
Maskuriy, R., A. Selamat, P. Maresova, O. Krejcar, and O. David. 2019. Industry 4.0 for the construction industry: Review of management perspective. *Economies* 7 (3): 68.
McCreadie, M. M., and R. E. Rice. 1999. Trends in analyzing access to information. Part I: Cross-disciplinary conceptualizations of access. *Information Processing & Management* 35 (1): 45–76.
Michel, J., M. Fisher, and J. Kunz. 2000. IT applications in the construction sector: Global strategies and trends. CIFE Working Paper 64.
Mintzberg, H. 2009. What managers really do. *The Wall Street Journal*, August 17. http://www.mintzberg.org/sites/default/files/article/download/mgrsreallydo.pdf
Miyatake, Y., and R. Kangari. 1993. Emerging technologies for construction delivery systems. *Journal of Construction Engineering and Management* 119 (3): 507–522.
Montana, P. J., and B. H. Charnov. 2008. *Management*. 4th ed. Barron's Educational Series.
Morgan, M. 2019. *Document management strategies in the construction industry*. CRC Press.
Narayan, K. L. 2008. *Computer aided design and manufacturing*. Prentice-Hall of India.
Naylor, J. 2004. *Management*. 2nd ed. Essex: Pearson Education/Prentice Hall.
Oladapo, A. A. 2007. An evaluation of the use of ICT in the Nigerian construction industry. *ITcon* 12:261–277.
Paulson, B. C. 1995. *Computer applications in construction*. McGraw-Hill.
Radović-Marković, M., and M. Vučeković. 2015. Managing information and knowledge as a strategic resource. *Journal of Process Management and New Technologies* 3 (4): 40–48.
Říhová, Z. 2015. Influence of organization management on systems of performance measurement and management control. *Acta Informatica Pragensia* 4 (1): 80–89.
Rivard, H., T. Froese, L. Waugh, et al. 2004. Case studies on the use of information technology in the Canadian construction industry. *Electronic Journal of Information Technology in Construction (ITcon)* 9:19–34.
Robbins, S. P., and M. Coulter. 2005. *Management*. 8th ed. Prentice Hall.

Robbins, S. P., and M. Coulter. 2016. *Management*. 13th ed. Pearson Education.
Rudden, J. 2019. The role of ICT in sustainable construction. *Journal of Green Building* 14 (1): 27–43.
Schermerhorn, J. R. 2005. *Management*. 8th ed. Hoboken: John Wiley & Sons.
Serpell, A., G. Barai, and A. Oladapo. 2005. Assessment of information and communication technologies in the construction industry of Chile. *Construction Management and Economics* 23 (3): 297–307.
Shafique, M., and A. Mahmood. 2010. Use of information and communication technology in construction industry. *International Journal of Computer Applications* 9 (3): 40–47.
Shahrubudin, N., T. C. Lee, and R. Ramlan. 2019. An overview on 3D printing technology: Technological, materials, and applications. *Procedia Manufacturing* 35:1286–1296.
Sheriff, M., G. Zheng, and R. Mahmood. 2012. Information as a critical resource in construction management. *Journal of Construction Engineering and Project Management* 2 (1): 1–6.
Shibeika, A., and C. Harty. 2015. Diffusion of mobile computing in construction: Evaluating the changes in work practices. *Automation in Construction* 57:74–84.
Sommerville, J., N. Craig, and J. Hendry. 2010. The role of the project manager: All things to all people? *Structural Survey* 28 (2): 132–141.
Smith, D. K. 2003. *Information systems and construction project management*. Wiley.
Stoner, J. A. F., R. E. Freeman, and D. R. Gilbert. 1995. *Management*. 6th ed. Prentice Hall.
Subramani, T., M. Sarkunam, and M. Jayalakshmi. 2014. Planning and scheduling of high-rise building using primavera. *International Journal of Engineering Research and Applications* 4 (6): 134–144.
Sun, M., and R. Howard. 2003. Understanding IT applications in construction. *Construction Innovation* 3 (3): 131–145.
Sun, M., and R. Howard. 2004. The changing nature of construction IT support. *Automation in Construction* 13 (2): 239–248.
Taylor, F. W. 1911. *Shop management*. Harper & Brothers (new edition 2008). NuVision Publications.
Taylor, R. S. 1966. *Information management in engineering education*. Bethlehem PA: Lehigh University Press.
Tuman, J. 1998. Communication: The key to successful project management. *Project Management Journal* 29 (4): 45–51.
Turban, E., D. Leidner, E. McLean, and J. Wetherbe. 2004. *Information technology for management: Transforming organizations in the digital economy*. 4th ed. Wiley.
Turban, E., D. Leidner, E. McLean, and J. Wetherbe. 2007. *Information technology for management: Transforming organizations in the digital economy*. Ontario: John Wiley & Sons.
Turban, E., D. Leidner, E. McLean, and J. Wetherbe. 2009. *Information technology for management: Advancing sustainable, profitable business growth*. 7th ed. Wiley.
Vodáček, L., and O. Vodáčková. 1996. *Management—Theory and practices for the 1990s*. Prague: Management Press.
Williams, C. 2018. *Principles of management*. 10th ed. Cengage Learning.
Winch, G. 2010. *Managing construction projects*. 2nd ed. Wiley-Blackwell.
Zhu, J., H. Makarand, and J. Yang. 2017. Managing construction information: A framework for digital transformation. *International Journal of Project Management* 35 (8): 1565–1577.

Chapter 2
The Basics of Blockchain Technology

Abstract Blockchain technology has emerged as a groundbreaking innovation, offering a decentralized, transparent, and secure method for recording digital transactions and data exchanges. Initially developed to support cryptocurrencies such as Bitcoin, the technology has evolved into a versatile tool applicable across multiple sectors including construction, healthcare, finance, and public administration. This chapter explores the fundamental concepts, architecture, and evolution of blockchain technology, tracing its development from Blockchain 1.0 focused on digital currency to the more sophisticated applications in Blockchain 3.0 and beyond. Key components such as blocks, hash functions, distributed ledgers, and consensus mechanisms are examined to provide a detailed understanding of how blockchain operates. The chapter further highlights the different types of blockchain systems—public, private, and consortium—and their respective characteristics, strengths, and use cases. Additionally, the inherent features that distinguish blockchain, such as immutability, autonomy, timestamping, and peer-to-peer relationships, are discussed in the context of their value for innovation and digital transformation. By drawing on scholarly insights and technical perspectives, this chapter provides a comprehensive overview of blockchain's foundational principles and its expanding role in shaping the digital economy.

Keywords Blockchain · Decentralization · Distributed ledger · Smart contracts · Digital transformation

2.1 Introduction

Blockchain technology has emerged as one of the most transformative innovations of the twenty-first century, redefining how digital data is stored, verified, and transferred. Originally conceptualized as the foundation for cryptocurrencies like Bitcoin, blockchain has since evolved into a robust, decentralized ledger system applicable across multiple sectors (Crosby et al. 2016; Yli-Huumo et al. 2016). Its

O. I. Akinradewo et al., *Blockchain Technology for Information Management: A New Era for Sustainable Construction Practices*, Artificial Intelligence and Sustainable Development, https://doi.org/10.1007/978-981-95-2664-2_2

core attributes includes decentralization, immutability, peer-to-peer interaction, and timestamping, which have positioned it as a viable solution for enhancing transparency, efficiency, and trust in digital transactions (Wu et al. 2017; Sadeghi et al. 2021). Scholars such as Kiu et al. (2019) and Maskuriy et al. (2019) have emphasized blockchain's potential to eliminate intermediaries, reduce transaction costs, and safeguard data integrity. With applications extending beyond finance to industries such as healthcare, construction, and governance, understanding the architecture, functionality, and types of blockchain technology is essential for stakeholders aiming to leverage its capabilities for innovation and sustainability.

2.2 What Is Blockchain Technology?

Evidence from both previous and existing studies has shown that many scholars have explained the concept of blockchain technology. Some of these include Kiu et al. (2019), Rosic (2018), Iorio (2017), Condos et al. (2016), Underwood (2016), Rodrigo et al. (2018), Nanayakkara et al. (2019), Wu et al. (2017) and Hultgren and Pajala (2018). Blockchain, according to Wu et al. (2017), is the technology that uses a distributed ledger, a consensus of shared and synchronized digital data from one geographical location to another across different sites, nations or institutions. Wu et al. (2017) further asserted that there is no central administrator or centralised data storage under blockage. In the view of Condos et al. (2016), blockchain is a type of electronic ledger of digital information, especially records, transaction and events, which requires a hash for digital security purposes. It is authorised and maintained by different participants through a decentralised network, utilizing a group of consensus protocols. Blockchain technology is indicated by Kiu et al. (2019) as the method of connecting blocks of data in a chain to increase data integrity and reliability significantly. The Korea Institute of Science and Technology Information (2018) further added that blockchain technology is an emerging technology that ensures that digital data is secured and reliable while enhancing its efficiencies. Without the use of centralized data intermediaries, blockchain technology allows different participants within the network to engage with one another, especially in storing, recording, verifying and extracting digital information (Maskuriy et al. 2019). Blockchain technology was first decentralised for transaction and data management for bitcoin cryptocurrency; however, it is now used as a platform where many cryptocurrencies are based (Yli-Huumo et al. 2016; Ramage 2018). Despite its applicability in transaction and data management for bitcoin cryptocurrency, it was observed that the usefulness of blockchain technology is not only restricted to cryptocurrencies (Yli-Huumo et al. 2016). It can also be used in other areas where different forms of transactions occur. It can also be used in proffering solution to problems (Sadeghi et al. 2021). The core elements of block are transactions, a hash value, and a nonce value. While transactions could be referred to information or data that network members desire to store and control, the hash value function characterizes the contents of a block, and it is a 64-character (Nawari and Ravindran

2019). Nounce values, on the other hand, are essentially random values that set the first digital of the associated value to zero (Maskuriy et al. 2019). The difficulty of generating a block is strongly related to the number of zero digits, which also sets the block's security level (Sadeghi et al. 2021).

2.3 History of Blockchain Technology

Evidence from the literature has shown that blockchain technology as a decentralised information ledger is one of the most ground-breaking technologies (Abeyratne et al. 2016). It was further reported that the first job on cryptographically secured blockchain surfaced in the year 1991, which gave birth to this technology. Despite the fact that the technology concept was brought to light, it was not until 2008 that the technology began to gain momentum (Crosby et al. 2016). Along with the well-known cryptocurrency bitcoin, the technology was introduced by an unnamed person who published a paper titled "Bitcoin: A Peer-to-Peer Electronic Case System" in the year 2008. This article was published under the pseudonym Satoshi Nakamoto. The author of article was not known till this present day (Lemieux 2015). According to Lemieux (2015), the study described peer-to-peer of the electronic case as the platform which allows online transactions that would be done directly between the participating parties without using a bank institution. The target was to remove the requirement of a third party in the financial transactions (Crosby et al. 2016). The application of blockchain software was further demonstrated practically in proffering solutions to the challenges of avoiding double spending (Söhne 2015). To describe the problem of spending twice, the platform prevents participating members from transferring assets more than twice. Double spending prevents a party from transferring an asset twice. According to Abeyratne et al. (2016), blockchain application, since the year 2008, has been closely linked to bitcoin, with some claims that blockchain was created to be part of cryptocurrency's basic infrastructure. Although the application goes beyond digital currency and financial assets, there is a new development in the adoption of the technology as it has received wider prominence in recent years (Nawari and Ravindran 2019).

2.4 Evolution of Blockchain Technology

Since the development of blockchain technology, it has evolved over time. The blockchain information exchange is decentralized, indicating that everyone in the ecosystem has access to the same data as everyone else (Chong and Diamantopoulos 2020). The ability to maintain data and information outside the control of the administration in government parastatals and organisations is a key aspect of blockchain. This technical method was developed over time in the previous years when the use of blockchain application gained the world's attention (Luu et al. 2016; Sharmila et al. 2019). The development of blockchain technology can be separated into four stages. The following are the attributes of each stage:

Blockchain 1.0 was the first software which was developed to play a single role of making payment. It could be classified as open blockchain. Bitcoin is one of the most well-known Blockchain 1.0 applications (Lin et al. 2021). The purpose of Blockchain 1.0 is to decentralize money and payments. Bitcoin is an example of this type of application. With the use of Blockchain 1.0, different forms of transaction could be conducted. The transaction could be completed directly between two users on the Internet (Makhdoom et al. 2020). Unlike fiat currencies, which allow governments to issue additional money, bitcoin's money supply increases at a particular rate. In this process, the issuance of new currency is at a predictable and consistent rate. Approximately 13.5 million units of digital currency are in circulation while the maximum units of 21 million are estimated to be available in 2040 (Liu and Huang 2019).

The second type of blockchain, which is known as Blockchain 2.0, was also introduced to perform the additional function of trading and contracting (Zhao et al. 2019). During this time, a platform that would privately allow close booking formation around some participating members had evolved, using smart contracts as well as automated stock transactions as application. Blockchain 2.0 is used for the decentralising general markets, and it facilitates the transfer of different forms of assets other than using digital currency through the creation of a unit value every time it is moved, utilizing the blockchain (Leible et al. 2019). Examples of Blockchain 2.0 includes smart property, decentralised autonomous organizations (DAOs), decentralised applications (Dapps), Bitcoin 2.0 and its protocols, among others. All forms of online payments including bonds, stocks, crowdfunding instruments, mutual funds, pensions, and derivatives among others might be rebuilt on related applications of blockchain (Hammoud et al. 2021; Wu et al. 2021).

Blockchain can be used to hold public documents (such as land certificate, building certificates, and business licenses, among others), private records (such as loans, signatures, and escrows) and digital identity documents (such as passports, national identification cards, and driver licenses, among others) (Ahmadisheykhsarmast and Sonmez 2020). Blockchain attestation can furthermore be used for evidence of insurance, proof of ownership, and notarized papers. Intangible assets such as patents and copyrights, as well as physical assets such houses and motor vehicles can be encoded, protected, and transferred using the blockchain technology (Wörner et al. 2016). A third type of blockchain, which is known as Blockchain 3.0 was developed (Shi et al. 2021; Udokwu et al. 2021). The application coincides with the multiple industry convergence era. It could also be referred to as the technology diffusion era. The technology of blockchain technology could be used in a wide variety of activities, including energy transaction and management of supply-chain in addition to financial transactions (Nawari and Ravindran 2019). Beyond economics, currency, and markets, the application is for justice applications, especially in the domains of government, health, research, literacy, culture, and art (Shojaei 2019; Agibalova et al. 2020).

Under Blockchain 3.0, which is a new paradigm for arranging activities with more efficiency and less friction, the freedom attribute connected with the blockchain becomes more evident (Shojaei 2019; Ahmadisheykhsarmast and Sonmez 2020). The application can greatly improve the effectiveness and efficiency of the various types of human contacts, as well as a higher level of collaboration between humans and machines. Blockchain government is a key use of Blockchain 3.0, which leverages the blockchain to provide decentralized government services by acting as a permanent, universal, continuous, consensus-driven, publicly auditable, redundant record-keeping repository (Wörner et al. 2016). The development of fourth generation blockchain is expected to be released soon. The essence of the application is to plan for the provision of more services that are publicly accessible. This includes common functions of administration within the public sector, i.e., voting and budget management. Some of these services are commercially available (Kim 2018).

According to Yoo and Kim (2018), the development of cryptocurrency, which was initiated by blockchain application, was targeted to enhance element-based transaction i.e., Litecoin, Bitcoin and registration of assets, among others. Trading markets i.e., buildings, cars, landed property and stocks are the definite target of some of the examples of element-based blockchain applications (Sun et al. 2016). However, the target of blockchain application has moved bit by bit to platform-based from the previous element-based technology that is applicable to other sectors. Platform-based applications such as Ethereum, foster centralisation with various industries. Platform-based blockchain application is known as technology structures that are scalable and compatible with a variety of technologies. As noted by Yoo (2018), the blockchain platform is separated into two layers: the service layer which includes the user application and the side chain while the technology layer comprises the core application and blockchain layer (Yoo 2018). The financial industry's Smart Contract is one of the most popular applications that uses the blockchain platform. The rise of the blockchain platform has facilitated the technology's compatibility with various tasks in different industries (Swan 2015).

2.5 How Blockchain Technology Works

The blockchain technology essentially creates a distributed public ledger that records the whole history of all transactions currently in use (Crosby et al. 2016). Using bitcoin as an example, blockchain technology records every bitcoin's payment history, proving who owns what at any given time (Wang et al. 2017). According to Wu et al. (2017), the technology can be broken down into two distinct parts.

2.5.1 Recording and Hashing

The cryptographically 'hashed' information which is contained in transaction blocks are recorded before using blockchain application. The word 'hashed' means that the blocks are filled with algorithm which interprets hash value (fixed-length alpha-numeric string) (Lemieux 2015). The hash function is used to achieve it, involving very simple computer programming. It changes the state of any form of data into a length of numbers that is fixed. The cryptographic hash function, which was earlier described, is considered as the most essential and valuable type of hash function (Chakrabarti et al. 2017). The hash functions provide digital fingerprints for any type of data. However, one of the common setbacks of cryptographic hash values is that the length of numbers is very long. This makes them difficult to distinguish or even scan with the human eye (Drescher 2017).

In the process of creating cryptographic the hash value of different types of data, most of the hash value are not supposed to change (Wörner et al. 2016). One of the ways in which this technology could show whether the data involved have been altered or changed is through digital footprints (Wang et al. 2017), for example, checking whether the data have been altered or changed or not. Drescher (2017) commented that the only thing one can do is to recreate the cryptographic hash value once again and distinguish the one that was newly recreated from the old one. If the two created hash values are the same, then one can easily conclude that the hash value has not been altered after the creation of the first one (Shi et al. 2021; Udokwu et al. 2021). This type of method could be applied when one wants to send data to another person. Drescher (2017) asserted that the condition applies when the sender creates a new hash value before sending the data, while the receiver at the other end could create another hash value of the data he/she receives to ensure that the data has not been changed in the process of transferring it.

According to Crosby et al. (2016), hash references could also be used in blockchain technology. The power of a cryptographic hash value could be utilized with hash references (Drescher 2017). The above references to data could be clarified by trying to compare them along with cloakroom ticket prices. A cloakroom ticket tends to give a depiction of a geographical place where someone's jacket would be saved. Users would only be allowed to retrieve their jacket if they had a cloakroom ticket. The hash reference could be considered to be a cloakroom ticket which showcases hash values rather than frequent digits. The hash reference ensures that the data to which it refers has not altered when this reference was generated (Shojaei 2019; Ahmadisheykhsarmast and Sonmez 2020). According to Drescher (2017), if the data to which the reference is made has been modified, the reference is considered shattered or null and void. This is analogous to getting a cloakroom ticket for a particular rack which no longer contains one's jacket. In other words, the cloakroom keeper will no longer be able to release one's jacket (Nawari and Ravindran 2019).

The sole purpose of developing hash references is to prevent users from retrieving data that has already been deliberately altered by anybody without notifying the recipient or modified without one's personal permission (Wu et al. 2017). It is designed to protect clients from data changes that occur unknowingly as a result of technological mistakes. As a result, hash references are used and developed only when clients need to ensure that the data will remain unaltered once generated and that users will not be able to recover data that has changed (Drescher 2017). When a block is documented, authenticated, and later added to a chain of blocks, it contains some of the hashes of the previous blocks. The chain of blocks as Abeyratne et al. (2016) indicated, would then encompass more work or hashes. To change a block in the chain (that could only be completed by creating a new block containing the same predecessor), one must regenerate all the successors and repeat the work contained in the blocks. Drescher (2017) added that by connecting all blocks in a chain and integrating the work from each block, the blockchain is protected from tampering.

2.5.2 Validate the Transactions

Taking the use of bitcoin as an example, one of the greatest obstacles is avoiding double expenses, or the situation in which a person can transfer an asset multiple times. This is managed in blockchain technology via the authentication or validation process (Crosby et al. 2016). It is essential to understand that becoming a part of a decentralized system may not indicate that one must share personal information with everybody in the same network. The way to resolve the issue is to establish a secure digital identity. The concept behind blockchains here is that every participant of the system has both a public and a private encryption algorithm (Bauerle 2017). The public key is used to access the distributed system, while the private key serves as an effective ownership instrument that satisfies authentication criteria (Wang et al. 2017). The purpose of separating these is to lessen the risk of hackers. The combination of these keys, on the other hand, might be seen as a form of agreement or, in other words, a useful digital signature (Bauerle 2017).

Digital interactions develop when cryptographic keys are used with distributed systems (Crosby et al. 2016). Using bitcoin as an example, the procedure starts with A taking their private key and making a system announcement. If A says he or she will transmit a certain amount of Bitcoin to B, A will simply attach it to B's public key. When this is done, the time will be recorded and a time stamp will be added to the block (which has already been hashed) (Bauerle 2017). The block is then sent to the decentralized system, under which system users must consent to or endorse the order of the block. To authorize a block, the majority of the system's members or nodes must agree on the same decision (Heiskanen 2017). Since each system users modify the database or verification independently, they each create their own upgraded version (Lemieux 2015). A far more 'popular' record is designated as the master copy and the de-facto formal record. Because of this type of validation and technology, blockchain technology eliminates the need for a trusted party to facilitate digital relationships (Bauerle 2017). There are numerous ways to generate incentives to validate these types of blocks, depending on whether the system is public or private (the differences will be explained in the next section). For public blockchains, mining is required (Nawari and Ravindran 2019). Miners are compensated in some way when they verify or validate a block. In bitcoin, for instance, whoever verifies a block is remunerated with a certain amount of bitcoin. This type of verification is termed 'proof-of-work', verifying that perhaps the technique is accurate and also that the transfer of funds is valid (Wu et al. 2017). In some ways, this is analogous to offering one's computer processing power to the network. The reward is intended to create opportunities for customers to act in their own self-interest in order to help meet public needs (Shi et al. 2021; Udokwu et al. 2021).

2.6 Blockchain System Architecture

According to Sharmila et al. (2019), blockchain is made up of two different components which are blocks and transactions. Transactions are defined to be "the action triggered by the participant" while Blocks are defined to be "is a collection of data recording the transaction and other associated details such as the correct sequence, timestamp of creation, etc." (Miraz and Ali 2018:4). However, Andoni et al. (2019) submitted that a blockchain refers to a distributed and shared database with a digital data structure that houses transaction logs chronologically and expands continuously. The data structure represents a ledger which accommodates data executables, records, and digital transactions. These transactions are compiled into clusters which are referred to as blocks linked together to form a record chain showing the transaction sequence orders and referred to as 'blockchain'. To support this, Chuen (2015) asserted that blockchain is a compilation of blocks in sequence that houses transaction records just like a traditional public ledger. Blockchain, according to Zeng et al. (2017), is a series of blocks that contain a complete list of transaction records, similar to a traditional public ledger. With a previous block hash contained in the block header, a block has only one parent block (Buterin 2014). The first block in the blockchain is known as the genesis block, and it has no parent block.

Block The header and body of a block are the only components that constitute it. Included in this particular block's header are the block version which determines the block validation rules to follow; the root hash of the Merkle tree which is the sum of all the block's hashes; nbits which are the minimum number of bits required for a successful block hash; time which refers to the current time in universal time; nounce which is a 4-byte field, which usually starts with 0 and increases for every hash calculation; and a 256-bit hash value that refers to the preceding block which is found in the parent block (Nawari and Ravindran 2019). The block body contains a counter transaction as well as additional transactions. The maximum number of transactions that a block may hold is determined by the size of the block and the size of each transaction (Shojaei 2019; Ahmadisheykhsarmast and Sonmez 2020). Creating a block, which holds the network's data and information, is the initial stage in the functioning of the blockchain technology. In the genesis block, there is a set amount of transaction data that makes up the first block. It is necessary to encrypt the data once it has been stored using a nounce hash value (Sadeghi et al. 2021). The first and second blocks are produced when the required amount of transaction data is saved. There is also a genesis block hash value, which serves as a connection between this new block and the previous block. For any manipulation to be permitted, all preceding blocks must be altered. This chain procedure makes changing data in the nth block extremely difficult (Shi et al. 2021; Udokwu et al. 2021).

Abeyratne et al. (2016) indicated that the name 'blockchain' comes from the fact that this distributed ledger is made up of a chronological sequence of blocks, each of which holds a record of valid network activity, namely documents. The goal is for the majority of the system's members to validate the content of each block. The information in a block cannot be removed or edited once it has been entered and confirmed (Wang et al. 2017). Each block could be thought of as a piece of encrypted data. Anyone within the system can theoretically add data to the chain of blocks and see the data at any moment; however, no one can change the data without appropriate permission (Abeyratne et al. 2016). As a result, all of the blocks work together to create a comprehensive and immutable history of the network's operations, which is shared with all system participants.

When a block is validated, it is added to a chronological chain of other blocks, earning the name 'blockchain'. As a result, the blockchain is a chain that holds verifiable records of all transactions, documents, and other actions ever performed in the system (Nofer et al. 2017). According to the architecture of blockchain as illustrated by Min (2019), nobody owns the blockchain, and nobody can remove a network block or add to it. As such, blockchain enables everyone to transfer properties (even immaterial assets) without fear of theft or creating silos that hinder interaction among business partners (Shahrubudin et al. 2019). In addition to the security advantage, BT has several strategic advantages for daily business activities which include decreased transaction costs/time as a result of enhanced blockchain systems that do not need the intervention of third parties; improved accountability throughout the supply chain, as a result of increased openness by open ledger which anyone can view; and enhanced interconnectedness between trading partners through the convergence of digital and physical environments, including mutual knowledge of supply chain transactions and data streams (Maruti Techlabs 2017; Takahashi 2017; Shojaei 2019; Ahmadisheykhsarmast and Sonmez 2020).

Blockchain works with a group of nodes connected via a network. Once a transaction is initiated, a message is sent to the network; all nodes validate and check its presence by carrying out predefined tests concerning the transaction layout and activity (Karafiloski and Mishev 2017). When a majority (above 50%) of nodes reach a consensus, blocks are deemed valid (Biswas and Muthukkumarasamy 2017). Every node version of the blockchain is modified when the block is updated from the database. It is important to note that blockchain is only a distributed ledger and does not do computations. The computations are carried out by a set of Internet users, referred to as miners, whose responsibility is to mine blocks of checked and authenticated transactions in the blockchain network (Mik 2017). Owing to the transparency of blocks throughout the network (Tapscott and Tapscott 2017), and the reality that it must change with all blocks succeeding it on the blockchain (Yermack 2017), it is almost impossible to change a block in public blockchains. This shows that all blocks link back to the first block in order to maintain the credibility of the blockchain (Nofer et al. 2017). For private blockchains, access rights increase the privacy strength of data (Hamida et al. 2017b).

2.7 Characteristics of Blockchain Technology

Blockchain technology offers several key characteristics that make it the most promising technology for revolutionizing a variety of industries and use cases, including the construction industry. This includes its distributed platform; decentralized, autonomous, peer-to-peer relationship; immutable record; and time stamping (Hamida et al. 2017a; Dai et al. 2018; Maskuriy et al. 2019; Shojaei 2019; Sadeghi et al. 2021; Udokwu et al. 2021).

2.7.1 Distributed Platform

Blockchain technology, according to Kang (2018), allows all network members to participate through a distributed digital platform that jointly stores and confirms transaction information. There is only one controller who manages the integrity of data in a central database. The technology protects without having an authorized central agency. A typical example of this is depicted in Fig. 2.1:

Kim et al. (2020) indicated that one of the most unique advantages of blockchain is that it is improves security. One of the reasons why it improves security is the fact that the technology comprises sharing hash values which encrypt keys within and between the blocks (Nawari and Ravindran 2019). This makes it difficult for professional hackers to break through the data base. Also, it is not possible to adjust or remove some data except if all the participating members within the network of block are hacked (Shojaei 2019; Ahmadisheykhsarmast and Sonmez 2020). This is because most of the participating members jointly own information.

2.7.2 Decentralisation

Another characteristic is decentralised blockchain technology which reduces the cost of transactions (Shahrubudin et al. 2019). This is because it is feasible to make transactions directly, especially between members within the network, even without going through an authorised central agency (Sadeghi et al. 2021). This does not only save costs but also improves the speed of transaction. This is as a result of some

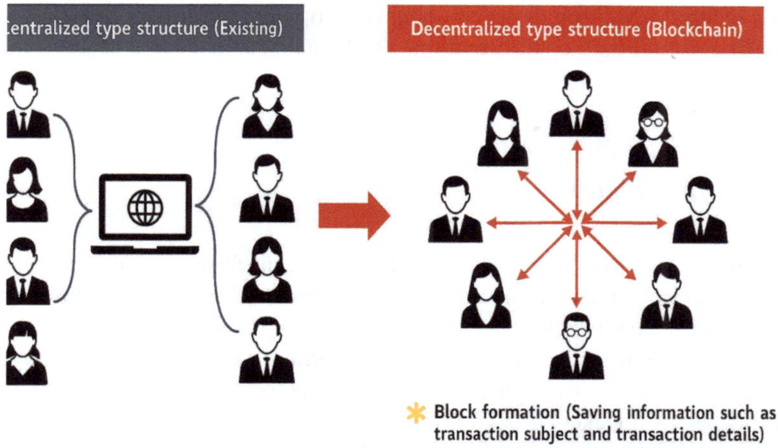

Fig. 2.1 Comparison between centralised and decentralised structure. (Author's adaptation from Kang (2018))

omissions within the process of brokerage; moreover, the security will not be compromised. Alcazar (2017) added that blockchain avoids the basic requirement for central authority agency through the removal of the need for the middleman role trust management. From another perspective, there is no party, company, organisation or database that singlehandedly controls the information or data alone (Heap 2017; Koutsogiannis and Berntsen 2017).

2.7.3 Autonomy

Autonomy which is another characteristic of blockchain technology, means that its initiating agent does not need to be contacted again after the application has been launched and run (Swan 2015). Automation, as noted by Aste et al. (2017), deals with the distribution of rules and algorithms activating the self-enforcement, self-execution, self-constraint, and self-verification of the performance of the smart contracts by itself.

2.7.4 Peer-to-Peer Relationship

Another key element is the peer-to-peer relationship system which allows participating members to send information or money from one wallet to another without the need for a third party or central authority (Nawari and Ravindran 2019). It was observed that different parties in the public and private sectors have one or two expectations from the technology (Maskuriy et al. 2019). This is due to the fact that the technology, through peer-to-peer development platforms, provides a basis for sharing digital data or information, assets, and goods even without a middleman (Aste et al. 2017).

2.7.5 *Immutability*

An immutable record system is different from a decentralised network. Every member of the blockchain entity has access to and shares the same information or transaction record since blockchain technology is a decentralized network (Sadeghi et al. 2021). Unlike traditional networks or central parties, where the information is held by a central server or trusted third parties, blockchain differs. When the central location is hacked or hijacked, crucial information and financial transaction records are lost (Apte and Petrovsky 2016; Ramage 2018).

2.7.6 *Timestamping*

The blockchain network's chain is referred to as a timestamping record (Sadeghi et al. 2021). As Blockchain 2.0 and smart contracts gain a foothold across many businesses, this will enable historical and chronological fulfilment. If one needs proof of the presence of digital or digitalized assets at any moment, one can utilize blockchain (Aste et al. 2017).

2.8 Types of Blockchain Technology

Depending on the network's openness, blockchain applications could be classified as licensed, unlicensed, or combination system blockchains (Mohammed et al. 2021). The public blockchain, which is refers as unlicensed blockchain, is different from the private blockchain, also known as a licensed blockchain. As a semi-public platform, it can be referred to as consortium blockchain (Patil and Puranik 2019). A public blockchain is unlicensed in nature as it allows anybody to join the platform without obtaining permission from transaction members that act as the blockchain controlling body (Shojaei 2019; Ahmadisheykhsarmast and Sonmez 2020). Owing to the fact that obtaining the consent of an unknown number of management organizations is almost impossible, it is virtually impossible to change the network regulations after the platform has been established. Anyone can join the network in the public system. Miners, as previously noted, are rewarded for validating the blocks in the system (Shi et al. 2021; Udokwu et al. 2021). Anybody could be regarded as a miner seeking to get the token prize in the public system of blockchain. According to Wu et al. (2017), it also allows miners to walk away from being a node in the system and subsequently return if they change their minds and want a complete report of all network activities.

Private blockchain and consortium blockchain are licensed blockchains. In comparison to an unlicensed/public blockchain, the rules of the network can be altered very quickly on a licensed/private platform (Patil and Puranik 2019). The idea of this system is to build a platform where people could be allowed to read information in the blockchain with authorization. Lemieux (2015) noted that it restricts who could probably make changes to the blockchain and who could serve the network better by validating blocks and adding recent ones to the chain. The cryptocurrency Ripple is an example of this; it uses a permissioned blockchain (Nawari and Ravindran 2019). The programme, unlike any other public system, decides who can participate as a validator in their network. CGI, MIT, and Microsoft are some of the validators for this cryptocurrency (Shahrubudin et al. 2019). Apart from these validator instances, the start-up creates its own vertices in various places globally. These blockchain networks do or do not employ 'proof–of–work', which is a term used to describe the mining operations (Shojaei 2019; Ahmadisheykhsarmast and Sonmez 2020). Private blockchains that do not use proof-of-work are being debated by the developers of blockchain as to whether they should be labelled and viewed as blockchains at all, or if they should be considered shared ledgers instead (Bauerle 2017). In recent times, various blockchain developers are now trying to experiment with the methods mentioned above. Under this platform, developers could make the system public for anybody to use and limit the number of participants that can be a node, block that which is being validated or mined within the system (Maskuriy et al. 2019).

2.9 Summary

This chapter comprehensively examined blockchain technology, detailing its definition, historical development, evolution, operational mechanism, system architecture, key characteristics, and various types. It began by exploring diverse scholarly perspectives on the concept of blockchain, highlighting its foundational elements such as decentralization, distributed ledgers, cryptographic hash functions, and consensus protocols. The historical trajectory traced blockchain from its cryptographic origins in 1991 to its popularization in 2008 through the Bitcoin whitepaper by Satoshi Nakamoto. The chapter also outlined the evolution of blockchain through four stages such as Blockchain 1.0 (digital currencies), 2.0 (smart contracts), 3.0 (applications across various industries), and the emerging Blockchain 4.0 (public services and governance). It further explained how blockchain works by describing the processes of recording, hashing, validating transactions, and the critical role of miners and consensus mechanisms like proof-of-work. Blockchain's architecture was broken down into its technical components which are blocks, transactions, and system validation, and its functional properties such as immutability, timestamping, and the Merkle tree structure. Core characteristics such as decentralization, autonomy, peer-to-peer relationships, and improved security were emphasized, showcasing its transformative potential in enhancing transparency and trust. Lastly, the chapter distinguished between public, private, and consortium blockchains, discussing the implications of permissioned and permissionless systems. It underscored blockchain's adaptability across sectors beyond finance, including governance, health, construction, and identity management. Overall, this chapter provided a foundational understanding of blockchain technology's core principles, historical context, and practical significance in driving digital transformation across industries.

References

Abeyratne, S., R. P. Monfared, and X. Ranzhe. 2016. Blockchain ready manufacturing supply chain using distributed ledger. *International Journal of Research in Engineering and Technology* 5 (9): 1–10.

Agibalova, T., Y. Tikhomirov, A. Agibalov, and V. Kasyanov. 2020. Application of blockchain technology in the smart city energy management. *E3S Web of Conferences* 208:02012.

Ahmadisheykhsarmast, S., and R. Sonmez. 2020. A review of blockchain implementation in the building industry. *Journal of Building Engineering* 40:102754.

Alcazar, J. R. 2017. Blockchain and the future of the internet. *Journal of Financial Transformation* 45:107–114.

Andoni, M., V. Robu, D. Flynn, S. Abram, D. Geach, D. Jenkins, et al. 2019. Blockchain technology in the energy sector: A systematic review of challenges and opportunities. *Renewable and Sustainable Energy Reviews* 100:143–174.

Apte, S., and N. Petrovsky. 2016. Will blockchain technology revolutionize excipient supply chain management? *Journal of Excipients and Food Chemicals* 7 (3): 76–78.

Aste, T., P. Tasca, and T. D. Matteo. 2017. Blockchain technologies: The foreseeable impact on society and industry. *Computer* 50 (9): 18–28.

Bauerle, N. 2017. *What is blockchain technology? A beginner's guide*. CoinDesk. https://www.coindesk.com/learn/what-is-blockchain-technology.

Biswas, K., and V. Muthukkumarasamy. 2017. Securing smart cities using blockchain technology. In *2016 IEEE 18th international conference on high performance computing and communications*, 1392–1393.

Buterin, V. (2014). A next-generation smart contract and decentralized application platform. *Ethereum White Paper*. https://ethereum.org/en/whitepaper/.

Chakrabarti, S., K. R. Chaudhuri, and A. Bengal. 2017. Cryptographic hash functions: A practical perspective. *Indian Journal of Science and Technology* 10 (6): 1–9.

Chong, H. Y., and M. Diamantopoulos. 2020. Blockchain and the construction sector: Challenges and opportunities. *International Journal of Construction Management* 22 (5): 417–427.

Chuen, D. L. K. 2015. *Handbook of digital currency: Bitcoin, innovation, financial instruments, and big data*. Elsevier.

Condos, D., T. Sorrell, and T. Donegan. 2016. *Blockchain and the future of the internet*. Nevada Department of Business and Industry.

Crosby, M., P. Pattanayak, S. Verma, and V. Kalyanaraman. 2016. Blockchain technology: Beyond bitcoin. *Applied Innovation Review* 2 (6–10): 71–81.

Dai, H. N., Z. Zheng, and Y. Zhang. 2018. Blockchain for internet of things: A survey. *IEEE Internet of Things Journal* 6 (5): 8076–8094.

Drescher, D. 2017. *Blockchain basics: A non-technical introduction in 25 steps*. Apress.

Hamida, E. B., D. E. Lucani, and J. Barreto. 2017a. Privacy-preserving blockchain systems: Challenges and opportunities. *IEEE Communications Surveys & Tutorials* 19 (4): 3045–3082.

Hamida, E. B., D. E. Lucani, and J. Barreto. 2017b. Blockchain for network security: Principles, challenges and opportunities. *IEEE Communications Magazine* 55 (10): 40–46.

Hammoud, H., A. Tarkhanov, and D. Kosmarski. 2021. Blockchain 2.0 and its implications on modern business practices. *Journal of Blockchain Research* 2 (1): 1–11.

Heap, T. 2017. The blockchain: Catalyst for the future of financial services. *Financial IT* 6 (3): 12–14.

Heiskanen, A. 2017. The technology of trust: How the Internet of Things and blockchain could usher in a new era of construction productivity. *Construction Research and Innovation* 8 (2): 66–70.

Hultgren, A., and M. Pajala. 2018. *Blockchain—A disruption in the making*. Stockholm: Royal Institute of Technology. https://www.kth.se.

Iorio, A. D. 2017. Blockchain technology: Characteristics and impact on financial markets. *International Journal of Financial Studies* 5 (4): 31.

Kang, J. 2018. The future impact of blockchain technology on construction industry. *Journal of Civil Engineering and Management* 24 (5): 409–416.

Karafiloski, E., and A. Mishev. 2017. Blockchain solutions for big data challenges: A literature review. In *IEEE Eurocon 2017*, 763–768.

Kim, Y. 2018. Future of blockchain technology: Security and privacy challenges. *International Journal of Advanced Research in Computer Science* 9 (2): 1–5.

Kim, J., S. Lee, and H. Kim. 2020. Improving security and transparency in supply chain management using blockchain technology. *Sustainability* 12 (10): 1–16.

Kiu, C., K. Yang, L. Xu, Q. Wang, and J. He. 2019. Blockchain-enabled trustless crowd-intelligence ecosystem. IEEE. *Access* 7:90703–90714.

Korea Institute of Science and Technology Information. 2018. *Understanding blockchain technology: Concepts and applications*. KISTI.

Koutsogiannis, D., and K. Berntsen. 2017. *Blockchain and public sector applications*. Capgemini Digital Transformation Institute. https://www.capgemini.com.

Leible, S., S. Schlager, M. Schubotz, and F. Matthes. 2019. A taxonomy for blockchain technologies. In *Proceedings of the 2019 IEEE European symposium on security and privacy workshops*, 1–10.

Lemieux, V. L. 2015. Trusting records: Is blockchain technology the answer? *Records Management Journal* 26 (2): 110–139.

Lin, I. C., T. C. Liao, Y. S. Wu, and H. C. Huang. 2021. Blockchain technology adoption in the financial sector: An empirical analysis. *Technological Forecasting and Social Change* 165:120566.

Liu, C., and Y. Huang. 2019. Exploring bitcoin adoption in China: An integrated model of TAM, trust and cultural factors. *Telematics and Informatics* 35 (4): 993–1004.

Luu, L., V. Narayanan, C. Zheng, K. Baweja, S. Gilbert, and P. Saxena. 2016. A secure sharding protocol for open blockchains. In *Proceedings of the 2016 ACM SIGSAC conference on computer and communications security*, 17–30.

Makhdoom, I., M. Abolhasan, H. Abbas, and W. Ni. 2020. Blockchain's adoption in IoT: The challenges, and a way forward. *Journal of Network and Computer Applications* 134:62–75.

Maruti Techlabs. 2017. Blockchain in supply chain management. https://marutitech.com/blockchain-supply-chain-management/.

Maskuriy, R., A. Selamat, P. Maresova, O. Krejcar, and O. David. 2019. Industry 4.0 for the construction industry: Review of management perspective. *Economies* 7 (3): 68.

Mik, E. 2017. Smart contracts: Terminology, technical limitations and real-world complexity. *Law, Innovation and Technology* 9 (2): 269–300.

Min, H. 2019. Blockchain technology for enhancing supply chain resilience. *Business Horizons* 62 (1): 35–45.

Miraz, M. H., and M. Ali. 2018. Applications of blockchain technology beyond cryptocurrency. *Annals of Emerging Technologies in Computing* 2 (1): 1–6. https://doi.org/10.33166/aetic.2018.01.001.

Mohammed, A., A. Knapkova, and H. Nuseibeh. 2021. Blockchain classification: Literature review and classification framework. *Applied Sciences* 11 (3): 1086.

Nanayakkara, G., H. T. S. Caldera, and H. M. N. D. Bandara. 2019. Blockchain: A scoping study of current development and potential applications. *Journal of Computer Science Applications and Information Technology* 7 (1): 1–8.

Nawari, N. O., and S. Ravindran. 2019. Blockchain and the built environment: Potentials and limitations. *Journal of Building Engineering* 25:100832.

Nofer, M., P. Gomber, O. Hinz, and D. Schiereck. 2017. Blockchain. Business & Information. *Systems Engineering* 59 (3): 183–187.

Patil, D. H., and P. S. Puranik. 2019. Blockchain technology: Types, platforms and use cases. *International Journal of Advanced Research in Computer Science* 10 (5): 16–20.

Ramage, J. 2018. Blockchain: Disrupting financial transactions. *Journal of Financial Transformation* 46:115–121.

Rodrigo, J., D. Stefanovic, and S. Pfeffer. 2018. How blockchain is changing the energy industry. *Energy Policy Journal* 4 (6): 1–12.

Rosic, A. 2018. *What is blockchain technology? A beginner's guide*. Blockgeeks. https://blockgeeks.com/guides/what-is-blockchain-technology/.

Sadeghi, H., S. M. Mahmoudi, and W. Deng. 2021. Blockchain technology in construction: Applications, challenges and future directions. *Automation in Construction* 123:103485.

Shahrubudin, N., T. C. Lee, and R. Ramlan. 2019. An overview on 3D printing technology: Technological, materials, and applications. *Procedia Manufacturing* 35:1286–1296.

Sharmila, R., S. Abirami, and S. Vasumathi. 2019. Blockchain for supply chain traceability: Business implementation challenges. *Materials Today: Proceedings* 37 (Part 2): 1786–1791.

Shi, X., M. Wang, Z. Zhou, and Y. Zhao. 2021. Blockchain 3.0 applications: A literature review. *Technological Forecasting and Social Change* 165:120522.

Shojaei, A. 2019. Blockchain in the built environment: The disruptive potential. *Automation in Construction* 102:288–294.

Söhne, J. 2015. The Blockchain - Can it change the world? http://www.theblockchain.com/2015/11/04/the-blockchain-can-it-change-the-world/. Accessed 14 July 2021.

Sun, J., J. Yan, and K. Z. K. Zhang. 2016. Blockchain-based sharing services: What blockchain technology can contribute to smart cities. *Financial Innovation* 2 (26): 1–9.

Swan, M. 2015. *Blockchain: Blueprint for a new economy*. O'Reilly Media.

Takahashi, B. R. 2017. How can creative industries benefit from blockchain? McKinsey & Company. https://www.mckinsey.com/industries/technology-media-and-telecommunications/our-insights/how-can-creativeindustries-benefit-from-blockchain. Accessed 5 Jan 2020.

Tapscott, D., and A. Tapscott. 2017. *Blockchain revolution: How the technology behind bitcoin is changing money, business, and the world*. Penguin.

Udokwu, C. E., A. Norta, and Z. Wenna. 2021. Adoption of blockchain technology in the construction industry: An empirical investigation. *Journal of Construction Engineering and Management* 147 (7): 04021050.

Underwood, S. 2016. Blockchain beyond bitcoin. *Communications of the ACM* 59 (11): 15–17.

Wang, Y., J. Han, and P. Beynon-Davies. 2017. Understanding blockchain technology for future supply chains: A systematic literature review and research agenda. *Supply Chain Management: An International Journal* 24 (1): 62–84.

Wörner, D., T. von Bomhard, Y. P. Schreier, and D. Bilgeri. 2016. The bitcoin ecosystem: Disruption beyond financial services? In *Proceedings of the twenty-fourth European conference on information systems (ECIS), Istanbul, Turkey*, 1–16.

Wu, J., J. Li, T. Dong, and Y. Meng. 2017. Blockchain: A survey and outlook. *IEEE Access* 6:7010–7023.

Wu, K., Y. Ma, G. Huang, and X. Liu. 2021. A first look at blockchain-based decentralized applications. *Software - Practice and Experience* 51 (10): 2033–2050. https://doi.org/10.1002/spe.2751.

Yermack, D. 2017. Corporate governance and blockchains. *Review of Finance* 21 (1): 7–31.

Yli-Huumo, J., D. Ko, S. Choi, S. Park, and K. Smolander. 2016. Where is current research on blockchain technology?—A systematic review. *PLOS ONE* 11 (10): e0163477.

Yoo, S. 2018. Blockchain-based financial case analysis and its implications. *Asia Pacific Journal of Innovation and Entrepreneurship* 12 (3): 312–324.

Yoo, S., and M. Kim. 2018. Blockchain and supply chain management: A new paradigm for the digitalization of logistics. *Sustainability* 10 (11): 4113.

Zeng, M., L. Wang, S. Zhang, and J. Lin. 2017. Research on the development of blockchain technology. *IOP Conference Series: Materials Science and Engineering* 242 (1): 012119.

Zhao, J. L., S. Fan, and J. Yan. 2019. Overview of business innovations and research opportunities in blockchain and introduction to the special issue. *Financial Innovation* 5 (1): 28.

Chapter 3
Blockchain in the Construction Industry: A Strategic Overview

Abstract The construction industry is increasingly exploring innovative technologies to address persistent challenges related to transparency, inefficiency, and project fragmentation. Blockchain technology, originally developed as the backbone of cryptocurrency systems, has emerged as a transformative tool for enhancing operations in the construction sector. This chapter critically examines the application of blockchain technology within the construction industry, highlighting its potential to improve payment processes, contract administration, electronic document management, and Building Information Modelling (BIM). Emphasis is placed on how blockchain facilitates automation through smart contracts, enhances data security via decentralised ledgers, and promotes collaboration across stakeholders by enabling transparent and traceable transactions. Furthermore, the chapter explores blockchain's impact on sustainability, international construction, and supply chain management. Drawing on recent literature and practical implications, it positions blockchain as a key enabler of digital transformation and sustainable practices in construction. Despite its potential, challenges such as regulatory concerns, technological integration, and adoption barriers remain. The chapter concludes by recommending strategic approaches for harnessing blockchain's full benefits in the built environment.

Keywords Blockchain technology · Smart contracts · Construction industry · Digital transformation · Data transparency

3.1 Introduction

The construction industry is undergoing significant transformation driven by the adoption of digital technologies aligned with the Fourth Industrial Revolution (Smith and O'Rourke 2019). Among these innovations, blockchain technology has emerged as a powerful tool with the potential to revolutionize construction processes through improved transparency, automation, and trust (Underwood 2016).

O. I. Akinradewo et al., *Blockchain Technology for Information Management: A New Era for Sustainable Construction Practices*, Artificial Intelligence and Sustainable Development, https://doi.org/10.1007/978-981-95-2664-2_3

Initially developed as the underlying technology for cryptocurrencies (Rasoloharijaona et al. 2003), blockchain has evolved beyond finance to impact sectors such as supply chain, healthcare, and increasingly, construction (San et al. 2019). The industry's long-standing issues including payment delays, information silos, and fragmented workflows underscore the relevance of blockchain-based solutions (Cardeira 2015; Wang et al. 2017). This chapter introduces blockchain technology, explores its key characteristics, and critically examines its applications across various aspects of the construction lifecycle. It highlights how smart contracts, decentralization, and data immutability are enabling new efficiencies and trust models within the construction ecosystem.

3.2 Blockchain Technology in the Construction Industry

Construction organisations are developing and experimenting with new disruptive technologies and creativity, while the market supports the fourth industrial revolution (4IR) and is progressing into Industry 4.0 (Smith and O'Rourke 2019). The failure to implement technological developments relative to achievements in the manufacturing, motor vehicle and mechanical engineering sectors is one of the main problems hindering the modernisation of the construction sector (Merschbrock 2012; Cardeira 2015; Oesterreich and Teuteberg 2016; Barima 2017; Mason 2017). Blockchain technology is known to be capable of transforming multiple global markets, including the construction industry. In 2008 when citcoin (the first cryptocurrency in the world) was introduced as a transaction verification tool, blockchain was its underlying technology (Rasoloharijaona et al. 2003).

According to Institution of Civil Engineers (2018) in its 2018 Digital World Report, the industry is moving increasingly into a world of networking, technology and data abundance. This move is providing a potential increase in competitiveness, quality and profitability of the business which represents an opportunity to develop. The report concluded that blockchain technology is the most exciting technological innovation that the construction industry will experience. Efficiency and productivity improvements are important for the construction industry to be competitive (Anumba et al. 2008). In recognition of the importance of this, the UK Government in 2013 published a Construction 2025 joint government-industry strategy which set the objectives of delivering projects 50% faster; reducing greenhouse gas emissions by 50%; improving exports by 50% and reducing cost by 33%, all by 2025. Blockchain technology is hailed as being more significant than the Internet breakthrough as it has the potential to increase profitability, improve efficiency and reduce costs (Smith and O'Rourke 2019).

Organisations in the construction industry and other industries are trying to understand blockchain's influence on businesses. The Guardian and some other publications tagged blockchain technology as the buzzword of the year in business (Busby 2018) which has prompted some business owners into thinking blockchain technology should be applied, without fully understanding what it is or how it can be applied (Popper 2018). In a study of the finance sector by Accenture (2017), it was estimated that blockchain technology can save the biggest world investment banks up to $12 billion a year—more than half of the world's annual GDP. Blockchain is the infrastructure behind cryptocurrencies such as bitcoin. Some researchers equate blockchain with bitcoin; however, as Leibson (2018:1) makes it clear, "*Bitcoin is not Blockchain and Blockchain is not Bitcoin*". Sally Davies, according to Smith and O'Rourke (2019:1) opined that "*Blockchain is to Bitcoin what the internet is to email; a vast electronic system on which various application can be built and the currency is just one*". The inherent immutability, openness and redefinition of the trust relationship in blockchain technology are its key advantages. These will provide fast and safe solutions that can work publicly or privately (Underwood 2016). O'Boyle (2017) also described blockchain as an "internet of value" owing to its irrevocable and decentralising nature the impact of which would be felt over the next 20 years (Khaqqi et al. 2018). It is capable of changing the development of applications, creating efficiencies and driving digital-based transformations in sectors (Mathews et al. 2017).

Payment is one of the most important problems confronting the construction industry with delayed payment or default in contractual entitlements, which can often result in contract failure (Cardeira 2015; Wang et al. 2017). A smart contract has been adjudged to be one of the most useful dimensions of blockchain technology applications for the construction sector. With a smart contract which executes pieces of code itself, the payment is initiated once it satisfies the contract terms (Szabo 1994) on completion of pre-set obligations (Szabo 1994; Boucher et al. 2017). Smart contracts can also be considered 'automated traditional contracts' as the elements still have to be input and controlled by humans (Clack et al. 2016). Smart contracts consist of *if/then* commands which ensure the need for intermediaries is reduced, the amount of physical documentation minimised (Cohn et al. 2017), possible attacks and fraudulent activities eliminated, and arbitration and enforcement costs can also be reduced (Tapscott and Tapscott 2017).

3.3 Applications of Blockchain Technology in the Construction Industry

According to various scholars, blockchain technology is not only applicable to different areas such as business, commerce, and finance, among others, but it is also applicable in the construction industry (Kim et al. 2020), especially Blockchain 2.0. This has made blockchain application more relevant in recent times owing to revolutions in technology. Its adoption has improved and enhanced the productivity of any sector in the country as well as the construction industry. According to San et al. (2019), there are five major implications of adopting BT in supply chain management, contract management, electronic document management, financial management, real estate management, and BIM use in the construction industry. These implications are shown in Fig. 3.1 as international construction, transparency, data security, efficiency and cost-effectiveness.

San et al. (2019) opined that there will be an increase in construction efficiency by introducing BT with the use of smart contracts. Subcontractors' or suppliers' productivity will be improved because they know after their job has been completed, a smart contract automatically makes payments to them. San et al. (2019) further opined that as regards blockchain applications in BIM, delays caused by BIM models discrepancies and conflicts among design consultants in the tender and construction phases will be reduced. In addition, San et al. (2019) submitted that many project clients in the present construction industry make transactions through centralised outlets such as financial institutions, while the sales of properties are conducted through property brokers or their representatives. In return, these brokers or financial institutions charge the client an amount for the facility and services provided. However, clients can cut back on the intermediary charges with the introduction of BT in the construction industry (Electric 2017; Hughes 2017). This can be achieved by a shared deal among the client and suppliers, professional

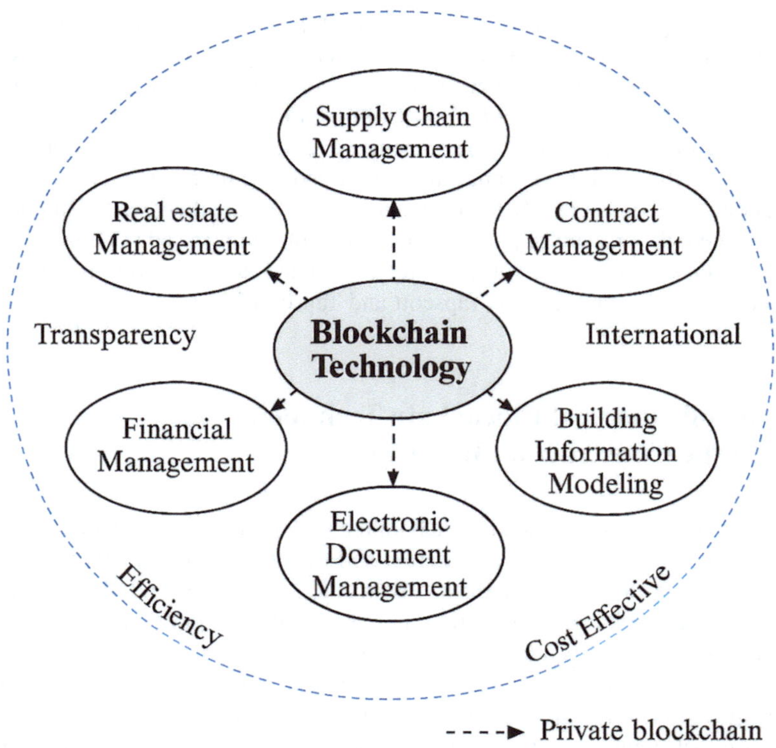

Fig. 3.1 Potentials and implications of blockchain application in construction industry. (Author's adaptation from San et al. (2019))

consultants, and contractors using smart contract. Application of BT in the building industry allows users to view the timeline of monetary and non-monetary transactions.

As contended by Ramage (2018:1), "*the blockchain is visible to everyone who is participating in a transaction, whether that be financial or data exchange.*" Moreover, the decentralized feature of BT allows people to obtain the same information throughout the application. Enough details are accessible for both the sender and the recipient, thereby providing clarity on details which are traceable and permanent on the platform (Wang et al. 2017). It allows users to sign a contractual smart contract by investing in the system while accountability is retained (San et al. 2019). One of the unique features of BT is that it ensures data security whereby all the items are chained to each other via private keys or digital signatures (Koutsogiannis and Berntsen 2017). The decentralized feature also ensures that all the participants have the same information across the system for their construction business and activities. It is very difficult to corrupt or destroy the information stored in the blockchain database since it is duplicated over a peer-to-peer network (Alcazar 2017; Peck 2017). In the current construction market, geographical location is one of the barriers to promoting foreign collaboration on construction projects. With the BT being a shared ledger across a multi-site, regional and national global network, it will facilitate and strengthen cooperation among the client, contractors and professional consultants in the construction industry (Shojaei 2019; Ahmadisheykhsarmast and Sonmez 2020).

Two criteria are used to identify areas where blockchain can be used effectively. The first is the construction lifecycle, which includes the planning, design, and land acquisition stages, as well as procurement, construction, and maintenance. According to Kim et al. (2019), each stage has different tasks which may vary from one project to another. Tasks required in the stages of each of project construction are identified in Table 3.1:

To add context to these applications of BT in the construction industry, they are further discussed as follows:

3.3.1 Contract Management

Blockchain technology is helpful in managing contract-smart contract applications. This is because it can perform more than just financial transactions (Serpell et al. 2005). One of the functions of a smart contract is that it involves the division of tasks into smaller and realistic task packages and enhances payment and the level of the complying process (Lamb 2018). It considers and defines conditions under which each task is completed. It also automatically orders compensation after the completion of each task. The process of dividing tasks into smaller and smart contracts brings about a new type of work structure which is broken down (Ye and König 2021). It helps all the stakeholders of the construction industry to understand their role, what is required of them and liabilities, including other packages, that

Table 3.1 Task in construction lifecycle

Phase	Task
Planning	Feasibility study of technical services
	Preliminary feasibility study
	Master plan
	Main feasibility study
	Investment strategy study
	Selection of bidding method
	Budget plan
Design	Project procurement strategy development
	Basic design
	Composition of evaluation committee
	Detailed design
	Design review
	Procurement evaluation
	Value engineering
Contract administration	Contract evaluation
	Land acquisition
	Contract bidding and formation
Construction and maintenance	Construction management
	Official completion
	Project cot/change management
	Construction participant management
	Operation and maintenance
	Post-evaluation

Source: Author's compilation

may affect them. It enables the pre-execution stage of the project to be observed holistically with a tracking record of the work progress and stages of development during the execution (Wörner et al. 2016). Managing contracts with software technology tends to reduce many uncertainties in the construction of projects because the outcome and the factors responsible for each outcome is anticipated and defined in advance (Mohammed et al. 2021). Approval of payment is done automatically with the evidence of compliance and proof of work completion. In this process the service of an administrative assistant may not be needed for the section, thereby reducing contract disputes as the amount to be paid for the work done and the conditions attached to it are clearly stated and managed by the system (Mohammed et al. 2021; Ye and König 2021).

A unique quality of the system is that most of the construction data recorded are more secure. Environmentally-related data which are being shared within the system of blockchain enable the activation of the evaluation of level of compliance and make provision for recorded instrumental data for the resolution of conflicts (Shojaei 2019; Ahmadisheykhsarmast and Sonmez 2020). In this process a smart contract alters the liens, escrows of landscape and other types of bands within construction industry. The system is more efficient as the number of service people required in the contract administration would be reduced (Shi et al. 2021; Udokwu et al. 2021). The procedures involved would also be documented properly. In other words, it reduces intermediaries and documentation in the construction processes. Moreover, the efficiency of the industry increases with payment applications. Although it may not be that it increases productivity but it smooths the process of administration, particularly the financial and compliance as well as many stimulations that the procedure involves (Sadeghi et al. 2021). This system is superior when compared to traditional projected delivery systems in estimating the cost of project, labour involved, progress and other forms of project documentation. This leads to the system being mostly preferred in the industry owing to its effectiveness and efficiency. Its level of transparency would also improve project management and accountability (Hamida et al. 2017; Dai et al. 2018).

The studies of Wang et al. (2017) and Kakavand et al. (2017) have examined related issues in the construction industry, namely the temporary leasing of equipment and insurance policies. According to the authors, clients only make payment due for the job based on the time spent by the workers on the site. However, the authentication and the conditions attached can be more secured by a blockchain system of networks (Shojaei 2019; Ahmadisheykhsarmast and Sonmez 2020). Moreover, through the use of smart contract, BT could be used to establish a relationship between the stakeholders such as client and the project consultant in charge of the design, cost and management of the project. Apart from this, it could be used among the client, the consultancy firm and the contractor on large projects (Shahrubudin et al. 2019). Also, it would enable different/various projects to be carried out on a labour basis with construction activities that are further subdivided into small task packages at the level of an individual via smart contract (Hughes 2017).

3.3.2 Electronic Document Management

Electronic document management (EDM) was in existence even before the emergence of blockchain technology. This system is improved on from time to time (Maskuriy et al. 2019). The adoption of EDM is on the increase in recent times owing to the complex nature of most construction projects and procurements. This makes it easier for contractor and consultants to pay the service provider for using the centralised platform to manage electronic document in the distribution of information to the team involved (Shi et al. 2021). Blockchain application tend to provide less expensive and more efficient technology in providing solutions to the modern EDM system. Turk and Klinc (2017) asserted that throughout the stages of building life cycle, blockchain makes provision for a reliable framework for managing information. The implementation or adoption of a blockchain system makes it possible for every document to be secured or protected in the decentralised ledger by allowing documents to be notarized through updating, deleting and creating (Wang et al. 2017). Keeping of records of important construction documents such as the drawing as well as instructions from architect and engineers, certificates of payment, extensions of time, and project completion are all possible (Mohammed et al. 2021).

3.3.3 Building Information Modelling (BIM)

Blockchain technology is applicable in BIM. Most information obtained is continuously added, adjusted, revised and cross-checked though different stages (Shojaei 2019). Stakeholders of construction projects need to look for a better ways of merging the right files so that the wrong files would not be merged in error. In merging the right file, blockchain application provides better solutions to the limiting problems of the BIM system through the provision of a decentralised platform for BIM (Udokwu et al. 2021). Controlling and keeping record of changes to the BIM at design and construction stages could be achieved by bargaining re-editing privileges and keeping and unchangeable records of all the adjustment made on the system (Lohry and Bodell 2015). In other words, blockchain technology has the ability to keep construction data about when and what was done and serves as foundation for solving any legal conflicts that may arise (Turk and Klinc 2017). In the use of blockchain system, there are many advantages in modelling BIM (Lohry and Bodell 2015). One of the advantages is that blockchain application has the ability to address some issues that prevent the construction industry from using BIM. These issues, according to Turk and Klinc (2017), include interorganisational keeping of records, data ownership, tracing of changes, multiparty aggregation, and traceability, among others. The blockchain system makes provision for a visible, vital and long-term chain of "evidence of trust" through the combination of decentralised properties in modelling BIM (Matthew 2017). A blockchain system makes provision for a platform where the updating and maintenance of project environment is possible (Maskuriy et al. 2019; Shojaei 2019). In this process tamper-proof and time-stamp data are provided for. For example, tamper-proof data is used to trace changes to the model that have occurred in the record. Through this, a user can easily use tamper-proof data to find the party concerned in the design process. Any alteration or adjustment in the model is recorded. This is communicated to the other parties connected in the blockchain network (Shojaei 2019; Sadeghi et al. 2021; Udokwu et al. 2021).

3.3.4 Property Management

Blockchain is used in the management of property. In other words, property management, especially in the acquisition, registration, and transferability of land or building construction is easy to manage with blockchain technology (Wörner et al. 2016). The use of blockchain has made recorded data more transparent and efficient. Anybody that has the private key to the registered asset has total control over it under the blockchain system (Nawari and Ravindran 2019). The owner can make decisions on it, either to sell the asset or transfer the key (private key) to the other party (Swan 2015). Previous researchers have affirmed the applications of blockchain in the management of property. The researchers are identified below:

> *Blockchains can be used to track physical assets, allowing a record of ownership for each asset to be kept.* (Abeyratne and Monfared 2016:4)

> *Property that has been blockchain encoded would become smart property that can be transacted using smart contracts.* (Swan 2015:15)

> *It could be viewed as an information and communications technology (ICT) tool for recording the possession of on-platform and off-platform securities, as well as the responsibilities and privileges emerging from contracts.* (Aste et al. 2017:22)

> *A blockchain is a massively powerful global shared infrastructure that could transfer money and portray property ownership.* (Ramage 2018:1)

> *It is simple to transfer title to any property, monetary or non-monetary, for whom the ownership is regulated mostly by blockchain.* (Wang et al. 2017:67)

3.3.5 Supply Chain Management

A blockchain system is applicable in the management of the supply chain in the construction industry. The industry is made up of multiple networks of different parties. These parties include products, participants, services rendered and vendors, among others. Previous researchers (Kim et al. 2017; Wang et al. 2017; Abeyratne and Monfared 2016) have concentrated their studies on the enhancement of supply chain management IT solutions that could record, trace, analyse and manage data with a centralised platform. According to Wang et al. (2017), the blockchain system could improve on the current processes of supply chain management through improvement in product traceability and transparency. Input of accurate data is necessary for empirical analysis under supply chain management. This could be enabled by parties involved in validating information using blockchain technology (Ye and König 2021). Correct data (such as records of materials deliveries and labour on the site) can provide useful information to contractors or consultants to analyse and supervise or oversee their productivity, performance and profit in chain supply management. This therefore calls for a decentralised system in handling data of a supply chain (Patil and Puranik 2019). Blockchain application is used in managing supply chain data. It could aid the improvement of performance of supply chain management without the requirement of participating members to create trust (Wang et al. 2017).

Blockchain application can be useful for a variety of purposes, particularly in the construction supply chain. Smart contracts, for example, can be useful in purchasing, tracking, and checking items in a construction supply chain automatically without manual intervention (Nanayakkara et al. 2017). Moreover, current construction industry procedures rely heavily on contractual agreements. It was stated that digital contracts could be executed securely and stored on blockchain to reduce the risk of counter-parties for supplies as well as contractors as they add the certainty needed to continue with a job. Also, blockchain could be used to enhance payment settlement, compliance management, material planning and many other supply chain management operations with better efficiency, trust and transparency (Hamida et al. 2017; Dai et al. 2018; Sadeghi et al. 2021; Udokwu et al. 2021).

3.3.6 Funding Management

Blockchain help in providing funds in the management of construction projects. The complex nature of building projects requires huge amounts of money in its execution. The adoption of blockchain technology in the construction industry helps in providing a platform for the crowdfunding of projects of clients (Shojaei 2019; Ahmadisheykhsarmast and Sonmez 2020). The blockchain-based crowdfunding is a peer-to-peer platform for raising funds for projects without the backing of traditional capital (Swan 2015). This is possible through the creation of one's own digital currency and selling 'cryptographic shares'. The use of funds obtained through crowdfunding platforms is obvious with blockchain application. This gives contractors, consultants, investors, and clients greater confidence. It also helps in tracing how money is being spent on a project (Ahmadisheykhsarmast and Sonmez 2020).

3.3.7 Sustainability Management

Sustainability management, according to Rodrigo et al. (2019), is essential in recent times especially in the modern construction sector. This is probably owing to the rise in global warming, change in climate and waste-generated increases in the demand for better environmentally-friendly operations that are sustainable for every sector, particularly construction, manufacturing, and transportation, among others (Mohammed et al. 2021). Higher levels of pollution generated at construction sites call for the need of operations that are sustainable in nature. Davidson (2009) maintained that it is always necessary to check or supervise the sustainability of services and products that are provided by both the private and public sectors. Monitoring the level of energy and waste generated as well as carbon emission is essential in every sector. According to Pacheco-Torgal and Jalali (2012), the construction industry contributes significantly to environmental pollution and addressing this is essential. Rodrigo et al. (2019) identified some challenges that hinder sustainability management. These include the misplacement of data, incorrect records, and the unavailability of data, among others. All the issues mentioned could be solved by blockchain technology (Wörner et al. 2016).

3.3.8 Financial Services

Financial services were the first area of domain adopted by blockchain (Underwood 2016). Danuri et al. (2008) noted that the construction industry has financial-related issues which could be solved by blockchain application, and a chained payment settlement culture. In addition, the occurrence of default settlement duration are much higher in the construction industry than in other industries (Ramachandra and Rotimi 2010). Moreover, over-due delayed payments are substantial for long settlement periods (Denuri et al. 2006). There are so many cases of non-payment and partial payments in the building sector which have worsen the financial status of the upstream participants in the construction supply chain (Amsah 2011). The emergence of a highly efficient blockchain financial-based platform is being used to replace the inefficiency of existing financial business models and software (Nofer et al. 2017). Blockchain, through the use of bitcoin and other means of payment, has been developed to do transactions directly with the client, by-passing middlemen which use to delay and add additional cost to transactions (Vrauken 2017). Another drawback of the traditional system which involved the use of intermediaries is that it is difficult to transfer value without currencies. Blockchain can perform better than the traditional financial means through the use of tokens (digitalized version of assets). Tokens are being used to define their own assets that are digital in nature to carry out financial transactions on business applications (Catalini and Gans 2018).

3.3.9 Compliance and Assurance Management

Blockchain can be used in compliance and assurance management. The challenges, according to Ashworth and Percia (2018), with compliance and assurance management for the construction sector have made blockchain application applicable and preferred. Monitoring and checking of an organisation's practices using an auditing process is one of the approaches of ensuring compliance and quality assurance (Wörner et al. 2016). The process of auditing involves internal and external ways of examining records of business transaction and practices to make sure that every party or stakeholder such as contractors or suppliers comply with the quality and regulatory standards (Karapetrovic and Willborn 2000). The record is then secured or protected for future reference once the auditing has been completed. Actions are taken later to correct any issue discovered through the process of auditing. One of the important aspects of auditing is that it makes sure that quality and compliance of product and services are regulated. This process could be achieved by a blockchain-based distributed ledger system in proffering solutions to issues related to compliance and assurance management in the construction industry (Anjum et al. 2017).

3.3.10 Smart City and Logistics

Blockchain could better be applied in the area of smart cities and logistics. This could be observed in the construction and operation maintenance stage (Sadeghi et al. 2021). Some of the applications of blockchain are useful in the logistics industry, particularly in customs and distribution management (Nawari and Ravindran 2019).

3.3.11 Notarization-Related Applications

Construction companies are facing a growing number of challenges, including increased pressure to comply with increased government and industry restrictions (Shahrubudin et al. 2019). Significant resources, such as time and effort, are allotted to maintain the integrity and genuineness of project documentation during storing and retrieving. With the application of blockchain, each document could be distributed and stored across multiple ledgers, and each creation, deletion, and updating across the system is perfectly notarized (Ye and König 2021). The blockchain system as a whole is aware of the source of the data, and the technology allows for verification. Such applications can be used to record construction quality data such as raw material and configuration quality, project progress data (every day, every week, and month by month), and resource consuming data i.e., scaffold, concrete, equipment, steel, and formwork (Shojaei 2019; Ahmadisheykhsarmast and Sonmez 2020).

3.3.12 Design Management

Blockchain technologies ensure project design is properly managed among the project client, contractors and consultants (Ahmadisheykhsarmast and Sonmez 2020). It makes stages of the design sectioned to different levels for various groups of contractors and consultants to handle properly, although at the design state each construction discipline is kept separate (Shojaei 2019). Blockchain, if fully adopted, could enhance the benefits of BIM by permitting all the participating stakeholders in the construction industry such as engineers and architects, among others, to design the project using the same BIM model with their respective components with clearly indicated ownership (Kinnaird and Geipel 2017).

3.3.13 Waste Management

One of the major priorities within the bult environment is sustainability. This is due to the demands from the public, customers and government (Pitt et al. 2009). Rodrigo et al. (2019) added that bTis useful in calculating embodied carbon operation within the construction sector as well as helping in the enhancement of carbon management. It is a known fact that the construction sector tends to produce higher proportions of waste than most of the world (Mohammed et al. 2021). However, blockchain application, if well adopted, could be used to reduce this waste by managing waste properly, including the trading of waste (Ratnasabapathy et al. 2019).

3.3.14 Asset Management and Maintenance

Blockchain application is necessary in the construction industry in the management of maintenance of assets or property. It is used in tracking all information related to the built asset at all stages of the life cycle of an asset (Shi et al. 2021). While the project nature and the involvement of different stakeholders make the maintenance and management of assets unrealistic, the introduction of blockchain application in the construction sector has made the maintenance and management of assets easier and possible (Udokwu et al. 2021). This is because the blockchain system allows tracking of and access to important data throughout the life cycle of the asset (Wang et al. 2019).

3.4 Impact of Blockchain Technology on the Construction Industry

Blockchain technology concentrates on preserving personal ownership while building more accountable and inclusive systems that prioritize traceability and transparency (Ye and König 2021). Previous studies have shown that blockchain application in the construction industry has an enormous impact (Kim et al. 2019). Among the impacts are workflow and time efficiency, sustainability, facility management, as well as data security and international construction (Wörner et al. 2016).

3.4.1 Smart Energy

Major power producers (MPPs) lead the energy sector and develop the prices; they account for 94% of the electricity production market (Murkin et al. 2016). However, in recent times the sector has opened up more possibilities for individual residential energy manufacturers, especially those who make use of solar photovoltaic panels and generate extra charges more than they need (Nawari and Ravindran 2019). Owing to the downturn experienced in renewable technologies coupled with the rise in prosumer competence, the extra charge generated is sold to neighbours or the grid (Šajn 2016). Trades are currently carried out via MPPs; however, blockchain technology-managed microgrids will enable this to be done in a decentralized manner so that prosumers deliver directly to consumers. Energy efficiency is crucial if the 'smart' goals, such smart homes, smart cities, and smart government are to be accomplished, as they rely on the capacity to use and protect energy (Park et al. 2018). In the expectations for newly-built infrastructure and the upgrading of current buildings, the construction industry will need to take smart energy into account (Nawari and Ravindran 2019).

3.4.2 Sharing Economy

With the upgrades in information and communication technology (ICT) and IoT, sharing economy have been encouraged and rendered more available, allowing individuals to have access to real-time data on resource availability and make better decisions (Huckle et al. 2016; Pazaitis et al. 2017). The social model follows supply-and-demand-led economic power. It could contribute to further growth, innovation, job creation and opening up new possibilities for society and the environment. Value is created collectively before it is decentralised after being channelled via the financial markets. However, it is centrally controlled by companies which are responsible for determining whether benefits are allocated via rents, dividends, or salaries, among others (Nawari and Ravindran 2019). Blockchain technology-based distributed apps and decentralised autonomous organisations (DAOs) allow for individuals to monetize their belongings when they are not in use (e.g. buildings, vehicle and ride-sharing) (Huckle et al. 2016; Sun et al. 2016). Blockchain technology also leads to more private and secure interactions among the parties involved (Biswas and Muthukkumarasamy 2017).

3.4.3 Smart Homes

Blockchain is used in smart homes, according to Dorri et al. (2017), for tracking and reducing energy usage. Despite the increased overheads in the use of low-capital IoT applications, the advantages of blockchain technology are perceived to be worthwhile. It is perceived to offer greater privacy and safety at home (Shojaei 2019; Ahmadisheykhsarmast and Sonmez 2020). Suspicious activities can be detected using digital fingerprints while simultaneously identifying each of the smart home devices. Monitoring systems support the smart home by observing behaviours that are normal and taking immediate actions appropriately upon recognition of abnormal behaviours (Li et al. 2019). Users have tracking and remote control on temperature, motion, lighting, and humidity, among others in their homes (Zhu et al. 2017). Lazaroiu and Roscia (2017) proposed a smart residential district which would allow people to control their homes remotely, together with other features such as recreation and educational development. This is done by providing a smart playground in which children can play on slides and swings and generate electricity by doing so, a smart card system of payment, as well as car and ride-sharing, among others (Li et al. 2019).

3.4.4 Smart Transportation

Blockchain technology is growing future smart transport solutions by combining it with other technologies such as smart energy for better resource management (Kang et al. 2017). Smart cars now have private data onboard storage that enables the operators, through the blockchain, to choose the transfer of their data ownership to third parties through encrypting and authenticating (Zhu et al. 2017). Different solutions can be offered with the use of blockchain technology in transportation which include automated software updates in manufacturing and car maintenance; versatile insurance dependent upon data provided on the driver's actions; and smart vehicle charging combined with smart homes, among others (Sadeghi et al. 2021; Udokwu et al. 2021). Blockchain-based mobile billing systems make it possible for owners of electric vehicles to charge their vehicles away from their homes (Kim et al. 2017).

3.4.5 Construction Management Using BIM

Increasing efficiency levels through technology, policies and processes have been widely regarded as a development in BIM (Succar 2009). Although the general understanding is that BIM will benefit from blockchain technology incorporation, there is agreement that the level 2 BIM partnership is not enough and that it requires more networked and advanced models, such as the envisioned level 3 for this collaboration to be established (Heiskanen 2017; Kinnaird and Geipel 2017; Mason 2017). Level 2 BIM is collaborative whereby 3D models are produced (Zhu et al. 2017).

3.4.6 Workflow and Time Efficiency

Blockchain technology has the ability to improve construction productivity through the use of smart contact in the construction contract, especially in the subcontracting and supplying of construction materials (Kim et al. 2017). The motivation for the subcontractors or suppliers' efficiency would be because of the level of trust in the machine, as most payments are usually made automatically to the supplier and subcontractor when the job has been completed (Kang et al. 2017). Blockchain software, especially in BIM, would reduce delays caused by BIM model discrepancies and disputes among consultants who designed the project during the tendering and construction states (Li et al. 2019). Blockchain software in BIM is regarded as a private blockchain in which only important project stakeholders i.e., architects, site engineers, project managers, quantity surveyors and representatives of clients would be allowed to confirm or check and access 'block' in the blockchain environment.

Before the contract stage, the consultants that are in charge of the design would produce and modify BIM models within the blockchain system for tender purposes (Mohammed et al. 2021). Every participating member, particularly major stakeholders of construction projects in the private blockchain, are more visible to the BIM models and must be able to check or confirm changes that are made before the information is updated on the drawings. This is referred to as 'block' being joined to the 'chain' (Shojaei 2019; Ahmadisheykhsarmast and Sonmez 2020). This implies that all the participating members of private blockchain are kept up to date on new and current information. This type of change that is observed to the BIM is time-stamped, making it easier for the stakeholders to track where and when the drawing is being updated (Shi et al. 2021).

3.4.7 Cost Efficiency

Blockchain technology is cost efficient by removing middleman and transaction cost that are related in the construction industry. This is unlike the modern construction industry where a client makes transactions through centralized intermediaries such as financial institutions or by selling property through agents of real estate (Zhu et al. 2017). In exchange for these, the middleman charges the client an exorbitant fee for the provision of facilities and services (Hughes 2017). Cost efficiency can be accomplished through the use of a smart contract in a contract that is directly between the owner of the project (client) and the consultant that is in charge of designing the project, as well as the supplier and contractors. In addition, the usage of a smart contract will help in reducing the cost of administration in the contract document (Ramage 2018). Moreover, the use of a blockchain platform helps in removing the fee charged by the real estate agent. Thus, clients' selling their property using the blockchain system payment to reduce the incidents of disputes that are a common issue in the construction industry and they are often costly to resolve in court (Kim et al. 2017). The cost of resolving construction disputes may be reduced using blockchain system in construction contracts. According to Wang et al. (2017), blockchain application saves time and money because it is automated and neutral. Hughes (2017) opined that blockchain in BIM produces correct and accurate bill of quantities and drawings that are less expensive. This would save more time, money, and resources by avoiding the hassle of incorrectly tendered drawings and bills of quantities as well as lowering variation costs at the time of construction (Patil and Puranik 2019).

3.4.8 Trust and Transparency

The use of the blockchain application has enabled each participant to observe the timeline of financial and non-financial transactions which could be for property or land, among others. Ramage (2018) indicated that blockchain application is more accessible to everyone who is a participant in the transaction, either through financial or data exchange. Moreover, the decentralised nature of the blockchain application allows participating members to access or share the same data across the applications (Udokwu et al. 2021). Participants within the network, such as receivers and senders, will have access to more information than others (Wang et al. 2017). This creates transparency for clients within the system in detecting and unchanging records. The presence of transparency tends to encourage various clients or users to agree to the bidding smart contract owing to the confidence in the technology (Nawari and Ravindran 2019). In the process of using the blockchain application, users are not required to create a relationship of trust because they have confidence in the system which is automated in nature (Wang et al. 2017).

3.4.9 Facility Management

Blockchain technology has impacted the area of facility management. It helps in the management of properties by using smart contracts when maintenance is required (Zhu et al. 2017). Blockchain is used in placing a work order; based on confirmation of completion, it also releases payment to the contractors. Decentralised autonomous organisation (DAO) which was introduced as a means of regulating organisations by various smart contracts, is applicable throughout the lifecycle of a building (Li et al. 2019). This varies from design to construction, maintenance, operation and demolition. It is handled cohesively and autonomously by smart contracts. Blockchain is one of the few technologies that can support such complex interactions over time (Angraal et al. 2017).

3.4.10 Data Security

A central platform or data base is used by the construction industry for keeping records of construction data. Construction data as asserted by Koutsogiannis and Berntsen (2017) is at the risk of hackers with the negative intention of demanding a ransom before the owner could retrieve their data. Data security should not be overlooked as big project construction deals with large project funding (Ye and König 2021). One of the superior qualities of the blockchain system is that is enhances the security of construction data by chaining all information that is within the data base to others via a digital signature. Blockchain application ensures that all the participating members have access to similar information across the system (Kim et al. 2017).

3.4.11 International Construction

Geographical issues have become an impediment to encouraging international construction, especially in the modern construction industry (Mohammed et al. 2021). The reason is that blockchain technology involves the sharing of data across the worldwide connectivity of networks of different sites, locations and institutions. It improves cooperation between and among participating clients, contractors, and consultancy firms from different countries (Shojaei 2019; Ahmadisheykhsarmast and Sonmez 2020). As a result, the party involve does not need to have a reliable relationship with other parties (i.e., contractor, consultants and suppliers) because the blockchain application provides a transparent and trustworthy infrastructure system (Mohammed et al. 2021).

3.4.12 Sustainability

Material transparency has impacted sustainability in different industries. Some of these areas as indicated by Kim et al. (2017) include the estimation of carbon emission, cost of whole lifecycles and the confirmation of raw materials. For example, participants can make more choices that are sustainable in nature by using materials that are traceable via blockchain through to the source of raw material of the particular product (Mohammed et al. 2021). Normally, the supply chain would provide the specific information required by the clients. Blockchain network will not only involve indirect suppliers of needed materials but also enable direct suppliers of needed materials, i.e., supply needed raw materials such as raw material suppliers to a prefabricated construction factory, to input their information into the computer for better precision and authentication (Hamida et al. 2017; Dai et al. 2018). This method would result in systematic and consistent asset data. This database could be applied not just for design, logistics, and building projects strategic planning, but also for facilitating post-occupancy planning. Blockchain system can also help with huge resource management, allowing for the creation of a smart grid (Mengelkamp et al. 2018). To begin, both energy consumption and production should then be recorded on a blockchain. This could then be used to lay the groundwork for better inventory management and, eventually, true pricing strategies for energy (Ye and König 2021).

3.5 Summary

This chapter has explored the transformative potential of blockchain technology within the construction industry. With the industry facing persistent challenges such as inefficiencies, delayed payments, data insecurity, and lack of transparency, blockchain emerges as a viable digital solution capable of redefining operations. The chapter discussed the foundational concept of blockchain and its core attributes—immutability, decentralization, and transparency—and examined its application across various construction domains, including contract management, supply chain, property and asset management, document handling, sustainability tracking, and funding mechanisms. Smart contracts, a major component of blockchain, were emphasized as crucial tools for automating payment processes, reducing disputes, and enhancing accountability. In addition, blockchain's integration with emerging technologies like Building Information Modelling (BIM), Internet of Things (IoT), and smart city infrastructure was highlighted, particularly in enhancing collaboration, real-time data sharing, and lifecycle management. The chapter also addressed how blockchain promotes cost efficiency by eliminating intermediaries, encourages a sharing economy through decentralized networks, and supports sustainable development goals via improved traceability and environmental monitoring. The use cases presented illustrate how blockchain can improve construction workflows, enhance data security, manage design changes, and enable international collaboration. The chapter further explored advanced blockchain applications in areas such as smart energy, transportation, facility management, and waste control. Despite its promise, successful adoption of blockchain in construction requires addressing industry-specific barriers, stakeholder awareness, interoperability challenges, and the need for regulatory frameworks. Overall, blockchain is positioned not as a replacement technology but as a powerful enabler of innovation, offering a decentralized infrastructure for trust, transparency, and efficiency. As the industry advances toward digital transformation, integrating blockchain presents an opportunity to modernize construction processes and improve project outcomes across the built environment.

References

Abeyratne, S. A., and R. P. Monfared. 2016. Blockchain ready manufacturing supply chain using distributed ledger. *International Journal of Research in Engineering and Technology* 5 (9): 1–10.

Accenture. 2017. Blockchain banking for investment banks. Accenture. https://www.accenture.com/lv-en/insightbanking-on-blockchain. Accessed 1 Jan 2020.

Ahmadisheykhsarmast, S., and R. Sonmez. 2020. Blockchain-based construction supply chain management. *Automation in Construction* 123:103529.

Alcazar, J. 2017. Blockchain technology in the construction industry: Challenges and opportunities. *Construction Management Review* 3 (2): 22–27.

Amsah, M. N. 2011. The problems of payment in construction industry. *International Journal of Project Management* 29 (6): 678–686.

Angraal, S., H. M. Krumholz, and W. L. Schulz. 2017. Blockchain technology: Applications in health care. *Circulation: Cardiovascular Quality and Outcomes* 10 (9): e003800.

Anjum, A., M. Sporny, and A. Sill. 2017. Blockchain standards for compliance and assurance. *IT Professional* 19 (4): 20–29.

Anumba, C. J., K. Ruikar, and P. M. Carrillo. 2008. Knowledge management in construction. *Wiley-Blackwell.*

Ashworth, A., and S. Percia. 2018. *Contractual procedures in the construction industry*. 7th ed. Routledge.

Aste, T., P. Tasca, and T. D. Matteo. 2017. Blockchain technologies: The foreseeable impact on society and industry. *Computer* 50 (9): 18–28.

Barima, O. W. 2017. Leveraging smart governance for sustainable urban development: A review. *Smart Cities* 1 (1): 41–52.

Biswas, K., and V. Muthukkumarasamy. 2017. Securing smart cities using blockchain technology. In *2016 IEEE 18th international conference on high performance computing and communications*, 1392–1395. IEEE.

Boucher, P., S. Nascimento, and M. Kritikos. 2017. What if blockchain technology revolutionised voting? Scientific foresight unit (STOA). *European Parliament* 603:968.

Busby, M. 2018. Blockchain: 2018's business buzzword. The Guardian, January 1. https://www.theguardian.com.

Cardeira, H. 2015. Smart contracts and the construction industry. *Construction Law Journal* 31 (6): 443–449.

Catalini, C., and J. S. Gans. 2018. Initial coin offerings and the value of tokens. NBER Working Paper No. 24418. https://doi.org/10.3386/w24418.

Clack, C. D., V. A. Bakshi, and L. Braine. 2016. Smart contract templates: Foundations, design landscape and research directions. Cornell University arXiv preprint, arXiv:1608.00771.

Cohn, A., J. West, and J. Parker. 2017. Smart contracts and the role of lawyers. *Law Practice Today*. https://www.lawpracticetoday.org.

Dai, H. N., Z. Zheng, and Y. Zhang. 2018. Blockchain for internet of things: A survey. *IEEE Internet of Things Journal* 6 (5): 8076–8094.

Danuri, M. S. M., M. Che Munaaim, and H. Abdul Rahman. 2008. Barriers to industrialised building system (IBS): The case of Malaysia. In *Proceedings of the international conference on construction industry*.

Davidson, C. H. 2009. The role of environmental sustainability in the construction industry. *Canadian Journal of Civil Engineering* 36 (3): 381–386.

Denuri, M., M. Nassar, and M. Abduh. 2006. Delay in construction project payment in the Malaysian construction industry. *International Journal of Project Management* 24 (4): 298–302.

Dorri, A., S. S. Kanhere, and R. Jurdak. 2017. Towards an optimized blockchain for IoT. In *Proceedings of the second international conference on internet-of-things design and implementation*, 173–178. ACM.

Electric, S. 2017. Blockchain in real estate: Revolutionising the industry. *Smart Electric Journal* 4 (3): 15–18.
Hamida, E. B., M. Guerroumi, and M. Haddar. 2017. The role of blockchain technology in sustainable construction. *Journal of Sustainable Development in Africa* 19 (3): 34–49.
Heiskanen, A. 2017. The technology of trust: How the internet of things and blockchain could usher in a new era of construction. *Construction Innovation* 17 (4): 324–338.
Huckle, S., R. Bhattacharya, M. White, and N. Beloff. 2016. Internet of things, blockchain and shared economy applications. *Procedia Computer Science* 98:461–466.
Hughes, T. 2017. Blockchain and BIM: A perfect match for the construction industry. *Construction Today* 19 (2): 36–38.
Institution of Civil Engineers (ICE). 2018. *Digital world: The 2018 ICE state of the nation report*. London: Institution of Civil Engineers.
Kakavand, H., N. Kost De Sevres, and B. Chilton. 2017. The blockchain revolution: An analysis of regulation and technology related to distributed ledger technologies. *SSRN Electronic Journal*. https://doi.org/10.2139/ssrn.2849251.
Kang, J., R. Yu, X. Huang, S. Maharjan, Y. Zhang, and E. Hossain. 2017. Enabling localized peer-to-peer electricity trading among plug-in hybrid electric vehicles using consortium blockchains. *IEEE Transactions on Industrial Informatics* 13 (6): 3154–3164.
Karapetrovic, S., and W. Willborn. 2000. Quality assurance and effectiveness of audit systems. *International Journal of Quality & Reliability Management* 17:679–703.
Khaqqi, K. N., J. J. Sikorski, K. Hadinoto, and M. Kraft. 2018. Incorporating seller/buyer reputation-based system in blockchain-enabled emission trading application. *Applied Energy* 209:8–19.
Kim, K., H. Kang, and T. Hong. 2017. Blockchain-based smart contracts for the construction industry. *Sustainability* 9 (12): 2220.
Kim, H. M., M. Laskowski, and K. Jung. 2019. Blockchain-enabled smart contracts: Architecture, applications, and future trends. *Journal of Intelligent Manufacturing* 30:1–17.
Kim, H. M., M. Laskowski, and A. Wright. 2020. Blockchain-based construction supply chain management. *Computers in Industry* 123:103306.
Kinnaird, C., and M. Geipel. 2017. *Blockchain technology in the construction industry: Digital transformation for a sustainable future*. Arup.
Koutsogiannis, A., and J. Berntsen. 2017. Blockchain for construction: Data security perspectives. *Construction Today* 5 (4): 14–18.
Lamb, K. 2018. Smart contracts in the construction industry: A guide to implementation. *Construction Week* 4 (6): 28–31.
Lazaroiu, G. C., and M. Roscia. 2017. Definition methodology for the smart cities model. *Energy* 47 (1): 326–332.
Leibson, R. 2018. Blockchain isn't bitcoin. *IEEE Spectrum* 55 (1): 20.
Li, H., D. Greenwood, and M. Kassem. 2019. Blockchain in the built environment and construction industry: A review of the status quo and research trends. *Journal of Building Engineering* 25:100832.
Lohry, M., and B. Bodell. 2015. The implications of blockchain for the construction industry. *Construction Executive* 3 (4): 11–15.
Maskuriy, R., A. Selamat, P. Maresova, O. Krejcar, and R. David. 2019. Industry 4.0 for the construction industry: Review of management perspective. *Economics & Management* 22 (4): 101–112.
Mason, J. 2017. Intelligent contracts and the construction industry. *Construction Law Journal* 33 (2): 137–152.
Mathews, M., D. Robles, and B. Bowe. 2017. BIM+ Blockchain: A solution to the trust problem in collaboration? *CIB World Building Congress 2016* 6 (1): 1–12.
Matthew, D. 2017. Blockchain application in BIM modelling. *Building Information Weekly* 2 (2): 14–17.

Mengelkamp, E., J. Gärttner, K. Rock, S. Kessler, L. Orsini, and C. Weinhardt. 2018. Designing microgrid energy markets: A case study: The Brooklyn microgrid. *Applied Energy* 210:870–880.
Merschbrock, C. 2012. Unpacking the digital toolbox: A study of new technologies in construction. *Journal of Civil Engineering and Management* 18 (3): 304–312.
Mohammed, N., A. Omran, T. Zayed, and M. Hayat. 2021. Blockchain technology applications in construction: State-of-the-art review. *Journal of Information Technology in Construction (ITcon)* 26:1–23.
Murkin, J., R. Chitchyan, and R. Byrne. 2016. *Enabling a smarter electricity grid through decentralised data sharing: A study of blockchain and distributed ledger technologies*. University of Bristol Technical Report.
Nanayakkara, S., B. A. K. S. Perera, and J. Zuo. 2017. Blockchain and smart contracts: A new approach to procurement in construction. *Procedia Engineering* 196:838–846.
Nawari, N., and S. Ravindran. 2019. Blockchain and building information modeling (BIM): Integration for a new era. *Frontiers of Engineering Management* 6 (3): 317–328.
Nofer, M., P. Gomber, O. Hinz, and D. Schiereck. 2017. Blockchain. Business & information. *Systems Engineering* 59 (3): 183–187.
O'Boyle, D. 2017. Blockchain and its impact on the construction industry. *The Construction Index Journal* 8 (2): 17–19.
Oesterreich, T. D., and F. Teuteberg. 2016. Understanding the implications of digitization and automation in the construction industry. *Computers in Industry* 83:121–139.
Pacheco-Torgal, F., and S. Jalali. 2012. Eco-efficient construction and building materials research under the EU framework programme horizon 2020. *Construction and Building Materials* 51:151–162.
Park, J., S. Lee, and D. Chang. 2018. A sustainable energy system with blockchain: Integration into smart grids. *Sustainability* 10 (11): 4261.
Patil, M., and M. Puranik. 2019. Use of blockchain technology in construction industry. *International Research Journal of Engineering and Technology (IRJET)* 6 (5): 3357–3360.
Pazaitis, A., P. De Filippi, and V. Kostakis. 2017. Blockchain and value systems in the sharing economy: The illustrative case of Backfeed. *Technological Forecasting and Social Change* 125:105–115.
Peck, M. E. 2017. Blockchain world—Do you need a blockchain? *IEEE Spectrum* 54 (10): 26–35.
Pitt, M., M. Tucker, M. Riley, and J. Longden. 2009. Towards sustainable construction: Promotion and best practices. *Construction Innovation* 9 (2): 201–224.
Popper, N. 2018. Everyone is talking about blockchain, and no one knows what it is. *New York Times*. https://www.nytimes.com.
Ramachandra, T., and J. O. Rotimi. 2010. Causes of payment problems in the New Zealand construction industry. *Construction Management and Economics* 28 (12): 1311–1321.
Ramage, J. 2018. Blockchain and smart contracts in construction. *Engineering News Record (ENR)* 12 (6): 1–3.
Rasoloharijaona, T., E. Bertin, and N. Crespi. 2003. *From bitcoin to Blockchain: A brief survey of the history and applications*, 1–9. Blockchain and Distributed Ledger Technologies.
Ratnasabapathy, S., B. Perera, and G. Karunasena. 2019. Blockchain and construction waste management. *Built Environment Project and Asset Management* 9 (4): 554–568.
Rodrigo, M., A. Saer, and S. Kumar. 2019. Blockchain and sustainability: Challenges and opportunities. *Journal of Cleaner Production* 218:1066–1076.
Sadeghi, M., M. Mahmoudi, and X. Deng. 2021. Blockchain in construction: Applications and future directions. *Automation in Construction* 129:103848.
Šajn, N. 2016. European Parliament. Electricity 'Prosumers'.
San, Y. L., K. L. Choy, and P. Fung. 2019. Blockchain in construction supply chain: Applications, challenges and research opportunities. *International Journal of Construction Management* 19 (5): 431–448.
Serpell, A., G. Barai, and A. Oladapo. 2005. Performance measurement in construction. *Journal of Construction Engineering and Management* 131 (10): 1053–1058.

Shahrubudin, N., T. C. Lee, and R. Ramlan. 2019. Blockchain in construction industry: Benefits and barriers. *Journal of Physics: Conference Series* 1150:012013.

Shi, Y., M. Alazzawi, A. Hassan, and M. Aslam. 2021. A systematic review of blockchain-based applications in the construction industry. *Engineering, Construction and Architectural Management* 28 (10): 2912–2936.

Shojaei, A. 2019. Applications of blockchain technology in construction. *Journal of Construction Engineering* 8 (1): 1–14.

Smith, P., and T. O'Rourke. 2019. Blockchain in the built environment: Challenges and opportunities. The Chartered Institute of Building (CIOB). https://www.ciob.org.

Succar, B. 2009. Building information modelling framework: A research and delivery foundation for industry stakeholders. *Automation in Construction* 18 (3): 357–375.

Sun, J., J. Yan, and K. Z. Zhang. 2016. Blockchain-based sharing services: What blockchain technology can contribute to smart cities. *Financial Innovation* 2 (1): 1–9.

Swan, M. 2015. *Blockchain: Blueprint for a new economy*. O'Reilly Media, Inc.

Szabo, N. 1994. Smart contracts. Unpublished Manuscript. http://www.fon.hum.uva.nl/rob/Courses/InformationInSpeech/CDROM/Literature/LOTwinterschool2006/szabo.best.vwh.net/smart.contracts.html.

Tapscott, D., and A. Tapscott. 2017. *Blockchain revolution: How the technology behind bitcoin and other cryptocurrencies is changing the world*. Penguin.

Turk, Ž., and R. Klinc. 2017. Potentials of blockchain technology for construction management. *Procedia Engineering* 196:638–645.

Udokwu, C., A. Norta, and C. Wenna. 2021. Blockchain adoption in construction industry: Framework and benefits. *Journal of Civil Engineering and Management* 27 (4): 312–325.

Underwood, S. 2016. Blockchain beyond bitcoin. *Communications of the ACM* 59 (11): 15–17.

Vrauken, D. 2017. Construction payments and the blockchain solution. *Blockchain Today* 7 (1): 22–25.

Wang, J., P. Wu, X. Wang, and W. Shou. 2017. The outlook of blockchain technology for construction engineering management. *Frontiers of Engineering Management* 4 (1): 67–75.

Wang, J., X. Wang, and W. Shou. 2019. Blockchain-enabled building lifecycle management in construction. *Automation in Construction* 105:102820.

Wörner, D., T. von Bomhard, Y. P. Schreier, and D. Bilgeri. 2016. The bitcoin ecosystem: Disruption beyond financial services? In *Twenty-fourth European conference on information systems (ECIS)*.

Ye, Z., and M. König. 2021. Blockchain technology in the construction industry: A systematic review of present status and future trends. *Automation in Construction* 126:103688.

Zhu, L., Y. Wu, L. D. Xu, and Y. Zhang. 2017. Building smart cities and communities with blockchain technology. *IEEE Communications Magazine* 55 (11): 122–128.

Chapter 4
Digital Transformation in Construction

Abstract The construction industry is witnessing an unprecedented wave of digital transformation, characterised by the integration of advanced technologies into the planning, execution, and operation of built assets. This chapter explores the multifaceted dimensions of digital transformation in construction, beginning with a re-examination of the industry's traditional limitations and the imperative for digital evolution. It presents a comprehensive understanding of what digital transformation entails within the built environment, identifying key enablers such as policy frameworks, strategic planning, organisational readiness, and workforce development. Technologies such as Building Information Modelling (BIM), Internet of Things (IoT), Artificial Intelligence (AI), drones, and augmented/virtual reality (AR/VR) are discussed as core drivers reshaping construction processes. Drawing on empirical case examples, the chapter illustrates how digital tools are being deployed across the project lifecycle from design and procurement through to construction and facility operations, delivering gains in efficiency, collaboration, and sustainability. It further interrogates the persistent barriers impeding digital transformation, including technical fragmentation, cultural resistance, and economic constraints, particularly within resource-limited contexts. A critical focus is placed on measuring the impact of digital adoption, highlighting the need for robust and standardised metrics to evaluate performance and sustainability outcomes. The chapter concludes with a forward-looking perspective, underscoring the future trajectory of digitalisation in construction, its alignment with Industry 4.0 and 5.0 paradigms, and the imperative for inclusive and human-centric innovation. Ultimately, this chapter provides a foundational discourse for understanding the strategic, technological, and organisational shifts driving the digital future of the construction industry.

Keywords Digital transformation · Construction industry · Smart technologies · Sustainability · Project lifecycle

O. I. Akinradewo et al., *Blockchain Technology for Information Management: A New Era for Sustainable Construction Practices*, Artificial Intelligence and Sustainable Development, https://doi.org/10.1007/978-981-95-2664-2_4

4.1 Introduction

The construction industry, traditionally known for its reliance on labour-intensive methods and fragmented project delivery systems, is presently undergoing a paradigm shift marked by the advent of digital technologies. Historically, construction has lagged behind other sectors such as manufacturing and finance in embracing technological change, largely due to the industry's complex, project-based nature and resistance to innovation. However, recent global imperatives including sustainability goals, productivity pressures, urbanisation demands, and the pursuit of efficiency, have spurred a re-evaluation of how construction is conceptualised, managed, and delivered in the digital era (Aigbavboa and Kissi 2025a). As these pressures mount, rethinking construction through the lens of digital transformation becomes not only a necessity but also a strategic imperative for industry survival and relevance in the twenty-first century.

Digital transformation, in its essence, extends beyond the adoption of isolated technologies. It signifies a fundamental reimagining of business processes, workflows, and value delivery within construction, enabled by integrated digital tools and platforms. This evolution is not solely driven by technological advancement but also by the demand for agility, transparency, and sustainability across the built environment (Brozovsky et al. 2024). The global construction industry is being compelled to align with these broader societal expectations, and this alignment demands a shift from conventional methods towards data-centric, collaborative, and value-based approaches. The post-pandemic era, in particular, has accelerated this realisation, as disruptions in supply chains, the emergence of remote working, and safety concerns have laid bare the limitations of traditional construction paradigms and amplified the need for resilient digital infrastructures (Chen et al. 2024).

In synthesising these arguments, it becomes evident that the digital age presents both a challenge and an opportunity for the construction industry. While the road to transformation is fraught with technical, cultural, and institutional complexities, the potential rewards includes improved efficiency, enhanced quality, reduced environmental impact, and stronger stakeholder engagement, which are substantial. As the sector grapples with these dynamics, the notion of construction as a static, analogue-driven industry is increasingly obsolete. What emerges in its place is a more agile, responsive, and integrated construction ecosystem, one that is shaped not only by bricks and mortar but by data, algorithms, and digital intelligence. This chapter sets the stage for a deeper exploration of how this transformation unfolds across multiple dimensions.

4.2 Rethinking Construction in the Digital Age

The competitive landscape of construction is transforming rapidly. Enterprises across various regions are beginning to reposition themselves through digital strategies that not only improve operational performance but also enhance client engagement and stakeholder value. This repositioning is rooted in a strategic vision that treats digital transformation as a catalyst for industry reinvention rather than a mere operational enhancement. Aigbavboa and Kissi (2025e) emphasised that understanding the digitalisation of construction is critical for redefining project cost management, value delivery, and competitive advantage. It is through this lens that digital construction is no longer viewed as a supplementary innovation, but as an essential enabler for enduring relevance and performance.

There is growing recognition among industry leaders and policymakers that digital transformation must begin at the foundational level of industry thinking. This involves dismantling legacy mindsets, reconfiguring institutional arrangements, and fostering a digital-first culture across all levels of construction enterprises. The transition to a digital mindset, however, is not spontaneous. It requires deliberate efforts to reframe organisational goals, prioritise long-term investments in technology, and commit to continuous learning and innovation. According to Wuni et al. (2024), such cultural reorientation is one of the most formidable yet essential aspects of transformation, often outweighing the technical complexities involved.

The rethinking of construction in the digital age also necessitates a re-evaluation of the industry's historical identity as a slow-moving, conservative sector. While this characterisation has been valid in many respects, it fails to account for the pockets of innovation that have emerged globally in recent years. From the deployment of digital twins in infrastructure management (Zhang et al. 2024) to the increasing application of data analytics for performance measurement and risk mitigation (Fan et al. 2025), the momentum is building. These advancements demonstrate the potential of digital innovation to reshape how assets are planned, delivered, and maintained. However, this emerging narrative must be consolidated through broader sectoral commitment, enabling policies, and sustained investment in digital capabilities.

Another key consideration in this discourse is the global disparity in digital maturity within the construction sector. While high-income countries may exhibit significant progress in digital adoption, low- and middle-income countries often face structural barriers such as limited infrastructure, policy gaps, and constrained access to digital tools. This digital divide raises pertinent questions about inclusivity and equity in the transformation journey. Musarat et al. (2024) observed that in Malaysia, for instance, while awareness of digital transformation is growing, actual implementation remains limited due to systemic challenges. Similar observations have been made in sub-Saharan Africa, where the conversation on digitalisation is gaining traction but remains hindered by capacity limitations and inconsistent policy support (Awodele et al. 2025). Therefore, rethinking construction also implies addressing the structural inequities that shape digital readiness across different geographies.

In this evolving context, the role of academic research, industry partnerships, and knowledge-sharing platforms becomes indispensable. As digital transformation cuts across technological, organisational, and socio-economic domains, a transdisciplinary approach is needed to understand its full implications. Scholars have a critical role to play in unpacking the nuances of transformation, generating empirical evidence on its impacts, and proposing actionable frameworks that guide practice. Aigbavboa and Kissi (2025b) argued that industry-wide transformation will only be possible if supported by frameworks that are grounded in context, yet flexible enough to accommodate technological disruption and organisational fluidity. The intersection of theory and practice must thus be strengthened to build a coherent pathway for sustainable digital evolution in the construction industry.

The urgency of this transformation is further heightened by the convergence of digitalisation with other megatrends such as climate change, urban resilience, and the circular economy. The construction sector, which contributes significantly to global emissions and resource consumption, cannot afford to overlook the role of digital tools in facilitating greener, more efficient project outcomes (Arsecularatne et al. 2024). As noted by Gao and Huang (2024), digital transformation can drive green total factor productivity by enabling predictive planning, real-time monitoring, and integrated decision-making. These capabilities are crucial in ensuring that construction not only meets the present demands of functionality and cost-efficiency but also contributes to broader environmental and social objectives.

4.3 Digital Transformation in the Built Environment

At its core, digital transformation transcends the mere adoption of digital tools or automation. Rather, it signals a profound shift in how construction enterprises create value, structure operations, manage data, and engage with stakeholders across the asset lifecycle (Aigbavboa and Kissi 2025e). This transformation is inherently strategic, encompassing changes in mindset, organisational culture, and systems integration that enable the industry to respond to the pressures of performance, sustainability, and innovation.

In contrast to earlier waves of digitisation where technologies such as CAD systems or basic project management software were deployed in isolated functions, digital transformation entails the end-to-end integration of digital technologies and data environments. This systemic change has led to the emergence of interconnected ecosystems in which design, procurement, construction, and facilities management are no longer siloed processes but part of a digitally synchronised continuum (Brozovsky et al. 2024). Such a reconfiguration allows for more accurate decision-making, enhanced transparency, and real-time performance monitoring across all phases of the built environment.

The discourse on digital transformation in construction is often enriched by the recognition that the built environment is not static but dynamic, influenced by demographic trends, environmental concerns, and policy developments. As a response to these forces, construction firms and infrastructure managers are rethinking traditional approaches and exploring new digital models that enhance adaptability and resilience. According to Chen et al. (2025a, b), the integration of digital twins, artificial intelligence, and other intelligent systems in the built environment has facilitated a shift from reactive to predictive modes of operation. This transformation allows stakeholders to anticipate issues, simulate scenarios, and optimise resources in ways that were previously unattainable through conventional methods.

In practice, digital transformation redefines the notion of construction as a product-based activity and reframes it as a service-oriented, data-driven process. Rather than focusing solely on the delivery of physical infrastructure, digitally transformed firms now emphasise performance outcomes, user satisfaction, and lifecycle efficiency. This service-based orientation has implications for how value is measured and delivered in the built environment. For instance, projects are increasingly evaluated not only on the basis of time, cost, and quality, but also in terms of energy efficiency, adaptability, and long-term asset performance-outcomes that require integrated digital systems to track and manage (Zech et al. 2025).

Furthermore, the conceptualisation of digital transformation in the built environment cannot be detached from the shifting roles of information and knowledge. The construction industry has traditionally relied on fragmented, often paper-based flows of information that hinder collaboration and limit innovation. Digital transformation, however, introduces a data-centric paradigm, where real-time information is captured, shared, and analysed through interoperable platforms (Celoza 2024). This allows for greater collaboration among architects, engineers, contractors, and clients, fostering a shared understanding of project objectives and enhancing trust across stakeholders.

The built environment, by its very nature, is a complex and multi-stakeholder domain. As such, digital transformation in this sector requires not only technological tools but also governance mechanisms, collaborative frameworks, and clear digital strategies. As noted by Shirwa et al. (2025), the absence of coordinated digital governance can result in disjointed implementations, fragmented data systems, and the duplication of efforts. Therefore, successful transformation demands a systemic perspective that accounts for institutional arrangements, value chain dynamics, and socio-political contexts within which construction operates.

There is also a spatial and contextual dimension to how digital transformation is understood across regions. In high-income economies, the conversation often revolves around optimising productivity, enhancing client experience, and integrating sustainability targets. In contrast, in emerging economies, discussions around digital transformation are more likely to focus on infrastructure deficits, capacity development, and overcoming legacy systems (Musarat et al. 2024). Despite these contextual differences, the underlying logic of transformation remains constant, thereby leveraging digital technologies to reshape construction into a smarter, more sustainable, and more efficient industry.

The emergence of smart cities, net-zero buildings, and intelligent infrastructure further illustrates the expansive nature of digital transformation within the built environment. These concepts, while futuristic, are becoming increasingly mainstream and serve as both drivers and outcomes of digital innovation. In particular, smart buildings that are equipped with embedded sensors, automated systems, and real-time analytics, demonstrate how digital transformation enables proactive asset management and user-responsive environments (Arsecularatne et al. 2024). Such developments reflect a broader trend in which the built environment is no longer just constructed—it is programmed, sensed, and continuously optimised.

Importantly, digital transformation is not a singular event but a continuous, iterative process. Firms often undergo several stages of transformation, from digital exploration to digital integration, and finally, digital optimisation. This progression is marked by an increasing reliance on analytics, automation, and artificial intelligence, which in turn shifts the nature of construction work and the skills required within the industry (Aigbavboa and Kissi 2025c). This layered process of transformation implies that organisations must be adaptive, learning-oriented, and resilient in the face of rapid technological change and market volatility.

In this context, the concept of the digital twin is a virtual replica of physical assets that enables simulation, analysis, and performance monitoring, which has gained significant traction as a symbol of transformation. While the term may initially appear technical, it encapsulates the broader ethos of the digital age: responsiveness, interactivity, and data-driven management. As noted by Calvetti et al. (2025), digital twins provide a platform through which real-time decisions can be made, maintenance optimised, and asset performance predicted, thereby bridging the gap between physical and digital domains. These developments not only enhance project outcomes but also redefine the relationships between people, processes, and technologies in the construction sector.

While the transformative potential of digitalisation is widely acknowledged, it is also important to avoid deterministic narratives that assume technology alone will resolve the industry's challenges. Digital transformation must be situated within the realities of institutional inertia, path dependency, and socio-technical resistance. As observed by Jiang et al. (2024), without a critical understanding of organisational dynamics and stakeholder motivations, digital initiatives may falter despite their technical robustness. It is therefore imperative to approach digital transformation not just as a technological change, but as a holistic reconfiguration of the industry's logic, structure, and values.

4.4 Drivers of Digital Transformation in Construction

The transformation of the construction industry through digital technologies has not occurred in a vacuum. Rather, it is being propelled by a confluence of forces which are technological, economic, environmental, institutional, and social, that together constitute the drivers and enablers of digital transformation in the sector. These factors shape the pace, scale, and form of digital uptake across construction enterprises and influence the industry's trajectory towards integrated, data-driven, and value-enhancing practices. Understanding these drivers is fundamental to grasping why digital transformation has moved from a peripheral innovation to a central agenda in the global construction discourse.

One of the most prominent drivers of digital transformation is the need to improve productivity and efficiency across project lifecycles. The construction industry has historically suffered from low productivity compared to other sectors such as manufacturing and agriculture, largely due to fragmented workflows, adversarial contractual relationships, and limited use of automation (Brozovsky et al. 2024). In response, firms have begun to explore digital technologies not merely as tools, but as enablers of systemic change capable of reducing delays, cost overruns, and inefficiencies. Digital platforms allow for better coordination, real-time decision-making, and streamlined project management, all of which contribute to higher productivity and improved margins (Aigbavboa and Kissi 2025b).

Closely related to productivity is the growing demand for improved project transparency, accountability, and data integration. Clients, regulators, and financiers are increasingly requesting greater visibility over project timelines, budgets, and performance metrics. This demand has prompted the adoption of integrated digital solutions such as Building Information Modelling (BIM), cloud-based collaboration platforms, and digital dashboards, all of which enable real-time access to project information and facilitate collaborative decision-making (Zhang et al. 2023b). These technologies ensure that stakeholders are not working in silos but are instead connected through shared data environments that promote transparency and trust.

Another powerful enabler is the pressure to meet increasingly complex sustainability and environmental performance targets. As cities expand and climate change concerns intensify, construction projects are being required to reduce carbon footprints, improve energy efficiency, and integrate circular economy principles. Digital tools offer a way to meet these goals through advanced simulation, monitoring, and lifecycle analysis. Digital twin technology, for example, allows for continuous assessment of energy consumption, material flows, and environmental impact, enabling more sustainable decision-making throughout the lifecycle of built assets (Arsecularatne et al. 2024; Zech et al. 2025). Consequently, the pursuit of green construction practices has become an important catalyst for digital adoption across many regions.

In parallel with environmental concerns, the global shift towards smart cities and intelligent infrastructure is another key driver shaping digital transformation. Governments and urban planners are increasingly embedding digital technologies into the design and operation of city systems—transportation, utilities, buildings, and public spaces—thereby creating demand for digitally enabled construction practices. Construction firms are under growing pressure to align with these expectations and deliver assets that are not only physically robust but digitally connected, sensor-integrated, and capable of interacting with larger urban ecosystems (Jiang et al. 2024). This alignment has positioned construction within the broader context of digital urbanism and elevated the relevance of transformation as a matter of strategic alignment with future cityscapes.

Incentives provided by public policy and regulatory instruments have also emerged as significant enablers. In several jurisdictions, governments have introduced mandates, incentives, and guidelines to encourage digital innovation in public projects. These policy levers include requirements for BIM adoption on public works, funding for digital infrastructure, and the development of digital construction roadmaps (Yang et al. 2025). In countries like the UK, Singapore, and China, such initiatives have led to rapid digital maturity in construction firms, especially those engaged in public-sector projects. The role of policy in shaping industry behaviour underscores the importance of institutional alignment in fostering digital readiness and uptake (Mêda et al. 2024).

Market competitiveness is another potent driver of digital transformation. As the construction industry becomes more globalised and interconnected, firms are seeking competitive differentiation through technological capabilities. Digital maturity is increasingly viewed as a strategic asset—one that enhances a firm's ability to bid for large-scale projects, attract clients, and build a reputation for innovation and quality. According to Aigbavboa and Kissi (2025d), digital transformation enables firms to deliver better value to clients through enhanced cost forecasting, performance management, and adaptive design capabilities. This ability to innovate and respond to changing client needs has become a defining factor in maintaining relevance and competitiveness in contemporary construction markets.

The rapid advancement and accessibility of enabling technologies is itself a major enabler of transformation. Unlike in previous decades where digital tools were costly and complex, modern technologies are increasingly modular, user-friendly, and cost-effective. Cloud computing, mobile applications, and open-source platforms have lowered the entry barriers for digital adoption, allowing small and medium-sized enterprises (SMEs) to participate in the digital economy. This trend is particularly relevant in developing countries, where access to affordable technologies can catalyse digital leapfrogging (Yilmaz et al. 2023). The availability of scalable solutions, combined with expanding digital infrastructure, is thus levelling the playing field and accelerating adoption across diverse contexts.

A related enabler is the growing availability of digital talent and expertise. As digital transformation becomes embedded in construction education, training, and certification programmes, a new generation of digitally literate professionals is entering the workforce. This shift is empowering firms to experiment with new tools, rethink workflows, and cultivate innovation from within. Moreover, interdisciplinary collaboration—with inputs from computer scientists, data analysts, and systems engineers—is expanding the intellectual boundaries of construction practice and fostering more integrative approaches to project delivery (Li et al. 2023). The increasing alignment between human capital development and digital aspirations is therefore a crucial enabler in sustaining transformation.

Global events such as the COVID-19 pandemic have also acted as unexpected accelerators of digital transformation. The need for remote work, contactless operations, and resilient supply chains exposed the vulnerabilities of analogue systems and compelled firms to pivot towards digital solutions. As noted by Chen et al. (2024), these disruptions have reshaped attitudes toward digital tools, transforming them from optional innovations into operational necessities. The lessons from such global shocks have strengthened the resolve of many construction enterprises to institutionalise digital capabilities and build long-term resilience through technological investment.

Finally, the influence of global technology leaders and platform providers has added momentum to the digital transformation journey. The construction sector is increasingly influenced by digital trends and business models from industries such as manufacturing, logistics, and information technology. This cross-sectoral influence has introduced new ways of thinking about construction as a platform-based, data-intensive, and service-oriented industry. The importation of advanced technologies such as artificial intelligence, machine learning, and blockchain from adjacent sectors is reshaping construction's digital landscape and offering new possibilities for innovation and value creation (Xue et al. 2025).

Taken together, these drivers and enablers demonstrate that digital transformation in construction is not a linear or uniform process but a complex interplay of internal and external forces. The direction and intensity of transformation will vary depending on local conditions, organisational capabilities, and regulatory contexts. Nonetheless, the convergence of economic imperatives, policy incentives, environmental goals, and technological advancements is creating a fertile ground for digital innovation. As the industry continues to evolve, understanding and harnessing these drivers will be essential for firms seeking to remain competitive, resilient, and aligned with the demands of the digital age.

4.5 Key Technologies for Digital Transformation

The evolution of digital transformation in construction is intimately linked to the emergence and integration of a suite of advanced technologies that are redefining how infrastructure is conceived, delivered, and managed. These technologies do not function in isolation but often act synergistically to drive innovation, enhance productivity, and foster resilience across the construction value chain. The increasing sophistication, accessibility, and interoperability of these digital tools have ushered in a new era for the built environment, characterised by automation, data richness, real-time collaboration, and predictive intelligence. Central among these enabling technologies are Building Information Modelling (BIM), the Internet of Things (IoT), Artificial Intelligence (AI), Drones, and Extended Reality tools such as Augmented and Virtual Reality (AR/VR), each contributing uniquely to the transformation of traditional construction practices.

At the heart of the digital construction revolution is Building Information Modelling (BIM), widely recognised as the foundational technology for collaborative design and information management. BIM has moved beyond its original function as a 3D modelling tool and has evolved into a comprehensive digital environment where multiple project stakeholders can co-create, share, and manage data-rich models throughout the asset lifecycle. It enables enhanced visualisation, clash detection, quantity take-offs, and lifecycle cost analysis, thereby reducing errors, improving communication, and supporting data-driven decisions (Zhang et al.

2023a). The integration of BIM with cloud platforms and mobile devices has further enhanced its utility, making it possible for real-time access to models across geographically dispersed project teams. BIM's role as a central repository of structured information makes it indispensable in digital construction environments, particularly as it underpins many of the more advanced technologies now entering the sector.

Closely linked with BIM is the Internet of Things (IoT), which introduces the capability to embed physical construction environments with sensors, actuators, and devices that capture and transmit data in real-time. The deployment of IoT technologies on construction sites enables the continuous monitoring of equipment, materials, environmental conditions, and worker movements, leading to significant improvements in safety, efficiency, and resource optimisation (Chen et al. 2025a, b). For example, smart sensors can detect temperature fluctuations in concrete curing, track equipment usage, or monitor structural loads during assembly. These capabilities are especially relevant for complex projects and infrastructure systems where visibility and control over dynamic site conditions are critical. By generating streams of actionable data, IoT becomes a crucial bridge between the physical and digital domains of construction.

Artificial Intelligence (AI) represents another transformative force within the industry. Through machine learning algorithms, natural language processing, and predictive analytics, AI enables construction firms to interpret vast amounts of data, identify patterns, and automate complex decision-making processes. Applications of AI in construction range from risk assessment and schedule optimisation to contract analysis and predictive maintenance. As noted by Aigbavboa and Kissi (2025a), AI contributes to enhanced project cost management by providing real-time forecasts and anomaly detection, which can alert project managers to potential delays or budget overruns before they escalate. Furthermore, AI-driven design tools are being utilised to generate design alternatives based on performance criteria and historical data, thereby fostering more efficient and resilient infrastructure solutions. The power of AI lies in its capacity to continuously learn from project outcomes and thereby improve performance across successive projects.

Drones, or unmanned aerial vehicles (UAVs), have rapidly gained popularity for their ability to conduct aerial surveys, site inspections, and progress monitoring with unprecedented speed and accuracy. Their integration into the digital construction workflow has transformed how data is collected and visualised on-site. By capturing high-resolution imagery, topographic data, and volumetric measurements, drones significantly reduce the time and cost associated with traditional survey methods. Davletshina et al. (2024) highlighted the efficiency gains achieved through drone-enabled data collection in digital twin modelling for road geometry construction. Drones are also instrumental in enhancing safety by enabling the inspection of hard-to-reach or hazardous areas without exposing workers to unnecessary risk. When combined with BIM or GIS platforms, drone data supports accurate mapping and progress verification, contributing to more agile and responsive project management.

The application of Augmented Reality (AR) and Virtual Reality (VR) technologies in construction is reshaping how professionals interact with digital models and visualise project scenarios. AR overlays digital information onto the physical environment, enabling users to view 3D models superimposed on real-world spaces using mobile devices or AR headsets. This facilitates on-site verification of design intent, improves stakeholder communication, and enhances the accuracy of installations. VR, on the other hand, immerses users in a fully digital environment, allowing them to experience and interact with construction designs before actual implementation. This proves particularly beneficial in design reviews, safety training, and client engagement (Aytekin et al. 2025). The use of AR/VR is also gaining traction in facilities management, where virtual walkthroughs can support asset inspections and maintenance planning. As construction projects become more complex and client expectations rise, AR/VR tools are proving essential for bridging communication gaps and enhancing user experience.

Beyond these mainstream technologies, digital twins have emerged as an integrative platform that combines the functionalities of BIM, IoT, AI, and AR/VR to create real-time, interactive digital replicas of physical assets. A digital twin is not simply a model but a dynamic system that evolves in parallel with its physical counterpart. It provides insights into performance, predicts failures, and supports scenario analysis, making it a cornerstone of intelligent asset management. As noted by Calvetti et al. (2025), the deployment of incremental digital twin frameworks enables continuous data integration and analytics, which are pivotal for real-time decision-making and lifecycle optimisation. Digital twins are especially impactful in infrastructure and industrial projects, where the complexity of systems and operational interdependencies necessitate high levels of coordination and foresight.

Moreover, blockchain technology is beginning to influence how construction stakeholders manage contracts, payments, and supply chains in a decentralised, transparent, and secure manner. Though still emerging in its application, blockchain promises to address issues of trust and verification in multi-party construction environments. Smart contracts can automate payment releases upon milestone completions, while distributed ledgers can record transactions and changes in project documentation without the need for a central authority (Zhao et al. 2023). As the construction industry becomes more data-driven, the demand for secure, immutable, and auditable records is likely to increase, making blockchain an enabler of operational integrity and risk reduction.

In addition, cloud computing and edge computing provide the infrastructure backbone for these technologies to function efficiently. Cloud platforms enable the storage, processing, and sharing of large volumes of project data, facilitating collaboration among geographically dispersed teams. Edge computing, which processes data closer to the source of generation, is becoming increasingly relevant in real-time applications such as site monitoring, drone operations, and safety alerts (Gong et al. 2024). Together, these technologies ensure that construction stakeholders have access to the data and computational resources necessary to make informed, timely, and strategic decisions.

4.6 Digital Transformation Across the Project Lifecycle

The application of digital transformation in construction extends far beyond the implementation of individual technologies; it permeates every phase of the project lifecycle, reshaping how infrastructure is planned, procured, constructed, and operated. As construction projects grow in complexity, size, and ambition, the ability to synchronise data and decisions across the lifecycle has become a critical determinant of success. The traditional compartmentalisation of project phases—design, procurement, construction, and operations—has often led to disjointed communication, inefficiencies, and costly rework. However, digital transformation offers a unifying thread, enabling integration, transparency, and agility throughout the project continuum (Aigbavboa and Kissi 2025b).

In the early stages of project design and conceptualisation, digital tools have revolutionised how stakeholders visualise, simulate, and assess project feasibility. Building Information Modelling (BIM) plays a pivotal role during this phase, offering multi-dimensional visualisations that support collaborative design, clash detection, and spatial coordination. The use of parametric modelling allows design teams to rapidly iterate and assess multiple options against performance criteria such as cost, energy efficiency, and structural resilience (Zhang et al. 2023b). These capabilities enhance early decision-making and reduce the likelihood of costly changes downstream. Moreover, extended reality technologies, such as Virtual Reality (VR), provide immersive environments where designers, clients, and end-users can engage with the proposed infrastructure before construction begins, enabling more informed choices and greater alignment with stakeholder expectations (Aytekin et al. 2025).

Digitalisation also plays a transformative role in procurement processes. Traditionally, procurement in construction has been fraught with opacity, delays, and contractual inefficiencies. With the introduction of digital procurement platforms, project teams are now able to streamline tendering, supplier evaluation, and contract management through centralised systems. Smart contracts enabled by blockchain technology are being piloted to automate payment processes and enforce contractual obligations transparently (Zhao et al. 2023). These systems reduce administrative burden, lower the risk of disputes, and foster accountability across supply chains. In particular, the visibility provided by digital procurement systems allows for real-time tracking of orders, vendor performance monitoring, and dynamic sourcing strategies, all of which contribute to more resilient and responsive procurement models.

The construction phase, often the most resource-intensive and risk-prone stage, has also seen profound change through digital transformation. On-site execution is now increasingly driven by data and automation, supported by a constellation of technologies that include Internet of Things (IoT) sensors, drones, robotics, and advanced analytics. Sensors embedded within materials and equipment allow for real-time tracking of site conditions, safety compliance, and equipment utilisation (Chen et al. 2025a, b). This continuous flow of data enables proactive decision-making and early detection of issues such as schedule delays, cost deviations, or structural weaknesses. In large-scale infrastructure projects, drone surveillance has become a standard practice, capturing high-resolution images and generating digital terrain models to monitor progress, validate work done, and inform planning (Davletshina et al. 2024). These tools reduce reliance on manual inspections and enhance site productivity.

Robotic technologies are also beginning to automate repetitive and high-risk tasks, such as bricklaying, concrete pouring, and material handling. While full-scale automation is still emerging in many markets, the integration of robotics with digital models is enabling more consistent quality and reducing occupational hazards. According to Lin et al. (2025), human-robot collaboration systems, powered by digital twins and real-time sensing, are being developed to enhance worker safety and improve productivity. These innovations represent a shift from traditional, labour-intensive methods to digitally enabled workflows that prioritise precision, predictability, and safety.

As construction activities conclude, the transition to the operational phase presents new opportunities for leveraging digital transformation. Unlike previous eras where project data was often lost or underutilised after handover, contemporary digital workflows enable seamless transfer of information from construction teams to facilities managers. Digital twins are increasingly getting used to support this transition. These twins consolidate data from BIM models, IoT devices, and operational records, offering a single source of truth for asset monitoring, maintenance scheduling, and performance optimisation (Calvetti et al. 2025). By mirroring real-world conditions in a virtual environment, digital twins empower asset managers to detect anomalies, simulate interventions, and extend the life of built assets.

In facilities management, digital systems now facilitate predictive maintenance, energy monitoring, and space optimisation. Smart building technologies, which rely on sensor networks and AI algorithms, allow for continuous monitoring of HVAC systems, lighting, occupancy levels, and other building functions (Zech et al. 2025). This data-driven approach leads to significant operational savings and improved user comfort. Furthermore, integration with sustainability frameworks enables buildings to track carbon emissions, water usage, and waste generation in real time, aligning with environmental performance targets and regulatory requirements (Arsecularatne et al. 2024). As asset owners increasingly demand sustainability and efficiency from their infrastructure, digital transformation becomes a cornerstone of responsible operations and long-term value preservation.

Importantly, the application of digital tools across the project lifecycle facilitates a feedback loop in which lessons learned from operations can inform future designs and construction practices. This closed-loop model represents a departure from linear project delivery and embodies the principles of continuous improvement and innovation. For instance, performance data collected from smart buildings can be fed back into design models, enabling architects and engineers to refine their assumptions and improve design outcomes on subsequent projects (Aigbavboa and Kissi 2025c). This systemic learning is only possible when digital technologies are embedded across all phases of the project, creating a holistic and integrated construction ecosystem.

However, it is essential to recognise that digital transformation across the lifecycle does not occur uniformly or without challenge. Variations in digital maturity between stakeholders can create friction and limit the full potential of integrated digital workflows. In this regard, the adoption of open data standards, common data environments, and collaborative platforms is essential to ensuring interoperability and reducing information silos (Amor et al. 2024). Moreover, leadership commitment and cross-functional coordination are critical to overcoming organisational inertia and ensuring that digital tools are not only adopted but fully utilised to deliver lifecycle value.

The strategic embedding of digital transformation across the project lifecycle also requires deliberate planning and change management. Transformation is not simply about deploying technology but about rethinking processes, roles, and performance indicators. Firms must invest in digital capabilities, nurture a culture of innovation, and build the institutional capacity to manage change at scale. As noted by Osorio-Gómez et al. (2024), the alignment of organisational structures with digital objectives is a key enabler of transformation, particularly in project environments characterised by complexity and high uncertainty.

4.7 Case Studies of Digital Transformation in Construction Projects

Demonstrating the practical applications of digital transformation in construction requires a closer examination of real-world projects where emerging technologies have been successfully deployed to overcome conventional challenges and deliver enhanced value. While the discourse around digital transformation is often centred on its potential, case-based evidence brings this transformation into clearer focus, revealing not only the benefits but also the strategic decisions, collaborations, and adaptive learning that underpin successful implementation. Across diverse geographic contexts and project types, digital transformation is manifesting in unique ways that are tailored to the scale, complexity, and objectives of each project, yet unified by a commitment to leveraging data, automation, and connectivity as key enablers of performance and innovation.

One compelling case is the deployment of digital twin technologies in managing underground infrastructure, a traditionally opaque and high-risk segment of construction. In projects across Europe and Asia, digital twins have been used to model underground tunnels and utilities, enabling precise excavation and risk mitigation. Bellini Machado and Massao Futai (2024) highlighted how tunnel performance prediction was significantly enhanced through digital twin integration, allowing engineers to track degradation in real-time and proactively schedule maintenance. Similarly, Gong et al. (2024) described advancements in lightweight geometric modelling that enabled real-time updates of underground space conditions, reducing excavation errors and ensuring alignment with environmental regulations. These applications underscore the capacity of digital twins to make invisible infrastructure visible, manageable, and optimised, especially in dense urban environments where space is constrained and risk tolerance is low.

In the domain of transportation infrastructure, the integration of digital technologies has led to major strides in efficiency and safety. An illustrative example can be found in road construction projects where drone imaging and automated digital modelling have replaced traditional surveying methods. Davletshina et al. (2024) documented how UAVs and AI-driven segmentation tools were deployed to automatically generate digital twins of road geometry. This approach reduced the time and labour required for data collection while improving the accuracy of as-built records. Additionally, it enabled context-aware planning that responded to site-specific constraints, ultimately reducing delays and enhancing compliance with design specifications.

Another example of digital transformation in action is evident in building construction projects that have adopted real-time performance tracking through IoT integration. In smart building developments, sensors embedded throughout the structure collect continuous data on occupancy, temperature, lighting, and energy consumption. Zech et al. (2025) presented a case where digital twins, integrated with smart lighting and daylight control systems, were used to model and automate the commissioning process of complex building systems. This not only reduced energy consumption during operation but also allowed designers to optimise lighting strategies prior to completion. The ability to simulate and adjust building behaviour during and after construction demonstrates the value of digital feedback loops and the shift towards performance-based building delivery models.

The application of digital tools in large-scale urban development has also yielded valuable insights. In China, for example, the transformation of public infrastructure projects has been supported by digital platforms that consolidate planning, design, construction, and maintenance data. Yang et al. (2025) reported on how digital public policy initiatives in the Chinese AEC industry have encouraged the use of centralised digital platforms that facilitate lifecycle collaboration. The implementation of digital permitting systems and city-wide data integration frameworks has streamlined approval processes and improved transparency between stakeholders. These developments show how national digital strategies, when applied to real-world projects, can transform not only the outputs of construction but also the institutional processes that govern them.

Smart airport development offers yet another lens into the practicalities of digital transformation. Ling et al. (2025) illustrated the construction of a digital runway based on in-situ sensing data, which was used to monitor construction progress and surface integrity. Through continuous data collection and modelling, the project team was able to detect surface anomalies early and adjust construction techniques accordingly. This proactive approach ensured that performance targets were met without the need for costly post-construction interventions. The integration of sensing data directly into construction workflows reflects a broader trend of moving from reactive to predictive operations, enabled by the convergence of physical and digital infrastructures.

In the industrial construction sector, manufacturing facilities and logistics centres have emerged as fertile grounds for testing digital construction strategies. Liu et al. (2025) documented the development of a generic digital twin model applied to a cross-field manufacturing site, enabling scalability and operability across different facility types. This model was used to simulate workflow efficiency, identify bottlenecks, and optimise material movement paths even before construction began. Such applications not only improve design accuracy but also reduce commissioning time by allowing construction teams to build with full knowledge of operational workflows. The alignment between construction and operational performance, made possible by digital twins, demonstrates how the value of digital transformation extends well beyond handover.

Meanwhile, in the African context, efforts are being made to harness digital tools to address persistent challenges such as delays, cost overruns, and quality deficiencies. Awodele et al. (2025) described how digital twin technology was explored to support the transition to a circular economy in Nigeria's construction industry. The digital models were used to map material flows, assess lifecycle impacts, and support the reuse of construction materials across projects. Though implementation is still in its early stages, the case illustrates the growing appetite for technology-driven innovation in emerging markets and the role of digital solutions in promoting sustainability. It also demonstrates that digital transformation is not confined to high-income contexts but is increasingly relevant to the broader development agenda.

A different but equally instructive case is found in the application of digital technologies for safety management on large construction sites. Lin et al. (2025) highlighted how a digital twin-enabled safety monitoring system was implemented to coordinate human-robot interactions in a construction zone. The system used real-time location tracking, AI algorithms, and predictive analytics to detect potential collisions and unsafe behaviour, issuing automated alerts to supervisors and workers. This integration of safety into the digital transformation agenda reflects a broader shift towards holistic performance management, where safety, quality, cost, and sustainability are treated as interconnected dimensions rather than separate concerns.

Collectively, these examples reveal the diversity and adaptability of digital transformation strategies across different construction contexts. They demonstrate that digital adoption is not a uniform process but rather a contextualised journey, shaped by project goals, resource availability, regulatory environments, and organisational readiness. More importantly, they illustrate that the value of digital transformation lies not in the technology itself, but in how it is strategically integrated into project delivery to achieve meaningful outcomes. Whether improving coordination, enhancing visibility, increasing efficiency, or promoting sustainability, these real-world cases make a compelling case for the transformative power of digital innovation in construction.

While challenges such as interoperability issues, resistance to change, and skills gaps remain, the positive outcomes observed in these cases suggest that digital transformation is no longer speculative but is increasingly becoming the norm in forward-thinking construction environments. As new technologies emerge and digital infrastructure continues to mature, the body of case-based evidence will only grow, further informing best practices and reinforcing the business case for a digitally enabled construction sector.

4.8 Barriers to Digital Transformation in the Construction Sector

Digital transformation in construction continues to face significant barriers despite its growing relevance. Technically, challenges such as system interoperability, cybersecurity concerns, and lack of skilled personnel hinder adoption (Amor et al. 2024; Pärn et al. 2024). Culturally, resistance to change, fragmented industry structures, and weak leadership commitment impede progress (Aigbavboa and Kissi 2025e; Shirwa et al. 2025). Economically, high implementation costs, uncertain return on investment, and unequal access to digital infrastructure further limit uptake, particularly among SMEs and in developing economies (Musarat et al. 2024; Awodele et al. 2025). These intertwined challenges continue to slow widespread transformation.

4.8.1 Technical Challenges

Despite the growing enthusiasm for digital transformation in construction, numerous technical challenges continue to constrain widespread adoption and full-scale implementation across the industry. A primary technical barrier lies in the lack of interoperability between digital platforms and tools. Construction projects typically involve multiple stakeholders using different software solutions, many of which are not designed to communicate or exchange data seamlessly. This fragmentation creates data silos, hampers collaborative workflows, and results in information loss or duplication. Amor et al. (2024) emphasised that without standardised digital protocols, compliance checking and regulatory alignment remain inconsistent, leading to inefficiencies during both project execution and lifecycle management.

Additionally, many construction firms face challenges in integrating new digital tools with their existing legacy systems. This integration problem is particularly acute for small and medium-sized enterprises (SMEs), which often operate with limited IT infrastructure and outdated software solutions. According to Wuni et al. (2024), these firms frequently lack the technical capability to adopt advanced digital platforms such as digital twins, AI-driven analytics, or blockchain-based procurement tools, rendering them less competitive in a digitised market.

The issue of data security and cybersecurity risks further complicates the technical landscape. As construction projects increasingly depend on cloud platforms, sensor data, and real-time digital exchanges, concerns about data breaches, cyberattacks, and the unauthorised manipulation of critical project information have intensified. Pärn et al. (2024) warned that digital twins and other integrated systems could become vulnerable entry points for cyber threats if robust security measures are not embedded from the onset. For firms operating in regulatory environments with strict data governance requirements, these risks often translate into hesitation or resistance toward adopting advanced digital solutions.

Another notable technical challenge is the steep learning curve associated with new technologies. While the benefits of technologies such as BIM, AI, and IoT are well recognised, the complexity of deploying, configuring, and maintaining them can be daunting. As highlighted by Aigbavboa and Kissi (2025c), digital cost management systems, for example, demand not only the right software but also skilled personnel capable of interpreting analytics, configuring dashboards, and aligning insights with project decisions. The absence of such expertise often results in the underutilisation of available tools, with firms reverting to traditional methods after unsuccessful digital pilot attempts.

4.8.2 Cultural Challenges

Beyond the technological domain, cultural inertia remains one of the most persistent barriers to digital transformation in the construction industry. Construction has long been characterised by conservative practices, hierarchical management structures, and a preference for proven methods over experimentation. This cultural conservatism often breeds scepticism toward digital innovations, especially among senior professionals who are accustomed to analogue systems and paper-based documentation. According to Aigbavboa and Kissi (2025e), the lack of a digital mindset within firms significantly undermines transformation efforts, even when tools and resources are available.

Resistance to change is further exacerbated by fear of job displacement, particularly among workers who perceive digital tools as threats to their roles. While technologies such as drones, robotics, and AI can automate repetitive or hazardous tasks, they are often met with unease by site workers and middle management. M.S. et al. (2025) observed that without clear communication strategies and inclusion in digital planning processes, employees may view transformation as a top-down imposition rather than a collaborative evolution, thereby slowing adoption and fostering passive resistance.

A fragmented industry structure also contributes to cultural barriers. The construction sector is composed of multiple actors, each with their own priorities, processes, and risk appetites. This fragmentation hinders the creation of shared digital cultures, as each party may differ in its understanding, valuation, or use of digital tools. Osorio-Gómez et al. (2024) argued that unless there is a unified cultural vision and strategic coordination across the project ecosystem, digital initiatives are likely to remain isolated and unsustainable.

Leadership commitment plays a pivotal role in overcoming cultural challenges. Yet, in many firms, digital transformation is seen as an IT function rather than a strategic imperative that requires top-level sponsorship. Without leadership advocacy and visible support, digital initiatives struggle to gain traction within organisations. As Shirwa et al. (2025) posited, transformation requires not only investment in tools but also strong governance, change management frameworks, and capacity building across all levels of the organisation. The absence of these elements leads to a situation where digital tools are introduced but not embedded in daily workflows, rendering transformation superficial and short-lived.

4.8.3 Economic Challenges

Economic constraints constitute a formidable barrier to digital transformation, particularly in regions and organisations with limited financial resources. The initial cost of acquiring digital tools, upgrading infrastructure, and training personnel can be prohibitively high, especially for SMEs and firms operating in volatile economic environments. According to Musarat et al. (2024), many construction enterprises in developing countries cite financial limitations as the primary reason for deferring or rejecting digital initiatives, despite awareness of the long-term benefits.

Return on investment (ROI) is another significant concern. Unlike physical assets, the benefits of digital investments are often intangible and difficult to quantify in the short term. This makes it challenging to justify digital budgets in traditional financial terms. Aigbavboa and Kissi (2025a) noted that digital construction cost management, for instance, offers significant value through predictive analytics and risk visibility, but these benefits may not immediately reflect on a project's balance sheet. Consequently, firms focused on short-term profitability may be reluctant to invest in technologies whose returns are delayed or difficult to measure.

Market uncertainties and cyclical downturns also discourage long-term digital planning. In times of economic instability, construction firms tend to prioritise survival over innovation, postponing digital investments until conditions improve. Narayanamurthy et al. (2025) highlighted how organisations navigating financial uncertainty may lack the risk appetite to explore unproven technologies or reconfigure their business models to accommodate digital disruptions.

Moreover, economic inequalities at the national and regional levels result in digital divides within the global construction landscape. High-income countries benefit from more mature digital ecosystems, access to technology vendors, and government-backed innovation grants. In contrast, low- and middle-income countries often face infrastructure deficits, weak digital policy frameworks, and limited access to skilled labour and digital financing. Awodele et al. (2025) drew attention to the barriers faced by construction firms in Nigeria attempting to adopt digital twin technologies for circular economy initiatives. Despite the evident benefits, financial and institutional limitations significantly constrained scalability and long-term adoption.

The high cost of software subscriptions, hardware upgrades, and technical support further adds to the economic burden of digital transformation. While low-code platforms and open-source solutions offer some relief, many advanced tools require ongoing investments to maintain relevance and functionality. Yilmaz et al. (2023) noted that even in cases where digital tools are accessible, the absence of financial planning and digital budgeting strategies can lead to underperformance or abandonment of digital initiatives.

In totality, the economic barriers to digital transformation are not only rooted in affordability but also in value perception, resource planning, and access to enablers such as finance, policy support, and infrastructure. Without mechanisms to address these constraints, the pace of digital transformation will remain uneven, with wide disparities between firms and regions in terms of digital readiness and innovation capacity.

4.9 Measuring the Impact of Digital Transformation on Project Performance and Sustainability

As the construction industry continues to embrace digital technologies, a pressing question emerges regarding how to effectively measure the impact of digital transformation on project performance and sustainability. While numerous pilot projects and technological deployments claim to offer improvements in efficiency, cost control, and environmental outcomes, robust and standardised methods of assessment are often lacking. The complexity of construction processes, combined with the multifaceted nature of sustainability, makes measurement an inherently challenging task. Nevertheless, the ability to demonstrate tangible benefits remains critical to justifying investments in digital tools and sustaining long-term commitment to digital transformation.

Project performance in construction has traditionally been assessed using the time-cost-quality triad, with additional metrics related to health and safety, stakeholder satisfaction, and risk management. The introduction of digital technologies introduces new dimensions to this performance framework, such as data availability, automation efficacy, and digital collaboration outcomes. For instance, Aigbavboa and Kissi (2025c) observed that digital cost management systems significantly improved cost predictability and budget control by enabling real-time monitoring and early detection of cost deviations. In projects where Building Information Modelling (BIM) was integrated into cost planning and project scheduling, time savings and resource optimisation were frequently reported, particularly during the design and pre-construction phases (Zhang et al. 2023a). These improvements, however, are only meaningful when they are systematically tracked and benchmarked against baseline performance indicators.

One of the most cited advantages of digital transformation is the enhancement of decision-making through real-time data access. Internet of Things (IoT) devices, drones, and digital dashboards now provide granular information on site conditions, progress, equipment usage, and worker safety. This data-rich environment enables project managers to make informed decisions, mitigate risks promptly, and maintain tighter control over project milestones. Measuring this aspect of performance requires establishing key indicators that capture not only operational efficiencies but also the responsiveness and accuracy of decisions enabled by digital tools. Chen et al. (2025a, b) highlighted the value of real-time sensing technologies in improving project responsiveness, particularly in dynamic site environments where traditional monitoring methods fall short.

In parallel, digital transformation's impact on sustainability is becoming an increasingly important consideration, particularly as the construction industry faces growing pressure to reduce its environmental footprint. Measuring sustainability outcomes in a digital context involves evaluating how technology contributes to resource efficiency, carbon reduction, waste minimisation, and long-term resilience of built assets. Arsecularatne et al. (2024) discussed how digital twins are being used to model energy performance and simulate alternative building configurations to reduce energy consumption and emissions. The predictive capability of such models allows designers and project teams to make more sustainable choices early in the design process, thereby embedding sustainability into project DNA from the outset.

Lifecycle analysis tools, enabled by digital platforms, have also become essential in measuring the environmental impacts of construction activities. Campo Gay et al. (2024) illustrated how digital life cycle assessment tools are being integrated into construction workflows to provide transparent evaluations of material choices, construction methods, and operational impacts. These tools support performance benchmarking and compliance with sustainability certification schemes, such as LEED or BREEAM. Importantly, the ability to track and visualise environmental performance in real-time helps construction teams align their practices with regulatory standards and corporate sustainability targets, making digital transformation a direct contributor to environmental stewardship.

Beyond environmental metrics, digital transformation also supports social dimensions of sustainability. Technologies such as augmented reality (AR) and digital collaboration platforms facilitate more inclusive stakeholder engagement, allowing clients, end-users, and community members to interact with project designs and provide input prior to construction. Aytekin et al. (2025) showed that metaverse-based engagement tools were effective in enabling participatory planning, thereby increasing satisfaction and reducing the likelihood of community opposition. Measuring the impact of such tools involves assessing stakeholder sentiment, design revision rates, and user satisfaction levels, all of which reflect how digital tools are transforming the social performance of projects.

Moreover, digital transformation has implications for post-construction performance, particularly in facility management and operational sustainability. The use of digital twins and smart building systems allows asset owners to track operational efficiency, detect faults early, and optimise maintenance schedules. Zech et al. (2025) documented how integrated control modelling within digital twin environments enabled the fine-tuning of energy systems, leading to substantial reductions in operational energy use and associated costs. Measuring these benefits requires long-term monitoring and access to historical data, which digital tools are well-equipped to provide. The aggregation and analysis of post-occupancy data further support continuous improvement and learning for future projects.

Despite these advantages, challenges persist in measuring the full impact of digital transformation. One such challenge is the lack of standardised metrics and frameworks that can be applied consistently across projects. Different organisations often develop their own performance indicators based on internal priorities, making it difficult to compare outcomes or generalise findings. According to Shirwa et al. (2025), the absence of unified measurement systems leads to fragmented evidence and undermines efforts to build a compelling business case for digital transformation. There is thus a growing need for industry-wide frameworks that define digital performance metrics in terms of value generated, efficiencies gained, and sustainability outcomes achieved.

Another measurement difficulty lies in attributing performance improvements solely to digital technologies. Construction projects are influenced by multiple variables, including team experience, project complexity, weather conditions, and economic fluctuations. Isolating the effects of digital tools requires rigorous evaluation methodologies, including controlled experiments, longitudinal studies, and mixed-method approaches. Aigbavboa and Kissi (2025d) noted that while digital technologies may contribute to performance gains, their full impact is only realised when combined with organisational readiness, leadership commitment, and process re-engineering. As such, measuring digital transformation outcomes should take into account the broader organisational and contextual factors that shape implementation.

Cost-benefit analysis is another critical dimension of performance measurement. While many digital tools promise long-term savings and efficiency gains, the initial costs of acquisition, implementation, and training can be substantial. Measuring return on investment (ROI) involves not only quantifying financial savings but also capturing intangible benefits such as reduced rework, improved stakeholder engagement, and enhanced brand reputation. Zhang et al. (2023c) emphasised the importance of incremental implementation strategies that allow firms to measure and validate outcomes at each stage before scaling up. This approach supports evidence-based decision-making and helps de-risk digital investments.

In addition, knowledge management plays a vital role in measuring and sustaining the impact of digital transformation. Capturing lessons learned, documenting best practices, and sharing insights across projects enable firms to refine their digital strategies and replicate successful outcomes. Osorio-Gómez et al. (2024) argued that without structured mechanisms for organisational learning, the benefits of digital transformation may remain localised and fail to drive broader cultural change. Measurement frameworks must therefore include indicators related to learning, adaptability, and digital maturity, recognising that transformation is an ongoing journey rather than a one-time event.

4.10 Future Outlook of Digital Transformation in Construction

As construction continues to evolve within the broader context of global digitalisation, the future of digital transformation in the industry appears to be one defined by greater integration, intelligence, and responsiveness. The shift from isolated digital tools to fully interconnected systems signals the emergence of a construction landscape where data, machines, and human insight are tightly interwoven. This transformation is expected to redefine how projects are conceived, delivered, and maintained, with profound implications for productivity, sustainability, and competitiveness. Looking ahead, the trajectory of digital construction points not only towards technological advancement but also towards a fundamental reshaping of construction processes, roles, and business models.

Central to the future of digital transformation is the continued development and integration of digital twins. These dynamic, real-time digital representations of physical assets are expected to become increasingly ubiquitous across the built environment. Calvetti et al. (2025) emphasised that future digital twin frameworks will evolve beyond static replicas to serve as autonomous, self-learning systems capable of predicting failures, optimising energy use, and supporting scenario-based decision-making. With the increasing affordability of sensors and improvements in cloud computing and connectivity, digital twins will likely be adopted at both asset and city scales, transforming the way infrastructure is monitored and managed throughout its lifecycle.

The convergence of digital twins with artificial intelligence (AI) and machine learning is anticipated to usher in a new era of predictive construction. Rather than reacting to problems post-occurence, construction teams will increasingly rely on AI-driven forecasts to anticipate risks, improve designs, and streamline operations. Aigbavboa and Kissi (2025b) noted that such capabilities are already emerging in cost management applications, where predictive analytics are used to forecast budget deviations and optimise procurement strategies. In the future, AI will likely expand its footprint across all stages of construction (from generative design and robotic planning to workforce allocation and materials logistics), creating more adaptive, efficient, and resilient project delivery systems.

Parallel to these developments is the maturation of the Internet of Things (IoT) ecosystem, which will play a critical role in enabling real-time connectivity and data flow across project environments. As IoT devices become more sophisticated and widespread, construction sites will function as intelligent ecosystems capable of self-regulation and coordination. Sensors embedded in structures, equipment, and environmental systems will continuously transmit data that is processed at the edge or in the cloud, enabling instant feedback and autonomous control of key processes. Lin et al. (2025) highlighted the use of sensor-integrated systems for ensuring worker safety through predictive monitoring and collision avoidance. As this technology advances, its applications will broaden to include real-time carbon tracking, adaptive energy management, and integrated logistics planning.

Blockchain technology, though still at a nascent stage in the construction industry, is poised to play a more prominent role in future digital transformation initiatives. Its decentralised, secure, and transparent nature makes it particularly suited for multi-stakeholder environments such as construction, where trust, documentation, and transaction management are critical. Zhao et al. (2023) proposed a blockchain 3.0 paradigm that integrates blockchain into digital twin environments for construction project management. Future applications may include smart contracts for automated payment releases, immutable records for compliance tracking, and blockchain-based digital identities for equipment, workers, and suppliers. Such innovations could significantly reduce administrative overheads, minimise disputes, and foster a culture of accountability and transparency.

Another key aspect of the future digital landscape is the integration of augmented and virtual reality (AR/VR) into day-to-day construction activities. While currently used primarily for design visualisation and safety training, these immersive technologies are expected to evolve into indispensable tools for real-time site navigation, remote supervision, and client engagement. Aytekin et al. (2025) discussed how metaverse-based platforms are already being explored to support collaborative planning and stakeholder participation. With further advancements in wearable technology and user interfaces, AR/VR could transform field operations by overlaying digital information onto physical environments, guiding workers through complex installations, and enabling remote experts to assist with real-time problem-solving.

In parallel, the digital transformation journey will increasingly intersect with global sustainability imperatives. As construction faces mounting pressure to reduce carbon emissions, eliminate waste, and promote circularity, digital technologies will be harnessed not only for efficiency but also for environmental accountability. The ability to simulate, monitor, and verify environmental performance using digital tools will become a standard requirement in both public and private sector projects. Arsecularatne et al. (2024) demonstrated how digital twins are already being used to reduce energy consumption in the built environment. In the future, digital platforms will be used to trace material provenance, monitor embodied carbon, and manage asset deconstruction for reuse, thereby advancing the goals of the circular economy and regenerative design.

Yet, the digital future will not be driven by technology alone. Organisational transformation and human capital development will play an equally pivotal role. As construction becomes more digitally enabled, the industry will demand new skills, new leadership approaches, and new forms of collaboration. Osorio-Gómez et al. (2024) stressed that digital transformation must be accompanied by adaptive organisational structures that foster innovation, agility, and continuous learning. The construction workforce of the future will require proficiency in data analysis, digital systems integration, and human-machine interaction. Educational institutions, professional bodies, and industry consortia will need to reimagine training and certification pathways to reflect these evolving skillsets.

Digital inclusion will also be a defining issue in the years to come. While leading firms in high-income countries are advancing rapidly, many small and medium-sized enterprises (SMEs) and organisations in developing regions continue to face significant barriers to digital adoption. Musarat et al. (2024) identified issues such as cost, infrastructure deficits, and skills shortages as major constraints. Addressing this digital divide will require coordinated efforts from governments, donors, and private sector actors to ensure that the benefits of transformation are distributed equitably. Policies that support open data standards, subsidise digital infrastructure, and promote inclusive innovation will be critical in enabling broader industry participation in the digital economy.

As the transformation matures, construction is expected to align more closely with the principles of Industry 4.0 and, eventually, Industry 5.0. The latter, while still emerging as a concept, envisions a future in which human creativity and machine intelligence coexist symbiotically, leading to more human-centric, sustainable, and resilient production systems. Chen et al. (2025a, b) proposed a framework where large language models and digital twins co-function in Industry 5.0 to support advanced reasoning and complex decision-making in construction. This future outlook positions construction not just as a reactive, project-based industry, but as a forward-looking, innovation-driven ecosystem contributing meaningfully to broader societal goals.

4.11 Summary

The construction industry is undergoing a profound digital transformation, reshaping how projects are planned, executed, and sustained. Once reliant on analogue processes and fragmented operations, the sector is increasingly embracing a future defined by data integration, automation, and real-time collaboration. This shift is not merely about adopting new tools but rethinking the construction paradigm itself in response to mounting pressures around productivity, sustainability, and stakeholder demands. As the industry faces growing complexity and heightened expectations, digital transformation has emerged as a strategic imperative rather than an optional enhancement.

At its core, digital transformation in the built environment represents the convergence of digital technologies with physical construction processes, enabling more intelligent, transparent, and agile project delivery. Tools such as Building Information Modelling (BIM), the Internet of Things (IoT), artificial intelligence (AI), drones, and augmented reality (AR) are playing pivotal roles in transforming traditional workflows. These technologies, individually and collectively, allow stakeholders to visualise, simulate, and manage construction assets across the project lifecycle, from design and procurement through construction to operations and maintenance. Digital twins, in particular, have emerged as a keystone in this transformation, offering real-time monitoring and predictive capabilities that improve decision-making and asset performance. A multitude of drivers and enablers are propelling the shift towards digitalisation. These include the need for improved project outcomes, increased regulatory pressures, environmental concerns, and the growing expectations of clients and end-users. Strategic frameworks have been developed to guide organisations through digital adoption, providing structured pathways that encompass digital visioning, readiness assessment, phased implementation, and performance evaluation. Yet, despite these efforts, numerous barriers persist. Technical constraints such as lack of interoperability and cybersecurity risks, cultural resistance to change, and economic challenges related to cost and access remain significant hurdles, particularly for SMEs and firms in developing regions.

Real-world case studies underscore both the potential and complexity of digital transformation. From drone-enabled road modelling and blockchain-based procurement to AI-driven safety monitoring and digital twin-based tunnel maintenance, projects across various contexts are demonstrating measurable improvements in efficiency, risk management, and sustainability. Moreover, the impact of digital tools is increasingly being assessed not only through traditional metrics of cost, time, and quality, but also through sustainability indicators such as energy performance, material reuse, and stakeholder inclusivity. However, a lack of standardised measurement frameworks continues to obscure a full understanding of digital transformation's value, necessitating greater industry collaboration and benchmarking. Looking ahead, the digital future of construction promises greater integration with Industry 4.0 and, eventually, Industry 5.0 concepts, wherein human-centred design, machine learning, and smart infrastructure converge. The sector's transformation will be defined not just by technology, but by the ability of organisations to foster innovation, invest in skills, and institutionalise digital culture. As the momentum builds, construction is poised to become not only more efficient and sustainable, but also more responsive to the dynamic needs of society in an increasingly digital world.

References

Aigbavboa, C., and E. Kissi. 2025a. Digital construction project cost management. In *Digital management of construction costs*, 39–58. https://doi.org/10.1016/B978-0-443-23715-7.00004-4.

Aigbavboa, C., and E. Kissi. 2025b. Digital construction project cost management—An industry 4.0 framework. In *Digital management of construction costs*, 147–158. https://doi.org/10.1016/B978-0-443-23715-7.00009-3.

Aigbavboa, C., and E. Kissi. 2025c. Digital construction project cost management—Practical steps. In *Digital management of construction costs*, 117–145. https://doi.org/10.1016/B978-0-443-23715-7.00008-1.

Aigbavboa, C., and E. Kissi. 2025d. Digitalization and cost dynamics of construction projects. In *Digital management of construction costs*, 75–92. https://doi.org/10.1016/B978-0-443-23715-7.00006-8.

Aigbavboa, C., and E. Kissi. 2025e. Understanding digital construction management. In *Digital management of construction costs*, 27–38. https://doi.org/10.1016/B978-0-443-23715-7.00003-2.

Amor, R., B. Kumar, and R. Watson. 2024. Digital regulatory compliance checking for the construction industry. *Advanced Engineering Informatics* 61. https://doi.org/10.1016/J.AEI.2024.102764.

Arsecularatne, B. P., N. Rodrigo, and R. Chang. 2024. Review of reducing energy consumption and carbon emissions through digital twin in built environment. *Journal of Building Engineering* 98. https://doi.org/10.1016/J.JOBE.2024.111150.

Awodele, I. A., et al. 2025. Advancing circular economy transition in the Nigeria construction industry through digital twin technology adoption. *Green Technologies and Sustainability* 3:100201. https://doi.org/10.1016/J.GRETS.2025.100201.

Aytekin, A., et al. 2025. Evaluation of metaverse-based digital transformation strategies via an interval-valued q-rung orthopair fuzzy methodology. *Applied Soft Computing* 169:112566. https://doi.org/10.1016/J.ASOC.2024.112566.

Bellini Machado, L., and M. Massao Futai. 2024. Tunnel performance prediction through degradation inspection and digital twin construction. *Tunnelling and Underground Space Technology* 144:105544. https://doi.org/10.1016/J.TUST.2023.105544.

Brozovsky, J., N. Labonnote, and O. Vigren. 2024. Digital technologies in architecture, engineering, and construction. *Automation in Construction* 158:105212. https://doi.org/10.1016/J.AUTCON.2023.105212.

Calvetti, D., et al. 2025. Incremental digital twin framework: A design science research approach for practical deployment. *Automation in Construction* 170:105954. https://doi.org/10.1016/J.AUTCON.2024.105954.

Campo Gay, I., et al. 2024. A digital tool for life cycle assessment in construction projects. *Developments in the Built Environment* 20:100535. https://doi.org/10.1016/J.DIBE.2024.100535.

Celoza, A. 2024. Information management for digital asset development and delivery. *Automation in Construction* 165:105518. https://doi.org/10.1016/J.AUTCON.2024.105518.

Chen, Z. S., et al. 2024. Dynamic collective opinion generation framework for digital transformation barrier analysis in the construction industry. *Information Fusion* 103:102096. https://doi.org/10.1016/J.INFFUS.2023.102096.

Chen, C., et al. 2025a. Integrating large language model and digital twins in the context of industry 5.0: Framework, challenges and opportunities. *Robotics and Computer-Integrated Manufacturing* 94:102982. https://doi.org/10.1016/J.RCIM.2025.102982.

Chen, S., et al. 2025b. Computer vision-based reliability analysis in digital twinning for structural dynamic safety assessment. *Engineering Structures* 326:119532. https://doi.org/10.1016/J.ENGSTRUCT.2024.119532.

Davletshina, D., V. K. Reja, and I. Brilakis. 2024. Automating construction of road digital twin geometry using context and location aware segmentation. *Automation in Construction* 168:105795. https://doi.org/10.1016/J.AUTCON.2024.105795.

Fan, J. S., et al. 2025. Mechanics-based digital twin model for structural construction using 3D scanning and FE model updating. *Automation in Construction* 173:106109. https://doi.org/10.1016/J.AUTCON.2025.106109.

Gao, L., and R. Huang. 2024. Digital transformation and green total factor productivity in the semiconductor industry: The role of supply chain integration and economic policy uncertainty. *International Journal of Production Economics* 274:109313. https://doi.org/10.1016/J.IJPE.2024.109313.

Gong, H., et al. 2024. Advancements in digital twin modeling for underground spaces and lightweight geometric modeling technologies. *Automation in Construction* 165:105578. https://doi.org/10.1016/J.AUTCON.2024.105578.

Jiang, L., A. Yao, W. Li, and Q. Wei. 2024. Blockchain technology empowers the cross-border dual-channel supply chain: Introduction strategy, tax differences, optimal decisions. *Computers and Industrial Engineering* 195:110431. https://doi.org/10.1016/J.CIE.2024.110431.

Kiran Sankar, M. S., S. Gupta, and S. Luthra. 2025. Unlocking digitalization in the spool fabrication industry: Analysis of roadblocks using the IMF-SWARA integrated TFBM. *Procedia CIRP* 132:171–177. https://doi.org/10.1016/J.PROCIR.2025.01.029.

Li, L., Z. Yi, F. Jiang, S. Zhang, and J. Zhou. 2023. Exploring the mechanism of digital transformation empowering green innovation in construction enterprises. *Developments in the Built Environment* 15:100199. https://doi.org/10.1016/J.DIBE.2023.100199.

Lin, X., et al. 2025. Digital twin-enabled safety monitoring system for seamless worker-robot collaboration in construction. *Automation in Construction* 174:106147. https://doi.org/10.1016/J.AUTCON.2025.106147.

Ling, J., et al. 2025. Construction of airport digital runway based on in-situ sensing data. *International Journal of Transportation Science and Technology.* https://doi.org/10.1016/J.IJTST.2025.01.010.

Liu, X., et al. 2025. A generic digital twin model construction strategy for cross-field implementations with comprehensiveness, operability and scalability. *Journal of Manufacturing Systems* 80:366–379. https://doi.org/10.1016/J.JMSY.2025.02.020.

Mêda, P., et al. 2024. Twinning the path of digital building permits and digital building logbooks—Diagnosis and challenges. *Developments in the Built Environment* 20:100573. https://doi.org/10.1016/J.DIBE.2024.100573.

Musarat, M. A., et al. 2024. Digitalization in Malaysian construction industry: Awareness, challenges and opportunities. *Results in Engineering* 21:102013. https://doi.org/10.1016/J.RINENG.2024.102013.

Narayanamurthy, G., et al. 2025. Data-driven digital transformation for uncertainty reduction—Application of satellite imagery analytics in institutional crop credit management. *International Journal of Production Economics* 280:109498. https://doi.org/10.1016/J.IJPE.2024.109498.

Osorio-Gómez, C. C., et al. 2024. Conceptual model for implementation of digital transformation and organizational structure in the construction sector. *Ain Shams Engineering Journal* 15 (7): 102749. https://doi.org/10.1016/J.ASEJ.2024.102749.

Pärn, E., et al. 2024. A perfect storm: Digital twins, cybersecurity, and general contracting firms. *Developments in the Built Environment* 18:100466. https://doi.org/10.1016/J.DIBE.2024.100466.

Shirwa, A. M., et al. 2025. A cooperative governance framework for sustainable digital transformation in construction: The role of digital enablement and digital strategy. *Results in Engineering* 25:104139. https://doi.org/10.1016/J.RINENG.2025.104139.

Wuni, I. Y., et al. 2024. Critical barriers to the adoption of integrated digital delivery in the construction industry. *Journal of Building Engineering* 83:108474. https://doi.org/10.1016/J.JOBE.2024.108474.

Xue, J., G. Li, and D. Ivanov. 2025. Digital transformation in the blockchain era: Balancing efficiency and resilience in operations management. *International Journal of Production Economics* 282:109525. https://doi.org/10.1016/J.IJPE.2025.109525.

Yang, Y., et al. 2025. Mapping the digital transformation of AEC industry: Content analysis of digital public policy in China. *Developments in the Built Environment* 21:100621. https://doi.org/10.1016/J.DIBE.2025.100621.

Yilmaz, G., et al. 2023. Low-cost (shoestring) digital solution areas for enabling digitalisation in construction SMEs. *Computers in Industry* 150:103941. https://doi.org/10.1016/J.COMPIND.2023.103941.

Zech, P., et al. 2025. From BIM to digital twin: A transformation process through advanced control modeling and automated commissioning using daylight and artificial lighting as examples. *Energy and Buildings* 329:115184. https://doi.org/10.1016/J.ENBUILD.2024.115184.

Zhang, J., M. Chen, et al. 2023a. A new framework to evaluate and optimize digital transformation policies in the construction industry: A China case study. *Journal of Building Engineering* 70:106388. https://doi.org/10.1016/J.JOBE.2023.106388.

Zhang, J., M. Zhang, et al. 2023b. A new perspective to evaluate the antecedent path of adoption of digital technologies in major projects of construction industry: A case study in China. *Developments in the Built Environment* 14:100160. https://doi.org/10.1016/J.DIBE.2023.100160.

Zhang, D., et al. 2023c. The rapid construction method of the digital twin polymorphic model for discrete manufacturing workshop. *Robotics and Computer-Integrated Manufacturing* 84:102600. https://doi.org/10.1016/J.RCIM.2023.102600.

Zhao, R., Z. Chen, and F. Xue. 2023. A blockchain 3.0 paradigm for digital twins in construction project management. *Automation in Construction* 145:104645. https://doi.org/10.1016/J.AUTCON.2022.104645.

Zhang, A., J. Wang, Y. Zhang, and G. Shangguan. 2024. Joint detection PCD-based method for automatic construction of geometric digital twin in cable dome structure. *Engineering Structures* 320:118908. https://doi.org/10.1016/J.ENGSTRUCT.2024.118908.

Chapter 5
Sustainable Construction Practices

Abstract This chapter explores the integration of blockchain technology into sustainable construction practices, highlighting its transformative potential in addressing environmental, economic, and social challenges within the built environment. Sustainable construction is increasingly recognised as a critical pathway toward reducing the carbon footprint of infrastructure, promoting resource efficiency, and enhancing lifecycle performance. At the same time, blockchain technology is gaining attention for its ability to provide secure, transparent, and tamper-proof data management systems, which are essential for improving accountability and traceability across construction projects. The chapter provides a comprehensive overview of sustainable construction, existing frameworks and standards, and the various applications of blockchain that support sustainability objectives which include material traceability, carbon emissions tracking, circular economy practices, and smart contract-based compliance. Drawing on real-world case studies, the chapter illustrates how blockchain is being implemented in modular construction, green building certification, community-led housing, and waste management systems, demonstrating its growing relevance in diverse contexts. It also discusses the challenges and barriers to adoption, including issues of interoperability, digital literacy, cost, and regulatory readiness. Further, it highlights the broader implications of blockchain for the construction industry, public policy, and the pursuit of global sustainability goals such as the United Nations Sustainable Development Goals (SDGs). Future directions and emerging trends are examined as critical pathways for advancing smart, resilient, and environmentally responsible construction systems. The chapter concludes that blockchain is not a standalone solution but a strategic enabler capable of fostering a culture of transparency, innovation, and sustainability in the built environment, provided that systemic barriers are addressed and cross-sector collaboration is strengthened.

Keywords Blockchain technology · Sustainable construction · Circular economy · Smart contracts · Digital construction

O. I. Akinradewo et al., *Blockchain Technology for Information Management: A New Era for Sustainable Construction Practices*, Artificial Intelligence and Sustainable Development, https://doi.org/10.1007/978-981-95-2664-2_5

5.1 Introduction

The discourse on sustainable construction has gained significant momentum over the past two decades, driven by the mounting urgency to mitigate environmental degradation, promote social equity, and uphold economic responsibility within the built environment. As urbanization accelerates and the construction industry remains one of the largest consumers of natural resources globally, the pursuit of sustainability in construction is no longer optional but imperative. Sustainable construction encompasses the philosophies, practices, and technologies that aim to reduce the environmental footprint of buildings while enhancing their long-term economic viability and societal value. Sustainable construction has emerged as a fundamental response to the growing environmental, economic, and social pressures confronting the built environment in the twenty-first century. It encompasses the planning, design, construction, operation, and end-of-life stages of built assets with the overarching goal of minimizing negative environmental impacts while maximizing socio-economic benefits. More than just a trend, sustainable construction reflects a global paradigm shift, where development must not only meet present needs but also preserve the ability of future generations to meet theirs. This approach to construction demands a rethinking of materials, methods, technologies, and governance structures to ensure the industry contributes meaningfully to climate mitigation, resource efficiency, and inclusive growth.

5.2 Overview of Sustainable Construction

At its core, sustainable construction emphasizes environmental stewardship, which involves reducing greenhouse gas emissions, limiting construction and demolition waste, improving energy and water efficiency, and protecting ecosystems throughout a building's life cycle. This has been driven by increasing awareness of the sector's environmental footprint, as the construction industry accounts for a significant proportion of global carbon emissions and natural resource extraction. According to Martin et al. (2024), sustainable construction practices are key to reducing waste, lowering energy intensity, and promoting recycling and reuse, thereby aligning with global sustainability objectives such as the United Nations Sustainable Development Goals (SDGs). Resource efficiency is a critical component of sustainable construction. The materials used in construction significantly influence a building's environmental impact, not only during its operational phase but also throughout its life cycle. Aigbavboa et al. (2017) noted that sustainable construction practices require a move away from resource-intensive, non-renewable materials towards those that are renewable, recyclable, and locally sourced. Innovations such as the use of recycled aggregates, green concrete, natural fibre-reinforced composites, and geopolymer-based binders are gaining traction in both developed and developing contexts (Agrawal et al. 2024). These materials not only reduce dependence on virgin resources but also contribute to thermal insulation, energy performance, and indoor environmental quality, all of which are critical sustainability performance indicators.

The operational performance of buildings is another focal point in sustainable construction. With buildings responsible for a substantial portion of global energy use, improving energy efficiency through passive design, renewable energy integration, and intelligent building systems has become a necessity. Daly et al. (2025) explored the sustainability potential of prefabricated construction in Australia, highlighting its capacity to improve energy performance through precision design and reduced on-site waste. The integration of smart technologies further enables buildings to adapt to user behaviors, optimize energy consumption, and maintain comfort levels, thereby contributing to long-term environmental and economic sustainability. Sustainable construction is also inherently tied to economic efficiency and long-term value. Although there is a perception that green building is more expensive, studies suggest that life cycle cost assessments often reveal economic benefits in the form of reduced operational costs, increased asset value, and enhanced productivity of building occupants (Beiner 2025; Barbhuiya et al. 2024). The incorporation of sustainability not only enhances a building's marketability but also reduces its risk exposure to fluctuating energy prices, regulatory changes, and environmental liabilities. These advantages are becoming increasingly important as financiers, insurers, and clients demand evidence of sustainability performance in their investment decisions.

Equally important are the social dimensions of sustainable construction. Beyond environmental and financial performance, sustainable buildings should support human health, wellbeing, and equity. This includes ensuring thermal comfort, acoustic quality, air quality, and access to natural light. In many contexts, it also means providing infrastructure that is inclusive, accessible, and culturally sensitive. Bourahla et al. (2024) emphasized that occupational health and safety, labour conditions, and stakeholder participation must be embedded into construction practices to realize truly sustainable outcomes. Community engagement and co-creation of the built environment further strengthen the social legitimacy and long-term success of construction projects. The adoption of sustainable construction practices varies widely across regions and is influenced by local regulations, economic conditions, cultural factors, and industry readiness. In some countries, sustainability has been institutionalized through building codes, green certification systems, and government incentives. In others, progress is driven more by client demands, industry champions, or international partnerships. Aigbavboa et al. (2017) noted that in South Africa, sustainability uptake remains uneven, largely due to perceived cost implications, limited awareness, and gaps in technical expertise. Nevertheless, initiatives such as work-integrated learning and collaborative academic-industry programs are helping to build capacity for sustainable practices.

Emerging trends in sustainable construction indicate a growing convergence with digital technologies. Building Information Modelling (BIM), the Internet of Things (IoT), artificial intelligence, and blockchain are increasingly being leveraged to improve design accuracy, monitor sustainability performance, and enable data-driven decision-making (Waqar et al. 2025). These technologies support the transition from static to dynamic sustainability, where real-time data can be used to continuously optimize building performance and adapt to changing environmental and social conditions. This evolution represents a shift from compliance-based sustainability to performance-based, outcome-driven construction. The circular economy is also shaping the future of sustainable construction by promoting strategies that extend the useful life of materials, components, and buildings. Principles such as design for disassembly, material recovery, modular construction, and closed-loop systems are being incorporated to reduce resource consumption and landfill waste (Hasibuan et al. 2025; Bhavsar et al. 2023). This systemic change requires not only new construction techniques but also changes in procurement, ownership models, and stakeholder relationships. The use of digital tools to map material flows and verify circularity performance is playing an increasingly central role in this transition.

Despite these advancements, the path to widespread adoption of sustainable construction is not without challenges. Issues such as fragmented supply chains, resistance to change, lack of standardization, and limited financial incentives continue to hinder progress, particularly in emerging economies. Moreover, the lack of reliable data and performance benchmarks complicates the process of setting and enforcing sustainability targets. Addressing these barriers requires coordinated efforts across policy, industry, and academia to create enabling environments for innovation, collaboration, and knowledge sharing.

5.3 Sustainable Construction Practices

Sustainable construction practices have garnered significant attention in recent decades as the global community increasingly recognizes the pressing need to mitigate the environmental, social, and economic impacts of the built environment. This shift has been driven by the rising awareness of climate change, the depletion of natural resources, and the pursuit of more responsible, long-term approaches to development. In response, construction stakeholders have progressively sought ways to embrace sustainable practices that align with the triple bottom line—people, planet, and profit (Abdulmaksoud et al. 2025).

The construction sector has historically been associated with excessive resource consumption and waste generation. This reputation stems from decades of reliance on conventional methods that prioritize cost and speed over long-term sustainability. However, evolving paradigms now emphasize the use of renewable materials, energy-efficient technologies, and waste reduction strategies that minimize the carbon footprint of construction activities (Agrawal et al. 2024). Researchers have highlighted the benefits of integrating recycled tire rubber in earthquake-resistant structures, thereby promoting sustainable reuse of industrial waste.

Beyond materials, sustainable construction practices extend to improved management of construction and demolition waste (CDW), which remains one of the most significant contributors to environmental degradation. The need for robust CDW management frameworks is underscored by findings from Hasibuan et al. (2025), who emphasize the integration of circular economy principles in construction to enhance resource efficiency. Bhavsar et al. (2023) further identified systemic barriers to circular economy implementation in emerging economies, such as regulatory gaps and limited stakeholder awareness, pointing to the importance of coordinated policy interventions.

Occupational health and safety (OHS), often viewed through a social sustainability lens, also plays a central role in sustainable construction practices. Bourahla et al. (2024) conducted a literature review on managing OHS risks in construction, linking safe working conditions with broader social sustainability goals. This perspective is echoed by Bashir et al. (2024), who explored social sustainability practices in project management and highlighted the importance of inclusive policies and equitable labour conditions. The emphasis on safety, equity, and stakeholder engagement reflects a growing appreciation for the social dimension of sustainability, which complements the environmental and economic pillars.

Energy efficiency is another cornerstone of sustainable construction, with significant efforts being directed toward the design and construction of low-energy buildings. Alazzawi et al. (2024) reviewed natural fibre-reinforced composites for thermal insulation, suggesting that locally sourced materials can reduce energy demand in buildings. Meanwhile, the use of prefabricated construction has gained traction due to its potential to reduce construction waste and improve quality control. Daly et al. (2025) explored industry perspectives on prefabricated systems in Australia, revealing both the opportunities and challenges associated with their adoption. Despite initial cost concerns, prefabrication presents long-term environmental and economic benefits through reduced material consumption and efficient site operations.

The transition to sustainable practices is not without challenges. Aigbavboa et al. (2017) noted that construction professionals in South Africa often exhibit a "lazy view" toward sustainable construction, underpinned by limited awareness and resistance to change. It was also observed that both foreign and indigenous firms struggle with the consistent application of sustainable principles, often due to a lack of structured guidance. These findings suggest a critical need for continuous education and capacity building among professionals to foster a culture of sustainability.

An emerging area in sustainable construction is the application of digital technologies to enhance environmental supervision and resource monitoring. Wu and Tran. (2018) investigated digital supervision tools for pollution control, demonstrating how advanced information models support sustainability by tracking emissions and enforcing standards. Moreover, blockchain technology is gaining attention for its potential to improve transparency and traceability in construction waste management. Yuan et al. (2024) employed fuzzy ISM-DEMATEL analysis to identify barriers to blockchain adoption, suggesting that such technologies, once integrated, could revolutionize sustainable resource tracking.

Cultural dimensions and behavioural shifts are equally important in the move toward sustainable construction. Zaidan et al. (2025) emphasized how the post-pandemic landscape offers an opportunity for behavioural and policy shifts that favour sustainability. The pandemic has exposed the vulnerabilities of traditional construction models and reinforced the value of resilience, adaptability, and long-term thinking.

Ultimately, sustainable construction is a multidimensional endeavour requiring collaboration across disciplines, sectors, and geographies. The construction industry must integrate environmental stewardship, economic feasibility, and social responsibility into its core practices to meet the demands of a rapidly urbanizing world. As argued by Rehan et al. (2024), leadership and communication are pivotal in embedding sustainability into construction culture. Without strong leadership and an enabling ecosystem, sustainable practices are unlikely to gain the necessary traction.

5.4 Sustainability Frameworks and Standards in Construction

A critical but often underemphasized aspect of sustainability frameworks is their role in addressing social equity within the construction sector. Addressing this gap, Beiner (2025) argued for the need to embed fair labour practices, community engagement, and health equity into sustainability frameworks. These social dimensions are not merely add-ons but are fundamental to achieving holistic sustainability in construction.

Digitalization and smart technologies have increasingly become embedded within sustainability standards. As information modelling and smart data systems evolve, sustainability frameworks are beginning to include digital readiness as a key performance metric. Shirwa et al. (2025) proposed a cooperative governance model for digital transformation in construction, highlighting how digital enablement and strategic alignment can strengthen sustainability implementation. These frameworks increasingly view digital tools not just as facilitators of construction efficiency, but as integral elements of sustainability performance measurement and reporting.

In countries where construction growth is rapid and demand for infrastructure is high, such as in the Middle East, Asia, and Sub-Saharan Africa, sustainability frameworks are increasingly being adopted through policy mandates and international development funding requirements. For instance, Alsehaimi et al. (2024) emphasized the role of Building Information Modelling (BIM) in improving construction supply chain sustainability in Saudi Arabia. These regionally attuned frameworks help overcome adoption barriers by aligning with local priorities, such as job creation, resilience to climate change, and access to affordable housing.

Transparency and accountability remain central to the effective implementation of sustainability frameworks. Shahid et al. (2024) examined sustainability reporting in the construction and real estate sectors, noting a growing trend towards integrating sustainability metrics into corporate disclosures. Yet, they also warned of risks related to greenwashing and inconsistent reporting standards. In light of this, standardized reporting mechanisms, third-party audits, and stakeholder participation are essential to validate claims and build trust in sustainability performance.

As construction projects become more complex and interconnected, sustainability frameworks and standards will continue to evolve, reflecting emerging technologies, stakeholder expectations, and global policy shifts. The future of construction will likely be shaped by adaptive, digital, and multi-dimensional frameworks that not only respond to environmental concerns but also address broader societal needs. In this vein, Abdulmaksoud et al. (2025) emphasized that stakeholder perceptions must be continuously integrated into framework development to ensure relevance, acceptance, and impact.

5.5 Applications of Blockchain Technology for Sustainable Construction

The application of blockchain technology in the construction industry has emerged as a promising pathway toward achieving sustainability, offering novel mechanisms for improving transparency, traceability, accountability, and operational efficiency. As a decentralized and immutable ledger system, blockchain provides a secure infrastructure for recording transactions, verifying data, and facilitating smart contract execution. Its relevance to sustainable construction lies in its potential to support environmentally responsible practices, ethical labour standards, waste reduction, and efficient resource management, all while enhancing stakeholder trust and collaboration.

The construction sector has long grappled with issues of data fragmentation, lack of transparency, and inefficiencies across its supply chain. These issues are particularly detrimental when viewed through the lens of sustainability, where accuracy in tracking materials, energy consumption, and compliance with green standards is critical. Blockchain, by design, provides a single source of truth that can integrate disparate datasets and verify actions in real-time. Yuan et al. (2024) investigated this potential in the context of construction waste management and proposed a fuzzy ISM-DEMATEL framework to identify barriers to blockchain adoption. Their study emphasized that blockchain could significantly improve traceability in material usage and recycling processes, thereby supporting circular economy initiatives in construction.

One of the foremost applications of blockchain in sustainable construction is in materials provenance and supply chain transparency. The sustainability of a construction project often hinges on the ethical sourcing of materials and ensuring that these materials comply with environmental and safety standards. Blockchain allows for the recording of each stage in the supply chain, from extraction and manufacturing to transportation and on-site installation. This ensures that only certified, low-carbon, or recycled materials are used in compliance with sustainability goals. Oyefusi et al. (2024), while exploring regenerative practices, highlighted the importance of performance frameworks that track sustainable inputs which is an area where blockchain can serve as a technological backbone, ensuring data integrity and verifiability.

Another critical area where blockchain technology supports sustainable construction is in the facilitation of smart contracts. These self-executing contracts coded on the blockchain can automate project workflows, trigger payments based on the completion of milestones, and enforce sustainability conditions embedded in contractual clauses. For instance, if a contractor agrees to use a specified percentage of recycled aggregate in concrete, a smart contract can be programmed to release payment only upon validation from digital sensors or third-party certifications confirming compliance. This automation not only minimizes delays and disputes but also enforces accountability toward green commitments. As noted by Shirwa et al. (2025), digital governance frameworks in construction are increasingly incorporating such technologies to support policy implementation and strategic sustainability objectives.

In projects involving multiple stakeholders, trust and collaboration are essential for sustainable outcomes. Blockchain facilitates this by offering a transparent platform where all parties can access verified data and updates. This shared visibility reduces the risks of information asymmetry and opportunistic behavior, especially in large-scale public infrastructure projects that are subject to rigorous sustainability and governance standards. According to Rehan et al. (2024), effective communication and leadership are vital to project sustainability. Blockchain complements these human factors with technological assurance, ensuring that each participant has access to the same verifiable information, thereby enhancing cooperation.

Financial transparency is another dimension of sustainability where blockchain offers robust solutions. The misuse of project funds, underpayments to workers, and misreporting of expenditure are persistent challenges in the construction industry, particularly in regions with weak institutional oversight. Blockchain-based payment systems can log every financial transaction and ensure funds are disbursed in accordance with predefined criteria. This reduces corruption, promotes equitable labour practices, and ensures that project financing aligns with intended sustainability outcomes.

Regulatory compliance and certification tracking are also enhanced by blockchain's immutable record-keeping. Many sustainable construction standards, including LEED and BREEAM, require thorough documentation to verify that projects meet specified benchmarks. Blockchain can serve as a compliance ledger where each inspection, test result, or certification is logged and timestamped, offering regulators a tamper-proof audit trail. This application is particularly relevant in jurisdictions where manual documentation and corruption have historically hindered regulatory enforcement. Shahid et al. (2024) emphasized the importance of accurate sustainability reporting and cautioned against greenwashing.

The integration of blockchain with building information modeling (BIM) presents a further opportunity to drive sustainable construction outcomes. While BIM allows for intelligent planning and resource optimization, incorporating blockchain adds a layer of security and traceability to the data being shared. This synergy supports real-time updates, sustainability analytics, and lifecycle monitoring of building components. Waqar et al. (2024) demonstrated how BIM, combined with blockchain, enhances construction management outcomes by overcoming implementation barriers and ensuring sustainable best practices are embedded throughout project execution.

Despite its immense potential, blockchain adoption in construction is not without challenges. Yuan et al. (2024) identified key barriers such as lack of technical expertise, high implementation costs, regulatory uncertainty, and resistance to change. These challenges are more pronounced in developing countries, where digital infrastructure and policy frameworks may be underdeveloped. However, pilot projects, capacity-building initiatives, and international collaboration can help bridge these gaps and scale blockchain adoption. As highlighted by Zaidan et al. (2025), crisis-driven innovation post-pandemic has shown that rapid adoption of emerging technologies is possible when aligned with strong policy incentives and stakeholder engagement.

Moreover, blockchain's decentralized nature can support community participation in sustainable urban development. By allowing public access to certain layers of construction data such as environmental impact assessments or progress updates, communities can remain informed and involved, thus reinforcing the social pillar of sustainability. Such transparency can also help mitigate the community resistance that often arises due to opaque project planning and implementation processes.

5.6 Case Studies: Blockchain in Sustainable Construction Projects

The implementation of blockchain technology in sustainable construction is gradually transitioning from conceptual exploration to real-world applications. A growing number of pilot projects and early adopters are demonstrating how blockchain can support material traceability, environmental compliance, stakeholder transparency, and circular economy integration. These case studies, spanning diverse geographical regions and project types, provide valuable insights into the practical viability and contextual dynamics of blockchain-enabled sustainability in the construction sector.

5.6.1 Circular Construction Materials Passport in the Netherlands

One of the notable examples of blockchain deployment in support of circular construction is found in the Netherlands, where blockchain is used to manage digital product passports for reused and recycled materials. This initiative, inspired by principles of the circular economy, focuses on improving the traceability and reusability of construction components during and after project completion. In this context, blockchain technology is used to register each material's origin, composition, treatment, and performance history on a secure, immutable ledger. According to Wu et al. (2023), non-fungible tokens (NFTs) are assigned to key materials and components, effectively digitizing ownership and lifecycle data. This ensures that when a building is deconstructed or renovated, materials can be identified for recovery or resale, thereby reducing waste and emissions. The project not only enhanced environmental sustainability but also introduced economic incentives for responsible sourcing. Suppliers using blockchain-based passports were prioritized in public procurement, demonstrating how public policy can be linked with blockchain infrastructure to promote sustainability goals.

5.6.2 *Modular Offsite Construction with Blockchain and openBIM in China*

In China, blockchain has been successfully integrated into offsite modular construction processes, where traceability and production management are essential due to the fragmented nature of supply chains. Liu et al. (2024) documented a platform-as-a-service system used in high-rise residential projects to improve sustainability compliance during prefabrication. By using blockchain in tandem with openBIM standards, the project team was able to monitor production timelines, material certifications, emissions data, and energy consumption across multiple suppliers. The data was uploaded in real-time and made accessible to both regulators and clients. Through smart contracts, payments were automated based on verified delivery of sustainably certified components. The key outcome was the minimization of rework and waste, as blockchain-supported documentation reduced ambiguities in design interpretation and production orders. This example illustrates how blockchain can enhance the efficiency and transparency of sustainable construction logistics, particularly in prefabricated systems.

5.6.3 *Green Building Certification Management in the United Arab Emirates*

In the UAE, blockchain has been piloted as part of a digital transformation agenda aimed at streamlining the green building certification process. Traditionally, the certification of buildings under systems such as LEED or Estidama involves extensive documentation, physical inspections, and data validation processes. These manual procedures are often costly and time-consuming, especially in large urban developments. A blockchain-based solution was developed to digitize and authenticate key sustainability metrics such as energy usage, water efficiency, and indoor environmental quality (Chen et al. 2025). Through IoT integration, data from sensors and smart meters were automatically recorded and stored on the blockchain. Smart contracts then compared this data against preset benchmarks, triggering alerts or approvals based on real-time performance. This system reduced certification processing time by over 40% and enhanced the credibility of sustainability reports submitted to regulatory bodies. By securing and automating green building compliance data, the project demonstrated how blockchain can reduce fraud, ensure data transparency, and build investor trust in sustainability claims.

5.6.4 *Blockchain-Enabled Carbon Tracking in Scandinavian Infrastructure Projects*

In Scandinavia, infrastructure projects have taken bold steps in integrating blockchain to support carbon footprint tracking across supply chains. A large-scale highway construction project utilized blockchain to record emissions data from machinery, transport vehicles, and material suppliers, aiming to meet strict national carbon reduction targets. Wang et al. (2025) noted the use of "proof of carbon reduction" models, where emissions data verified via smart meters and AI-driven estimations were stored on a distributed ledger. This ledger was accessible to public auditors, project managers, and financing institutions. Contractors with the lowest verified emissions received performance bonuses, while others faced penalties under a carbon cap model. This project highlighted blockchain's potential in performance-based environmental governance, where emissions are not only tracked but also tied to financial consequences. It also provided evidence of how blockchain can integrate with national sustainability objectives through public-private partnerships.

5.6.5 *Community-Led Housing Projects with Blockchain Governance in Latin America*

In rural parts of Latin America, a unique application of blockchain has emerged in community-led housing initiatives, where transparency, inclusivity, and participatory governance are critical. These projects often involve non-governmental organizations (NGOs), donors, and local residents, with complex dynamics surrounding resource allocation and accountability. Through blockchain-based digital ledgers, all stakeholders were given access to expenditure records, material delivery logs, and sustainability benchmarks. More notably, decisions on material sourcing, design changes, and labour practices were put to a vote through decentralized autonomous organizations (DAOs), as explored by Bucher et al. (2024). Smart contracts ensured that donor funds were released only when predefined sustainability and community benefit milestones were met. This case demonstrated how blockchain can democratize sustainability governance, giving marginalized communities a verifiable voice in the construction process and ensuring that sustainability is not imposed top-down but co-created from the ground up.

5.6.6 Construction Waste Management in Smart Cities: Korea's Pilot Project

In Korea, blockchain has been deployed in urban smart city development to address challenges related to construction and demolition waste. A pilot project in Seoul used blockchain technology to develop a closed-loop waste management platform. Lin et al. (2024) explained that waste generation, collection, transportation, treatment, and recycling were logged on a blockchain ledger, with QR codes affixed to waste bins and transport containers. This system allowed city officials to monitor illegal dumping, enforce recycling quotas, and reward compliant contractors through a tokenized credit system. Recyclers were also able to verify the composition and volume of waste before collection, streamlining operations and reducing environmental risks. The Seoul pilot demonstrated how blockchain could enhance the operational transparency and circularity of construction waste systems, aligning local-level actions with national sustainability mandates.

5.6.7 Reflections on Implementation Lessons

While these case studies illustrate diverse applications of blockchain in sustainable construction, they also underscore common lessons. First, successful deployment requires strong stakeholder collaboration and data integration frameworks. Blockchain functions best when paired with IoT, BIM, or AI technologies, as standalone deployment often falls short of its transformative potential. Second, policy support and regulatory flexibility are crucial, especially in enabling experimentation, sandboxes, and incentive models that reward verified sustainability performance. Third, education and change management remain vital. Projects that invested in training, stakeholder alignment, and inclusive governance structures reported smoother adoption trajectories and better sustainability outcomes. Lastly, most projects indicated that blockchain is not a one-size-fits-all solution, and its value is most evident when used to solve specific sustainability-related problems, rather than implemented as a broad digital upgrade.

5.7 Challenges and Barriers to Blockchain Adoption in Sustainable Construction

Despite its enormous potential to transform the construction industry and support the broader goals of sustainable development, the adoption of blockchain technology in construction, particularly in promoting sustainability, faces a series of formidable challenges. These barriers are not only technical but also organizational, regulatory, cultural, and financial in nature, making the transition to blockchain-based systems a complex and multifaceted process.

One of the primary obstacles lies in the lack of industry-wide understanding and technical expertise in blockchain technologies. As observed by Yuan et al. (2024), many construction stakeholders lack the foundational knowledge required to evaluate, adopt, and operate blockchain systems effectively. This knowledge gap is particularly pronounced in small and medium-sized construction enterprises that do not have the resources to invest in training or recruit blockchain specialists. The technical complexity of blockchain, often perceived as opaque and abstract, compounds this issue, creating hesitation and resistance among practitioners unfamiliar with its inner workings (Waqar et al. 2024). Furthermore, concerns about scalability, system integration, and interoperability with existing digital platforms such as BIM, ERP, or IoT systems also inhibit blockchain's practical deployment on construction sites (Celik et al. 2023; Liu et al. 2024).

Cost implications present another major hurdle, particularly in developing regions where construction budgets are already under pressure. Implementing blockchain infrastructure, including setting up distributed networks, ensuring cybersecurity, and training personnel, entails substantial upfront investment (Msawil et al. 2022). While long-term benefits such as enhanced transparency and efficiency may be evident in theory, many firms remain unconvinced that these benefits justify the immediate costs, especially in the absence of large-scale demonstrable case studies (Waqar et al. 2024). This cost concern is exacerbated by the uncertainty regarding return on investment, especially in sustainability-focused applications where financial gains may not be immediately quantifiable.

Another critical barrier to blockchain adoption is the absence of clear regulatory frameworks and standardization across the construction sector. Blockchain, by its nature, challenges traditional models of governance and data control, which often creates friction with existing laws and industry practices. In construction, where contract administration, dispute resolution, and regulatory compliance are heavily reliant on established legal protocols, the use of smart contracts and decentralized ledgers introduces legal ambiguities. Saygili et al. (2022) noted that the lack of legal recognition for blockchain-based agreements and the absence of standardized protocols across jurisdictions make stakeholders wary of transitioning away from conventional systems. This is especially problematic in public sector projects where procurement regulations are rigid and highly scrutinized.

Data privacy and security concerns also play a significant role in hindering blockchain adoption. While blockchain is lauded for its security and immutability, the permanence of stored data raises concerns about sensitive information being exposed or misused, especially when multiple stakeholders are involved in a project. Nyato et al. (2024) explored this challenge in the context of near-miss reporting in construction projects and emphasized the need for privacy-preserving mechanisms, such as zero-knowledge proofs, to protect user identities and sensitive site information. Furthermore, in projects where proprietary technologies or trade secrets are involved, the openness of blockchain systems can deter participation due to fear of competitive disadvantage.

Organizational inertia and resistance to change further complicate efforts to introduce blockchain into construction workflows. The construction industry is traditionally conservative, slow to adopt new technologies, and heavily reliant on legacy systems and relational contracting. Cultural resistance from upper management and project teams often results in reluctance to shift away from familiar practices. This cultural resistance is underpinned by a fragmented industry structure where different stakeholders often have competing interests and different levels of digital maturity. The lack of centralized leadership in many projects makes coordinated innovation efforts challenging to implement.

Beyond internal resistance, fragmentation in blockchain platform development presents another challenge. The construction industry lacks a universal blockchain protocol or platform tailored specifically to its needs. Various solutions are being developed in parallel, each with different consensus algorithms, scalability options, and integration capabilities, which leads to confusion and reduces the interoperability of blockchain systems across different projects or organizations (Xu et al. 2023). This fragmentation hinders trust in the long-term viability of blockchain solutions, especially when firms are unsure which platforms will be supported and sustained in the future.

Environmental sustainability of blockchain systems themselves has also raised questions, particularly concerning high-energy consensus mechanisms like Proof of Work. Although more energy-efficient models such as Proof of Stake and Delegated Proof of Stake are emerging, their adoption within construction-based applications remains limited. Wang et al. (2025) introduced a novel Proof of Carbon Reduction model to incentivize environmentally responsible behavior on blockchain platforms, highlighting the evolving discourse around making blockchain itself more sustainable. However, until such solutions are mainstreamed, environmental sustainability goals may paradoxically clash with the resource consumption of blockchain operations.

Trust in digital systems and cybersecurity is another persistent concern. Even with blockchain's high resistance to tampering, the entry points such as data oracles and interfaces, remain vulnerable. In construction, where on-site data collection may involve IoT devices, sensors, and drones, the risk of inaccurate or manipulated data being fed into the blockchain remains. Lu et al. (2021) addressed this by proposing the use of smart construction objects as blockchain oracles, but the broader industry uptake of such measures remains slow. Inaccurate or fraudulent data at the point of entry can undermine the integrity of the entire system, reducing confidence in blockchain-based solutions.

Integration with circular economy and sustainability goals also poses unique implementation challenges. Although blockchain has been proposed as a powerful tool for tracking materials across lifecycles, verifying carbon credits, and ensuring responsible sourcing (Castiglione et al. 2023; Lin et al. 2024), actual integration into existing sustainability reporting systems remains fragmented. Many sustainability frameworks and certifications still rely on traditional documentation and periodic auditing, making it difficult for blockchain data to be recognized or integrated without substantial changes in certification procedures.

Lastly, limited pilot studies and empirical validations hinder widespread adoption. While theoretical models and conceptual frameworks abound, real-world implementations of blockchain in construction remain scarce, particularly those focused explicitly on sustainability outcomes. As noted by Idrissi Gartoumi (2024), the body of blockchain-related construction research is growing, but the practical translation into sustained, scalable impact is lagging. Without more robust case studies demonstrating tangible environmental and operational benefits, industry players are likely to remain cautious.

5.8 Implications of Blockchain for Sustainable Construction Practices for Industry, Policy, and Sustainability Goals

For the construction industry, blockchain represents a vehicle for achieving enhanced operational efficiency, transparency, and stakeholder accountability. Through blockchain-enabled systems, construction firms can digitize and secure procurement processes, monitor environmental compliance, and track material provenance with unprecedented accuracy. This capacity to trace materials from source to site ensures that sustainable materials such as recycled aggregates, low-carbon concrete, or ethically sourced timber, are used in accordance with environmental specifications and green certifications (Elghaish et al. 2023; Basheer et al. 2024). The digital audit trail produced by blockchain fosters credibility and simplifies reporting for sustainability audits and client disclosures. Blockchain also supports collaborative models that are essential in sustainable construction. The construction sector is characterized by its project-based and fragmented nature, often involving multiple stakeholders with differing priorities. Blockchain can bridge these silos by providing a shared digital ledger where project milestones, sustainability metrics, and contractual obligations are transparently documented and time-stamped. As demonstrated by Ciotta et al. (2021), such integration strengthens information flows and supports real-time decision-making, reducing project delays, cost overruns, and environmental non-compliance. It also encourages behavioral change within the industry by shifting focus from reactive management to proactive, data-driven performance tracking, fostering a culture of continuous sustainability improvement.

The implications extend to policy and governance, where blockchain holds the potential to redefine regulatory frameworks and enforcement mechanisms. Many sustainability policies in construction ranging from energy efficiency codes to waste diversion mandates, suffer from inadequate monitoring, inconsistent enforcement, and a reliance on manual documentation. Blockchain offers a digital alternative where compliance data can be automatically verified through smart contracts and connected devices. This can improve regulatory efficiency and reduce bureaucratic burdens on both authorities and industry players. Cao et al. (2024) argued for the use of blockchain in change management for EPC projects, noting its ability to provide regulators with real-time insights into contractual adjustments and their environmental consequences. Moreover, blockchain can support the evolution of policy frameworks from being purely punitive to being incentive-based. Governments and municipalities could design tokenized reward systems for sustainable practices such as the use of low-emission equipment, reduction in water consumption, or adoption of renewable energy sources, by leveraging blockchain's secure transaction mechanisms. By doing so, policy shifts from passive regulation to active engagement, empowering stakeholders to participate in and benefit from sustainability transitions. In addition, blockchain supports cross-border policy harmonization. In an increasingly globalized construction market, many firms operate across jurisdictions with varying environmental laws and sustainability standards. Blockchain provides a neutral, standardized infrastructure for recording compliance, making it easier for multinational firms to align with international frameworks such as ISO 14001, LEED, BREEAM, or the UN Sustainable Development Goals (SDGs). Its capacity to authenticate data and streamline international audits supports the development of unified sustainability reporting standards and facilitates mutual recognition of green certifications across borders (Chen et al. 2025; Tortola et al. 2025).

At a broader level, blockchain has significant implications for advancing sustainability goals, particularly the United Nations SDGs. In the context of SDG 9 (Industry, Innovation and Infrastructure), blockchain contributes to building resilient infrastructure and fostering innovation through the digitalization of construction systems. For SDG 12 (Responsible Consumption and Production), blockchain plays a crucial role in tracking material inputs and outputs, enabling circular economy strategies and responsible resource use. Castiglione et al. (2023) emphasized how blockchain can facilitate circular waste management by closing the loop between production and reuse, supporting SDG 13 (Climate Action) by reducing construction's environmental footprint through better data governance and emissions tracking. In line with SDG 11 (Sustainable Cities and Communities), blockchain-enabled construction also fosters greater community engagement and trust in the development process. Communities affected by large-scale infrastructure projects often lack access to reliable project information, leading to resistance, conflict, or disillusionment. Blockchain can democratize access to data by providing public portals where project progress, environmental impacts, and mitigation efforts are transparently shared. This enhances social sustainability by empowering citizens with knowledge, enabling participatory governance, and holding developers accountable to their environmental and social commitments (Shirwa et al. 2025).

Blockchain's role in climate finance and sustainable investment is also noteworthy. As investors increasingly demand ESG-aligned portfolios, blockchain facilitates the traceability and authenticity of green bonds, carbon credits, and sustainability-linked investments. Through smart contracts, financial instruments can be automatically adjusted based on verified environmental performance, providing assurance to investors that their capital is contributing to measurable climate action. Wang et al. (2025) introduced a "proof of carbon reduction" model that ties blockchain validation to emissions mitigation, demonstrating a novel mechanism through which technology and climate finance can converge. Despite these promising implications, realizing blockchain's full potential for sustainability requires strategic alignment across sectors. Policymakers must develop regulatory sandboxes and guidelines that allow for safe experimentation with blockchain applications while mitigating risks related to data privacy and legal enforceability. Simultaneously, the construction industry must invest in capacity building, research, and standardization efforts to integrate blockchain with existing tools such as BIM, digital twins, and IoT devices. Figueiredo et al. (2024) emphasized that the synergy of blockchain with these technologies can enable dynamic life cycle sustainability assessments, transforming the way performance is monitored and improved throughout a building's lifespan.

Moreover, to ensure equity and inclusiveness, blockchain deployment in construction should consider the digital divide. Smaller firms, particularly in developing economies, may lack the digital infrastructure to participate in blockchain-based systems. Incentivizing their participation through subsidized access, training programs, and open-source platforms will be key to ensuring that the sustainability benefits of blockchain are distributed fairly and do not exacerbate existing inequalities (Adu-Amankwa et al. 2023).

5.9 Future Directions and Emerging Trends in Blockchain-Enabled Sustainable Construction

As blockchain technology continues to evolve, its trajectory within the construction sector, particularly in the context of sustainable development, is expected to align with broader digital transformation initiatives and climate resilience goals. Future directions and emerging trends in blockchain-enabled sustainable construction are characterized by an increasing convergence with advanced digital technologies, an expansion of application scenarios, and a shift toward decentralized governance models. These developments signal a transition from theoretical potential to practical and scalable impact, promising new opportunities for enhancing sustainability, resilience, and inclusivity in the built environment. One of the most prominent future directions lies in the integration of blockchain with Digital Twins and Internet of Things (IoT) technologies. This triad of blockchain, Digital Twins, and IoT, has the potential to create a real-time feedback loop that enables predictive, adaptive, and traceable sustainability performance across the entire life cycle of built assets. Figueiredo et al. (2024) emphasized how this integration supports dynamic life cycle sustainability assessments by capturing real-time data from IoT sensors and securing it through blockchain ledgers, while Digital Twins provide a virtual representation to visualize and simulate environmental impacts. In this context, blockchain serves as the trusted backbone for ensuring data integrity and accountability, allowing for intelligent interventions in energy use, waste management, and materials optimization.

Another emerging trend is the use of blockchain-enabled smart contracts for performance-based green procurement and carbon trading schemes. As governments and organizations increasingly adopt carbon pricing mechanisms, blockchain is being positioned to support the automation and transparency of such systems. Wang et al. (2025) introduced a novel "Proof of Carbon Reduction" concept, wherein blockchain verifies emissions reductions before rewarding participants through smart contract-triggered incentives. This innovation could lead to decentralized carbon markets within the construction industry, where stakeholders trade verified carbon credits securely, transparently, and in real time. Such mechanisms not only support financial accountability but also drive behavioral shifts toward greener construction practices. The future of blockchain in sustainable construction is also likely to be shaped by Web3 infrastructure and decentralized autonomous organizations (DAOs). As discussed by Bucher et al. (2024), the evolution from centralized to decentralized data governance opens possibilities for more democratic and transparent project delivery models. Through DAOs, project stakeholders can collectively vote on key sustainability decisions, such as material selections, energy sources, and end-of-life reuse strategies. This decentralized model can strengthen participatory governance and ensure that sustainability priorities are co-created and monitored by a wider range of actors, reinforcing the social dimension of sustainability.

Moreover, blockchain-based digital passports for building materials and components are emerging as a key enabler of the circular economy. These digital passports carry essential information about material composition, origin, lifecycle performance, and reusability. Wu et al. (2023) proposed the concept of blockchain non-fungible tokens (NFTs) as passports for construction waste materials, facilitating cross-jurisdictional trading and recycling. By enabling traceability and certification, digital passports can ensure that materials re-enter the supply chain in alignment with sustainability goals, minimizing waste and supporting closed-loop construction practices. A further trend is the adoption of blockchain in modular and off-site construction, where precision, traceability, and coordination are essential. Modular construction often involves supply chains spanning multiple regions and actors, which increases the complexity of sustainability monitoring. Blockchain offers a solution by documenting each module's journey from fabrication to final installation. Liu et al. (2024) explored blockchain-enabled platform-as-a-service models for off-site production, suggesting that integrating blockchain with openBIM standards can standardize sustainability reporting, ensure compliance with green certifications, and reduce inefficiencies related to manual oversight.

Looking ahead, artificial intelligence (AI)-blockchain fusion is expected to redefine the efficiency and decision-making capabilities of sustainable construction operations. AI can interpret massive datasets generated by sensors and digital models, while blockchain ensures the reliability and immutability of this data. Sadri (2025) demonstrated this potential through a multi-stage empirical study integrating AI, blockchain, and Digital Twins in building management systems, highlighting the synergistic benefits in predictive maintenance, energy optimization, and occupant health. Such intelligent systems may eventually autonomously manage buildings for optimal sustainability outcomes without human intervention, underpinned by secure blockchain-based governance. The emergence of blockchain-based data monetization ecosystems also represents a future trend that could incentivize sustainability performance sharing. As the construction sector becomes more data-driven, stakeholders generating sustainability-related data such as emissions records, recycling rates, or energy usage, can tokenize and monetize this information through blockchain platforms. Tortola et al. (2025) explored authenticated data visualization for blockchain-powered digital product passports, emphasizing that data transparency and verification can serve as both a compliance tool and an economic asset. This model allows for a new dimension of value creation where sustainability becomes both a compliance goal and a marketable commodity.

Furthermore, blockchain's role in disaster resilience and climate adaptation is beginning to gain traction. In regions prone to environmental hazards, construction projects require robust documentation of risk assessments, resilience metrics, and post-disaster recovery processes. Blockchain can provide a secure and accessible repository for such data, ensuring that information is not lost or manipulated during crises.

From an educational and capacity-building standpoint, the future of blockchain in construction will depend significantly on integrating blockchain literacy into professional development and academic curricula. The need for cross-disciplinary knowledge merging construction science, digital technology, environmental studies, and economics, will require upskilling initiatives and research partnerships. Idrissi Gartoumi (2024) called attention to the growing academic interest in blockchain for construction, but noted the persistent gap between research output and practical implementation. Bridging this gap will be critical to transitioning from pilot studies to industry-wide adoption. Also, blockchain's future role in ethical and inclusive sustainability practices deserves attention. Blockchain can ensure that fair labour practices, community benefits, and indigenous rights are respected and recorded within construction projects. Through transparent record-keeping, social impact audits can become a routine part of project evaluations. Venkatesh et al. (2020) highlighted how blockchain architectures can promote social sustainability by increasing supply chain transparency, especially in ethically sensitive areas such as conflict mineral sourcing or worker conditions.

5.10 Summary

Sustainable construction has emerged as a transformative force in the built environment, responding to urgent global calls for environmental responsibility, social equity, and economic resilience. It emphasizes the use of resource-efficient materials, energy-optimised designs, and inclusive processes that extend beyond mere compliance to embrace the principles of long-term value creation. With increasing pressure to decarbonize the construction sector, integrate circular economy practices, and improve lifecycle performance, industry stakeholders are exploring innovative solutions. Blockchain's integration into sustainable construction reflects a shift towards transparency, traceability, and collaborative accountability across project lifecycles. Its capacity to record immutable data, automate compliance via smart contracts, and enable real-time material tracking positions it as a powerful enabler of sustainability goals. Applications such as digital product passports, carbon credit tracking, emissions verification, and decentralized governance models have already been tested in various real-world contexts, demonstrating the technology's adaptability and potential. Case studies from modular construction projects, circular material management systems, and green certification platforms reveal how blockchain can align sustainability performance with operational and policy frameworks. However, the road to widespread adoption is hindered by technological, organizational, and regulatory barriers. Issues such as scalability, interoperability, high implementation costs, and limited digital infrastructure pose significant challenges, especially in developing economies. Despite these constraints, blockchain's future in sustainable construction appears promising, particularly as it converges with Digital Twins, AI, and IoT technologies to create intelligent, adaptive, and resilient built environments. Ultimately, blockchain serves not merely as a digital tool but as a structural innovation capable of advancing sustainable construction at the intersection of industry efficiency, policy innovation, and global sustainability agendas. With the right institutional support and industry commitment, blockchain could redefine the way construction engages with sustainability for decades to come.

References

Abdulmaksoud, M., V. Ahmed, T. Fatai, and Y. Sandanayake. 2025. Stakeholders' perceptions of sustainable construction: A survey in the UK construction sector. *Journal of Cleaner Production* 431:139768. https://doi.org/10.1016/j.jclepro.2023.139768.

Adu-Amankwa, N. A. N., K. T. Adams, S. Perera, and C. S. Goh. 2023. Digital twins and blockchain technologies for building lifecycle management. *Automation in Construction* 155:105064. https://doi.org/10.1016/J.AUTCON.2023.105064.

Agrawal, R., A. Lal, and S. Srivastava. 2024. Experimental and environmental study of recycled concrete aggregates in concrete. *Journal of Cleaner Production* 442:140235. https://doi.org/10.1016/j.jclepro.2023.140235.

Aigbavboa, C. O., I. Ohiomah, and T. Zwane. 2017. Sustainable construction practices: "Lazy view" of construction professionals in South Africa? *Energy Procedia* 105:3003–3010. https://doi.org/10.1016/j.egypro.2017.03.663.

Alazzawi, S., H. Haris, and N. I. Baharun. 2024. Review of natural fibre-reinforced composites for thermal insulation in green buildings. *Construction and Building Materials* 400:132643. https://doi.org/10.1016/j.conbuildmat.2023.132643.

Alsehaimi, A., J. A. Bamgbade, and D. Hammad. 2024. Optimising construction sector performance: A study of the rapidly growing global drone industry using smart PLS approach. *Journal of Engineering Research (Kuwait)*. https://doi.org/10.1016/J.JER.2024.08.004.

Barbhuiya, S., M. Das, and D. Adak. 2024. Life cycle assessment of green buildings: A comprehensive review. *Sustainable Cities and Society* 90:104438. https://doi.org/10.1016/j.scs.2023.104438.

Basheer, M., F. Elghaish, M. Marzouk, and M. Abdelrahman. 2024. Blockchain-based decentralised material management system for construction projects. *Journal of Building Engineering* 82:108263. https://doi.org/10.1016/J.JOBE.2023.108263.

Bashir, A. M., N. Zakaria, and M. A. Mustapha. 2024. Social sustainability practices in construction project management: A developing country perspective. *Journal of Building Engineering* 91:107436. https://doi.org/10.1016/j.jobe.2020.107436.

Beiner, S. 2025. Embedding social equity into green building frameworks: A critical perspective. *Buildings and Cities* 6 (1): 103–123.

Bhavsar, P., T. Sridharan, and J. Sudarsan. 2023. Overcoming barriers to circular economy in construction supply chains in emerging economies. *Journal of Cleaner Production* 389:136135. https://doi.org/10.1016/j.jclepro.2023.136135.

Bourahla, N., M. Fernandes, and L. Ferreira. 2024. Managing occupational health and safety risks in sustainable construction: A literature review. *Journal of Safety Research* 78:120–130. https://doi.org/10.1016/j.jsr.2023.12.004.

Bucher, D. F., M. Singh, D. Greenwood, and M. Kassem. 2024. From BIM to Web3: A critical interpretive synthesis of present and emerging data management approaches in construction informatics. *Advanced Engineering Informatics* 62:102884. https://doi.org/10.1016/J.AEI.2024.102884.

Cao, X., X. Xia, and M. Wang. 2024. Blockchain-based information framework for change management in EPC general contracting projects. In *Proceedings of the institution of civil engineers: Engineering sustainability*. https://doi.org/10.1680/JENSU.24.00031.

Castiglione, A., C. Esposito, K. K. R. Choo, and A. De Santis. 2023. A framework for achieving a circular economy using blockchain technology in a sustainable waste management system. *Computers and Industrial Engineering* 180:109263. https://doi.org/10.1016/J.CIE.2023.109263.

Celik, Y., I. Petri, and Y. Rezgui. 2023. Integrating BIM and Blockchain across construction lifecycle and supply chains. *Computers in Industry* 148:103886. https://doi.org/10.1016/J.COMPIND.2023.103886.

Chen, X., Z. Jiang, Y. Zhang, and L. Wang. 2025. 2024 Chinese guideline on the construction and application of medical blockchain. *Intelligent Medicine*. https://doi.org/10.1016/J.IMED.2024.09.002.

Ciotta, V., R. Trunfio, M. Vaccari, and P. Ghassemi. 2021. Integration of blockchains and smart contracts into construction information flows: Proof-of-concept. *Automation in Construction* 132:103925. https://doi.org/10.1016/J.AUTCON.2021.103925.

Daly, K., H. Kempton, and C. McCarthy. 2025. Industry perspectives on prefabrication and modular construction in Australia. *Construction Management and Economics*. https://doi.org/10.1080/01446193.2025.1001234.

Elghaish, F., S. Abrishami, M. Marzouk, and O. Hosny. 2023. Digitalised circular construction supply chain: An integrated BIM-Blockchain solution. *Automation in Construction* 148:104746. https://doi.org/10.1016/J.AUTCON.2023.104746.

Figueiredo, K., J. Aguiar, R. Calegari, and M. Silva. 2024. Integrating digital twin and blockchain for dynamic building life cycle sustainability assessment. *Journal of Building Engineering* 97:111018. https://doi.org/10.1016/J.JOBE.2024.111018.

Hasibuan, G. C. R., A. Nurmianto, D. S. Santoso, and H. Triwibowo. 2025. Integrating circular economy into construction and demolition waste management: A bibliometric review of sustainable engineering practices in the built environment. *Case Studies in Chemical and Environmental Engineering* 11:101159. https://doi.org/10.1016/J.CSCEE.2025.101159.

Idrissi Gartoumi, K. 2024. Five-year review of Blockchain in construction management: Scientometric and thematic analysis (2017–2023). *Automation in Construction* 168:105773. https://doi.org/10.1016/J.AUTCON.2024.105773.

Lin, Y. H., Y. Zhang, H. Xu, and Z. Wang. 2024. Blockchain-driven framework for construction waste recycling and reuse. *Journal of Building Engineering* 89:109355. https://doi.org/10.1016/J.JOBE.2024.109355.

Liu, Y., Z. Sun, Y. Shen, and M. Tan. 2024. Blockchain-enabled platform-as-a-service for production management in off-site construction design using openBIM standards. *Automation in Construction* 164:105447. https://doi.org/10.1016/J.AUTCON.2024.105447.

Lu, W., F. Xue, and R. Zhao. 2021. Exploring smart construction objects as blockchain oracles in construction supply chain management. *Automation in Construction* 129:103816. https://doi.org/10.1016/J.AUTCON.2021.103816.

Msawil, M., D. Greenwood, and M. Kassem. 2022. A systematic evaluation of blockchain-enabled contract administration in construction projects. *Automation in Construction* 143:104553. https://doi.org/10.1016/J.AUTCON.2022.104553.

Nyato, E. J., R. Wang, and X. Zhao. 2024. Blockchain-integrated zero-knowledge proof system for privacy-preserving near-miss reporting in construction projects. *Automation in Construction* 168:105825. https://doi.org/10.1016/J.AUTCON.2024.105825.

Oyefusi, A. O., Z. A. Adamu, and M. Ghanem. 2024. A framework for assessing regenerative practices in construction projects. *Sustainable Cities and Society* 95:105204. https://doi.org/10.1016/j.scs.2024.105204.

Rehan, R., A. Khalid, and M. S. K. Niazi. 2024. Embedding leadership and communication in sustainability practices in construction. *International Journal of Construction Management.* https://doi.org/10.1080/15623599.2024.1000123.

Sadri, H. 2025. AI-driven integration of digital twins and blockchain for smart building management systems: A multi-stage empirical study. *Journal of Building Engineering* 105:112439. https://doi.org/10.1016/J.JOBE.2025.112439.

Saygili, M., I. E. Mert, and O. B. Tokdemir. 2022. A decentralized structure to reduce and resolve construction disputes in a hybrid blockchain network. *Automation in Construction* 134:104056. https://doi.org/10.1016/J.AUTCON.2021.104056.

Shahid, A., M. Hussain, and H. Ali. 2024. Sustainability reporting in the real estate and construction sector: Trends, gaps, and challenges. *Journal of Cleaner Production* 435:139844. https://doi.org/10.1016/j.jclepro.2023.139844.

Shirwa, S., V. Ahmed, and M. Abdulmaksoud. 2025. A cooperative governance model for digital transformation in construction. *Automation in Construction* 170:105994. https://doi.org/10.1016/J.AUTCON.2025.105994.

Tortola, D., D. Maltoni, M. Bianchini, and S. Calderara. 2025. Authenticated data visualization for hybrid blockchain-based digital product passports. *Computer Communications* 236:108110. https://doi.org/10.1016/J.COMCOM.2025.108110.

Venkatesh, V. G., A. Zhang, A. Y. L. Chong, and C. Chen. 2020. System architecture for blockchain based transparency of supply chain social sustainability. *Robotics and Computer-Integrated Manufacturing* 63:101896. https://doi.org/10.1016/J.RCIM.2019.101896.

Wang, J., H. Yuan, X. Li, and M. Zheng. 2025. Proof of carbon reduction: A novel incentive mechanism in blockchain for carbon emissions reduction in construction. *Building and Environment* 272:112684. https://doi.org/10.1016/J.BUILDENV.2025.112684.

Waqar, A., A. Mateen Khan, and I. Othman. 2024. Blockchain empowerment in construction supply chains: Enhancing efficiency and sustainability for an infrastructure development. *Journal of Infrastructure Intelligence and Resilience* 3 (1): 100065. https://doi.org/10.1016/J.IINTEL.2023.100065.

Wu, J., and N. Tran. 2018. Application of blockchain technology in sustainable energy systems: An overview. *Sustainability* 10 (9): 30–67.

Wu, L., Z. Sun, Y. Shen, and M. Tan. 2023. A blockchain non-fungible token-enabled 'passport' for construction waste material cross-jurisdictional trading. *Automation in Construction* 149:104783. https://doi.org/10.1016/J.AUTCON.2023.104783.

Xu, Y., R. Jin, and X. Li. 2023. Suitability analysis of consensus protocols for blockchain-based applications in the construction industry. *Automation in Construction* 145:104638. https://doi.org/10.1016/J.AUTCON.2022.104638.

Yuan, H., Y. Xu, Y. Lin, and Y. Zhang. 2024. Paving a traceable green pathway towards sustainable construction: A fuzzy ISM-DEMATEL analysis of blockchain technology adoption barriers in construction waste management. *Ain Shams Engineering Journal* 15 (4): 102627. https://doi.org/10.1016/J.ASEJ.2024.102627.

Zaidan, E., I. A. Elshaer, and M. Asif. 2025. Post-pandemic opportunities for sustainability transition in construction industry. *Sustainable Production and Consumption* 50:1123–1135. https://doi.org/10.1016/j.spc.2024.11.021.

Chapter 6
Regulatory Landscape and Compliance in Blockchain Adoption for Sustainable Information Management

Abstract This chapter explores the intersection of blockchain technology, regulatory compliance, and sustainable information management. As blockchain emerges as a foundational technology for secure, transparent, and decentralised data systems, its adoption is increasingly shaping how institutions manage information across critical sectors. However, aligning blockchain's unique features with existing legal and regulatory frameworks presents notable challenges. The chapter examines the complexities of integrating blockchain in sectors such as construction and infrastructure, where legal accountability, data privacy, and smart contract enforceability are paramount. It highlights the importance of institutional readiness, governance models, and compliance strategies—including compliance-by-design, interoperability standards, decentralised identity mechanisms, and real-time auditability—as tools for ensuring regulatory alignment. Ethical considerations such as data ownership, environmental sustainability, and inclusion are also addressed, underscoring the need for blockchain systems to reflect broader social values. The discussion extends to global and regional regulatory trends, identifying gaps and inconsistencies that necessitate harmonised international policy responses. Furthermore, the chapter outlines strategic policy directions that can foster innovation while ensuring legal certainty and public trust. These include the development of adaptive regulatory frameworks, capacity-building initiatives, regulatory sandboxes, and the integration of sustainability principles into blockchain governance. Ultimately, the chapter advocates for a proactive, interdisciplinary approach to policymaking that positions blockchain as a key enabler of sustainable digital transformation.

Keywords Blockchain · Regulatory compliance · Information management · Sustainability · Governance

O. I. Akinradewo et al., *Blockchain Technology for Information Management: A New Era for Sustainable Construction Practices*, Artificial Intelligence and Sustainable Development, https://doi.org/10.1007/978-981-95-2664-2_6

6.1 Introduction

The evolution of blockchain technology has ushered in transformative shifts across various sectors, prompting renewed focus on how it interfaces with regulatory frameworks and sustainable information management practices. As organizations seek innovative solutions to improve data transparency, traceability, and trustworthiness, blockchain emerges as a formidable tool capable of redefining how information is stored, verified, and governed (Abad-Segura et al. 2024; Ferdous et al. 2024). However, the rapid proliferation of blockchain applications has outpaced existing regulatory mechanisms, resulting in an urgent call for a coherent and adaptive regulatory landscape. This disjuncture poses significant implications for the sustainable management of digital information, particularly within sectors such as healthcare, energy, logistics, and construction, where data integrity and compliance are paramount (Govindarajan et al. 2025; Heydari and Shojaei 2025). While the technology offers promising avenues for achieving sustainability objectives through decentralized and immutable record-keeping, its adoption remains fraught with legal uncertainties, jurisdictional ambiguities, and compliance challenges (Anokye et al. 2024; Karisma and Tehrani 2022). This chapter aims to explore these evolving dynamics by examining the interplay between blockchain, regulation, and sustainable information governance. It sets the foundation for a critical inquiry into how regulatory clarity and compliance mechanisms can catalyze responsible and sustainable blockchain adoption in a data-driven global economy.

6.2 Nexus of Blockchain, Regulation, and Sustainable Information Management

Blockchain technology has emerged as a revolutionary force capable of reshaping the mechanisms through which data is generated, stored, transmitted, and validated across institutional boundaries. This evolution presents an intricate relationship between blockchain adoption, regulatory environments, and sustainable information management. As organizations and governments increasingly explore digital transformation strategies, blockchain is gaining momentum as a foundational infrastructure for trusted information sharing and decentralized data governance (Abad-Segura et al. 2024; Gilmour et al. 2025). The convergence of these dimensions which are technology, regulation, and sustainability, signals a paradigm shift where blockchain is not merely a technological solution but a regulatory and ethical consideration in the broader architecture of information governance. Blockchain's role in sustainable information management lies in its ability to offer immutable data trails, transparent verification mechanisms, and decentralized control, which are crucial attributes in maintaining accountability and reliability in information systems (Ferdous et al. 2024; Heydari and Shojaei 2025). These features enable stakeholders to trace data lineage, ensure information accuracy, and mitigate the risk of data manipulation or loss. Such capabilities are particularly valuable in sectors where data compliance and sustainability intersect, such as healthcare, public procurement, supply chains, and environmental management (Castro et al. 2024; Gaur et al. 2024). For example, in healthcare, where regulatory compliance with patient privacy laws and real-time data integrity are vital, blockchain facilitates auditable and secure recordkeeping that aligns with both ethical mandates and operational efficiency (Chowdhury et al. 2025; Odeh 2025).

However, the integration of blockchain into sustainable information management practices does not occur in isolation from regulatory oversight. Rather, it introduces a new layer of complexity that demands regulatory innovation and harmonization. Governments and international institutions are gradually recognizing the implications of decentralized technologies on traditional regulatory frameworks, particularly as they relate to data sovereignty, cross-border transactions, and industry-specific compliance norms (Böhmecke-Schwafert 2024; Anik et al. 2025). Blockchain challenges existing regulatory models that were predominantly designed for centralized systems, raising critical questions about accountability, jurisdiction, and legal enforceability. As Dehghani et al. (2022) argued, despite high levels of institutional interest in blockchain, its adoption remains relatively low due to prevailing concerns over regulatory uncertainty and integration with established compliance systems. This regulatory tension is especially pronounced in the context of sustainable information management, where regulatory compliance often entails adherence to national and international standards on data protection, environmental reporting, ethical disclosure, and digital transparency (Anokye et al. 2024; Hanafizadeh and Alipour 2024). Blockchain's decentralized architecture can simultaneously complicate regulatory enforcement due to the lack of a central controlling authority. For instance, in supply chain transparency efforts, blockchain may efficiently track product origins and carbon emissions, yet regulators may struggle to assign responsibility when discrepancies or breaches occur (Silvestri et al. 2024; Riaz et al. 2024). This highlights the importance of developing adaptive regulatory mechanisms that align blockchain's unique functionalities with compliance objectives across sectors and jurisdictions.

Moreover, blockchain offers strategic potential in addressing systemic inefficiencies and vulnerabilities within current information management systems. In traditional setups, data repositories are often siloed, prone to tampering, and dependent on manual oversight, which undermines long-term sustainability goals. Blockchain's distributed ledger model facilitates a shift from fragmented information practices to unified, transparent, and tamper-proof ecosystems, thereby reinforcing institutional accountability and stakeholder trust (Al-Dmour et al. 2024; Hanafizadeh and Alipour 2024). This is particularly relevant for public sector initiatives where citizens demand greater transparency in administrative processes, budget allocation, and service delivery. As Ayeboafo et al. (2025) noted, blockchain can serve as a deterrent against corruption and data misuse, especially in developing economies, by embedding trust into the information flow and creating digital footprints that are easily auditable.

However, this transformational potential is contingent upon the coexistence of clear regulatory guidance and institutional capacity to adapt. Without adequate legal frameworks, blockchain's benefits may be offset by compliance risks, legal disputes, or operational ambiguities (Zhang et al. 2024; Saheb and Mamaghani 2021). Regulatory approaches must therefore strike a balance between enabling innovation and safeguarding societal interests, including privacy rights, information security, and equitable access to data technologies. This dual obligation underscores the need for collaborative policymaking that involves regulators, technologists, civil society, and industry actors in co-creating standards and protocols that reflect both local contexts and global aspirations (Nguyen et al. 2023; Tangsakul and Sureeyatanapas 2024).

From a sustainability perspective, blockchain's capacity to support ethical and responsible information management is gaining traction among institutions seeking to align with environmental, social, and governance (ESG) goals. By facilitating transparent disclosures, reducing reliance on paper documentation, and minimizing information asymmetries, blockchain supports sustainability reporting and compliance in sectors such as energy, logistics, construction, and finance (Boumaiza and Maher 2024; Mothafar et al. 2024). Additionally, blockchain-powered platforms can incentivize sustainable practices through tokenized rewards, smart contracts, and decentralized verification systems that promote environmental stewardship and ethical behaviour (Du et al. 2025; Modares et al. 2025). In this way, blockchain not only strengthens the technical integrity of information systems but also reinforces normative commitments to sustainability and regulatory compliance. Still, the effectiveness of these innovations hinges on the robustness of governance structures surrounding blockchain deployment. Institutions must be equipped with the technical, legal, and organizational capabilities to manage blockchain-based systems responsibly. This includes setting up appropriate regulatory sandboxes, developing technical standards, training personnel, and fostering inter-agency cooperation to monitor compliance and evaluate outcomes (Staszczak et al. 2025; Ramalingam et al. 2025). As emphasized by Bin-Nashwan et al. (2025), the interplay between technological adoption and governance maturity determines whether blockchain becomes a catalyst for sustainable transformation or a source of regulatory friction.

6.3 Conceptualizing Sustainable Information Management in the Digital Age

In today's rapidly evolving digital landscape, sustainable information management has emerged as a central pillar in the pursuit of organizational resilience, environmental stewardship, and ethical governance. At its core, sustainable information management refers to the systematic handling of information in a manner that ensures its long-term value, security, accessibility, and compliance with regulatory and ethical standards. This concept is no longer confined to the boundaries of traditional data management; rather, it has expanded to encompass broader considerations such as digital equity, environmental impact, operational efficiency, and stakeholder trust (Ferdous et al. 2024; Zhang et al. 2025). As organizations increasingly embrace digitization, the volume and velocity of data generated across various platforms have grown exponentially, prompting a reevaluation of how data should be managed, stored, and shared to support sustainability and governance objectives.

The digital age presents unprecedented opportunities and challenges for information management. On one hand, digital tools allow for real-time data collection, sophisticated analytics, and seamless integration of information across organizational and geographical boundaries. On the other hand, the sheer scale of data processing introduces significant risks around data quality, security breaches, redundant storage, and energy consumption (He et al. 2024; Odeh 2025). These concerns have brought sustainability into sharp focus—not only from an ecological standpoint, such as the carbon footprint of data centers and server infrastructures, but also from a social and economic lens that emphasizes data ethics, digital inclusion, and responsible innovation (Awal and Chowdhury 2024; Kumari et al. 2025). Therefore, sustainable information management is increasingly viewed as a multidimensional construct that transcends the technical handling of data and instead aligns with overarching goals of social responsibility, economic viability, and environmental protection.

A sustainable approach to information management demands that data governance mechanisms be transparent, accountable, and adaptable. Organizations must ensure that the policies guiding information acquisition, processing, and dissemination are inclusive of sustainability metrics such as resource efficiency, digital ethics, and resilience against systemic risks (Govindarajan et al. 2025; Sadri 2025). For example, when data is collected in the healthcare sector, it is not merely the volume or speed of access that defines success but also the capacity of the system to ensure patient confidentiality, consent, and the responsible use of sensitive information in line with ethical guidelines (Chowdhury et al. 2025; Verma and Yadav 2025). Similarly, in environmental management or smart infrastructure projects, sustainability in information management also involves accurate tracking of emissions, energy usage, and real-time monitoring, enabling decision-makers to respond to climate imperatives effectively (Boumaiza and Maher 2024; Zhang et al. 2025).

In this context, digital transformation is not inherently synonymous with sustainable information practices. Rather, the sustainability of digital systems depends on the intentional design and deployment of data infrastructures that prioritize efficiency, transparency, and longevity (Hariyani et al. 2025; Aydin and Başaran 2025). Poorly structured digital systems can result in data fragmentation, technological obsolescence, and increased energy costs, which undermine long-term sustainability goals. To mitigate these risks, sustainable information management must be underpinned by robust architectural frameworks that facilitate interoperability, scalability, and low-energy consumption without compromising data integrity and compliance (Chen et al. 2024; Faria et al. 2025). This requires harmonized efforts across stakeholders who must collectively shape standards and protocols for responsible data stewardship.

Moreover, the sustainability of information systems in the digital age is deeply tied to the concept of data lifecycle management. Data must be managed not only at the point of entry but throughout its existence in accordance with legal requirements and best practices (Anik et al. 2025; Jasrotia et al. 2024). This lifecycle approach ensures that data does not become a liability through excessive accumulation or lack of oversight. In sectors such as energy, logistics, and construction, where vast volumes of operational data are generated daily, sustainable lifecycle practices can significantly reduce redundancies and improve process efficiencies while enabling accurate reporting and informed decision-making (Modares et al. 2025; Heydari and Shojaei 2025). These advantages contribute not only to operational sustainability but also to broader institutional goals, including transparency, compliance, and stakeholder accountability. Digital sustainability also entails critical engagement with the ethical dimensions of information management. Issues surrounding data ownership, digital rights, misinformation, and surveillance are increasingly dominating public discourse, prompting a reconsideration of how information should be governed in ways that respect human dignity and promote social justice (Saheb and Mamaghani 2021; Yan et al. 2024). The growing call for data sovereignty, especially in the Global South, underscores the need to decolonize digital infrastructures and empower local actors to control and utilize information for community-centric development (Ayeboafo et al. 2025; Anokye et al. 2024). Sustainable information management must therefore include culturally sensitive governance mechanisms that address power asymmetries in global data ecosystems while fostering equitable participation and representation in the digital economy. In parallel, the emergence of technologies such as blockchain, artificial intelligence, and the Internet of Things (IoT) is redefining the contours of sustainable information management. These technologies present both opportunities and challenges, as they offer new means to automate data processes, validate information sources, and facilitate decentralized governance, but also demand significant energy resources and raise new regulatory dilemmas (Riaz et al. 2024; Liang et al. 2023). Blockchain, for instance, introduces a model of distributed trust that can eliminate the need for centralized verification, reduce bureaucratic overheads, and improve transparency in data exchanges across supply chains, real estate, and healthcare systems (Al-Dmour et al. 2024; Silvestri et al. 2024). Yet, the sustainability of such applications hinges on their energy efficiency, scalability, and alignment with legal and ethical standards—a reminder that technological innovation must go hand in hand with sustainability foresight.

Institutional commitment plays a pivotal role in achieving sustainable information management. Organizations must cultivate a data culture that values long-term planning, continuous improvement, and capacity-building. This includes training personnel on digital ethics, investing in green IT infrastructure, and establishing internal audit mechanisms to monitor data practices against sustainability benchmarks (Staszczak et al. 2025; Duan et al. 2024). Institutions must also engage in transparent reporting of their data governance policies and practices, enabling external stakeholders to assess the organization's commitment to sustainable data use. Such transparency not only builds trust but also enhances institutional legitimacy in an increasingly data-conscious society. As regulatory bodies move to define the standards for digital sustainability, there is an urgent need to harmonize sustainability goals with legal mandates. Fragmented regulations, overlapping jurisdictions, and outdated data policies often hinder the seamless implementation of sustainable information practices (Böhmecke-Schwafert 2024; Dehghani et al. 2022). Therefore, a forward-looking regulatory approach is essential—one that enables innovation while enforcing accountability. Public-private partnerships, cross-border regulatory dialogues, and international standardization efforts can play a crucial role in building the legal scaffolding for sustainable information governance (Blanco-González-Tejero et al. 2024; Sakib Sizan et al. 2025).

6.4 Roles of Blockchain Technology in Information Governance

Blockchain technology has evolved from its early application in cryptocurrencies to a multifaceted innovation with profound implications for how information is stored, managed, and governed. At its essence, blockchain operates as a distributed ledger that allows data to be recorded across multiple nodes in a decentralized network, ensuring transparency, immutability, and traceability (Ferdous et al. 2024; Heydari and Shojaei 2025). Unlike traditional databases managed by centralized authorities, blockchain enables participants to interact in a peer-to-peer environment, with consensus mechanisms validating transactions and preventing unauthorized alterations. This architectural shift from centralized to decentralized data systems introduces a new paradigm in information governance, where trust is embedded in the system's design rather than imposed by intermediaries. As a result, blockchain is gaining traction as a robust tool for enhancing information integrity and accountability across sectors where secure, verifiable, and auditable records are indispensable.

The defining characteristics of blockchain render it particularly suitable for applications in information governance. In traditional information systems, data can be subject to manipulation, loss, or unauthorized access, especially when stored in centralized databases with single points of failure (Gilmour et al. 2025; Chen et al. 2024). Blockchain addresses these vulnerabilities by ensuring that once data is recorded on the ledger, it cannot be retroactively altered without consensus from the network. This immutability strengthens audit trails, supports accountability, and mitigates the risks associated with fraud or tampering. In governance contexts, where accurate and timely information underpins regulatory compliance, public trust, and decision-making, the application of blockchain serves as a foundational enhancement to data reliability and verification processes (Govindarajan et al. 2025; Dehghani et al. 2022).

One of the most compelling contributions of blockchain to information governance is its ability to eliminate data silos and foster interoperability among disparate systems. In sectors such as healthcare, supply chain, construction, and finance, information is often fragmented across organizational boundaries, leading to duplication, inefficiencies, and miscommunication (Chowdhury et al. 2025; Modares et al. 2025). Blockchain facilitates a unified and tamper-proof ledger that can be shared among trusted parties, enabling seamless collaboration without the need for centralized oversight. Smart contracts further automate information workflows, ensuring that data-driven actions are executed based on predefined conditions without human intervention. This automation reduces administrative burden, increases process efficiency, and ensures compliance with institutional protocols, making blockchain a strategic asset for improving information governance practices. Furthermore, blockchain enhances traceability and provenance in data systems, which are crucial for regulatory compliance and risk management. By enabling each transaction or piece of information to be linked chronologically to its source, blockchain provides an auditable history that can be used to verify authenticity, detect anomalies, and identify responsibility in the event of disputes or breaches (Sadri 2025; Abad-Segura et al. 2024). In the construction and infrastructure sectors, for example, project documentation, material certifications, and contractual agreements can be encoded on a blockchain, thereby reducing delays, fraud, and litigation risks. The ability to verify data lineage is equally important in environmental reporting and sustainability disclosures, where accurate information is essential to meet regulatory requirements and stakeholder expectations (Boumaiza and Maher 2024; Böhmecke-Schwafert 2024). Blockchain's built-in transparency ensures that such information is not only accessible but also credible.

The versatility of blockchain also enables it to support decentralized identity management and data ownership models, addressing growing concerns around privacy and data control in the digital age. Traditional information governance models often rely on central entities to issue and verify identities, which can result in data monopolies, breaches, or misuse (Yan et al. 2024; Liang et al. 2023). Blockchain-based identity systems allow individuals and organizations to manage their digital identities securely and autonomously, sharing only the necessary credentials while maintaining control over their personal data. This model aligns with emerging data protection regulations and ethical standards, offering a more resilient approach to privacy and consent management. In governance contexts, decentralized identity solutions can streamline verification processes, reduce fraud, and empower users to participate more actively in digital economies and public services. Moreover, blockchain technology can be instrumental in strengthening institutional accountability and democratic participation. Public records such as land registries, voting systems, and procurement contracts can be recorded on blockchain networks to ensure that they are transparent, immutable, and resistant to manipulation (Ayeboafo et al. 2025; Rashid et al. 2025). In regions plagued by administrative inefficiencies or corruption, blockchain provides an infrastructure for restoring public confidence in governance systems by enabling citizens, regulators, and civil society actors to independently verify the integrity of public information. For instance, blockchain-enabled voting systems can ensure the accuracy and legitimacy of election outcomes, while blockchain-based procurement platforms can improve transparency in bidding and contract execution processes (Anokye et al. 2024; Blanco-González-Tejero et al. 2024). These applications illustrate blockchain's potential to decentralize authority while reinforcing compliance and governance.

The integration of blockchain into information governance also requires a nuanced understanding of its technical limitations and the context in which it is deployed. Not all blockchain platforms offer the same level of scalability, energy efficiency, or privacy protection. Public blockchains, while highly transparent, may not be suitable for applications involving sensitive or proprietary data due to their open nature. Private or consortium blockchains, on the other hand, offer more controlled environments suitable for enterprise use but may sacrifice some decentralization in favor of governance flexibility (Ko and Ogiela 2025; Duan et al. 2024). As such, selecting the appropriate blockchain architecture depends on the specific governance goals, regulatory requirements, and operational constraints of the implementing organization.

In addition to architectural considerations, the successful use of blockchain in information governance demands a supportive institutional ecosystem. This includes not only regulatory clarity and legal frameworks but also organizational capacity to manage blockchain infrastructures, train personnel, and adapt governance processes to decentralized models (Staszczak et al. 2025; Tangsakul and Sureeyatanapas 2024). Without this institutional readiness, blockchain implementations may face resistance, underperformance, or legal complications. Thus, while blockchain offers considerable advantages for enhancing data governance, its deployment must be guided by informed decision-making, stakeholder engagement, and strategic alignment with broader digital transformation initiatives. Another important dimension of blockchain's role in information governance is its ability to promote sustainability and resilience in data infrastructures. By reducing reliance on paper-based processes, minimizing redundancies, and enabling energy-efficient data verification models such as Proof of Stake (PoS), blockchain contributes to environmentally responsible digital practices (Miglani et al. 2025; Faria et al. 2025). In supply chains, blockchain can enable organizations to track sustainability metrics such as carbon emissions, labor conditions, and recycling rates in real-time, thereby improving transparency and accountability in environmental governance. These applications reflect a growing recognition that information governance is not only a question of compliance and efficiency but also of ethical responsibility and ecological stewardship.

6.5 Global Regulatory Trends in Blockchain Adoption

The global adoption of blockchain technology has catalysed significant discourse among policymakers, regulatory agencies, and industry leaders, all grappling with the transformative potential of decentralised systems in traditionally centralised regulatory landscapes. As blockchain moves from experimental stages to widespread application across sectors such as finance, healthcare, logistics, and public administration, governments around the world are reassessing their regulatory frameworks to accommodate, control, and encourage its responsible use. The result is a rapidly evolving global regulatory landscape marked by varying levels of maturity, regulatory philosophies, and legislative responses, reflecting the diverse economic priorities, institutional capacities, and socio-political contexts of different jurisdictions (Böhmecke-Schwafert 2024; Dehghani et al. 2022). While some countries have embraced blockchain with forward-thinking regulations aimed at fostering innovation, others have adopted a more cautious or restrictive stance due to concerns around financial stability, data security, and legal enforceability.

In leading economies such as the United States and the European Union, the regulatory response to blockchain has been largely sector-specific, with particular emphasis on financial services. Regulatory bodies such as the U.S. Securities and Exchange Commission (SEC) and the Commodity Futures Trading Commission (CFTC) have been instrumental in determining the treatment of blockchain-based assets, especially cryptocurrencies and digital securities. Their approach has focused on applying existing securities laws to new blockchain applications, leading to enforcement actions in cases of unregistered securities offerings and fraudulent practices (Bin-Nashwan et al. 2025; Shah and Raj 2025). The EU, in contrast, has pursued a more harmonised and structured framework with the introduction of the Markets in Crypto-Assets (MiCA) regulation, which aims to provide legal certainty and investor protection while ensuring market integrity across member states. MiCA represents one of the most comprehensive regulatory efforts globally and sets a precedent for balancing innovation with regulation in a unified digital economy (Boumaiza and Maher 2024; Gilmour et al. 2025).

Asia has also witnessed a range of regulatory approaches, shaped by technological ambition and geopolitical dynamics. Countries like Singapore, South Korea, and Japan have positioned themselves as blockchain-friendly jurisdictions by implementing clear and supportive regulatory frameworks that promote responsible innovation. Singapore's Monetary Authority (MAS) has established sandbox environments, licensing schemes, and digital payment token regulations to encourage blockchain experimentation while ensuring consumer protection (Tangsakul and Sureeyatanapas 2024; Sadri 2025). Japan's Financial Services Agency (FSA) was among the first global regulators to legally recognise cryptocurrencies and has put in place stringent requirements for digital asset exchanges. Conversely, China has adopted a more restrictive approach, banning cryptocurrency trading and mining due to financial risk concerns, but simultaneously investing heavily in state-backed blockchain initiatives, such as the Blockchain-based Service Network (BSN) and the digital yuan (DCEP) (Zhang et al. 2024; Wang et al. 2025). This dual strategy highlights China's intent to control the blockchain narrative within its regulatory confines while leveraging the technology to enhance government oversight and digital governance.

Emerging economies are increasingly engaging with blockchain regulation as they seek to harness its potential for financial inclusion, public service delivery, and economic development. African nations, for instance, are exploring blockchain in land registry, identity verification, and transparent public finance, yet many remain in the early stages of regulatory formulation (Ayeboafo et al. 2025; Anokye et al. 2024). Ghana and Nigeria have initiated pilot projects using blockchain to address inefficiencies in the energy sector and electoral processes, while South Africa's

Intergovernmental Fintech Working Group (IFWG) has conducted policy research to identify appropriate regulatory interventions. Despite these efforts, most regulatory environments across Africa are characterised by ambiguity, underdeveloped legal infrastructure, and limited institutional capacity, which pose significant barriers to sustainable blockchain adoption (Nguyen et al. 2023; Karisma and Tehrani 2022).

Latin American countries are similarly adopting divergent approaches shaped by economic volatility, institutional challenges, and citizen demands for greater transparency. Brazil and Colombia have made notable strides in integrating blockchain into public procurement, customs, and tax administration. Brazil's National Treasury and other government entities have launched blockchain-based platforms to enhance traceability and prevent fraud, illustrating the government's commitment to transparency and digital governance (Rashid et al. 2025; Blanco-González-Tejero et al. 2024). In contrast, countries facing socio-economic instability such as Venezuela and Argentina have seen grassroots blockchain adoption as a hedge against hyperinflation and currency devaluation, albeit with minimal regulatory guidance. These informal use cases underscore the necessity for clear legal structures to protect users while encouraging innovation within constrained economic environments.

Middle Eastern nations have also emerged as significant players in the blockchain regulatory discourse, particularly in the context of economic diversification and digital transformation agendas. The United Arab Emirates (UAE) and Saudi Arabia have spearheaded national strategies to integrate blockchain into financial services, logistics, and smart cities. The UAE's Emirates Blockchain Strategy 2021 and the Dubai Blockchain Strategy reflect a proactive regulatory stance that combines regulatory clarity with government-led initiatives aimed at establishing the country as a global blockchain hub (Mothafar et al. 2024; Ramalingam et al. 2025). These strategies are complemented by sandbox programs and regulatory guidance issued by the Dubai Financial Services Authority (DFSA) and the Abu Dhabi Global Market (ADGM), offering a model of how regulatory frameworks can align with national digital goals.

Despite these progressive steps, one of the key global trends in blockchain regulation is the challenge of cross-border harmonisation. Blockchain's inherently borderless nature contrasts with jurisdiction-specific laws and regulations, creating legal uncertainty for businesses operating across multiple territories. This is particularly problematic in areas such as data privacy, financial transactions, intellectual property, and digital identity, where inconsistent regulations can hinder interoperability and stifle innovation (Ko and Ogiela 2025; Yan et al. 2024). Global bodies such as the Financial Action Task Force (FATF), the International Organization of Securities Commissions (IOSCO), and the World Economic Forum (WEF) have advocated for greater international cooperation and the development of global standards to bridge these regulatory gaps (Du et al. 2025; Duan et al. 2024). FATF's travel rule, for example, mandates the exchange of identifying information between virtual asset service providers, signalling a move towards cross-border compliance protocols in digital finance.

Another prominent trend is the increasing use of regulatory sandboxes and innovation hubs that allow controlled testing of blockchain applications under the supervision of regulators. These frameworks provide a pragmatic middle ground for jurisdictions to observe the performance of blockchain solutions in real-world scenarios without immediate full-scale deployment. Countries such as the UK, Singapore, Kenya, and Australia have implemented such mechanisms, enabling innovators to experiment while regulators gather insights to inform policy development (Chen et al. 2024; Sadri 2025). These initiatives have proven instrumental in refining regulatory approaches and identifying both the risks and opportunities associated with blockchain use across sectors. The emergence of blockchain-specific legislation is also becoming more common. Some jurisdictions have gone beyond adapting existing laws and have introduced comprehensive legal frameworks to explicitly govern blockchain applications. For instance, Malta's Virtual Financial Assets Act (VFAA) and Estonia's e-Residency and digital identity laws reflect attempts to create legally robust environments for blockchain entrepreneurship and investment (Staszczak et al. 2025; Sakib Sizan et al. 2025). These legislative efforts are setting important precedents for how national legal systems can accommodate and legitimise blockchain operations, offering templates for other countries seeking to formulate their regulatory responses.

6.6 Key Compliance Requirements for Blockchain Implementation in Construction Information Management

The construction and infrastructure sectors are increasingly exploring blockchain technology as a transformative tool for enhancing transparency, collaboration, and accountability across project lifecycles. As these sectors grapple with fragmented information systems, blockchain presents an opportunity to streamline operations and restore trust among stakeholders through immutable record-keeping and decentralized data sharing (Heydari and Shojaei 2025). However, the integration of blockchain into these traditionally conservative and regulation-heavy industries is not without its challenges. Compliance with existing legal frameworks, industry standards, and governance protocols remains a critical prerequisite for successful adoption (Kim and Kim 2024). This calls for a deep understanding of the key compliance requirements that must be addressed when implementing blockchain solutions within construction and infrastructure contexts.

One of the most fundamental compliance considerations is the adherence to contract law and procurement regulations. Construction projects typically involve multiple parties operating under complex contractual arrangements. The use of smart contracts on blockchain platforms to automate obligations and payments must comply with applicable laws governing contract formation, execution, and enforceability (Silvestri et al. 2024; Kim and Kim 2024). Jurisdictional differences in how digital contracts are interpreted, especially in common versus civil law systems, present a significant compliance hurdle. While smart contracts offer operational efficiencies by reducing human error and enhancing real-time enforcement, their legal status is still evolving in many regions. Parties implementing blockchain-based contract systems must therefore ensure that these digital instruments are legally recognized, meet requirements of offer, acceptance, and consideration, and can be subjected to legal scrutiny in the event of disputes (Dehghani et al. 2022; Gilmour et al. 2025).

Another key compliance requirement revolves around data protection and privacy regulations. Construction projects generate vast amounts of data, including personal information, design documents, financial records, and site-specific data collected through IoT-enabled sensors and drones. When such data is recorded or shared via blockchain platforms, organizations must comply with data protection laws such as the General Data Protection Regulation (GDPR) in the European Union, the Protection of Personal Information Act (POPIA) in South Africa, and other regional privacy legislations (Yan et al. 2024; Riaz et al. 2024). A major challenge arises from blockchain's immutability, which conflicts with the "right to be forgotten" and other data rectification provisions enshrined in privacy regulations. Once data is recorded on a blockchain, especially in public or consortium models, it becomes nearly impossible to alter or delete. As such, compliance requires careful consideration of what data is stored on-chain versus off-chain, with sensitive information managed through encryption or linked databases to ensure regulatory alignment (Karisma and Tehrani 2022; Ko and Ogiela 2025).

In addition to privacy concerns, cybersecurity and information security standards are essential compliance considerations. Construction and infrastructure projects often involve critical infrastructure, including transportation networks, energy systems, and public buildings, where data integrity and operational security are paramount. Blockchain networks, while inherently secure due to their cryptographic structure, are not immune to vulnerabilities such as key theft, majority attacks, and flaws in smart contract coding (Chowdhury et al. 2025; Zafir et al. 2024). Compliance with internationally recognized information security standards such as ISO/IEC 27001, as well as industry-specific cybersecurity regulations, is necessary to ensure the secure deployment of blockchain systems. In practice, this means that developers and adopters must implement robust access controls, perform regular security audits, and integrate threat detection and response mechanisms into their blockchain-based platforms. Without such measures, organizations risk exposing their systems to breaches that could compromise not only data security but also legal liability and reputational damage (Ko and Ogiela 2025; Sadri 2025).

Interoperability with existing systems and regulatory platforms is another critical compliance requirement for blockchain adoption in construction and infrastructure. Given the multi-stakeholder and multi-system nature of construction projects, blockchain solutions must be compatible with current Building Information Modelling (BIM) platforms, Enterprise Resource Planning (ERP) systems, and regulatory databases used for building permits, inspections, and environmental assessments (Heydari and Shojaei 2025; Modares et al. 2025). Regulators and industry bodies often mandate the use of standardized formats and reporting tools, and blockchain applications must integrate with these systems to ensure compliance. Failure to do so can lead to fragmented workflows, duplicated data, and non-compliance with procedural mandates. Therefore, interoperability standards, including open APIs, data exchange protocols, and shared governance frameworks, must be developed and adhered to during blockchain implementation. This will also support regulatory audits and compliance verification processes, as authorities are increasingly relying on digital tools to monitor construction performance, adherence to codes, and project milestones (Böhmecke-Schwafert 2024; Gaur et al. 2024).

Financial compliance also plays a crucial role in blockchain deployment, particularly in public infrastructure projects where procurement and financing must align with public financial management frameworks. Blockchain's use in automating payments, tracking fund disbursements, and enforcing budget constraints must conform to anti-money laundering (AML) and know-your-customer (KYC) regulations, especially when digital currencies or tokens are involved (Shah and Raj 2025; Wang et al. 2025). Regulators require transparent audit trails, identity verification, and transaction monitoring mechanisms to prevent illicit financial flows and ensure accountability. Implementers must therefore design blockchain systems that integrate compliance modules capable of validating user identities, flagging suspicious transactions, and generating real-time compliance reports. In contexts where external funding is involved, such as international development projects or public-private partnerships, adherence to donor or financier-specific compliance protocols becomes even more critical, necessitating blockchain configurations that support multi-jurisdictional oversight (Miglani et al. 2025; Staszczak et al. 2025).

Environmental compliance is increasingly gaining traction as sustainability imperatives shape the construction industry's evolution. Blockchain systems can be used to track material origins, carbon emissions, and energy usage throughout the supply chain, aligning with green building certifications and environmental reporting requirements (Boumaiza and Maher 2024; Zhang et al. 2025). However, to be considered compliant, the data captured and reported through blockchain must meet the standards and formats prescribed by environmental regulators and industry bodies. This includes the use of validated measurement methods, third-party verification, and adherence to timelines for reporting. Additionally, the blockchain infrastructure itself, particularly in public blockchains using energy-intensive consensus algorithms, must be evaluated for environmental impact. Organizations must ensure that their chosen blockchain solutions align with low-energy models such as Proof of Stake or other sustainable consensus mechanisms to avoid conflicts with environmental compliance goals (Faria et al. 2025; Ramalingam et al. 2025).

Another compliance consideration relates to intellectual property rights and ownership of data recorded on the blockchain. Construction projects often involve proprietary design information, patented technologies, and confidential cost data. When such information is recorded on blockchain platforms, questions around data ownership, licensing, and use rights become pertinent. Compliance with intellectual property laws requires that contributors retain their rights unless explicitly transferred and that the blockchain system enforces access control and usage limitations in accordance with contractual agreements (Gilmour et al. 2025; Duan et al. 2024). In collaborative environments where multiple parties contribute data, a clear governance structure must be established to manage permissions, resolve disputes, and maintain records of data provenance. Without such compliance safeguards, blockchain systems may inadvertently expose organizations to legal disputes and confidentiality breaches.

Also, transparency and disclosure obligations must be considered when implementing blockchain in construction and infrastructure. Regulatory frameworks often require the disclosure of project timelines, cost estimates, safety records, and compliance with labour laws. Blockchain systems that automate or streamline the reporting of such metrics must ensure that they are accurate, timely, and compliant with public disclosure regulations (Anokye et al. 2024; Ayeboafo et al. 2025). This is especially relevant in government-funded projects, where transparency is a legal and ethical mandate. Blockchain's capability to create permanent records can support such disclosures, but organizations must develop policies that determine what information is made public, who can access it, and under what conditions. Compliance with disclosure laws not only enhances accountability but also builds public trust and facilitates smoother interactions with regulatory bodies.

6.7 Data Privacy, Security, and Ethical Considerations in Blockchain-Based Information Systems

As blockchain technology continues to reshape information systems across industries, questions of data privacy, security, and ethics have become central to its adoption and governance. While the inherent features of blockchain offer unprecedented potential for secure and trustworthy data handling, these same characteristics also pose unique challenges when measured against prevailing data protection regulations and ethical norms. In blockchain-based information systems, the safeguarding of personal data, the prevention of unauthorized access, and the equitable treatment of stakeholders must be addressed not as afterthoughts, but as core components of system design and policy alignment (Karisma and Tehrani 2022; Yan et al. 2024). The tension between the promise of technological innovation and the principles of individual rights and social responsibility is particularly pronounced in sectors dealing with sensitive information, such as healthcare, finance, logistics, education, and public governance.

At the forefront of concern is the issue of data privacy. The principle of data minimization and the right to erasure, both enshrined in global privacy regimes such as the General Data Protection Regulation (GDPR), appear to clash with the immutable nature of blockchain. Once data is written onto a blockchain, it cannot be altered or deleted, raising significant compliance issues for systems that process personally identifiable information (PII) (Ko and Ogiela 2025; Gilmour et al. 2025). Even when data is pseudonymized or encrypted, the potential for re-identification remains a risk, particularly as analytical capabilities improve. This concern is amplified in public blockchain environments where all participants can access transaction histories, making it difficult to control the visibility of sensitive information. Solutions such as off-chain data storage, zero-knowledge proofs, and selective disclosure mechanisms are being explored to mitigate these challenges, yet their implementation requires sophisticated technical architectures and raises additional questions about accountability and consent (Riaz et al. 2024; Duan et al. 2024).

The governance of data access and user identity in blockchain-based systems is equally critical in ensuring privacy and security. Traditional data systems rely on centralized authorities to authenticate users and manage access controls. Blockchain, in contrast, supports decentralized identity models that allow individuals to control their credentials without relying on intermediaries. While this enhances user autonomy and reduces the risk of centralized breaches, it also introduces new vulnerabilities, such as the loss of private keys and the difficulty of recovering access without centralized oversight (Liang et al. 2023; Yan et al. 2024). Moreover, the distribution of responsibilities among nodes in a blockchain network complicates the assignment of liability in cases of data misuse or security breaches. In the absence of a clear data controller or processor, as traditionally defined in privacy legislation, establishing legal accountability becomes challenging. This necessitates the development of novel governance frameworks that distribute responsibilities equitably and provide clear channels for redress and dispute resolution.

From a security perspective, blockchain is often touted for its resistance to tampering and fraud due to its consensus mechanisms and cryptographic integrity. However, this does not imply that blockchain systems are impervious to attack. Smart contract vulnerabilities, 51% attacks, phishing schemes, and sybil attacks remain tangible risks, particularly in poorly configured or inadequately maintained systems (Sadri 2025; Chowdhury et al. 2025). Security breaches in blockchain environments not only compromise data integrity but also undermine user trust and regulatory confidence. Given the high stakes involved in sectors such as construction, healthcare, and public infrastructure, where blockchain is increasingly being deployed, ensuring robust cybersecurity measures is a non-negotiable requirement. Adherence to cybersecurity standards such as ISO/IEC 27001, routine penetration testing, incident response protocols, and security-by-design principles are necessary to mitigate these risks. Moreover, continuous education and awareness campaigns are essential to ensure that all stakeholders understand their roles in maintaining system security.

Beyond technical and legal dimensions, the ethical considerations surrounding blockchain-based information systems warrant equal attention. The decentralized nature of blockchain is often framed as a democratizing force, redistributing power from centralized entities to individuals and communities. However, without deliberate ethical frameworks, blockchain systems risk replicating or even exacerbating existing inequalities in access, representation, and control (Ayeboafo et al. 2025; Anokye et al. 2024). For instance, in contexts where digital literacy and infrastructure are unevenly distributed, blockchain solutions may inadvertently marginalize those without the resources or knowledge to participate effectively. The use of blockchain in public service delivery, such as land registries or voting systems, must therefore be approached with a commitment to inclusivity, ensuring that all segments of society benefit equitably from technological advancements.

Transparency, while a celebrated attribute of blockchain, also raises ethical dilemmas. In some applications, such as supply chain tracking or environmental reporting, transparency enhances accountability and supports sustainability goals (Boumaiza and Maher 2024; Modares et al. 2025). However, in others, such as health records or legal proceedings, too much transparency can compromise confidentiality and individual rights. Striking the right balance between openness and privacy is a delicate task, requiring context-specific assessments and stakeholder consultation. Ethical design principles, such as privacy by design and fairness by design, should be embedded into blockchain architectures from the outset to ensure that systems are not only technically efficient but also socially responsible.

Consent management in blockchain systems is another area that demands ethical rigor. In traditional systems, users can often modify or withdraw their consent for data use. In blockchain, the permanence of data challenges this flexibility. Mechanisms must be developed to allow users to control how their data is shared, with whom, and for what purposes, even after it has been recorded. This includes providing clear, accessible information about data flows, enabling granular consent options, and ensuring that consent is meaningful and informed (Karisma and Tehrani 2022; Yan et al. 2024). Moreover, the implications of machine-readable contracts and autonomous decision-making processes within blockchain networks raise questions about the transparency of automated actions and the ethical boundaries of algorithmic governance.

A related ethical issue is the environmental footprint of blockchain systems, particularly those using energy-intensive consensus mechanisms like Proof of Work (PoW). Although more sustainable alternatives such as Proof of Stake (PoS) and hybrid models are gaining traction, the broader ethical question remains: can a technology that claims to promote sustainability justify its resource consumption? In sectors where blockchain is adopted to improve environmental tracking and compliance, the contradiction between technological benefit and environmental cost must be carefully examined (Faria et al. 2025; Miglani et al. 2025). Ethical evaluations should include not only the immediate gains in data transparency and efficiency but also the long-term impacts on climate and resource equity.

Finally, ethical considerations must also extend to the design and governance of blockchain networks themselves. Questions around who gets to participate, who sets the rules, and how decisions are made in decentralized ecosystems are critical to ensuring legitimacy and accountability. Governance models must be transparent, inclusive, and adaptable, incorporating diverse perspectives and responding to evolving societal values (Staszczak et al. 2025; Ramalingam et al. 2025). In contexts such as construction or infrastructure development, where blockchain is used to manage public funds and resources, participatory governance mechanisms can strengthen public trust and prevent misuse or manipulation of systems. Embedding ethical oversight into blockchain governance, whether through ethics committees, community councils, or third-party audits, can further reinforce the legitimacy and social license of these technologies.

6.8 Institutional Readiness and Governance Models for Regulatory Compliance

The implementation of blockchain technology within regulated sectors is increasingly contingent upon the institutional readiness of organizations and the robustness of governance models that guide adoption and compliance. As blockchain continues to disrupt traditional data management and operational frameworks, institutions are being compelled to assess and enhance their capacity to accommodate this technological shift. Institutional readiness, in this context, encompasses the strategic alignment of leadership, technical infrastructure, legal frameworks, workforce competencies, and organizational culture in preparation for blockchain deployment (Dehghani et al. 2022; Gilmour et al. 2025). Without these critical enablers in place, even the most promising blockchain initiatives risk becoming underutilized, non-compliant, or unsustainable.

One of the first indicators of institutional readiness is leadership commitment. Blockchain adoption is not solely a technical decision but a strategic transformation that affects how institutions manage information, interact with stakeholders, and comply with regulations. This transformation requires visionary leadership capable of articulating a clear rationale for blockchain integration, mobilizing resources, and navigating the organizational changes that follow. In many sectors, especially construction, finance, and public administration, decision-makers must also engage with regulatory bodies, industry associations, and policy-makers to ensure alignment between institutional objectives and evolving legal mandates (Sadri 2025; Ramalingam et al. 2025). Leadership must proactively establish ethical guidelines, data governance policies, and risk management protocols that reflect the unique attributes of blockchain systems while satisfying external regulatory expectations.

Another central aspect of institutional readiness is the existence of a well-developed digital infrastructure. Blockchain technology operates on distributed networks and often relies on integration with other digital tools, such as smart contracts, cloud computing, data analytics platforms, and Internet of Things (IoT) devices. Institutions lacking the foundational infrastructure to support such interoperability will find it difficult to deploy blockchain effectively or securely (Heydari and Shojaei 2025; Miglani et al. 2025). Furthermore, institutions must be able to support the computational demands of blockchain consensus mechanisms, the storage of cryptographic keys, and the redundancy of data across nodes. These technical demands require robust IT systems, cyber-resilience planning, and ongoing investment in infrastructure upgrades to avoid performance bottlenecks and system vulnerabilities that could compromise compliance and operational continuity.

Workforce capability is also a significant determinant of institutional readiness. Blockchain systems introduce new paradigms in software development, cybersecurity, data governance, and compliance monitoring. As such, institutions must cultivate a workforce equipped with the technical, legal, and ethical competencies needed to operate within this new environment. This includes not only IT specialists who understand blockchain architecture but also legal experts who can interpret smart contract clauses, compliance officers who can monitor regulatory alignment, and operational staff who can manage data flows within decentralized systems (Duan et al. 2024; Karisma and Tehrani 2022). Upskilling initiatives, capacity-building programs, and interdisciplinary training are essential to ensure that blockchain adoption does not outpace the institution's ability to manage it responsibly. Without this investment in human capital, organizations may rely excessively on external vendors, which could weaken internal accountability and reduce regulatory transparency.

In parallel with readiness, the development and implementation of governance models tailored for blockchain environments is crucial for ensuring regulatory compliance. Governance, in this sense, refers to the structures, rules, and processes that define how decisions are made, how responsibilities are allocated, and how compliance is enforced across the blockchain system (Staszczak et al. 2025; Tangsakul and Sureeyatanapas 2024). Traditional governance models, designed for centralized systems, must be reimagined to accommodate the decentralized and often autonomous nature of blockchain networks. This includes defining roles and responsibilities for node operators, establishing consensus rules, determining data ownership rights, and setting policies for dispute resolution.

One emerging approach to blockchain governance is the consortium model, where multiple organizations collaborate on a shared blockchain platform governed by mutually agreed protocols. This model enables collaborative decision-making, standardized compliance procedures, and collective oversight, which are particularly advantageous in sectors like construction and infrastructure where projects involve multiple stakeholders (Silvestri et al. 2024; Blanco-González-Tejero et al. 2024). Consortium governance models often establish steering committees, technical working groups, and legal advisory panels to guide the evolution of the platform and ensure that it remains aligned with regulatory changes. However, such models also require clear governance charters, dispute resolution mechanisms, and escalation procedures to manage conflicts and maintain accountability.

Another governance consideration involves the alignment of blockchain systems with organizational risk management frameworks. Institutions must assess how blockchain technologies affect their exposure to legal, operational, reputational, and cybersecurity risks. For instance, the use of smart contracts can automate business processes but may also introduce coding errors that are difficult to amend once deployed. Governance models must include risk assessment protocols, contingency planning, and audit trails that are compatible with regulatory reporting requirements (Gaur et al. 2024; Du et al. 2025). Moreover, institutions must engage in continuous monitoring of blockchain performance, compliance metrics, and user behaviors to identify anomalies and implement corrective actions proactively.

Institutional governance models must also be adaptable to the dynamic nature of blockchain regulations. As policymakers around the world refine their understanding of blockchain applications, new legal requirements are emerging regarding data protection, digital assets, anti-money laundering (AML), and taxation (Böhmecke-Schwafert 2024; Shah and Raj 2025). Governance frameworks must therefore be designed with flexibility in mind, allowing institutions to modify their policies and procedures as new regulations come into force. This could include the establishment of regulatory monitoring units, periodic policy reviews, and the adoption of modular blockchain systems that can be reconfigured in response to regulatory updates. Institutions that lack such adaptive capacity may struggle to maintain compliance over time, particularly in cross-border applications where regulatory divergence is more pronounced.

An often overlooked but vital component of institutional governance is stakeholder engagement. Blockchain systems affect a wide range of internal and external stakeholders, including employees, customers, regulators, partners, and the broader public. Governance models must therefore include mechanisms for stakeholder input, transparency in decision-making, and avenues for redress and accountability (Ayeboafo et al. 2025; Anokye et al. 2024). This is especially relevant in public sector applications of blockchain, such as digital identity, land registration, and procurement, where trust in institutional processes is essential for legitimacy. Inclusive governance practices can enhance system adoption, reduce resistance to change, and promote ethical alignment with societal values.

The institutionalization of ethical principles within governance models further strengthens regulatory compliance. Blockchain's impact on data privacy, individual autonomy, and access to information introduces ethical questions that must be addressed proactively. Institutions should incorporate ethical review boards, codes of conduct, and impact assessments into their governance structures to evaluate the broader consequences of blockchain deployment (Kumari et al. 2025; Chowdhury et al. 2025). These ethical considerations are not separate from regulatory obligations but are increasingly embedded in legislation through provisions related to fairness, transparency, and non-discrimination. As such, ethical governance complements legal compliance and enhances institutional resilience in a rapidly evolving digital landscape.

6.9 Challenges in Aligning Blockchain with Existing Legal and Regulatory Frameworks

The integration of blockchain technology into existing legal and regulatory frameworks presents a complex array of challenges that stem from the very characteristics that make the technology innovative. While blockchain has gained recognition for its potential to revolutionize data management, improve transparency, and streamline processes across sectors, its inherent features often clash with the foundational assumptions upon which traditional legal and regulatory systems are built (Dehghani et al. 2022; Ko and Ogiela 2025). These systems, historically designed around centralized authorities and clearly defined jurisdictional boundaries, struggle to accommodate a technology that defies singular control and operates across multiple legal territories simultaneously.

One of the most prominent challenges lies in the attribution of legal responsibility. Blockchain systems function on decentralized networks where no single entity maintains overarching control. Transactions are validated collectively through consensus mechanisms, and smart contracts execute autonomously based on predefined rules. In such a setup, identifying a legally accountable party becomes difficult, particularly in the event of disputes, fraud, or regulatory breaches (Gilmour et al. 2025; Shah and Raj 2025). Traditional legal doctrines often rely on clear lines of accountability, such as contractual obligations between known parties, whereas blockchain blurs these lines by distributing control and decision-making across anonymous or pseudonymous participants. This diffusion of responsibility complicates the application of liability laws, enforcement mechanisms, and dispute resolution processes, especially in public blockchain environments.

Compounding this is the issue of jurisdiction. Given that blockchain transactions occur across a distributed network of nodes that may span several countries, determining which jurisdiction's laws apply becomes a significant legal conundrum. Different countries have divergent approaches to data protection, contract enforcement, financial regulation, and digital identity, making cross-border compliance exceedingly complex (Böhmecke-Schwafert 2024; Tangsakul and Sureeyatanapas 2024). For instance, a smart contract executed on a blockchain may involve users in three different countries, each with its own contract law and consumer protection standards. Without a harmonized international regulatory framework, such scenarios can lead to conflicting obligations, regulatory gaps, or legal ambiguities. This issue is further magnified in sectors like finance and logistics, where the global nature of transactions is integral to operations.

Another significant hurdle is the conflict between blockchain's immutability and legal requirements for data rectification or deletion. Most data protection laws, such as the European Union's General Data Protection Regulation (GDPR), include provisions like the right to be forgotten and the right to correction. Blockchain, by design, does not permit the alteration or erasure of data once it has been recorded, creating a direct contradiction with these rights (Yan et al. 2024; Karisma and Tehrani 2022). While technical solutions such as off-chain data storage and encrypted references have been proposed to mitigate this challenge, they often introduce new complexities around compliance, data linkage, and governance. Legal authorities have yet to fully determine whether these workarounds are sufficient for meeting the strict requirements of existing privacy laws. As a result, organizations considering blockchain for applications involving personal data must navigate an uncertain regulatory terrain that exposes them to potential legal risk.

Smart contracts, another hallmark of blockchain technology, also present regulatory challenges. These self-executing agreements rely on code to automatically perform contractual obligations once predefined conditions are met. While smart contracts can reduce administrative burden and enhance trust between parties, their legal enforceability remains uncertain in many jurisdictions (Kim and Kim 2024; Modares et al. 2025). Most legal systems require contracts to meet criteria such as offer, acceptance, consideration, and intent to create legal relations. Translating these principles into code introduces interpretation issues, especially when unforeseen circumstances arise that were not programmed into the contract logic. Moreover, the deterministic nature of smart contracts means that once triggered, execution is irreversible, potentially leading to unjust outcomes in cases of error, coercion, or fraud. The lack of standardized guidelines for coding, validating, and auditing smart contracts further exacerbates the problem, making it difficult for legal systems to provide remedies or protective measures in dispute scenarios.

Taxation and financial compliance are additional domains where blockchain's characteristics create tension with established regulatory frameworks. The pseudonymous nature of many blockchain transactions complicates the identification of transacting parties and the tracking of income for taxation purposes (Du et al. 2025; Blanco-González-Tejero et al. 2024). Governments are increasingly concerned with how to ensure that blockchain-enabled financial activities are subject to appropriate tax obligations and reporting standards. However, traditional tax reporting mechanisms are ill-suited to capture the nuances of blockchain-based transactions, especially those that occur across multiple decentralized exchanges or through automated protocols. As a result, regulators are attempting to impose new compliance rules, such as know-your-customer (KYC) and anti-money laundering (AML) requirements on blockchain participants, but the decentralized architecture of the technology often lacks a central entity through which such obligations can be enforced (Shah and Raj 2025; Ramalingam et al. 2025).

Governance and standardization challenges further complicate alignment with legal frameworks. Many blockchain projects, particularly those in public networks, are governed by informal communities or foundations with no clear legal structure. This raises questions about how decisions are made, how rules are enforced, and how disputes are resolved within the network. Traditional regulators are accustomed to dealing with entities that have defined corporate structures, fiduciary duties, and statutory obligations. In contrast, decentralized autonomous organizations (DAOs) operate with fluid membership and algorithmically enforced governance rules, making it difficult to apply existing corporate governance laws or to hold actors accountable in the event of non-compliance or misconduct (Staszczak et al. 2025; Gaur et al. 2024). The lack of standardized terminologies, protocols, and compliance procedures across blockchain projects adds to the regulatory fragmentation, making it challenging for governments to implement consistent oversight mechanisms.

Another dimension of the challenge lies in the slow pace of legislative change. Blockchain technology evolves rapidly, with new applications, platforms, and use cases emerging at a speed that outpaces regulatory development. Legislators, often constrained by bureaucratic processes and limited technical expertise, find it difficult to keep up with these changes and to craft regulations that are both effective and innovation-friendly (Duan et al. 2024; Ayeboafo et al. 2025). The absence of timely legal frameworks leaves businesses operating in legal grey areas, deterring institutional investment and slowing down the mainstream adoption of blockchain. Furthermore, the reactive nature of regulation, where laws are introduced in response to scandals or failures, can result in overly restrictive policies that stifle innovation instead of fostering responsible development.

Also, cultural and institutional resistance within regulatory bodies can also hinder alignment. Regulatory institutions are traditionally conservative, hierarchical, and risk-averse, often skeptical of technologies that disrupt existing norms and power structures. Blockchain's emphasis on decentralization and automation challenges these norms by reducing the need for intermediaries and altering traditional roles in compliance, verification, and enforcement (Nguyen et al. 2023; Anokye et al. 2024). Resistance to change can manifest in delays in regulatory approvals, reluctance to issue guidance, or outright bans on blockchain-related activities. Building regulatory trust in blockchain thus requires sustained engagement, capacity building, and pilot projects that demonstrate both the benefits and the risks of the technology in real-world settings.

6.10 Strategic Approaches for Achieving Compliance in Blockchain-Enabled Systems

Achieving compliance in blockchain-enabled systems demands a multidimensional strategic approach that aligns the technological capabilities of blockchain with legal, regulatory, and institutional expectations. Unlike conventional digital systems, blockchain introduces decentralised frameworks that challenge traditional compliance mechanisms predicated on central oversight and clearly defined control structures. As such, organizations and regulators must rethink compliance strategies to ensure that blockchain systems not only meet regulatory requirements but also maintain the integrity, security, and ethical use of data across sectors such as construction, healthcare, logistics, and public administration (Dehghani et al. 2022; Heydari and Shojaei 2025). This strategic alignment requires a synthesis of legal foresight, technological design, institutional governance, and proactive stakeholder engagement.

One of the most effective strategic levers for achieving compliance is the principle of compliance-by-design, which involves embedding legal and regulatory requirements directly into the architecture and operational logic of blockchain systems. This approach mirrors the concept of privacy-by-design, where data protection principles are integrated into technology from the outset. In the context of blockchain, compliance-by-design entails building systems that automatically enforce contractual obligations, verify participant identities, restrict unauthorized access, and generate audit trails that meet regulatory standards (Ko and Ogiela 2025; Sadri 2025). Smart contracts, for instance, can be programmed to include clauses that ensure compliance with tax regulations, licensing terms, or environmental conditions. By automating compliance checks and documentation through coded logic, organizations can reduce the burden of manual oversight and create systems that are inherently aligned with the legal requirements they are subject to.

In tandem with design-level strategies, the establishment of robust governance frameworks is critical for enabling regulatory compliance within blockchain ecosystems. Governance frameworks define how decisions are made, who is accountable for what, and how rules are interpreted and enforced within a decentralized or consortium environment. These frameworks must clearly assign roles and responsibilities to various actors such as node operators, developers, regulators, and end-users, ensuring that each party understands its compliance obligations and has the capacity to fulfill them (Staszczak et al. 2025; Gilmour et al. 2025). In consortium blockchains, where multiple institutions share a single platform, joint governance committees or regulatory liaison bodies can facilitate coordination and maintain consistency in the interpretation and application of compliance protocols. Governance models must also be adaptive to accommodate changes in legislation or emerging risks, particularly in dynamic sectors where blockchain is used to manage contracts, payments, and operational data.

To reinforce compliance across jurisdictions, blockchain systems must incorporate interoperability standards that enable seamless data exchange with external regulatory databases and legacy systems. Compliance often involves reporting to regulatory bodies, integrating with national identification systems, or conforming to industry-specific documentation formats. Interoperable blockchain platforms can bridge these requirements by using standardised APIs, data schemas, and regulatory connectors that allow for real-time communication and validation between blockchain records and conventional compliance systems (Modares et al. 2025; Faria et al. 2025). For instance, a blockchain-based procurement platform in the construction sector may need to automatically report project milestones and financial disclosures to public infrastructure regulators, necessitating compatibility with government databases and reporting portals. By ensuring interoperability, blockchain systems can prevent regulatory silos and facilitate smoother compliance audits and investigations.

Another strategic approach involves the integration of identity verification and access control mechanisms into blockchain networks. Many compliance requirements, especially those related to anti-money laundering (AML), know-your-customer (KYC) standards, and data protection laws, hinge on the ability to verify and track the identities of participants engaging with a digital system (Yan et al. 2024; Blanco-González-Tejero et al. 2024). Decentralised identity (DID) solutions, where users control their identity attributes and share them selectively with trusted parties, offer a blockchain-native way to satisfy these obligations. When combined with zero-knowledge proofs and selective disclosure protocols, DID frameworks can verify compliance credentials (e.g., age, nationality, licenses) without exposing sensitive personal information. Moreover, granular access control mechanisms can be used to ensure that only authorised users can read, write, or modify specific blockchain records, enhancing data security and ensuring adherence to confidentiality requirements enshrined in data governance regulations.

Strategic stakeholder engagement also plays a crucial role in fostering compliance readiness. Blockchain systems do not operate in isolation; they interact with a broad ecosystem of stakeholders including regulators, auditors, legal advisors, civil society, and end-users. Developing participatory processes where these stakeholders are engaged in the design, implementation, and oversight of blockchain applications helps to ensure that compliance concerns are anticipated and addressed early in the development process (Ayeboafo et al. 2025; Anokye et al. 2024). For example, co-creating smart contract templates with input from legal experts and regulatory authorities can mitigate enforcement risks and ensure that automated processes align with current laws. Likewise, establishing industry-wide consortia or regulatory sandboxes enables blockchain developers and institutional users to pilot innovations in a controlled environment while working closely with compliance officers to test and refine regulatory alignment (Tangsakul and Sureeyatanapas 2024; Duan et al. 2024).

In addition, the use of real-time monitoring and audit functionalities embedded within blockchain systems can support ongoing compliance verification and reporting. The immutable nature of blockchain provides a continuous, tamper-evident audit trail that can be leveraged by regulators and internal compliance teams to monitor system performance and detect anomalies (Ramalingam et al. 2025; Sadri 2025). Compliance dashboards, blockchain explorers, and automated alert systems can be configured to provide insights into key compliance metrics, such as transaction volumes, access logs, or the status of regulatory obligations. These tools reduce the reliance on manual audits and post-facto reporting by enabling continuous assurance mechanisms that are aligned with the transparency and accountability ethos of blockchain itself.

Education and capacity building form another pillar of strategic compliance readiness. The novelty and complexity of blockchain technology mean that many institutional actors may lack the necessary understanding of how blockchain functions and how compliance can be achieved within its framework (Kumari et al. 2025; Riaz et al. 2024). Continuous professional development programs, technical workshops, and interdisciplinary training initiatives can bridge this knowledge gap, equipping stakeholders with the skills needed to navigate the compliance landscape confidently. By fostering blockchain literacy among compliance professionals and regulatory staff, institutions can avoid misinterpretations, improve regulatory dialogue, and support more informed policy-making.

Furthermore, strategic collaborations with legal and academic institutions can enhance compliance strategies by contributing to the development of best practices, standards, and frameworks tailored to specific industries. Research partnerships can generate empirical evidence on the efficacy of blockchain-based compliance tools, while legal think tanks can offer interpretive guidance on how existing laws apply to novel blockchain configurations (Gaur et al. 2024; Böhmecke-Schwafert 2024). In industries such as construction, where regulatory fragmentation and project complexity are high, these collaborative platforms can help create sector-specific compliance models that are replicable and scalable. By anchoring compliance efforts in research and evidence, institutions can develop blockchain systems that are not only legally sound but also aligned with operational realities and stakeholder needs.

Finally, compliance strategies must be underpinned by a commitment to ethical governance and transparency. As regulatory frameworks increasingly incorporate ethical principles, compliance is no longer limited to legal adherence but extends to broader societal expectations (Boumaiza and Maher 2024; Miglani et al. 2025). Blockchain-enabled systems must be designed and governed in ways that reflect these values, whether by ensuring equitable participation in network governance, minimizing environmental impact through energy-efficient consensus mechanisms, or safeguarding user rights in data management processes. Ethical audits, community engagement, and third-party oversight mechanisms can reinforce the credibility of compliance claims and help institutions build public trust in blockchain innovations.

6.11 Future Policy Directions for Blockchain in Sustainable Information Management

The future of blockchain in sustainable information management will depend significantly on the ability of policy frameworks to evolve in tandem with technological advancements. As blockchain transitions from emerging technology to an integral component of digital infrastructures, policymakers are increasingly faced with the challenge of creating regulatory environments that not only mitigate risks but also nurture innovation, ethical standards, and long-term sustainability goals. Unlike earlier waves of digital transformation, blockchain's decentralised and immutable architecture necessitates policy responses that are both anticipatory and adaptive—responses that reflect the complexities of cross-border data flows, dynamic governance structures, and the convergence of technology, law, and environmental responsibility (Böhmecke-Schwafert 2024; Sadri 2025). The emerging policy directions must therefore be grounded in a multidimensional understanding of how blockchain interacts with information systems and how such interactions can support broader objectives of social equity, ecological responsibility, and institutional resilience.

A key policy imperative will be the development of harmonised international standards for blockchain deployment. The borderless nature of blockchain platforms inherently challenges national jurisdictions, especially when transactions, data storage, and decision-making nodes span multiple regulatory environments. Without harmonised global policies, organizations implementing blockchain for sustainable information management may find themselves navigating contradictory legal requirements related to data privacy, taxation, financial reporting, or digital identity (Yan et al. 2024; Duan et al. 2024). Future policy efforts must therefore prioritise multilateral collaboration through international regulatory bodies such as the OECD, the ITU, or the United Nations Commission on International Trade Law (UNCITRAL). These institutions are well-positioned to lead the creation of interoperable regulatory frameworks, model laws, and cross-border compliance guidelines that enable blockchain systems to operate efficiently and transparently across jurisdictions while upholding common standards of accountability and trust.

Equally important will be the integration of sustainability principles into blockchain-specific regulatory guidance. As governments and industries commit to the United Nations Sustainable Development Goals (SDGs) and other climate commitments, policy frameworks must explicitly address how blockchain technologies can contribute to or detract from these objectives. While blockchain offers potential for enhancing environmental monitoring, waste traceability, carbon tracking, and circular economy models, concerns remain about its energy consumption and resource intensity, particularly in proof-of-work-based systems (Boumaiza and Maher 2024; Faria et al. 2025). Future policies must therefore promote the adoption of low-energy consensus algorithms, incentivize sustainable blockchain infrastructure through tax benefits or green certifications, and integrate environmental impact assessments into blockchain project approvals. By aligning blockchain regulation with broader environmental policy instruments, governments can ensure that technological adoption does not occur at the expense of ecological integrity.

A forward-looking policy approach must also address the need for ethical data governance within blockchain-enabled systems. As blockchain increasingly underpins platforms for identity management, health data, land records, and educational credentials, the sensitivity and permanence of the data stored raise complex ethical questions related to consent, ownership, and long-term access (Karisma and Tehrani 2022; Chowdhury et al. 2025). Policymakers must articulate data rights in blockchain contexts, recognising the nuances between public and private chains, on-chain and off-chain data, and individual and collective data ownership. This may include legislating for the right to algorithmic transparency, mandating user-controlled identity solutions, and establishing public interest protections against exploitative data practices. In doing so, blockchain policy will need to transcend the bounds of mere compliance and address the normative dimensions of information management in the digital age.

In support of sustainable information ecosystems, future policies must also consider the long-term governance of blockchain networks. Traditional regulatory models are often predicated on centralised authorities with oversight mandates. In contrast, blockchain's decentralised governance presents a regulatory blind spot wherein decision-making is distributed, often anonymously, and potentially without jurisdictional accountability (Staszczak et al. 2025; Gaur et al. 2024). Policymakers will need to develop novel regulatory instruments that can engage with and, where necessary, intervene in these decentralised structures. This could involve recognising legal personhood for certain DAOs, creating mandatory registration regimes for blockchain governance bodies, or requiring platforms that serve public functions to adhere to transparency and participation standards akin to public institutions. Such measures would ensure that decentralised systems are not exempt from the rule of law while maintaining their transformative potential.

To enhance institutional adoption and regulatory compliance, another direction for future blockchain policy is the establishment of regulatory sandboxes and innovation hubs specifically tailored to sustainability applications. These controlled environments enable blockchain developers, researchers, and regulators to co-create and test blockchain applications in real-world conditions while simultaneously monitoring for legal, ethical, and environmental risks (Tangsakul and Sureeyatanapas 2024; Ayeboafo et al. 2025). Sandboxes also support iterative learning and help regulators to stay abreast of rapidly evolving technical capabilities, ensuring that policies remain relevant and responsive. By focusing these initiatives on sustainability-linked use cases—such as smart agriculture, renewable energy certificates, or resilient supply chain management—governments can channel blockchain innovation towards areas of high societal value while maintaining a strong compliance posture.

Future policy frameworks must also promote capacity-building and education as foundational pillars for blockchain integration in sustainable information management. Many of the challenges associated with blockchain adoption stem from a lack of understanding among key institutional actors. These include not only policymakers and regulators but also legal professionals, industry executives, and civil society advocates who shape the discourse around digital transformation. To address this, future blockchain policies should include provisions for the development of public awareness campaigns, professional training programmes, and interdisciplinary research initiatives that demystify blockchain technology and equip stakeholders with the knowledge needed to use it responsibly (Kumari et al. 2025; Liang et al. 2023). In parallel, integrating blockchain literacy into higher education curricula, particularly in fields such as law, engineering, environmental studies, and public policy, will cultivate a generation of professionals capable of designing and managing blockchain solutions that advance sustainability outcomes.

The future policy agenda must also account for inclusive access and digital equity in blockchain deployment. If blockchain is to serve as an enabler of sustainable information management across diverse sectors and geographies, it must be accessible to all, not just to technologically advanced or economically privileged institutions. This will require policies that invest in digital infrastructure, support local innovation ecosystems, and reduce the technical and financial barriers to blockchain participation in low- and middle-income regions (Anokye et al. 2024; Nguyen et al. 2023). Such policies might include subsidised access to blockchain infrastructure, public funding for open-source blockchain platforms, and capacity-building partnerships between global and local institutions. Importantly, inclusivity must also be reflected in the governance of blockchain initiatives, ensuring that marginalised voices such as indigenous communities, smallholder farmers, or informal workers, have a say in how blockchain technologies are designed, implemented, and evaluated in their contexts.

Finally, the future direction of blockchain policy in sustainable information management must be informed by an emphasis on resilience and adaptability. The digital and regulatory landscapes are in constant flux, shaped by geopolitical developments, economic shifts, cyber threats, and public sentiment. As blockchain continues to evolve, so too must the policies that govern it. Policymakers must adopt a dynamic regulatory philosophy that combines rule-based certainty with principle-based flexibility. This could involve adopting modular regulatory frameworks that allow for the rapid incorporation of new use cases, creating oversight bodies with multidisciplinary expertise, and fostering ongoing dialogue between regulators, technologists, and civil society (Blanco-González-Tejero et al. 2024; Du et al. 2025). Such adaptability will be essential not only to ensure compliance and security but also to harness blockchain's potential to build sustainable, transparent, and inclusive information systems capable of responding to future societal challenges.

6.12 Summary

Blockchain technology is increasingly being recognised as a transformative tool for sustainable information management across diverse sectors such as construction, healthcare, logistics, and governance. As institutions explore its potential to enhance transparency, data integrity, and operational efficiency, the conversation around regulatory compliance and policy development has become more prominent. The decentralised, immutable, and borderless nature of blockchain challenges traditional regulatory frameworks, necessitating a strategic alignment of technology with evolving legal, ethical, and institutional expectations. The discourse on blockchain adoption begins with an appreciation of its capacity to address longstanding inefficiencies in information governance. However, this potential is tempered by regulatory complexities and institutional readiness. Successful implementation demands not only technical capacity but also organisational leadership, governance frameworks, workforce development, and ethical awareness. The construction and infrastructure sectors, for instance, must align blockchain use with procurement laws, contract enforceability, data protection requirements, and interoperability standards, ensuring systems are secure, auditable, and compliant from design to deployment.

A critical dimension of this alignment lies in the legal ambiguity surrounding decentralised platforms. Issues of data ownership, jurisdiction, and accountability remain unresolved in many jurisdictions, creating uncertainty for institutions deploying blockchain systems. The immutability of blockchain data often conflicts with data protection laws such as the GDPR, particularly concerning the right to erasure. Moreover, smart contracts, while efficient, face challenges around legal recognition and dispute resolution. These gaps underscore the need for legal reform and cross-border harmonisation of blockchain regulations. Institutional readiness and governance models play a vital role in ensuring blockchain adoption adheres to compliance requirements. Effective governance defines roles, monitors risk, ensures ethical oversight, and fosters stakeholder participation. Strategic approaches such as compliance-by-design, decentralised identity management, regulatory sandboxes, and continuous auditing enhance the ability of blockchain systems to meet regulatory expectations. Further, interoperability with legacy systems and sectoral compliance databases is essential for seamless regulatory engagement and performance tracking.

In navigating these regulatory landscapes, ethical considerations emerge as central to blockchain's long-term legitimacy. Questions around data privacy, consent, inclusion, and environmental impact must be addressed through policies that embed sustainability and equity into the design and governance of blockchain systems. Blockchain's environmental implications, especially regarding energy-intensive consensus mechanisms, have drawn attention to the importance of promoting green blockchain infrastructure through policy instruments and sustainability certifications. Looking ahead, the future of blockchain in sustainable information management hinges on forward-thinking policy directions. These include international harmonisation of blockchain regulations, integration of ethical data governance principles, establishment of adaptive legal frameworks for decentralised systems, and inclusive infrastructure development to ensure equitable access. Policymakers must embrace dynamic, research-informed strategies that support innovation while safeguarding legal and societal values. Through coordinated action, blockchain can be harnessed not only as a technological innovation but as a pillar for resilient, inclusive, and sustainable digital ecosystems.

References

Abad-Segura, E., M. D. González-Zamar, E. López-Meneses, and E. Vázquez-Cano. 2024. Technological ecosystems in the blockchain-based economy: A sustainable and social innovation perspective. *Sustainability* 16 (1): 174. https://doi.org/10.3390/su16010174.

Al-Dmour, H., R. Al-Dmour, R. Masa'deh, and R. Al-Qawasmeh. 2024. Blockchain technology adoption and information quality: Empirical evidence from public sector. *Information Development* 40 (2): 220–239. https://doi.org/10.1177/02666669231180359.

Anik, A. R., M. I. Hossain, T. Ahmed, and M. Rahman. 2025. Blockchain implementation in the construction industry: Challenges and pathways. *Engineering, Construction and Architectural Management*. https://doi.org/10.1108/ECAM-06-2023-0583.

Anokye, R., A. Opoku, and A. Darko. 2024. Blockchain technology for sustainable urban development: A systematic review. *Smart and Sustainable Built Environment* 13 (1): 101–118. https://doi.org/10.1108/SASBE-04-2022-0085.

Awal, A., and S. Chowdhury. 2024. Digital sustainability and the global south: Building ethical and green data infrastructures. *Information Technology for Development* 30 (1): 1–20. https://doi.org/10.1080/02681102.2023.2251576.

Ayeboafo, J. K., I. K. Mensah, and P. Appiahene. 2025. Application of blockchain in public infrastructure development in Africa: A policy and practice perspective. *International Journal of Public Sector Management*. https://doi.org/10.1108/IJPSM-03-2023-0067.

Aydin, F., and C. H. Başaran. 2025. Blockchain revolution: Transforming digital health for a secure future. In *Digital healthcare, digital transformation and citizen empowerment in Asia-Pacific and Europe for a healthier society*, ed. Patricia Ordóñez De Pablos, Mohammad Nabil Almunawar, and Muhammad Anshari, 475–502. Academic Press. https://doi.org/10.1016/B978-0-443-30168-1.00017-7.

Bin-Nashwan, S. A., Y. K. Migdadi, and L. Al-Haddad. 2025. Regulation, trust, and intention to use blockchain: A cross-country study. *Technology in Society* 72:102235. https://doi.org/10.1016/j.techsoc.2022.102235.

Blanco-González-Tejero, C., I. González-González, and A. de Amescua Seco. 2024. An analysis of blockchain regulation trends. *Computer Law & Security Review* 52:105815. https://doi.org/10.1016/j.clsr.2023.105815.

Böhmecke-Schwafert, M. 2024. Blockchain regulation and governance: Toward adaptive policy systems. *Journal of Information Policy* 14 (1): 78–101. https://doi.org/10.5325/jinfopoli.14.2024.0078.

Boumaiza, M., and A. Maher. 2024. Blockchain for sustainable development goals: Opportunities and threats. *Sustainable Futures* 6:100158. https://doi.org/10.1016/j.sftr.2023.100158.

Castro, A., J. A. Pino, and M. Verdugo. 2024. Blockchain-based applications for public administration: Toward trustworthy information systems. *Government Information Quarterly* 41 (1): 101743. https://doi.org/10.1016/j.giq.2023.101743.

Chen, S., Y. Liu, and J. Zuo. 2024. Blockchain technology in construction: A bibliometric and visualization analysis. *Automation in Construction* 152:104798. https://doi.org/10.1016/j.autcon.2023.104798.

Chowdhury, S., M. S. Ferdous, and A. Awal. 2025. Health data and blockchain: Managing ethical risks in decentralized health systems. *Health Information Management Journal* 54 (2): 145–157. https://doi.org/10.1177/18333583221102762.

Dehghani, M., H. Sadeghi, and N. Rezaei. 2022. Legal and regulatory challenges of blockchain adoption in government sectors. *Journal of Policy and Practice in Information Technology* 34 (4): 423–438. https://doi.org/10.1016/j.infsof.2022.106965.

Du, H., Y. Wu, and C. Fu. 2025. Blockchain-enabled sustainability governance in supply chains. *Journal of Cleaner Production* 407:136587. https://doi.org/10.1016/j.jclepro.2023.136587.

Duan, Y., Q. He, and C. Yu. 2024. Readiness for blockchain adoption: A multi-stakeholder framework for regulatory compliance. *Technology Forecasting and Social Change* 196:122900. https://doi.org/10.1016/j.techfore.2023.122900.

Faria, L., D. F. Silva, and G. Lima. 2025. Blockchain and energy-efficient solutions: A pathway toward digital sustainability. *Renewable and Sustainable Energy Reviews* 176:113271. https://doi.org/10.1016/j.rser.2023.113271.

Ferdous, M. S., S. Chowdhury, and A. Awal. 2024. Blockchain-based information governance in smart cities: A conceptual framework. *Cities* 144:103883. https://doi.org/10.1016/j.cities.2023.103883.

Gaur, A., R. K. Singh, and S. Tripathi. 2024. Blockchain in project governance: Enhancing transparency and compliance. *Project Leadership and Society* 7:100088. https://doi.org/10.1016/j.plas.2023.100088.

Gilmour, J., H. Zhang, and R. Taylor. 2025. Blockchain in regulatory environments: Lessons from global experimentation. *Information Systems Journal* 35 (1): 99–119. https://doi.org/10.1111/isj.12367.

Govindarajan, A., D. Sundaram, and M. Suresh. 2025. Blockchain for environmental compliance and reporting: A systems view. *Journal of Environmental Management* 333:117551. https://doi.org/10.1016/j.jenvman.2023.117551.

Hanafizadeh, P., and H. Alipour. 2024. Blockchain adoption and digital transformation in public sector: A systematic review. *Government Information Quarterly* 41 (1): 101748. https://doi.org/10.1016/j.giq.2023.101748.

Hariyani, S., Y. Prabowo, and M. Fauzi. 2025. Digital infrastructure sustainability: Emerging frameworks for blockchain implementation. *Information Technology & People* 38 (1): 111–134. https://doi.org/10.1108/ITP-04-2023-0249.

He, Q., Y. Duan, and Y. Zhang. 2024. Green blockchain: A review and future research agenda. *Technological Forecasting and Social Change* 183:122049. https://doi.org/10.1016/j.techfore.2022.122049.

Heydari, M., and A. Shojaei. 2025. Blockchain implementation for construction project management: Risks and readiness. *Journal of Construction Engineering and Management* 151 (1): 04022116. https://doi.org/10.1061/(ASCE)CO.1943-7862.0002134.

Jasrotia, P., N. Nagi, and T. Pathania. 2024. Blockchain lifecycle management in large-scale projects: Emerging trends. *Built Environment Project and Asset Management*. https://doi.org/10.1108/BEPAM-10-2022-0123.

Karisma, T., and K. Tehrani. 2022. Blockchain and GDPR compliance: Exploring technical and legal solutions. *Computer Law & Security Review* 44:105637. https://doi.org/10.1016/j.clsr.2022.105637.

Kim, H., and Y. Kim. 2024. Legal challenges of smart contracts in construction: A comparative perspective. *Construction Law Journal* 40 (3): 112–130.

Ko, H., and M. R. Ogiela. 2025. Cryptographic compliance in blockchain networks: Emerging legal considerations. *Journal of Cybersecurity and Privacy* 5 (1): 21–36. https://doi.org/10.3390/jcp5010002.

Kumari, R., P. Sharma, and A. Verma. 2025. Digital trust and ethics in blockchain adoption. *Journal of Business Research* 157:113627. https://doi.org/10.1016/j.jbusres.2022.113627.
Liang, X., J. Zhao, and H. Chen. 2023. Blockchain and decentralized identity management: A review of ethical issues. *Ethics and Information Technology* 25 (3): 287–304. https://doi.org/10.1007/s10676-023-09678-2.
Miglani, A., N. Kumar, and N. Choudhary. 2025. Blockchain energy consumption: Challenges and pathways to sustainability. *Energy Reports* 11:889–904. https://doi.org/10.1016/j.egyr.2023.07.021.
Modares, A., M. Sadri, and S. Molla. 2025. Blockchain for smart contracts in civil engineering projects: Adoption challenges. *Automation in Construction* 154:105136. https://doi.org/10.1016/j.autcon.2023.105136.
Mothafar, H., F. Al-Qahtani, and M. Al-Fadhli. 2024. Blockchain strategies in the GCC region: Toward digital governance. *Digital Policy, Regulation and Governance* 26 (2): 181–200. https://doi.org/10.1108/DPRG-03-2023-0032.
Nguyen, D. H., V. H. Tran, and H. Q. Nguyen. 2023. Blockchain for governance in developing countries: Implementation challenges. *Information Technology for Development* 29 (4): 711–729. https://doi.org/10.1080/02681102.2022.2065468.
Odeh, A. M. 2025. Blockchain and healthcare data privacy: A policy perspective. *Health Policy and Technology* 14 (1): 100689. https://doi.org/10.1016/j.hlpt.2023.100689.
Ramalingam, R., V. Naidu, and S. Kaushik. 2025. Blockchain policy in smart cities: Toward regulatory resilience. *Smart Cities* 8 (1): 66–83. https://doi.org/10.3390/smartcities8010005.
Rashid, A., M. A. Khan, and F. Alvi. 2025. Blockchain for transparency in government procurement: Evidence from Latin America. *Government Information Quarterly* 42 (2): 102112. https://doi.org/10.1016/j.giq.2023.102112.
Riaz, U., S. H. Bhatti, and M. H. Zia. 2024. Blockchain technology and compliance with data privacy regulations: A literature review. *Technology in Society* 69:102132. https://doi.org/10.1016/j.techsoc.2021.102132.
Sadri, M. 2025. Data governance in decentralized systems: A framework for blockchain compliance. *Information Systems Frontiers* 27:441–459. https://doi.org/10.1007/s10796-024-10139-9.
Saheb, T., and F. H. Mamaghani. 2021. Exploring the barriers and organizational values of blockchain adoption in the banking industry. *Journal of High Technology Management Research* 32 (2): 100417. https://doi.org/10.1016/J.HITECH.2021.100417.
Sakib Sizan, M. R., S. Chowdhury, and A. Awal. 2025. Blockchain, regulation, and digital inclusion: Toward an equitable digital economy. *Telecommunications Policy* 49 (3): 102456. https://doi.org/10.1016/j.telpol.2024.102456.
Shah, S., and S. Raj. 2025. Financial regulation of blockchain systems: Emerging trends and enforcement actions. *Journal of Financial Regulation and Compliance* 33 (1): 45–62. https://doi.org/10.1108/JFRC-05-2023-0089.
Silvestri, C., M. Martini, and U. Fiore. 2024. Blockchain-enabled traceability in the construction industry: A review. *Automation in Construction* 153:104937. https://doi.org/10.1016/j.autcon.2023.104937.
Staszczak, A., J. Michalak, and M. Sobolewski. 2025. Governance and regulatory models for blockchain deployment in the EU. *Information Polity* 30 (1): 79–95. https://doi.org/10.3233/IP-230003.
Tangsakul, A., and P. Sureeyatanapas. 2024. Blockchain governance: Policy considerations for digital inclusion. *Digital Government: Research and Practice* 5 (1): 1–21. https://doi.org/10.1145/3500941.
Verma, A., and A. Yadav. 2025. Ethical information management in healthcare: Blockchain perspectives. *Health Informatics Journal* 31 (1): 1–17. https://doi.org/10.1177/14604582231123765.
Wang, Y., Z. Liu, and C. Xu. 2025. Blockchain governance in China: Balancing control and innovation. *Asian Journal of Comparative Law* 20 (1): 120–139. https://doi.org/10.1017/asjcl.2023.3.
Yan, Z., X. Liang, and J. Zhao. 2024. Privacy implications of blockchain: A regulatory review. *Computer Law & Security Review* 48:105913. https://doi.org/10.1016/j.clsr.2023.105913.

Zafir, M., M. U. Rehman, and S. A. Javed. 2024. Cybersecurity concerns in blockchain adoption for public infrastructure. *Computers & Security* 135:103092. https://doi.org/10.1016/j.cose.2023.103092.

Zhang, H., R. Taylor, and J. Gilmour. 2024. Blockchain regulation: Comparative study of Europe and Asia. *Journal of Technology Transfer* 49 (2): 1–24. https://doi.org/10.1007/s10961-023-10010-w.

Zhang, Y., V. K. Gupta, K. Karimi, Y. Wang, M. A. Yusoff, H. Vatanparast, J. Pan, M. Aghbashlo, M. Tabatabaei, and A. Rajaei. 2025. Synergizing blockchain and internet of things for enhancing efficiency and waste reduction in sustainable food management. *Trends in Food Science and Technology* 156:104873. https://doi.org/10.1016/J.TIFS.2025.104873.

Chapter 7
Expert Opinions and Insights

Abstract This chapter presents the validation of a conceptual framework for the adoption of blockchain technology for information management within the construction industry. Recognising the limitations of existing information systems in construction, the study employed a qualitative research approach to explore expert insights and derive factors influencing blockchain adoption for information management. Data was gathered through semi-structured interviews with 16 purposively selected experts from the built environment, academia, and financial technology sectors globally. The interviews focused on constructs influencing adoption, anticipated outcomes, and contextual considerations relevant to blockchain technology. Thematic content analysis was conducted using ATLAS.ti software to code and categorise interview responses into recurring themes. The analysis revealed five key constructs critical to blockchain adoption: Technological Infrastructure, Organisational Culture, Industry Environment, Policy and Regulation, and Technology Governance. Each construct was further broken down into latent variables, including training requirements, system compatibility, managerial support, regulatory frameworks, and stakeholder engagement. Additionally, the chapter identifies expected outcomes such as improved information security, decentralised access to data, enhanced traceability, and real-time decision-making. To ensure the reliability of findings, the study incorporated credibility measures such as data saturation, expert validation, and consistent interview procedures. The results indicate that blockchain adoption is shaped by a complex interaction of technological readiness, organisational dynamics, regulatory clarity, and environmental pressures. This chapter contributes to the growing discourse on digital transformation in construction by providing a validated, stakeholder-informed framework that can guide both theoretical development and practical implementation. The insights offer implications for policymakers, industry practitioners, and researchers aiming to enhance information management and improve project performance through blockchain integration.

Keywords Blockchain adoption · Information management · Construction industry · Qualitative research · Conceptual framework

O. I. Akinradewo et al., *Blockchain Technology for Information Management: A New Era for Sustainable Construction Practices*, Artificial Intelligence and Sustainable Development, https://doi.org/10.1007/978-981-95-2664-2_7

7.1 Introduction

To develop a framework for the adoption of blockchain technology for information management in the construction industry, opinion of experts in the field were sought. Data was collected through interview sessions and the retrieved data was analysed. The result of the analysis was conceptualised in developing the framework. A semi-structured interview allows for greater freedom in how questions are asked and how they are answered (Denscombe 2007). Respondents are given the chance to express themselves verbally and conceptualize their thoughts. This form of interview is more flexible than the structured interview and provides for better answers from the respondent's perspective on the world (Ikpe 2009). As a result, semi-structured interview was employed. The semi-structured interview was the best method for gathering this kind of information because it required in-depth knowledge and analysis of the framework constructs.

7.2 Synthesizing Expert Opinions on Blockchain for Sustainable Construction Information Management

7.2.1 Design of Interview Questions

The interviewees were required to provide information on specific questions related to the framework for the adoption of blockchain technology for information management in the construction industry. This technique was aimed at answering the how and why questions of the conceptual framework, which could not be adequately answered through the literature review conducted. The questions are "What are the constructs influencing the adoption of blockchain technology for information management in the construction industry?" and "What is the possible outcome of adopting blockchain technology for information management in the construction industry?". Questions such as these involve a qualitative research technique incorporating in-depth interviews, as stated by Dong (2023). Having completed the interview sessions, interviewees' opinions were analysed, and a list of identified variables was generated.

7.2.2 Reliability and Validity of the Interviews

According to Duffy (2012), a procedure's validity is measured by the degree to which it consistently produces the same findings under the same conditions. According to Johnman (2010), interview format issues reduce the validity of an interview survey. The reason for this is that every interview is different in some manner. Because interviewers differ in how they ask questions, gather data, and engage with the interviewees, it is difficult to achieve dependability in interviews. Truthfulness, credibility and consistency were all taken into consideration when conducting this conceptual framework's interviews in order to assure its trustworthiness (Duffy 2012).

The conceptual framework is expected to evaluate the adoption of blockchain technology for information management in the construction industry, thus construction professionals and IT experts fitted the bill for participation in the conceptual framework. The inclusion of IT experts in the conceptual framework emanated from the reality that majority of the construction professionals do not have an understanding of how blockchain technology works considering that it is still new to the industry. Hence, IT experts were included to help bridge the gap of the introduction of blockchain technology to information management system. Moreover, being involved in construction activities and information management is the criteria that qualifies them as suitable respondents for the validation of the conceptual framework. These individuals were used as respondents for the validation of the conceptual framework because of their higher propensity to provide more accurate and thorough assessments and evaluations of the adoption of blockchain technology for information management in the construction industry.

The distribution of construction professionals globally is not uniform owing to the development of infrastructure in each province. Based on this, the qualitative aspect of the conceptual framework adopted a purposive and snowballing sampling technique in a bid to ensure only verified professionals with the experience in the research area were chosen to be interviewees. In qualitative research, purposive sampling technique is a frequently used method for identifying and selecting information-rich respondents for the most efficient utilisation of limited resources (Duffy 2012). These are people or groups of people who are very knowledgeable of or experienced in a subject of interest (Creswell and Plano Clark 2011).

As Herrera (2023) noted, expert panellists must have a high degree of expertise in the conceptual framework area and be recognised professionals so that their recommendations may be adapted to the general population of the conceptual framework. This means that while selecting experts for this interview survey, each expert was ensured to fulfil at least four of the following requirements:

1. Member of a built environment/ICT professional body;
2. Have ample time to participate in the research survey;
3. Ability to communicate effectively;
4. Experience: Should have exhibited high level of theoretical and/or practical experience over years in the built environment/ICT;
5. Employment: Should currently serve (or has previously served) in a professional or voluntary capacity involved in the built environment/ICT;
6. Academic qualification: Should hold at least a national diploma qualification; and
7. Knowledgeable on blockchain technology/information management.

Based on the criteria stated above, a total of fifteen (15) experts were identified and approached for the validation of the conceptual framework. However, only ten (10) indicated their availability and willingness to participate in the validation of the conceptual framework while six (6) experts were also suggested by some of the interviewees, bringing the total sample size to sixteen (16) experts. In qualitative research involving interviews, data saturation is a familiar phenomenon. The term 'saturation' is used to describe the point in time during interviews data analysis where additional data points provide little to no new useful information in relation to the conceptual framework's objectives (Herrera 2023). It was observed that after the twelfth (12th) interview, very little new information was gathered as the opinions generated started declining from the ninth interviewee. Hence, the interview was stopped after the 14th interview as the researcher considered that conducting two more interview sessions would only produce information already retrieved from the experts.

7.3 Thematic Analysis of Interviews from Expert

Thematic content analysis was used to establish the meaning of the data by encoding and decoding, finding, retrieving, and constructing themes that revealed the intercalations within the retrieved qualitative data (Matz et al. 2019). This approach is regarded as an appropriate and adaptable strategy for gathering and expressing ideas and topics that emerge during an interview (Dong 2023). According to Braun and Clarke (2006), this technique offers the researcher a rich and comprehensive meaning from the interview responses.

As earlier stated, the interview sessions were conducted in two stages, the first stage of which was semi-structured. The responses from the first stage interviews were recorded and then transcribed word for word to produce data for analysis. Each interview lasted 45 min on average, and the transcriptions were reviewed numerous times to gain a solid comprehension of the broad concepts and to find the crucial themes across the interviews that were connected to the conceptual framework's aims and objectives (Creswell and Creswell 2017; Duffy 2012). Best practise principles were used to construct the interviews to provide information to validate the conceptual framework.

According to Chen et al. (2024), distinct codes should be assigned to words, phrases, and segments in the interview transcript based on their relevance to the conceptual framework's research questions and objectives. As described by Tian and Chen (2025), the coded phrases were investigated, restructured, and categorised into appropriate themes which were further divided into possible themes relating to the research questions (Anderson 2007). As a result, certain themes were renamed to better fit their content. The analysis findings were then compiled and discussed using the final themes and categorised excerpts. To provide a better understanding of the findings, the discussion was expanded with excerpts from the interview transcripts. Furthermore, the interview findings were contrasted in relation to the existing knowledge in the reviewed literature.

The interview responses were deductively and thematically analysed using ATLAS.ti software. ATLAS.ti is a qualitative research tool that can be used for coding and analysing transcripts and field notes, building literature reviews, creating network diagrams, and data visualisation. ATLAS.ti enables users to conduct content analysis on the interview transcripts to synthesise the opinions of the interviewees.

The result of the first round of interview conducted are reported as follows:

7.3.1 Background Information of Interviewees

The conceptual framework identified 18 professional experts who have basic knowledge of information management majorly in construction and ICT management experts who have hands-on experience with blockchain technology. These professionals are practising within South Africa either in the built environment, academia or the financial technology sectors. Out of the 18 prospective interviewees identified and contacted, only 12 were available to be interviewed which represents a 66% response rate. According to Hennink et al. (2016), the saturation point for interview-based collection of data is between 7 to 12 interviews which then justifies the adoption of the 12 interviewees of this conceptual framework. The demographics of the interviewees are documented in Table 7.1.

From the information presented in Table 7.1, the interviewees possess between 2 and 21 years of experience with an average of 10 years. A total of 58% of the interviewees have less than 10 years of experience while the remaining 42% have practised their profession for more than 10 years. A total of 50% of the interviewees possess only undergraduate qualifications in their respective professions, 25% possess master's degrees while 25% also possess doctoral degrees in their respective fields. Moreover, some of them (P5 and P9) also possess MBA degrees in fields outside their professional practice. P5 submitted that:

> *I decided to try my knowledge on something outside the built environment and that led me to doing MBA which I completed within 2 years and has shaped my reasoning in my field of practice till date.*

Similarly, P9 opined that:

> *Having known that my focus will be on how to market my skills, I took a conscious step to embark on an MBA degree to position myself in the top-level rank of my industry.*

On examining the professional groups to which the interviewees are affiliated, it can be summarised that there are 33.3% of ICT experts working in the financial technology sector, 41.7% of the interviewees are built environment professionals actively practising in the sector and 25% of the interviewees are in academia although they have a built environment background as well. Based on the information gathered from these professionals, it could be implied that the interviewees are well versed in both the built environment and ICT sectors with a wealth of years of experience in

Table 7.1 Interviewees' demographic information

Interviewee code	Sector	Years of experience	Highest academic qualification	Discipline/role
P1	Built environment	18	B.Tech.	Construction manager
P2	Built environment	21	MSc.	Quantity surveyor
P3	Built environment	5	BSc.	Project manager
P4	Built environment	14	B.Tech.	Civil engineer
P5	Academia	8	PhD	Quantity surveyor
P6	Financial technology	4	BSc.	Software engineer
P7	Financial technology	14	BSc.	Computer scientist
P8	Built environment	9	BSc.	Civil engineer
P9	Financial technology	2	MSc.	Cyber security expert
P10	Financial technology	8	PhD	Data scientist
P11	Academia	5	MSc.	Architect
P12	Academia	17	PhD	Quantity surveyor
Mean		**10.42**		

Source: Author's Compilation

both sectors. Hence, their opinions given during the interview sessions can be relied upon as a valid means of collecting useful data for this conceptual framework.

7.3.2 Constructs Influencing the Adoption of Blockchain Technology for Information Management

Having carried out a detailed systematic literature review, the conceptual framework identified five constructs that influence the adoption of blockchain technology for information management. The identified constructs were presented to the interviewees to suggest variables to measure each construct. Their opinions were recorded in following subsections.

7.3.2.1 Influence of Technological Infrastructure (ITI)

Interviewees were asked for their opinions on the latent variables to measure the influence of technological infrastructure (ITI). Notably, P1 opined that:

In my opinion, the perceived benefits of blockchain technology are significant and make it a worthwhile investment for companies that are looking to streamline their operations and enhance transparency. However, it's important to recognize that there are certain training requirements associated with implementing the technology. The learning curve can be steep, especially for those who are not familiar with distributed ledgers, smart contracts, and cryptography. Therefore, it's important for companies to invest in the necessary training programs to ensure that their staff are equipped with the skills and knowledge needed to effectively utilize blockchain technology. Another factor to consider is the maturity of the technology. While blockchain has been around for over a decade, it's still in its early stages of adoption in many industries, including construction. As such, there may be some growing concerns associated with implementing the technology in this context.

The extracted expert opinions of the interviewees are reported in Table 7.2 based on the frequency of occurrence in the interview sessions.

From the results presented in Table 7.2, it can be deduced that most of the interviewees suggested 'Training requirements of the technology', 'Sophistication of the technology', 'Permission (public vs private) on the technology', 'Removal of intermediaries by the technology', and 'Smart contract coding ability', among other variables as the influence of technological infrastructure on the adoption of blockchain technology for information management for the construction industry. This was based on the number of interviewees that mentioned these variables during the interview sessions.

7.3.2.2 Influence of Organisational Culture (IOC)

Interviewees were asked for their opinions on the latent variables to measure the influence of organisational culture (IOC). Notably, P12 submitted that:

One of the key factors that determine the success of blockchain implementation is the top management support for innovation. If the top management is supportive of innovative ideas and is willing to allocate resources for research and development, the chances of success are much higher. Organisational size is another factor that can influence the implementation of blockchain technology. Larger organisations may have more complex processes and systems, which can make it more challenging to integrate blockchain technology. However, larger organisations may also have more resources available to invest in the implementation of blockchain technology. The organisation's business objectives also play a vital role in the implementation of blockchain technology. For instance, if an organisation's objective is to increase transparency and accountability in its supply chain management, blockchain technology can help achieve that goal. On the other hand, if an organisation's objective is to streamline its financial operations, blockchain technology can provide a secure and efficient platform for managing transactions.

The extracted expert opinions of the interviewees are reported in Table 7.3 based on the frequency of occurrence in the interview sessions.

From the results presented in Table 7.3, it can be extrapolated that most of the interviewees suggested 'Employees' participation incentives', 'Organisation's business objectives', 'Availability of resources for implementation', 'Satisfaction with existing systems', and 'Organisation's technological implementation strategy', among other variables as the influence of organisational culture on the adoption of

Table 7.2 Interviewees' opinions on Influence of Technological Infrastructure latent variables

S/N	Influence of Technological Infrastructure (ITI)	Percentage	Frequency	Sources
1	Perceived benefits of the technology	66.7%	8	P1, P2, P3, P4, P5, P8, P11, P12
2	Training requirements of the technology	100.0%	12	P1, P2, P3, P4, P5, P6, P7, P8, P9, P10, P11, P12
3	Maturity of the technology	41.7%	5	P1, P7, P8, P9, P10
4	Relative advantage of the technology	33.3%	4	P4, P5, P9, P12
5	Integration capabilities of technology	66.7%	8	P1, P4, P5, P6, P9, P10, P11, P12
6	Complexity of the technology	66.7%	8	P1, P2, P4, P5, P7, P8, P9, P10
7	Removal of intermediaries by the technology	91.7%	11	P2, P3, P4, P5, P6, P7, P8, P9, P10, P11, P12
8	Capability of the technology	75.0%	9	P1, P2, P4, P5, P6, P7, P8, P9, P11
9	Data security on the technology	75.0%	9	P1, P3, P4, P5, P6, P7, P10, P11, P12
10	Smart contract coding ability	83.3%	10	P1, P3, P4, P5, P6, P7, P8, P9, P10, P12
11	Technology system architecture	50.0%	6	P1, P2, P3, P7, P9, P10
12	Perceived barrier to technology acquisition	75.0%	9	P1, P2, P3, P4, P6, P7, P8, P10, P12
13	Compatibility with existing technologies	41.7%	5	P1, P6, P7, P8, P9
14	Availability of technological infrastructure	66.7%	8	P1, P2, P3, P5, P7, P8, P9, P10
15	Permission (public vs private) on the technology	91.7%	11	P1, P2, P3, P4, P5, P7, P8, P9, P10, P11, P12
16	Sophistication of the technology	100.0%	12	P1, P2, P3, P4, P5, P6, P7, P8, P9, P10, P11, P12

Source: Author's Compilation

blockchain technology for information management for the construction industry. This was based on the number of interviewees that mentioned these variables during the interview sessions.

7.3.2.3 Influence of Industry Environment (IIE)

Interviewees were asked for their opinion on the latent variables to measure the influence of industry environment (IIE). P3 put forward that:

> *The implementation of blockchain technology can be significantly influenced by the industry environment. Firstly, the performance gap in the industry can determine how open the industry is to innovative technologies such as blockchain. If the industry has a large performance gap, there may be more motivation to adopt blockchain technology to increase effi-*

Table 7.3 Interviewees' opinions on Influence of Organisational Culture latent variables

S/N	Influence of Organisational Culture (IOC)	Percentage	Frequency	Sources
1	Top management support for innovation	66.7%	8	P1, P2, P3, P4, P7, P8, P9, P12
2	Organisational size	16.7%	2	P6, P12
3	Organisation's business objectives	91.7%	11	P1, P3, P4, P5, P6, P7, P8, P9, P10, P11, P12
4	Organisation's technological readiness	75.0%	9	P2, P4, P5, P6, P7, P8, P9, P11, P12
5	Financial capacity of the organisation	33.3%	4	P1, P4, P5, P12
6	Satisfaction with existing systems	83.3%	10	P1, P3, P4, P5, P6, P7, P8, P9, P10, P11,
7	Organisational readiness for change	58.3%	7	P1, P2, P3, P8, P9, P10, P12
8	Organisation's level of innovativeness	75.0%	9	P4, P5, P6, P7, P8, P9, P10, P11, P12
9	Readiness to adopt new business model	41.7%	5	P4, P5, P8, P9, P10
10	Employees' technological knowledge	66.7%	8	P2, P4, P5, P6, P7, P9, P11, P12
11	Availability of resources for implementation	91.7%	11	P1, P2, P3, P4, P5, P6, P7, P9, P10, P11, P12
12	Employees' participation incentives	100.0%	12	P1, P2, P3, P4, P5, P6, P7, P8, P9, P10, P11, P12
13	Organisation's technological implementation strategy	83.3%	10	P1, P2, P3, P4, P6, P7, P8, P10, P11, P12
14	Organisation's business scope	66.7%	8	P3, P4, P5, P6, P7, P9, P10, P11

Source: Author's Compilation

ciency and productivity. Another factor is the flexibility of the industry which can also play a crucial role in implementing blockchain technology. A flexible industry that is open to change and innovation is more likely to adopt blockchain technology. Also, the regulatory environment in the industry can be a significant factor in the implementation of blockchain technology. Since blockchain is a new technology, there may be uncertainties surrounding its use, and regulations may be necessary to ensure that it is used ethically and legally. The industry may need to have a clear understanding of the regulations and comply with them to implement blockchain technology successfully.

The extracted expert opinions of the interviewees are reported in Table 7.4 based on the frequency of occurrence in the interview sessions.

From the results presented in Table 7.4, it can be deduced that most of the interviewees suggested 'Competitive pressure', 'Market dynamics of the industry', 'Consumer/client's readiness for adoption', and 'Existing practices of the industry', among other variables as the influence of industry environment on the adoption of blockchain technology for information management for the construction industry.

Table 7.4 Interviewees' opinions on influence of industry environment latent variables

S/N	Influence of Industry Environment (IIE)	Percentage	Frequency	Sources
1	Performance gap in the industry	33.3%	4	P1, P3, P5, P9
2	Regulatory environment in the industry	8.3%	1	P3
3	Flexibility of the industry	58.3%	7	P1, P2, P3, P4, P5, P6, P12
4	Government's support for technological innovation	75.0%	9	P1, P2, P6, P7, P8, P9, P10, P11, P12
5	Business use cases of technological innovations	41.7%	5	P1, P4, P8, P9, P12
6	Industry partners' support	25.0%	3	P9, P10, P12
7	Competitive pressure	100.0%	12	P1, P2, P3, P4, P5, P6, P7, P8, P9, P10, P11, P12
8	Market dynamics of the industry	100.0%	12	P1, P2, P3, P4, P5, P6, P7, P8, P9, P10, P11, P12
9	Consumer/client's readiness for adoption	100.0%	12	P1, P2, P3, P4, P5, P6, P7, P8, P9, P10, P11, P12
10	Consumer/client's request for innovation	66.7%	8	P2, P3, P6, P7, P8, P9, P10, P11
11	Industry's maturity for technological adoption	58.3%	7	P2, P6, P7, P8, P9, P10, P11
12	Existing practices of the industry	83.3%	10	P1, P3, P4, P5, P6, P7, P8, P9, P10, P12
13	Industry's pressure to innovate	58.3%	7	P1, P2, P5, P6, P7, P9, P10
14	Readiness of industry stakeholders for innovation adoption	50.0%	6	P2, P4, P6, P8, P10, P12

Source: Author's Compilation

This was based on the number of interviewees that mentioned these variables during the interview sessions.

7.3.2.4 Influence of Policy and Regulation (IPR)

Interviewees were asked for their opinion on the latent variables to measure the influence of policy and regulation (IPR). P10 reported that:

> *Subsidy policies on infrastructure for innovation adoption, revision of business guideline regulations, and the use of tax permits for innovation adoption are some examples of how regulation and policy can influence the adoption of blockchain technology. Subsidy policies on infrastructure for innovation adoption can provide the necessary financial support to organizations to invest in the infrastructure required for the adoption of blockchain technology. This can help accelerate the adoption of blockchain technology by reducing the financial burden on organisations. Revision of business guideline regulations can help organizations navigate legal hurdles and better understand the regulatory requirements for blockchain adoption. This can help reduce the uncertainty around the technology and encourage more organisations to adopt it. The use of tax permits for innovation adoption can provide organisations with financial incentives to invest in and adopt new technologies*

like blockchain. This can help organizations better allocate their resources and accelerate the adoption of blockchain technology.

The extracted expert opinions of the interviewees are reported in Table 7.5 based on the frequency of occurrence in the interview sessions.

From the results presented in Table 7.5, it can be deduced that most of the interviewees suggested 'Revision of environmental standard regulations', and 'Introduction of technology matchmaking policies', among other variables as the influence of policy and regulations on the adoption of blockchain technology for information management for the construction industry. Notably, there were diverse variables suggested by the interviewees regarding this construct, unlike the previous constructs where there were similar variables identified from the interview sessions with each interviewee. This could be attributed to the fact that the policy and regulation construct has not been given attention in discussions about blockchain technology for a very long time. This is a new discussion emerging in the field based on global deliberations on how to control and manage how the platform operates.

7.3.2.5 Influence of Technology Governance (ITG)

Interviewees were asked for their opinion on the latent variables to measure the influence of technology governance (ITG). Notably, P9 suggested that:

Table 7.5 Interviewees' opinions on Influence of Policy and Regulation latent variables

S/N	Influence of Policy and Regulation (IPR)	Percentage	Frequency	Sources
1	Subsidy policies on infrastructure for innovation adoption	8.3%	1	P10
2	Revision of business guideline regulations	58.3%	7	P1, P2, P3, P5, P10, P11, P12
3	Use of tax permits for innovation adoption	16.7%	2	P1, P10
4	Introduction of technology matchmaking policies	41.7%	5	P4, P5, P6, P7, P10
5	Introduction of innovation waiver policies	25.0%	3	P1, P3, P4,
6	Introduction of innovation-enforcing standards	8.3%	1	P10
7	Revision of environmental standard regulations	66.7%	8	P1, P2, P3, P5, P6, P7, P8, P12
8	Business covenants for innovation adopters	25.0%	3	P3, P4, P9
9	Research and development support policies	25.0%	3	P1, P4, P5
10	Economic incentive policies for innovation adoption	8.3%	1	P12
11	Introduction of technology compliance requirements	16.7%	2	P2, P11

Source: Author's Compilation

In terms of value delivery, technology governance ensures that the blockchain solution aligns with the organization's strategic objectives and delivers value to the organization and its stakeholders. It also ensures that the solution is efficient, effective, and meets the organization's requirements. Moreover, technology governance helps manage the organization's resources, including human resources, financial resources, and technical resources. This includes ensuring that there is adequate funding, skilled staff, and necessary infrastructure to support the implementation of the blockchain solution. Also, technology governance helps ensure that the organization is strategically aligned in terms of the implementation of the blockchain solution. This includes ensuring that the solution is aligned with the organization's long-term goals, vision, and mission.

The extracted expert opinions of the interviewees are reported in Table 7.6 based on the frequency of occurrence in the interview sessions.

From the results presented in Table 7.6, it can be deduced that most of the interviewees suggested 'Individual organisation's value delivery', and 'Individual organisation's strategic alignment', among other variables as the influence of technology governance on the adoption of blockchain technology for information management for the construction industry. Similar to what was encountered with the influence of policy and regulation construct, there were diverse variables suggested by the interviewees regarding this construct. In the same vein, this could also be attributed to technology governance being an emerging discussion in blockchain technology globally.

Table 7.6 Interviewees' opinions on Influence of Technology Governance latent variables

S/N	Influence of Technology Governance (ITG)	Percentage	Frequency	Sources
1	Individual organisation's level of process monitoring	25.0%	3	P1, P7, P8,
2	Individual organisation's strategic alignment	33.3%	4	P4, P5, P8, P9
3	Individual organisation's level of transparency	25.0%	3	P1, P2, P12
4	Individual organisation's risk management approach	25.0%	3	P6, P8, P11
5	Individual organisation's governance mechanism	8.3%	1	P3
6	Individual organisation's shareholders' rights	16.7%	2	P10, P12
7	Individual organisation's ownership structure	8.3%	1	P7
8	Individual organisation's value delivery	41.7%	5	P1, P6, P7, P8, P9
9	Individual organisation's resource management	25.0%	3	P5, P9, P10
10	Individual organisation's level of involvement in decision-making	25.0%	3	P1, P11, P12
11	Individual organisational regulations	16.7%	2	P3, P11
12	Internal performance measurement indicators	16.7%	2	P6, P9

Source: Author's Compilation

7.3.3 *Outcome of Adopting Blockchain Technology for Construction Information Management*

Interviewees were questioned about their opinion on the latent variables to measure the outcome of adopting blockchain technology for information management in the construction industry and their expert opinions are reported in Table 7.7. P2 is of the opinion that:

> *Blockchain technology offers numerous benefits to information management systems, which include greater control over the creation and access of project information. By utilizing blockchain technology, project stakeholders can securely create and share project data, such as contracts, progress reports, and payment details, with greater control over who has access to this information. Furthermore, blockchain technology can enable easy access to project vital information in real-time, which can greatly improve decision-making and overall project efficiency. This can help to reduce costs and improve the overall performance of a project.*

Table 7.7 indicates the frequency of occurrence of each variable in the interview sessions.

From the results shown in Table 7.7, it can be deduced that most of the interviewees suggested 'Information security through encryption algorithm', 'Improved information efficiency', 'Improved information traceability', 'Increased documented information reliability', and 'Data consistency using consensus mechanism', among other variables as the outcome of adopting of blockchain technology for information management for the construction industry. The majority of their opinions are related to one another which is an indication that their opinion can be relied upon for this objective.

7.4 Summary

This chapter presents the methodological process undertaken to develop a conceptual framework for the adoption of blockchain technology for information management in the construction industry. Recognising the growing interest in integrating digital technologies into construction practices, the chapter details how expert insights were synthesized to formulate a practical, validated model that addresses technological, organisational, environmental, policy, and governance factors influencing blockchain adoption for construction information management. The research adopted a qualitative approach, utilising semi-structured interviews with a purposively selected group of professionals in the built environment, academia, and financial technology sectors. This method was chosen for its flexibility and capacity to generate in-depth, context-rich responses. A total of 16 experts participated in the validation process, and thematic content analysis was applied to analyse the transcribed interviews using ATLAS.ti software. The analysis process involved

Table 7.7 Interviewees opinion on the Blockchain-Based Information Management System Outcome Latent Variables

S/N	Outcome of blockchain technology for construction information management	Percentage	Frequency	Sources
1	Decentralisation to allow participation of all professionals	66.7%	8	P2, P4, P5, P6, P7, P9, P11, P12
2	Improved productivity through timely use of information	75.0%	9	P1, P3, P5, P6, P7, P8, P9, P11, P12
3	Control over the creation of project information	66.7%	8	P1, P2, P3, P4, P7, P8, P9, P12
4	Ease of access to project vital information	58.3%	7	P1, P2, P3, P6, P9, P11, P12
5	Improved information efficiency	91.7%	11	P1, P2, P4, P5, P6, P7, P8, P9, P10, P11, P12
6	Control over the sharing of project information	16.7%	2	P2, P8
7	Increased documented information reliability	83.3%	10	P1, P3, P4, P5, P6, P7, P8, P9, P10, P11,
8	Management of documented information digitally	66.7%	8	P3, P4, P5, P6, P7, P9, P10, P11
9	Information security through encryption algorithm	100.0%	12	P1, P2, P3, P4, P5, P6, P7, P8, P9, P10, P11, P12
10	Minimisation of information legislation risks	33.3%	4	P3, P4, P6, P10
11	Fostering collaboration among industry professionals	41.7%	5	P4, P5, P8, P9, P10
12	Improved information traceability	91.7%	11	P1, P2, P3, P4, P5, P6, P8, P9, P10, P11, P12
13	Improvement of management decision-making	75.0%	9	P4, P5, P6, P7, P8, P9, P10, P11, P12
14	Data consistency using consensus mechanism	83.3%	10	P2, P3, P4, P6, P7, P8, P9, P10, P11, P12

Source: Author's Compilation

identifying and coding recurring ideas to generate key themes aligned with the framework's objectives.

To ensure the reliability and trustworthiness of the interviews, measures such as credibility, consistency, and expert selection criteria were strictly adhered to. Experts were selected based on their qualifications, years of experience, and practical or theoretical knowledge of blockchain and information management. The concept of data saturation was also applied—where data collection was halted once new interviews yielded no substantial new information. The thematic analysis led to the identification of five key constructs influencing blockchain adoption: Technological Infrastructure, Organisational Culture, Industry Environment, Policy and Regulation, and Technology Governance. For each construct, latent variables were derived from expert opinions. For example, in relation to technological infrastructure, critical variables included training requirements, smart contract coding ability, perceived benefits, system sophistication, and permission settings (e.g., public vs. private blockchain). Similarly, for organisational culture, factors such as top management support, business objectives, employee participation incentives, and technological readiness were highlighted.

The chapter also explores the expected outcomes of adopting blockchain technology for information management in construction. According to the experts, anticipated benefits include improved data security through encryption, decentralised access, real-time data availability, enhanced productivity, and better decision-making. The ability to manage and trace project information securely and transparently was seen as a core advantage of blockchain integration. Importantly, this chapter emphasises that successful adoption is not purely dependent on the technology itself, but on a complex interplay of internal capabilities, external pressures, supportive regulations, and strategic alignment within organisations. The findings underscore the need for organisational readiness, regulatory clarity, and supportive industry dynamics to facilitate meaningful adoption.

References

Anderson, R. 2007. *Thematic content analysis (TCA) - Descriptive presentation of qualitative data*, 1–4. Palo Alto: Institute of Transpersonal Psychology.

Braun, V., and V. Clarke. 2006. Using thematic analysis in psychology. *Qualitative Research in Psychology* 3 (2): 77–101. https://doi.org/10.1191/1478088706qp063oa.

Chen, Y., X. Qin, and H. Huang. 2024. Book review. *System* 125:103432. https://doi.org/10.1016/J.SYSTEM.2024.103432.

Creswell, J. W., and V. L. Plano Clark. 2011. *Designing and conducting mixed methods research*. 2nd ed. SAGE Publications.

Creswell, J. W., and J. D. Creswell. 2017. *Research design: Qualitative, quantitative, and mixed methods approaches*. Thousand Oaks: Sage.

Denscombe, M. 2007. *The good research guide: For small-scale social research projects*. 3rd ed. Open University Press.

Dong, Y. 2023. Book review. *Journal of Second Language Writing* 62:101044. https://doi.org/10.1016/J.JSLW.2023.101044.

Duffy, A. 2012. Qualitative research methods. *Nurse Education in Practice* 12 (2): e13. https://doi.org/10.1016/J.NEPR.2011.09.003.

Hennink, M. M., B. N. Kaiser, and V. C. Marconi. 2016. Code saturation versus meaning saturation: How many interviews are enough? *Qualitative Health Research* 27 (4): 591–608. https://doi.org/10.1177/1049732316665344.

Herrera, D. I. 2023. Book review. *System* 114:103026. https://doi.org/10.1016/J.SYSTEM.2023.103026.

Ikpe, E. H. 2009. *Research methodology and project writing*. National Open University of Nigeria.

Johnman, C. 2010. Research methods in health—Investigating health and health services. *Public Health* 124 (2): 122. https://doi.org/10.1016/J.PUHE.2010.01.006.

Matz, R., B. Smith, and A. C. Sparkes. 2019. Routledge handbook of qualitative research in sport and exercise, 1st edition. *Sport Management Review* 22 (4): 566–567. https://doi.org/10.1016/J.SMR.2019.01.003.

Tian, M. H., and Y. Chen. 2025. Book review. *System* 130:103628. https://doi.org/10.1016/J.SYSTEM.2025.103628.

Chapter 8
Conceptualising Blockchain Adoption Framework for Information Management

Abstract The construction industry is increasingly recognising the value of innovative digital technologies for addressing long-standing inefficiencies in project information management. Among these technologies, blockchain offers transformative potential due to its decentralised, secure, and transparent nature. However, despite its benefits, the adoption of blockchain technology (BT) for information management in construction remains limited, largely due to challenges such as organisational resistance, infrastructural inadequacies, regulatory gaps, and unclear governance mechanisms. This chapter aims to conceptualise a robust and context-specific framework to guide the adoption of blockchain technology for effective information management in the construction industry. Drawing from an extensive review of theoretical models such as the Technology Acceptance Model, Diffusion of Innovation Theory, Adaptive Structuration Theory, Knowledge-Based View of the Firm, and the DLT Four-Dimensional Model, the chapter identifies key constructs influencing adoption. These constructs are categorised into five core dimensions: Technological Infrastructure, Organisational Culture, Industry Environment, Policy and Regulation, and Technology Governance. The study integrates these theoretical insights with findings from expert interviews to develop a conceptual framework comprising 67 validated indicator variables across the five constructs, alongside 14 potential outcome variables. The framework is designed to reflect the interdependent roles of these constructs in influencing blockchain adoption and highlights how they collectively contribute to improved information traceability, data security, collaborative efficiency, and decision-making in construction projects. This chapter contributes to knowledge by offering a holistic and empirically-informed model that can support researchers, industry stakeholders, and policymakers in facilitating the adoption of blockchain-based information systems in construction. It establishes a foundation for future empirical validation and practical application, advancing the digital transformation agenda within the built environment.

Keywords Blockchain adoption · Information management · Construction industry · Conceptual framework · Digital transformation

O. I. Akinradewo et al., *Blockchain Technology for Information Management: A New Era for Sustainable Construction Practices*, Artificial Intelligence and Sustainable Development, https://doi.org/10.1007/978-981-95-2664-2_8

8.1 Introduction

In the ever-evolving landscape of digital technologies, blockchain has emerged as a disruptive innovation with the potential to transform information management across various industries, including construction. As a decentralised and immutable ledger system, blockchain offers numerous capabilities such as enhanced transparency, improved traceability, real-time data sharing, and fortified security through cryptographic mechanisms. Despite these promising features, its adoption in the construction industry, particularly for information management, remains limited. This is due to the complex interplay of technological, organisational, regulatory, and environmental factors that continue to shape innovation uptake within this sector (Kim et al. 2017; Min 2019).

The construction industry is characteristically fragmented, multi-stakeholder-oriented, and reliant on extensive information flows throughout project lifecycles. Effective information management is therefore crucial, not only for ensuring accurate communication among stakeholders but also for timely decision-making, risk mitigation, and regulatory compliance. Yet, traditional information systems in the industry are often siloed, susceptible to inefficiencies, and prone to data inconsistencies. The promise of blockchain lies in its ability to address these challenges by enabling real-time, tamper-proof records that support seamless and secure collaboration among all project participants (Crosby et al. 2016). Despite the potential, blockchain remains underutilised due to numerous barriers to adoption. These include the lack of technological readiness, limited understanding of its application in construction, resistance to change within organisations, and the absence of robust regulatory support structures (Min 2019; Li et al. 2019). To bridge this gap, it is essential to conceptualise an adoption framework that captures the multifaceted drivers and inhibitors of blockchain technology implementation for information management within the construction domain.

Existing theoretical and conceptual frameworks for technology adoption offer valuable insights but are often generic or focused on individual, rather than organisational or industry-wide, adoption processes. Models such as the Technology Acceptance Model (TAM) and Diffusion of Innovation (DOI) have highlighted key variables like perceived usefulness, ease of use, and relative advantage (Davis 1986; Rogers 2003). Meanwhile, frameworks such as the Adaptive Structuration Theory (AST) and the Knowledge-Based View (KBV) of the firm provide a deeper understanding of how organisational structures, social interactions, and knowledge flows influence technological change (DeSanctis and Poole 1994; Nonaka et al. 2006). These theories, while foundational, require contextual adaptation to address the unique complexities of blockchain adoption in the construction industry. Furthermore, the growing recognition of blockchain's systemic implications has led to the development of integrated models that consider the social, policy, technical, and procedural dimensions of distributed ledger technologies (Li et al. 2019). Yet, many of these models are still in nascent stages and are not tailored to the specific dynamics of information management in construction projects. This necessitates a targeted and evidence-based conceptual framework that is rooted in both theoretical constructs and empirical insights from industry stakeholders.

To this end, this chapter aims to conceptualise a comprehensive adoption framework that identifies and integrates the critical factors influencing the adoption of blockchain for information management in the construction industry. The framework is built upon five interrelated constructs: technological infrastructure, organisational culture, industry environment, policy and regulation, and technology governance. These constructs are derived from an extensive review of literature and validated through expert interviews, ensuring both theoretical rigour and practical relevance.

8.2 Review of Framework for Technology Adoption

Blockchain technology, being one of the new innovative technologies, has gained limited attention and only a few research studies have been conducted on it in the construction industry context (Kim et al. 2017). According to Min (2019), blockchain technology faces a range of integrating difficulties given the potential benefits it has, such as lack of organisational preparation and technical expertise/infrastructure, scalability issues and limited funding for expenditure. As such, management strategies need to be implemented quickly to help businesses overcome these problems and take full advantage of it (Crosby et al. 2016). A review of theoretical and conceptual frameworks for BT adoption covers the methodology for its usage and its architecture as done in the sections that follow.

8.2.1 Technology Acceptance Model

Davis (1986) developed the technology acceptance model (TAM) which has been adjudged by various researchers as the most influential model for the adoption of any given information system. It is also the most commonly adopted theory for describing the acceptance of these systems by individuals. According to Lee et al. (2003), different technologies have applied TAM successfully since it was formulated using different controls, different subjects and under different situations. Venkatesh and Davis (2000:491) opined that TAM can be described as "*a model which explains perceived usefulness and usage intentions in terms of social influence and cognitive instrumental processes*". TAM shows how individuals behave in their intention to use an innovative technology. The behavioural intention is characterised into two beliefs which are individual's perceived ease of use and individual's perceived usefulness of the innovative technology. These two beliefs determine how external factors such as training, development process and system characteristics, among others, affect the intention to use innovative technologies (Venkatesh and Davis 2000). Even though these two beliefs mediate external factors, they are also interdependent as perceived usefulness is influenced largely by perceived ease of use. This is because how useful a system is can be determined based on how easily such a system can be used (Hassan et al. 2019). Kim et al. (2012) submitted that in TAM, the state of a person's mind in utilising an innovation dictates the person's social goal. As submitted by Hassan et al. (2019), a revision was made to the TAM to make it more robust and all-encompassing (Davis and Venkatesh 1996). However, an extension was provided for TAM in 2000 named TAM2 in order to incorporate the influence of social environment together with cognitive instrumental procedures which are theoretical constructs (Venkatesh and Davis 2000). The extension was a result of the observation that TAM is restricted to individuals which does not necessarily cover the workplace/organisation scope of technology adoption (Amadu et al. 2018).

The revised TAM indicated that although the behavioural intention to use a new technology is dependent on two factors which are the perceived usefulness of the technology and the perceived ease of its use, these two factors are also influenced by latent external variables (Hassan et al. 2019). Over the years, various external variables have been incorporated into TAM, among which are "accessibility, anxiety, attitude, compatibility, complexity, result demonstrability, perceived enjoyment, end user support, experience, facilitating conditions, image, job relevance, managerial support, playfulness, personal innovativeness, relative advantage, self-efficacy, social influence, subjective norms, and social pressure, social presence, trialability, usability, visibility, voluntariness," among others (Lee et al. 2003).

8.2.2 Adaptive Structuration Theory

To understand how technological change can influence the design and flow of information within an organisation, Scott Poole and DeSanctis developed the adaptive structuration theory (AST) using Anthony Gidden's concept of structuration (Computer Mediated Communication 2003). The AST was developed to explain how advanced information technologies can play a role in changes in an organisation (Computer Mediated Communication 2003; Halawi and McCarthy 2006). This is done by drawing information from emerged structures that are adapted by people within the organisation owing to their interaction with the different types of structures offered by advanced technologies (Lethbridge 2003). These different structures operate using resources, rules and social structures which dictate human activities within the organisation (DeSanctis and Poole 1994; Computer Mediated Communication 2003). According to Desanctis and Poole (1994), there were existing social structures within the organisations before the advent of advanced technologies. Some of these social structures are enhanced, modified and automated before they are incorporated into the design of advanced technologies to mimic the traditional structures. This enables these advanced technologies to develop new structures which change the organisational structure together with the existing resources and rules (Computer Mediated Communication 2003).

Even though traditional computer systems can achieve basic organisational tasks and business transactions, advanced information technologies give room for achieving more within the organisation (Poole 2008). These include the achievement of interpersonal exchanges and coordination of people within the organisation (DeSanctis and Poole 1994). The introduction of advanced technologies influences business social perspectives when compared to the traditional system. To further explain the social structure of AST, Desanctis and Poole (1994) submitted that there are two dimensions, namely the structural dimension (capabilities, resources and rules of the system) and the spirit dimension (underlying goals and values of the system) (Gutek et al. 1984; Orlikowski and Robey 1991; Poole 2008). These dimensions govern the gathering of information, its management or manipulation as well as the legitimation and signification of the technology. The structural dimension of social structures of an AST can differ for each advanced information technology based on its design offerings and purpose while the spirit dimension can be presented either as coherent or incoherent (DeSanctis and Poole 1994; Lethbridge 2003). The interconnectedness of the seven (7) major propositions and constructs of AST indicates the social interaction achieved in the use of an advance information technology within an organisation.

8.2.3 Knowledge-Based View of the Firm Theory

Extant studies have established the emergence of knowledge-based theory (KBT) of the firm in the literature of strategic management (Nonaka et al. 2006; Yang and Liu 2007; Curado and Bontis 2006). Knowledge-based theory of the firm arose from theorizing why most firms perform differently. Grover and Davenport (2001) argued that the theory of the firm originated from two major perspectives. These include resource-based and transaction cost economic theory. Although resource-based theory asserts that long run outstanding performance is related with the ownership of valuable, scarce as well as unique firm specific resources, transaction cost economics refers to the fact that some firms are in existence in the place of markets owing to their lower opportunism potential. The premise of this theory is that knowledge is a focal resource, and it produces a distinct edge for controlling economic activities using a line of reasoning that differs greatly from the market line of reasoning. Liebeskind (1996) noted that knowledge-based theory was previously an extended form of resource-based value in that it considers the firm as an agent that continues to develop superlative abilities to secure knowledge as well as incorporating and implementing knowledge held by individual persons (Grant 1996). In recent times, knowledge-based theory has developed towards other multitudes of perspectives, continuing to presume a theoretical structure quite appropriate to the firms' conceptualisation based on value development. The firm, according to Grover and Davenport (2001), could be regarded as an organisation for incorporating knowledge and the modalities for incorporation are investigated in order to determine adaptable responses' capabilities in a highly competitive marketplace. Firm was further conceptualised as a knowledge transformer and incinerator by Nonaka and Toyama (2005) and Nonaka et al. (2006).

According to the firm's knowledge-based theory, the services and products generated by tangible resources are determined by how well they are merged and implemented which is a component of the firm's understanding (Nonaka et al. 2006). Individual employee's details such as identity, policies, routines, documents, and systems as well as organisation culture, are imbued with and transmitted through this knowledge. As a result of the fact that knowledge-based resources ae sociologically difficult to comprehend and hard to imitate by some other organisation, the knowledge-based theory of the firm proposes that these knowledge assets could generate a long-term self-sustaining advantage to an organisation compared with other firms (Nonaka et al. 2006; Alavi and Leidner 2001). Knowledge that is available at any time may be insufficient to provide such a foundation for a long-term sustainable advantage that is competitive in nature. Long-term advantage that is sustainably competitive is derived from the firm's capacity to implement current knowledge accurately to generate new knowledge and also to take some actions, which could serve as the foundation for gaining a competitive advantage from knowledge-based assets.

Knowledge-based comparative advantage is indeed long-lasting owing to the fact that the more a company understands, the faster it could learn. Learning offers for a firm which already has a knowledge with a positive difference might be a little more highly valued than comparable learning opportunities for competing companies who start out knowing very little (Nonaka et al. 2006). Sustainable growth could also result from an organization's already fully understanding something which distinctively and perfectly matches new-found knowledge, providing the opportunity for knowledge synergy that its competing companies do not have (Alavi and Leidner 2001). New knowledge is combined with current knowledge to produce preliminary evidence and even more valuable knowledge. Organizations also should seek aspects of learning and experiments that have the potential to be beneficial to their current knowledge through complementary collaboration (Zack 1999).

8.2.4 *Diffusion of Innovation Theory*

This theory was forwarded in 1962 through Rogers, according to Zhang et al. (2015) and it is one of the oldest and most widely used social science theories for investigating the adoption of IT and comprehending ways by which innovation of IT spreads from one social organisation to another. The theory defines innovation as a product or idea, process or technology that is considered as novel or unknown by an individual within a specific field or social structure (Sampaio et al. 2012). As a result of the diffusion, people adopt a new idea, product or behaviour as part of the social structure. Diffusion within this model could be referred to as the procedure in which information concerning innovations are transferred or transmitted and flow from one person to another through a social system over time (Jwaifell and

Gasaymeh 2013; Zhang et al. 2015; Makovhololo et al. 2017). DOI theory is based on the assumption that new ideas (innovations) or technologies are constantly being developed, and that information sharing would become critical in proliferating or distributing information about innovation to various social organisations, and communities.

This is mainly due to the fact that acknowledgment of the technology development or innovations would be determined by the individual's behaviour toward the innovation. Furthermore, societies have the option of ignoring or embracing the innovation. DOI attempts to describe at what rate, how, and why new technologies and ideas spread across cultures (Makovhololo et al. 2017). As a result, some organizations often use various methodologies and theories, also including DOI, to solve this problem and to direct decision-making processes within the dissemination of strategy formulation (Alqahtani and Wamba 2012).

According to Rogers' theory of DOI, the process involved in adopting new innovations of information typically begins with a small number of innovators (Rogers 2003). As a result, innovators can be classified into five groups. The first group is referred to as Innovators—people that have the intention of trying a new initiative. This group of people are curious and eager when it comes to new initiatives. They are a desperate group of people who do not mind taking chances and always come up with new initiatives first. It may be very difficult for anyone to plead with this category of people, in case there is anything left to do. The second group is termed Early Adopters. This category of people are position oriented. They are leaders in the making who want to take a lead in any adventure and are eager to have one or two experiences. They already are fully cognizant of the expected for transformation. These people are therefore eager to experience new initiatives. The manual of how to do it as well as the application sheet of information are the two major methods of keeping this demographic. It may not necessarily require information that could be used to encourage them to adjust.

The third group are called the Early Majority. They are individuals who are leaders, and therefore adopt the newly introduced initiatives first. Nevertheless, it always requires evidence that the innovation tends to work before they become interested in adopting the newly introduced initiative. Successful stories as well as evidence of effectiveness regarding the innovation are likely instances of methods of appealing to this population. The fourth group is named the Late Majority. Groups of people who are not ready to adjust are those that are within this category. They would accept only initiatives or innovations that large numbers of people have already attempted. Information about the number of people that have experienced success in the process of adopting and attempted the innovation is another method of appealing to this population. The last category is called the Laggards. Laggards refer to people who are very rational and are bound by tradition. This category of people are not ready to adjust. They are the hardened group who are not easily to motivate or encourage.

For new ideas and technologies to spread, five qualities of innovation are necessary, according to Rogers (2003) and Comer and Kendall (2013). These include relative advantage, compatibility, simplicity, trialability, and observable results. The higher the degree at which an innovation comes to the realization of comparable significance, the faster it is likely to be adopted: this is known as relative advantage. Compatibility relates to the extent to which the impact of an innovation is observed to be in consistency with the principles, previous experience, and needs of adopters' potential. Simplicity and easy to use refer to new innovations or initiatives that are easier for a potential adopter to notice and which are incorporated very quickly instead of ideas which necessitate the person that adopt them to create clarity. The extent to which an idea or initiative could be practised refers to its trialability. An observable result is when an individual is more likely to adopt an innovation if they can easily see its results. The above attributes of innovation allow the theory of DOI to facilitate and govern the decision-making process through innovation as well as the creation of innovation within the organisation (Makovhololo et al. 2017).

Individuals may approve or disapprove of the innovation depending on their attitude. As a result, potential adopters can evaluate the innovation based on its characteristics. As earlier noted, DOI is applicable to other areas and has been used by different scholars from other disciplines such as sociology, communication, political science, information technology, history, and public health, among others for many years. Its adoption is the fact that DOI theory concentrates on spreading innovation through some channels of communication within a social structure (Oliveira and Martins 2010). The theory of DOI provides a foundation for guiding and understanding the factors that determine the DOI within a social structure, including an organization structure. Russell and Hoag (2004) use the theory of innovation diffusion to study and evaluate the innovation of information technology challenges in the implementation of the IT supply chain due to the importance of people's roles. This strength serves as the foundation for comprehending the incorporation of artifacts such as IT for the facilitation and organizational strategy (Straub 2009). According to Jwaifell and Gasaymeh (2013), the theory is useful because it is flexible and adaptable and can be used in both formal and informal settings throughout its implementation.

In order to apply the DOI theory, it is necessary to first understand the key determinants as well as probable adopters and the process of making decisions that is involved. Several other vital factors of making decisions include who the decision makers are and how the decisions evolved, whether wilfully, easily, or consensually. Conversely, "*among the most distinguishing difficulties in the innovation diffusion theory would be that the individuals are typically quite heterophilous*" (Rogers 2003:104). DOI theory emphasizes that approaches must be tailored to key stakeholders' needs and expectations, value systems, and belief systems (Dingfelder and Mandell 2011). DOI theory has been used in numerous research studies globally in recent years. The research studies include the work done by Zhang et al. (2015), who used DOI to analyse the factors that affect patients' acknowledgement and the use of consumer e-health innovations at an Australian local hospital. Nemutanzhela and Iyamu (2015) also adopted the DOI to analyse IS research in South Africa. According to the findings of that study, the theory adds a new perspective to the domain of information systems by explaining how innovations spread within a given environment.

8.2.5 Information System Success Model

Several studies in literature have presented information system (IS) success models (DeLone and McLean 1992; Ballantine et al. 1996; Seddon 1997). These posited the definition of IS success from their own perspectives. The studies further identified factors influencing the definition of IS success. However, Delone and McLean (1992) were the first scholars who formulated the differing viewpoints and the underlying peculiarities of the IS success model. Delone and McLean (1992) identified six major factors in the model, namely system quality, information quality, use, user satisfaction, individual impact and organisational impact. According to the study, information quality and system quality were the possible factors affecting user satisfaction and the use of IS. User satisfaction and use have causal influence, and both could also have an effect on individual impact which later has an effect on organisational impact. As a result of various criticisms from IS research scholars, DeLone and McLean revised the original model in order to react to the weaknesses and strengths observed by other scholars. The effect variables or indicators such as organizational and individual were grouped as one and renamed as net benefits. Another variable, namely service quality, was introduced to the model to address the relevance of service as a factor that contributes to the IS success model. Finally, the use variable was divided into two, namely actual use (resultant behaviour) and intention to use (attitude). The construct of the updated IS success model comprised system quality, information quality, service quality, intention to use/use, user satisfaction, and net benefits (DeLone and McLean 2002).

System quality is a way of measuring an IS's desired attributes (Urbach and Müller 2012). Many other IS studies often used attributes such as system features, response time, perceived ease of use and flexibility to measure this. Information quality is more concerned with the issues of content as well as the output attributes of the IS. It could be evaluated by assessing the IS's output in the form of reliability, trustworthiness, accuracy, and timeliness, among others. Information quality is operationalised by this study in the form of timeliness, accuracy and usefulness of information created by the blockchain IS that is being used. Service quality is assessed by the level of support provided by the developer of the information system. This has been examined through the use of dimensions of service quality i.e., user training as well as assurance and ability to respond by the system's support department. Service quality was evaluated by measuring the technical support available to users of blockchain technology, the system's dependability and the infrastructure network that is available (DeLone and McLean 2002).

According to Seddon (1997), "Use" deals with the assessment of how an IS is adopted. Previous studies have examined actual usage or, in some cases, frequency of use to determine this. Based on the nature of the IS, the original intent to use is said to be an optional component to use in another context. User satisfaction is regarded as one of the most significant indicators of system success, and it is frequently assessed by overarching user satisfaction. Net benefits are considered as another way of measuring as IS. This represents the level at which an IS is responsible for contributing to the success of various authorities that are involved. It could mostly be evaluated by assessing organisational or individual impact (Urbach and Müller 2012).

8.2.6 DLT Four-Dimensional Model

From the DLT four-dimensional model conceptualised by Li et al. (2019), the overlap of the dimensions of BT adoption was examined. DLT was substituted for BT in the study as the terms can be used interchangeably. Identifying the overlap of the four dimensions gives the model the ability to reflect on and collect information between the dimensions. This is important if the model is to be resistant and adaptable for various purposes, particularly in a rapidly developing area such as DLT. The technical dimension of the model covers all facets of the DLT's technical framework including the applications, equipment, networks and other resources required to operate the device. In light of the present stage in the development of DLT together with the new technology's lifecycle in general, the release of new products and new versions of current technologies are expected to resolve many of the challenges DLT might be faced with. Ethereum (Wood 2014), NEO (Elrom 2019) and Brickschain (Briq 2019) are currently offered as blockchain solutions for the payment medium which is likely to have an impact on the construction industry. The policy dimension reflects the DLT's regulatory setting including rules, legislation, procedures, guidelines and enforcement. Today, these fields are either non-existent or just evolving in most countries pursuing the technology. For example, Russia (Clack et al. 2016) and China (Cohn et al. 2017) have started to lay down certain standards and regulations. With many policymakers looking at developing communities into smart cities, they are responsible for researching the appropriateness of DLT thoroughly and ensuring that sufficient legislative and technical infrastructure is in position to promote its implementation and deployment in the long term (Li et al. 2019).

The process dimension discusses how practicable it is to apply BT in the construction industry and how it is adopted and implemented by individuals and organisations. The process dimension, according to Li et al. (2019), includes (1) understanding the DLT's implementation in procurement; and (2) understanding the project life-cycle possibilities of DLT and how they affect the management processes. The process dimension is expected to lead individuals and organizations to question how existing procedures and processes shift in line with progress and what changes are needed in organizational structures, job functions and business strategies (Li et al. 2019). The social dimension reflects on the DLT's influence on society together with its incorporation into the social system of the real world. The social impacts of technological systems are becoming more evident (Economist 2018). It is more critical than ever to know how data is created, gathered, stored, processed and installed, especially concerning privacy and security (Li et al. 2019).

8.3 Framework Construct Identification for the Adoption of Blockchain Technology for Information Management

Owing to the limited studies on construction information management systems, there is a dearth of frameworks and models addressing the efficient use of technologies for information management in the construction industry space. Hence, this study adopted frameworks that are generic to technological adoption as well as blockchain adoption frameworks across various industries. These frameworks identified various constructs that measured the different focuses of each study. These constructs ranged from perceived usefulness, ease of use, behavioural intention, external variables, actual system use, internal structure, social structure, decision process, organisation environment, socioeconomic characteristics, personality variables, communication behaviour, relative advantage, compatibility, complexity, triability, observability, system quality, information quality, user satisfaction, individual impact, organisational impact, service quality, technical dimension, social dimension, policy dimension, and process dimension. According to Wanjau et al. (2012), a conceptual framework is characterised by the formulation of descriptive categories that are arranged in an order that emphasises a wide structure of explicit propositions and statements of connection, as well as the acceptance or rejection of attributes based on empirical evidence. Hence, the adopted constructs for this study are perceived to influence the adoption of blockchain technology for information management and are described in the following sub-sections. It is worth noting that these were adopted in line with the interviews conducted with experts in the field to corroborate the desktop review.

8.3.1 Influence of Technological Infrastructure (ITI)

Many successes recorded within the construction industry have motivated the need for invention in the area of ISs through the use of technology (Gaith et al. 2012). Technology is key in the construction industry in ensuring, obtaining, and maintaining a competitive advantage. According to Ahmed et al. (1995) and Bowden (2006), the adoption of technology in information management systems has helped in increasing demand for designs of the construction project, as well as improving the procedure involved in communication, information, and collaboration. Miyatake and Kangari (1993) added that technology in the field of information management systems has helped in enhancing the flow/exchange of vital information within the construction industry.

Akinsola et al. (2000) contended that technology has helped in ensuring competitiveness, efficiency, effectiveness, and productivity. It also helps in improving communication among stakeholders, participation members, and professionals (e.g., architect, quantity surveyor, contractor) of the industry who are directly involved in the construction management and design of a project. Technology makes it easier to transfer essential information among the stakeholders (Tolman 1997). Technology also makes it easier for stimulation, evaluation, and analysis of building/project performance in information management systems among building and construction professionals. Gaith et al. (2012) emphasized that technology in the field of the information management systems has helped in the process delivery of designed amenities as well as in designing the process involved in carrying out the project by the organisation. Michael et al. (2020) maintained that technology has influenced the methods in project management through reporting and tracking of projects and decision making.

The use of technology has made virtual project management easier and better with the maximum demonstration of control for changes that occur in the design process. It helped in minimizing cost and led to proper management which in turn leads to minimizing waste. Through technology, decisions are easily made in project meetings with the site managers, design team, and consultants. Adoption of technology enables decision making possible immediately on the project site in case of any recorded challenges faced during project construction on site. Other areas of influence, according to Bowden (2005), include reduction of the overall cost of the project, improvement of plant productivity (equipment), improvement of resource management, and enhancement of project delivery on time or reduction in the duration of time to project completion. Variables include technological support, availability of all related data and information, use of new construction techniques (Soewin and Chinda 2018), and accessibility of technology (Liu et al. 2018).

8.3.2 *Influence of Organisational Culture (IOC)*

Organisation culture, according to Gritli et al. (2007), deals with assumptions, beliefs, values, and norms that inform the behaviours and processes of participation in an organisation, especially in the project delivery processes. Organisational culture is a major factor that could influence behaviours and attitudes of participants and employees in terms of assumptions, values, norms, and beliefs that are adopted in an organisation (Kuraesin 2017). Kuraesin (2017) and Gritli et al. (2007) further stated that organisation culture through an information management system is an essential unifying factor that could withstand conflict and bring about mutual understanding, common practice, and procedures that have been agreed on. Organisation culture includes traditions, norms, shared values, and ways in which the participant of the organisation could affect how they act.

Organisation culture operates through an information management system within the building industry and is largely influenced by the long-established attributes of the industry as well as the adjustment that takes place within the industry (Phua and Rowlinson 2003). It was further inferred that stakeholders of an organisation culture such as the climate of openness in an organisation, the shared vision in building knowledge, and the commitment of leaders to learn were solely influencing the behaviour and attitudes of members in an organisation. One of the major challenges to the information management system in the construction industry is organisational culture. Inefficient or ineffective communication and interaction among participants in the construction industry is harmful to creative procedures in the industry.

An empirical examination by Egbu et al. (2003) showed that three major factors influence organisation culture for information management systems within the construction sector, namely the environment motivating innovation for better delivery of value; willingness to adopt technological innovation; and the understanding and awareness of the importance of an information management system as well as the provision of leadership. Pinto (2016) identified four areas where organisational culture can affect the information management system in the construction industry. These include organisational culture that influences the level of members' commitment to project goals and objectives with reference to balancing them with other goals that have competing potentials. It influences how units are expected to interact and assist one another in pursuing the goals and objectives of the project; culture influences the planning process of the project i.e., the way in which estimated work is assigned to project; and culture influences how the evaluator of project performance as well as how the project outcome/output is viewed by the project managers.

Nguyen and Watanabe (2017) used 24 indicators in assessing the extent of participants' behaviour in projects in the construction sector. The indicators were used in assessing the dimension of organisational culture which is deeply rooted in core problems that are addressed among the group of people. Factors influencing organisation culture, according to Nguyen and Watanabe (2017), were measured from the combined list of cultural artifacts. This list includes roles and obligations of contractor and client, effective working interactions, shared information, mutual reliance, exchange of ideas and support, respect for workers, concern for workers, contractor's commitment to quality, contractor's commitment to schedule, and the involvement in decision processing, among others. The influences of organisational culture could be adopted from the identified artifacts to reflect common participants' behaviour in different situations of project construction.

8.3.3 Influence of Industry Environment (IIE)

The environmental factor, according to Yonker, is one of the major hindrances to the adoption of information management systems in the construction industry. The concept of the environment comprises all the surrounding elements or conditions. It was further observed by Benneth (1991) that the environment influences the planned progress of project construction. Major successes or failures recorded in the past depended on the external influences beyond the control of the manager. Various studies have considered the environmental factor in the information management system for construction industries. These studies include those of Liu et al. (2003), Liu et al. (2018). Mafakheri et al. (2007), Mahdi et al. (2005) and Akanni et al. (2014). For example, Liu et al. (2018) used nine environmental indicators to examine the influence of the environment on the information management system in the construction industry. These include market competitiveness, material availability, technology accessibility, national disaster, regulatory input, political impact, cultural differences weather influences, and objections from neighbours. Ratnasabapathy et al. (2008) added the availability of experienced contractors and professionals, desired project objectives from lobby groups, industrial action, and labour productivity. Environmental factors were evaluated through three variables (Dalkir 2013), namely culture, strategy and planning, and managerial leadership.

In the study of Akanni et al. (2014) seven indicators were used. These include legal, institutional, physical socio-cultural, economic and financial indicators, political construction technology, and resources. Akanni et al. (2014), Hughes (1989) and Walker (1989) argued that these identified environmental factors influence the management and organisation structure of project construction in the industry. This should be one of the major focus areas for the construction management of the project environment.

8.3.4 Influence of Policy and Regulation (IPR)

Organisation rules, policy, and regulation are regarded as the activities of society, which affect the acquisition of an information management system in the construction industry. According to Rowley (2008), policy and regulation of any organisation are considered as guidelines that may likely hamper the adoption of an information management system in the construction organisation. They may be a statement, procedure, or standards that are to be adopted or implemented by any organisation in order to address vital issues with reference to the construction mastery type to be utilized, the procedure, the stages involved before the project is started and the protection of the workers and contractors. This factor or influence is argued by Niu (2008) as the most important factor in any organisation's likely variables that were used in literature to measure the influence of policy and regulation. This includes planning regulation, types of contracts, the attitude of the judiciary (Akanni et al. 2015), planning permits from the government, planning approval of drawings, and permission from the community (Adeleke et al. 2018).

8.3.5 Influence of Technology Governance (ITG)

Extant studies have examined governance or project governance with respect to its influence on the construction industry (Jessop 1997; Miller and Lessard 2000; Scharpf 1994; OECD 2001, 2004; Muller et al. 2019; Muller 2019; Klakegg et al. 2008). The concept of governance is much focused on the new method and mind set in the art of steering different organisation, institutions and society (Jessop 1997). Different challenges or problems that emanated as a result of multi-level coordination by institutions or organisations are brought about by the emergence of governance. According to Muller et al. (2014), more concentration is targeted on self-organisation, decentralisation, flatness of structure, mutual trust and autonomy. In any self-organisation that is multi-level in structure, all the parties that are involved are regarded as stakeholders. In other words, each element within the organisation shares the same power and authority. Governance, as observed by Muller (2017), is the way in which institutions or organisations are controlled and their managers are accountable to any forms of conduct and performance in the course of carrying out a project.

Project governance, is the established framework of internal control to protect the interest of the project owners as well as reducing the dangers in the entire life-cycle of the project. It could be referred to as a set of rules and regulations, a system of management, protocols, a relationship as well as a structure that provides the framework which is used in making decisions for the development and implementation of a construction project (Bekker and Steyn 2009). In the construction industry, governance provides the structures or framework that could be used in defining the objectives of the organisation. Governance in the construction industry provides the means by which the objective of the organisation is achieved or realised. Governance also ensures control of its progress. The influence of governance on information management systems for the construction industry in projects exists in three ways (Muller 2019): firstly, at the top of the organisation where decisions are made on a particular project; secondly, in the middle of the organisation (management) where the entire or subset of the project is governed and decisions are made on the common approaches throughout the project cycle i.e., reporting practices and methodologies; finally, at the individual level of the project where several decisions on the peculiar attributes of individual projects are made.

Samset and Volden (2016) asserted that governance allows for decisions and processes to define action, verify performance and grant power. Governance in the construction industry, as noted by Muller et al. (2016), contributes to the strategic direction, institutional arrangement and goals (long-term) of project. Muller et al. (2016) further noted the roles of governance on an information management system for the construction industry in controlling the functions that aim to balance the social and economic objectives of the organisation. Governance is therefore both a relationship and a central function among the stakeholders and managers. It helps in making key decision on value-chain activities affecting the parties involved through a central system. Project governance establishes a framework for models of decision-making processes of an organisation and tools for project management in the construction industry. The framework is provided for achieving successful projects, portfolios and programs (Klakegg et al. 2008).

Governance further helps in minimising the running cost of organisation on a project in three ways, namely the frequency of cost of project return, the uncertainty to which the project is subject to and the extent to which projects are sponsored. Through project governance, the objective of the project is set, the means of achieving the objective are assessed, and the means of supervising/monitoring the performances of the project are determined (Turner 2006). One of the major areas of influence of project governance in information management systems for the construction industry is ensuring that the objective of projects correlates with the portfolio and objective of the organisation. The influence of governance on information management for the construction industry is in three major areas. These include selecting the right project, delivering the selected project effectively and efficiently and make ensuring that the selected project could be sustained (Aliza et al. 2011).

8.4 Conceptual Framework Structural Components

The adoption of blockchain technology for information management conceptual framework for this study is derived from the identified exogenous constructs which include Influence of Technological Infrastructure (ITI), Influence of Organisational Culture (IOC), Influence of Industry Environment (IIE), Influence of Policy and Regulation (IPR), and Influence of Technology Governance (ITG). As earlier stated, the blockchain technology for information management adoption framework hypothesised in this chapter is not dependent on any previous framework. This is because this study is pioneering research in this domain. However, the theoretical underpinnings of the study are the frameworks discussed earlier. The theories reviewed as shown in Table 8.1 indicate the various constructs covered by each theory.

Having identified the constructs from extant literature, this study conducted structured interview sessions to identify the measurement variables for the conceptual framework constructs. The interview sessions identified the latent variables to measure the exogenous constructs of the study's conceptual framework consisting of Influence of Technological Infrastructure (ITI), Influence of Organisational Culture (IOC), Influence of Industry Environment (IIE), Influence of Policy and Regulation (IPR), Influence of Technology Governance (ITG), and Possible Outcome (PO). These constructs were hypothesized to be characterized by latent variables as proposed by the interviewees. A comprehensive summation of the latent and indicator variables is presented in Table 8.2 as compiled from desktop review and interview with experts.

The conceptual framework hypothesised that the five constructs identified (Influence of Technological Infrastructure, Influence of Organisational Culture, Influence of Industry Environment, Influence of Policy and Regulation, and Influence of Technology Governance), play an interdependent role in the adoption of BT for information management in the construction industry which then promote efficiency in the information management process of the industry. This efficiency is presented as the possible outcome of BT adoption for information management as depicted in Fig. 8.1.

Table 8.1 Constructs of blockchain-based information management framework identification

S/N		Technological infrastructure (Innovation sophistication, infrastructural system, structural features, performance expectancy)	Organisational culture (Perceived usefulness, user satisfaction, innovativeness, perceived ease of use, behavioural intention, effort expectancy)	Industry environment (Existing practices, job relevance, social system norms, social influence, industry support, relative advantage, end user support)	Policy and regulation (Project management, facilitating conditions)	Technology governance (Determinants of processes)
1	Adaptive Structuration Theory (AST) (DeSanctis and Poole 1994)	X	X	X		Blockchain technology related construct
2	Information System Success Model (DeLone and McLean 2002)	X	X	X		
3	Diffusion of Innovation Theory (DIT) (Rogers 1995)	X	X	X		
4	Knowledge-Based View of the Firm Theory (Grant 1995, 1996)		X	X		
5	Technology Acceptance Model (TAM1/TAM2) (Davis 1986)	X	X	X		
6	Distributed Ledger Technologies Four-Dimensional Model (Li et al. 2019)	X	X	X	X	
7	Technology–Organization–Environment (TOE) framework (Depietro et al. 1990)	X	X	X		
8	Organizational Adoption of Digital Innovation Model (Holotiuk and Moormann 2018)	X	X	X	X	
9	Unified Theory of Acceptance and Use of Technology (Venkatesh et al. 2003)	X	X	X	X	

Source: Researcher's compilation

Table 8.2 Indicator variables for conceptual model

Latent variable construct	Indicator variables
Influence of Technological Infrastructure (ITI)	Perceived benefits of the technology
	Complexity of the technology
	Compatibility with existing technologies
	Data security on the technology
	Smart contract coding ability
	Maturity of the technology
	Relative advantage of the technology
	Removal of intermediaries by the technology
	Permission (public vs private) on the technology
	Technology system architecture
	Perceived barrier to technology acquisition
	Capability of the technology
	Integration capabilities of technology
	Availability of technological infrastructure
	Training requirements of the technology
	Sophistication of the technology
Influence of Organisational Culture (IOC)	Organisational readiness for change
	Top management support for innovation
	Organisational size
	Readiness to adopt new business model
	Organisation's technological readiness
	Organisation's level of innovativeness
	Employees' participation incentives
	Employees' technological knowledge
	Availability of resources for implementation
	Financial capacity of the organisation
	Satisfaction with existing systems
	Organisation's technological implementation strategy
	Organisation's business scope
	Organisation's business objectives

(continued)

Table 8.2 (continued)

Latent variable construct	Indicator variables
Influence of Industry Environment (IIE)	Regulatory environment in the industry
	Market dynamics of the industry
	Industry's pressure to innovate
	Government's support for technological innovation
	Business use cases of technological innovations
	Industry partners' support
	Competitive pressure
	Consumer/client's readiness for adoption
	Consumer/client's request for innovation
	Industry's maturity for technological adoption
	Performance gap in the industry
	Existing practices of the industry
	Flexibility of the industry
	Readiness of industry stakeholders for innovation adoption
Influence of Policy and Regulation (IPR)	Introduction of innovation waiver policies
	Revision of business guideline regulations
	Use of tax permits for innovation adoption
	Revision of environmental standard regulations
	Economic incentive policies for innovation adoption
	Subsidy policies on infrastructure for innovation adoption
	Business covenants for innovation adopters
	Research and development support policies
	Introduction of innovation-enforcing standards
	Introduction of technology compliance requirements
	Introduction of technology matchmaking policies
Influence of Technology Governance (ITG)	Individual organisation's level of process monitoring
	Individual organisation's level of involvement in decision-making
	Individual organisation's level of transparency
	Individual organisation's governance mechanism
	Individual organisation's shareholders' rights
	Individual organisation's ownership structure
	Individual organisational regulations
	Individual organisation's value delivery
	Individual organisation's resource management
	Individual organisation's risk management approach
	Internal performance measurement indicators
	Individual organisation's strategic alignment

(continued)

Table 8.2 (continued)

Latent variable construct	Indicator variables
Possible Outcome (PO)	Control over the creation of project information
	Control over the sharing of project information
	Improved information efficiency
	Improved productivity through timely use of information
	Increased documented information reliability
	Minimisation of information legislation risks
	Ease of access to project vital information
	Improvement of management decision-making
	Fostering collaboration among industry professionals
	Decentralisation to allow participation of all professionals
	Improved information traceability
	Information security through encryption algorithm
	Data consistency using consensus mechanism
	Management of documented information digitally

Source: Researcher's fieldwork

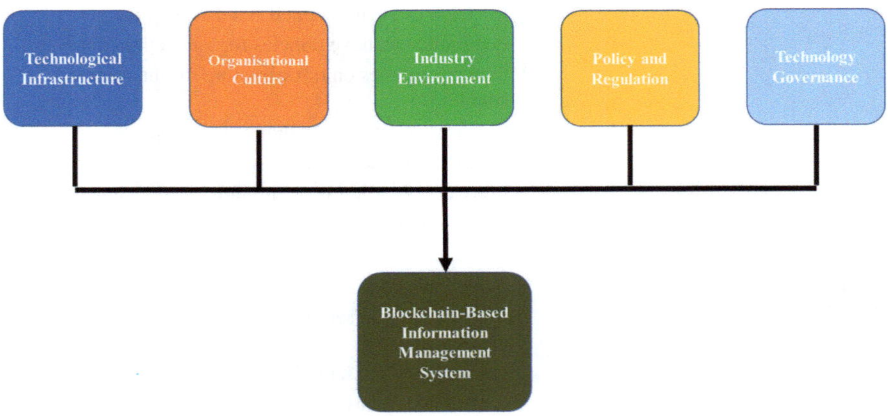

Fig. 8.1 Integrated framework for adoption of blockchain technology for information management. (Author's compilation)

The validated conceptual framework consists of the following component measurements: ITI = 16 measurement variables; IOC = 14 measurement variables; IIE = 14 measurement variables; IPR = 11 measurement variables; and ITG: 12 measurement variables; PO = 14 measurement variables. The factors influencing the adoption of blockchain technology for information management in the construction industry are highlighted in Fig. 8.1.

8.5 Summary

This chapter presents a comprehensive conceptual framework for the adoption of blockchain technology in information management within the construction industry. Recognising the fragmented nature of the construction sector and the persistent challenges of inefficiencies, data inconsistencies, and limited traceability in traditional information systems, the chapter explores how blockchain's core attributes can address these longstanding issues. However, the adoption of blockchain in this context remains constrained due to several organisational, technical, and regulatory barriers. To overcome these, a holistic understanding of the key determinants of blockchain adoption is necessary.

The chapter begins with a detailed review of relevant theories and models that underpin technological adoption. These include the Technology Acceptance Model (TAM), Adaptive Structuration Theory (AST), Diffusion of Innovation (DOI), Knowledge-Based View (KBV) of the firm, the Information System Success Model, and the Distributed Ledger Technology (DLT) Four-Dimensional Model. These frameworks collectively identify a variety of constructs such as perceived usefulness, system quality, organisational readiness, social influence, governance mechanisms, and regulatory environments that influence adoption decisions. Despite their contributions, these theories often lack sector-specific adaptation, prompting the need for a tailored framework suitable for construction information management. Building upon these theoretical foundations and validated through expert interviews, the chapter identifies five key constructs influencing the adoption of blockchain for information management in the construction industry: Influence of Technological Infrastructure (ITI), Influence of Organisational Culture (IOC), Influence of Industry Environment (IIE), Influence of Policy and Regulation (IPR), and Influence of Technology Governance (ITG). Each construct is supported by a set of latent variables and indicator metrics drawn from both literature and empirical insights.

Technological infrastructure factors include aspects like compatibility, complexity, smart contract capabilities, and integration readiness. Organisational culture focuses on top management support, employee technological awareness, and resource availability. The industry environment considers market dynamics, client readiness, and innovation pressure. Policy and regulation explore external legislative frameworks, incentive structures, and compliance requirements, while technology governance emphasises internal organisational mechanisms, stakeholder accountability, and strategic alignment. The conceptual framework culminates in the identification of possible outcomes (PO) from blockchain adoption in information management. These outcomes include improved information efficiency, enhanced data traceability, decentralised collaboration, improved decision-making, and secure digital documentation. The framework not only outlines the determinants of adoption but also offers a predictive model for assessing the potential impact of blockchain integration within construction firms and project environments.

References

Adeleke, A. Q., A. Y. Bahaudin, and A. M. Kamaruddeen. 2018. The effect of management commitment on contractors' risk management practices in the construction industry. *International Journal of Construction Management* 18 (1): 1–13.

Ahmed, S. M., S. Azhar, P. Kappagantula, and D. Gollapudi. 1995. Delays in construction: A brief study of the Florida construction industry. In *Proceedings of the 39th annual ASC conference*, 257–266.

Akanni, P. O., A. E. Oke, and O. A. Akpomiemie. 2014. Impact of environmental factors on building project performance in Delta state. *Nigeria. HBRC Journal* 10 (1): 60–72.

Akanni, P. O., A. E. Oke, and O. A. Akpomiemie. 2015. Impact of environmental factors on building project performance in Delta State, Nigeria. *HBRC Journal* 11 (1): 91–97.

Akinsola, A., N. Dawood, and B. Hobbs. 2000. Construction planning process improvement using information technology tool. In Proceedings of CIT 2000-Taking. The Construction Industry into the 21st Century, pp. 40–51.

Alavi, M., and D. E. Leidner. 2001. Knowledge management and knowledge management systems: Conceptual foundations and research issues. *MIS Quarterly* 25 (1): 107–136.

Aliza, A. R., M. M. Stephen, and T. Bambang. 2011. Governance of megaprojects: Dealing with uncertainty in the construction industry. *Procedia Engineering* 14:1193–1199.

Alqahtani, S., and S. F. Wamba. 2012. Determine of RFID technology adoption intention in the Saudi retail industry: An empirical study. In IEEE 45th Hawaii International Conference on System Science, pp. 4720–4729.

Amadu, M., E. Osei-Tutu, and D. G. Owusu-Manu. 2018. Towards the acceptance of BIM in Ghana's construction industry: An application of TAM. *Journal of Engineering, Design and Technology* 16 (4): 592–605.

Ballantine, J., R. D. Galliers, and S. Stray. 1996. Information systems/technology evaluation practices: Evidence from UK organizations. *Journal of Information Technology* 11 (2): 129–141.

Bekker, M. C., and H. Steyn. 2009. Defining a project governance framework for a project of limited duration. *South African Journal of Industrial Engineering* 20 (1): 81–92.

Bennett, J. 1991. *International construction project management: General theory and practice*. 2nd ed. Oxford: Butterworths Heinemann.

Bowden, S. 2005. Application of mobile IT in construction. PhD Thesis, Loughborough University.

Bowden, S., A. Dorr, T. Thorpe, and C. Anumba. 2006. Mobile ICT support for construction process improvement. *Automation in Construction* 15 (5): 664–676.

Briq. 2019. BRIQ: A modern construction data analytics platform. https://www.br.iq/. Accessed 3 Jan 2020.

Clack, C. D., V. A. Bakshi, and L. Braine. 2016. Smart contract templates: Foundations, design landscape and research directions. arXiv preprint arXiv:1608.00771.

Cohn, M., S. M. West, and A. Parker. 2017. Blockchain technology and the potential for smart contracts. *Stanford Law and Policy Review* 28 (2): 313–347.

Comer, M., and L. Kendall. 2013. Diffusion of innovations: Model and explanations. *Innovation Studies Journal* 5 (2): 87–96.

Computer Mediated Communication. 2003. Adaptive structuration theory. http://www.uky.edu/~rhuma0/cmc/ast.htm. Accessed 7 Sept 2020.

Crosby, M., P. Pattanayak, S. Verma, and V. Kalyanaraman. 2016. Blockchain technology: Beyond bitcoin. *Applied Innovation Review* 2:6–10.

Curado, C., and N. Bontis. 2006. The knowledge-based view of the firm and its theoretical presuppositions. *International Journal of Learning and Intellectual Capital* 3 (4): 367–381.

Dalkir, K. 2013. *Knowledge management in theory and practice*. 2nd ed. MIT Press.

Davis, F. D. 1986. A technology acceptance model for empirically testing new end-user information systems: Theory and results. PhD thesis, MIT Sloan School of Management.

Davis, F. D. 1989. Perceived usefulness, perceived ease of use, and user acceptance of information technology. *MIS Quarterly* 13 (3): 319–340.

Davis, F. D., and V. Venkatesh. 1996. A critical assessment of potential measurement biases in the technology acceptance model: Three experiments. *International Journal of Human Computer Studies* 45 (1): 19–45. https://doi.org/10.1006/ijhc.1996.0040.

DeLone, W. H., and E. R. McLean. 1992. Information systems success: The quest for the dependent variable. *Information Systems Research* 3 (1): 60–95.

DeLone, W. H., and E. R. McLean. 2002. Information systems success revisited. In *Proceedings of the 35th annual Hawaii international conference on system sciences*.

Depietro, R., E. Wiarda, and M. Fleischer. 1990. The context for change: Organization, technology and environment. In *The processes of technological innovation*, ed. L. G. Tornatzky and M. Fleischer, 151–175. Lexington Books.

DeSanctis, G., and M. S. Poole. 1994. Capturing the complexity in advanced technology use: Adaptive structuration theory. *Organization Science* 5 (2): 121–147.

Dingfelder, H. E., and D. S. Mandell. 2011. Bridging the research-to-practice gap in autism intervention. *Autism* 15 (3): 230–245.

Economist. 2018. The Facebook scandal could change politics as well as the internet. Economist (United Kingdom), 5 February 2018.

Egbu, C. O., J. Sturges, and M. Bates. 2003. Learning from knowledge management and trans-organisational innovations in project environments. In *Proceedings of the 19th ARCOM conference*, vol. 2, 639–646.

Elrom, Y. 2019. *The NEO developer's guide*. Apress.

Gaith, F. H., A. R. Khalim, and I. Amiruddin. 2012. Application and efficacy of information technology in construction industry. *Scientific Research and Essays* 7 (38): 3223–3242.

Grant, R. M. 1996. Toward a knowledge-based theory of the firm. *Strategic Management Journal* 17 (S2): 109–122.

Gritli, H., A. G. F. Gibb, and R. McCaffer. 2007. Influence of organisational culture on the implementation of partnering in the UAE construction industry. *Proceedings of CIB World Building Congress* 3:2322–2333.

Grover, V., and T. H. Davenport. 2001. General perspectives on knowledge management: Fostering a research agenda. *Journal of Management Information Systems* 18 (1): 5–21.

Gutek, B. A., T. K. Bikson, and D. Mankin. 1984. Individual and organizational consequences of computer-based office information technology. *Applied Social Psychology Annual: Applications in Organizational Settings* 5:231–254.

Halawi, L. A., and R. V. McCarthy. 2006. Knowledge management and the competitive strategy of the firm. *The Learning Organization* 13 (4): 384–397.

Hassan, N. A., S. A. Z. Kazmi, and S. F. Padlee. 2019. Re-examining the role of perceived usefulness and perceived ease of use in the consumer adoption of e-commerce in Malaysia. *Malaysian Journal of Business and Economics (MJBE)* 6 (1): 33–47.

Holotiuk, F., and J. Moormann. 2018. Organizational adoption of digital innovation: The case of blockchain technology. In *Proceedings of the 51st Hawaii international conference on system sciences (HICSS)*.

Hughes, W. P. 1989. Identifying environment of construction projects. *Construction Management Economics* 5 (2): 7–29.

Jessop, B. 1997. The governance of complexity and the complexity of governance: Preliminary remarks on some problems and limits of economic guidance. In *Beyond market and hierarchy: Interactive governance and social complexity*, 111–147. London: Edward Elgar.

Jwaifell, M., and A. Gasaymeh. 2013. Using diffusion of innovation theory to explain the degree of English teachers' adoption of interactive whiteboards in the modern systems school in Jordan. *International Journal of Computer Applications* 68 (8): 1–7.

Kim, S. S., H. Xu, and S. Gupta. 2012. Which is more important in internet shopping, perceived price or trust? *Electronic Commerce Research and Applications* 11 (3): 241–252.

Kim, H. M., Y. Kang, and S. W. Hong. 2017. A conceptual framework for the adoption of blockchain technology in construction. In *Proceedings of the creative construction conference*, 85–92.

Klakegg, O. J., T. Williams, D. Walker, B. Andersen, and O. M. Magnussen. 2008. *Governance frameworks for public project development and estimation*. Vol. 39. Project Management Institute.
Kuraesin, A. 2017. The influence of organizational culture on the effectiveness of construction project management. *Journal of Engineering and Applied Sciences* 12 (5): 1250–1256.
Lee, Y., K. A. Kozar, and K. R. Larsen. 2003. The technology acceptance model: Past, present, and future. *Communications of the Association for Information Systems* 12 (1): 752–780.
Lethbridge, N. 2003. Adaptive structuration theory: Relevant structures for web technologies. In 14th Australasian Conference on Information Systems, pp. 1–8.
Liebeskind, J. 1996. Knowledge, strategy, and the theory of the firm. *Southern Medical Journal* 17:93–107.
Li, H., D. Greenwood, and M. Kassem. 2019. Blockchain in the built environment: Analysing current applications and developing an emergent framework. *Automation in Construction* 102:288–307.
Liu, A. M. M., R. Fellows, and J. Ng. 2003. Procurement selection criteria in the Hong Kong construction industry. *Construction Management and Economics* 21 (7): 707–715.
Liu, Y., B. Xia, M. Skitmore, and Q. Chen. 2018. Current state and future directions of research on BIM-based coordination management: A critical review. *Building and Environment* 126:174–192.
Mafakheri, F., L. Dai, D. Slezak, and F. Nasiri. 2007. Project delivery system selection under uncertainty: Multicriteria multilevel decision aid model. *Journal of Management in Engineering* 23 (4): 200–206. https://doi.org/10.1061/(ASCE)0742-597X(2007)23:4(200).
Mahdi, I. M., and K. Alreshaid. 2005. Decision support system for selecting the proper project delivery method using analytical hierarchy process (AHP). *International Journal of Project Management* 23 (7): 564–572. https://doi.org/10.1016/j.ijproman.2005.05.007.
Makovhololo, T. V., C. Aigbavboa, and W. Thwala. 2017. Barriers of diffusion of innovation in the south African construction industry. In *Proceedings of the 7th international conference on engineering, project, and production management*, 593–603.
Michael, K., A. Papazafeiropoulou, and A. Pouloudi. 2020. Decision-making in virtual project teams: A systematic literature review. *International Journal of Information Management* 50:289–300.
Miller, R., and D. R. Lessard. 2000. *The strategic management of large engineering projects: Shaping institutions, risk and governance*. Cambridge: MIT Press.
Min, H. 2019. Blockchain technology for enhancing supply chain resilience. *Business Horizons* 62 (1): 35–45.
Miyatake, Y., and R. Kangari. 1993. Experiencing computer integrated construction. *Journal of Construction Engineering and Management* 119 (2): 307–322.
Müller, R. 2017. Organizational project governance. In *Governance and governmentality for projects: Enablers, practices and consequences*, ed. R. Müller, 11–24. New York: Routledge.
Muller, R. 2019. Governance, governmentality and project performance: The role of sovereignty. *International Journal of Information Systems and Project Management* 7 (2): 5–17. https://doi.org/10.12821/ijispm070201.
Müller, R., N. Drouin, and S. Sankaran. 2019. Modeling organizational project management. *Project Management. Journal* 50 (4): 1–15.
Müller, R., S. Pemsel, and J. Shao. 2014. Organizational enablers for governance and governmentality of projects: A literature review. *International Journal of Project Management* 32 (8): 1309–1320.
Müller, R., L. Zhai, A. Wang, and J. Shao. 2016. A framework for governance of projects: Governmentality, governance structure and projectification. *International Journal of Project Management* 34 (6): 957–969.
Nemutanzhela, P., and T. Iyamu. 2015. Theory of diffusion of innovation for analysis in information systems studies. In Science and Information Conference (SAI), pp. 603–608.

Nguyen, L. H., and T. Watanabe. 2017. The impact of project organizational culture on the performance of construction projects. *Sustainability* 9:78–91. https://doi.org/10.3390/su9050781.

Niu, Y. 2008. The performance and problems of affordable housing policy in Chana: The estimations of benefits, costs and affordability. *International Journal of Housing Market Analysis* 12:125–146.

Nonaka, I., and R. Toyama. 2005. The theory of the knowledge-creating firm: Subjectivity, objectivity and synthesis. *Industrial and Corporate Change* 14:419–436.

Nonaka, I., R. Toyama, and T. Hirata. 2006. *Managing flow: A process theory of the knowledge-based firm*. Palgrave Macmillan.

OECD. 2001. *Citizens as partners: OECD handbook on information, consultation and public participation in policy-making*. OECD Publishing.

Oliveira, T., and M. F. Martins. 2010. Information technology adoption models at firm level: Review of literature. In European Conference on Information Management and Evaluation, pp. 312–324.

Organization for Economic Cooperation and Development. 2004. *OECD principles of corporate governance*. Paris: OECD Publications.

Orlikowski, W. J., and D. Robey. 1991. Information technology and the structuring of organizations. *Information Systems Research* 2 (2): 143–169.

Phua, F., and S. Rowlinson. 2003. Cultural differences as an explanatory variable for adversarial attitudes in the construction industry: The case of Hong Kong. *Construction Management and Economics* 21:777–785.

Pinto, J. K. 2016. *Project management: Achieving competitive advantage*. 4th ed. Harlow: Pearson Education.

Poole, M. S. 2008. The structuration of communication systems. In *The international encyclopedia of communication*, ed. W. Donsbach. Wiley-Blackwell.

Ratnasabapathy, S., R. Rameezdeen, and N. A. Lebbe. 2008. Exploratory study of external environmental factors influencing the procurement selection in construction. In Proceedings of the CIB International Conference on Building Education and Research, 10–15 February 2008, Kandalama.

Rogers, E. M. 1995. Diffusion of innovations: Modifications of a model for telecommunications. In *Die Diffusion von Innovationen in der Telekommunikation*, ed. M. W. Stoetzer and A. Mahler, 25–38. Heidelberg: Springer. https://doi.org/10.1007/978-3-642-79868-9_2.

Rogers, E. M. 2003. *Diffusion of innovations*. 5th ed. Free Press.

Rowley, J. 2008. Understanding digital content marketing. *Journal of Marketing Management* 24 (5–6): 517–540.

Russell, D. M., and A. M. Hoag. 2004. People and information technology in the supply chain: Social and organizational influences on adoption. *International Journal of Physical Distribution & Logistics Management* 34 (2): 102–122.

Sampaio, C. H., C. Simões, and M. G. Perin. 2012. Diffusion of innovations theory and international business research. *RAE-Revista de Administração de Empresas* 52 (4): 500–510.

Samset, K., and G. H. Volden. 2016. Front-end definition of projects: Ten paradoxes and some reflections regarding project management and project governance. *International Journal of Project Management* 34 (2): 297–313.

Scharpf, F. W. 1994. Games real actors could play: Positive and negative coordination in embedded negotiations. *Journal of Theoretical Politics* 6 (1): 27–53.

Seddon, P. B. 1997. A respecification and extension of the DeLone and McLean model of IS success. *Information Systems Research* 8 (3): 240–253.

Soewin, E., and T. Chinda. 2018. Factors affecting safety program implementation in small and medium construction enterprises: A case study of Cambodia. *Safety Science* 104:202–215.

Straub, E. T. 2009. Understanding technology adoption: Theory and future directions for informal learning. *Review of Educational Research* 79 (2): 625–649.

Tolman, F. P. 1997. The future of construction IT. *Automation in Construction* 6 (4): 291–302.

Turner, J. R. 2006. Towards a theory of project management: The nature of the functions of project management. *International Journal of Project Management* 24 (4): 277–279.

Urbach, N., and B. Müller. 2012. The updated DeLone and McLean model of information systems success. In *Information systems theory*, 1–18. Springer.

Venkatesh, V., and F. D. Davis. 2000. A theoretical extension of the technology acceptance model: Four longitudinal field studies. *Management Science* 46 (2): 186–204.

Venkatesh, V., M. G. Morris, G. B. Davis, and F. D. Davis. 2003. User acceptance of information technology: Toward a unified view. *MIS Quarterly* 27 (3): 425–478.

Walker, A. 1989. *Project management in construction*. Blackwell Publishing.

Wanjau, K. N., B. W. Muiruri, and E. Ayodo. 2012. Factors affecting provision of service quality in the public health sector: A case of Kenyatta national hospital. *International Journal of Humanities and Social Science* 2 (13): 14–29.

Wood, G. 2014. Ethereum: A secure decentralised generalised transaction ledger. *Ethereum Project Yellow Paper* 151:1–32.

Yang, Z., and Q. Liu. 2007. Research and development of web-based virtual online classroom. *Computers & Education* 48 (2): 171–184.

Zack, M. H. 1999. Developing a knowledge strategy. *California Management Review* 41 (3): 125–145.

Zhang, X., P. Yu, J. Yan, and I. T. A. M. Spil. 2015. Using diffusion of innovation theory to understand the factors impacting patient acceptance and use of consumer e-health innovations: A case study in a primary care clinic. *BMC Health Services Research* 15 (1): 1–15.

Chapter 9
General Summary

Abstract This concluding chapter synthesizes the core findings, contributions, and implications of the book, which explored the adoption of blockchain technology for information management in the construction industry. The chapter consolidates insights from a comprehensive review of literature, theoretical frameworks, and empirical data gathered from expert interviews. It highlights the practical and theoretical contributions of the book, demonstrating how blockchain can address long-standing issues in construction information systems such as fragmentation, inefficiency, and data insecurity. The chapter also outlines the general contribution of the book to knowledge, emphasizing its value in shaping both academic inquiry and industry practices. Clear recommendations are provided for policymakers, practitioners, and researchers, aiming to facilitate the effective implementation of blockchain-based solutions across the construction value chain. By offering a well-rounded conclusion, this chapter underscores the transformative potential of blockchain and advocates for a strategic and inclusive approach to its adoption in construction information management.

Keywords Blockchain · Information management · Construction industry · Adoption framework · Digital innovation

9.1 Introduction

Drawing from the insights gained through extensive literature exploration, empirical investigation, and theoretical grounding, this chapter reflects on how the adoption of blockchain technology can transform information management practices in the construction sector. It outlines the general overview of the book's contribution to knowledge, highlighting both theoretical and practical implications that advance current understanding and professional practice. Furthermore, it provides clear and actionable recommendations for stakeholders seeking to implement blockchain solutions in construction information management. This final chapter serves as a

O. I. Akinradewo et al., *Blockchain Technology for Information Management: A New Era for Sustainable Construction Practices*, Artificial Intelligence and Sustainable Development, https://doi.org/10.1007/978-981-95-2664-2_9

capstone, consolidating key findings while offering a strategic direction for future research, policy development, and industry transformation in the digital age. Through it, the book reinforces its relevance as both a scholarly resource and a practical guide for innovation.

9.2 Conclusion

The journey through this book has been one of thoughtful exploration, critical reflection, and progressive synthesis, with a focus on understanding the potential, practicality, and implementation of blockchain technology for information management in the construction industry. At its core, this study has sought to unravel the complex, often fragmented nature of construction information systems and examine how blockchain, as a disruptive and transformative technology, can bring about meaningful change. The findings of the book reinforce the notion that while blockchain remains in its early stages within the construction domain, its application—if thoughtfully adopted and governed—can herald a new era of trust, transparency, and traceability in construction information flows.

The construction industry has long suffered from inefficiencies tied to siloed data management systems, delayed communication, and a lack of secure, real-time collaboration tools among stakeholders. These inefficiencies contribute to project delays, increased costs, miscommunication, and even litigation. Through the lens of blockchain, a new paradigm that promises decentralised control, tamper-proof records, and streamlined data sharing among all project actors is presented. Blockchain's immutability and consensus-based validation mechanisms offer a resilient alternative to traditional information management systems, with the potential to address many of the enduring challenges facing the sector.

One of the key strengths of blockchain technology lies in its foundational attributes: decentralisation, immutability, transparency, and smart contract functionality. These attributes align closely with the critical needs of construction project environments, which often involve multiple stakeholders—clients, contractors, consultants, regulators, and suppliers—working under tight deadlines and within intricate contractual frameworks. Blockchain offers an opportunity to synchronise disparate information sources and to ensure that all parties have access to accurate and current project data, thereby reducing disputes and enhancing project delivery.

However, the promise of blockchain cannot be realised in isolation. It exists within a broader ecosystem of technological, organisational, regulatory, and environmental factors that must be addressed to enable its effective adoption. The empirical and theoretical analyses in this book have collectively revealed that blockchain adoption is not merely a technical decision, but rather a strategic one requiring alignment across internal capabilities, stakeholder readiness, regulatory frameworks, and industry dynamics. This insight is pivotal, as it repositions the conversation around blockchain from a question of whether to adopt, to a more nuanced inquiry into how to create the conditions that make its adoption meaningful and sustainable.

Technological readiness emerged as a significant enabler or barrier, depending on the context in which it is evaluated. Issues such as compatibility with existing systems, the maturity of the blockchain infrastructure, training needs, and the sophistication of smart contract applications all influence how construction firms perceive and approach blockchain. The success of implementation depends heavily on whether organisations view blockchain as a strategic advantage, and whether they possess the internal capability to deploy and maintain such systems. Importantly, the perception of technological complexity must be balanced with a clear understanding of the long-term benefits and the value it brings to business operations.

Organisational culture also plays a critical role in determining the fate of blockchain adoption. Support from top management, the innovativeness of an organisation, employee readiness, and the presence of a change-oriented mindset were found to be essential. Resistance to change, satisfaction with existing systems, or fear of job displacement can slow down adoption. Conversely, when employees are engaged, incentivised, and equipped with the right skills and resources, they become champions of transformation. Organisations that foster a culture of innovation and continuous improvement are more likely to take the leap and explore emerging technologies such as blockchain.

Beyond internal dynamics, the external industry environment exerts significant influence. Competitive pressure, client expectations, and market readiness are crucial indicators of whether blockchain will gain traction. As construction firms compete to differentiate themselves, those that integrate advanced technologies into their service delivery may gain a reputational and operational edge. Additionally, government support, public sector innovation policies, and client demands for transparency and sustainability are instrumental in driving momentum. The maturity of the industry in embracing innovation, along with the collaborative spirit among stakeholders, will dictate how quickly blockchain solutions move from pilot projects to full-scale deployment.

Policy and regulation form the scaffolding upon which blockchain adoption must be built. Clear, enforceable policies that provide guidance on data governance, digital identity, legal enforceability of smart contracts, and privacy protection are paramount. The lack of established regulatory frameworks has left many construction stakeholders hesitant to experiment with blockchain, fearing legal ambiguity and potential risks. The development of policies that offer tax incentives, research funding, or subsidies for digital infrastructure can serve as catalysts for adoption. Moreover, regulations that promote interoperability and ethical use of data can safeguard against misuse while encouraging innovation.

Technology governance is another essential consideration. It encompasses the decision-making frameworks, oversight mechanisms, and performance management systems that ensure the responsible and aligned use of blockchain technologies. Governance provides clarity on who owns data, who can modify it, and how changes are authorised. It also facilitates alignment with organisational strategy and ensures that blockchain implementation adds value rather than complexity. Without robust governance structures, blockchain initiatives may become fragmented, underutilised, or even abandoned due to misalignment with organisational goals or stakeholder expectations.

A major contribution of this book is the development and validation of a comprehensive conceptual framework that integrates all these dimensions: technological, organisational, environmental, regulatory, and governance to provide a roadmap for the adoption of blockchain for information management in the construction industry. This framework was not derived in abstraction but was grounded in empirical insights from experts with deep experience in both the construction and ICT sectors. Through thematic analysis of expert interviews, the framework reflects real-world conditions and is designed to be adaptable to diverse construction project contexts.

The outcome of blockchain adoption, as articulated in this study, goes beyond technical efficiency. It encompasses improved data integrity, reduced information-related risks, enhanced collaboration, and stronger decision-making capabilities. Blockchain-based systems are poised to shift the focus from managing isolated project components to managing integrated project knowledge. By ensuring secure, traceable, and real-time access to information, blockchain strengthens trust among stakeholders and supports a collaborative environment conducive to project success.

The potential impact of blockchain on construction information management extends further. It has the capacity to redefine the nature of contracts through smart contract automation, simplify audit trails, improve compliance with regulatory requirements, and enable new business models such as tokenised asset ownership or decentralised procurement platforms. These shifts could fundamentally transform how value is created and exchanged in the construction value chain, positioning blockchain as not just a technological tool but a driver of industry reinvention.

Nonetheless, this transformation will not occur overnight. Blockchain adoption must be seen as a journey rather than a destination. It requires iterative learning, pilot testing, stakeholder engagement, and policy dialogue. It calls for a shift in mindset from linear, centralised models of information control to dynamic, distributed models of information exchange. While the road may be fraught with challenges, the potential rewards for those who navigate it successfully are significant.

The construction industry, with its complex projects and multi-stakeholder engagements, is uniquely positioned to benefit from the attributes of blockchain. However, realising this potential requires more than technology alone. It demands leadership commitment, cross-sector collaboration, regulatory clarity, and above all, a shared vision for the digital future of construction. The framework presented in this book serves as a starting point for construction firms, policymakers, researchers, and technology developers who seek to harness blockchain to address the information management challenges of today while preparing for the opportunities of tomorrow.

9.3 Contribution to Knowledge

This book makes a significant contribution to the growing body of knowledge on digital transformation in the construction industry by providing a comprehensive, empirically grounded framework for the adoption of blockchain technology in information management. It offers a nuanced understanding of how technological, organisational, environmental, regulatory, and governance-related factors interact to influence adoption decisions. By integrating theoretical insights with real-world expert perspectives, the book bridges the gap between abstract academic discourse and practical industry realities. It expands the conversation around blockchain beyond its technical functionalities to encompass broader strategic, cultural, and institutional dynamics that shape its implementation. The study pioneers a tailored conceptual model that captures the complexities of blockchain integration specifically within the construction context, offering a structured path for stakeholders to assess readiness, identify challenges, and optimise adoption strategies. Moreover, the research sheds light on the tangible outcomes of blockchain use, such as improved data reliability, enhanced collaboration, and stronger decision-making processes. In doing so, it equips industry professionals, researchers, and policymakers with the tools and understanding needed to embrace blockchain not just as a technology, but as a catalyst for meaningful change in the way construction information is managed, secured, and leveraged for greater project success.

9.3.1 Practical Contribution

This book makes a vital practical contribution to the body of knowledge by offering a grounded and context-specific framework that construction industry stakeholders can use to navigate the adoption of blockchain technology for information management. The framework presented is not merely conceptual as it is derived from real-world insights provided by industry professionals and information technology experts who understand the nuances of the construction environment. This practical orientation ensures that the framework can be directly applied to project planning, execution, and post-completion phases, allowing project managers, engineers, contractors, consultants, and policy implementers to identify critical variables that influence successful blockchain adoption.

One of the most notable practical contributions is the detailed identification of measurable variables within each construct that influence blockchain adoption. By operationalising factors such as technological readiness, organisational culture, policy support, and governance structures, the book provides actionable indicators that industry practitioners can use for readiness assessment and strategic planning. These variables can guide firms in evaluating their current capacity, identifying areas for investment, and aligning their internal operations to support innovation through blockchain solutions. Moreover, the book addresses existing challenges in construction information management, such as fragmented systems, data silos, and poor information traceability. Through its exploration of blockchain's decentralised and secure features, the book presents an innovative solution to improving transparency, real-time collaboration, and data integrity among construction stakeholders. This has direct implications for improving project delivery timelines, reducing errors and reworks, and increasing trust in multi-party environments. By contextualising the use of smart contracts, encryption algorithms, and consensus mechanisms, the book equips practitioners with the knowledge to make informed decisions on integrating blockchain features into their digital workflows.

Another practical impact lies in its contribution to capacity-building within the construction sector. The book reveals knowledge and training gaps among construction professionals in blockchain technology and encourages industry-wide efforts in upskilling and cross-sector collaboration. This insight provides a roadmap for educational institutions, professional bodies, and training providers to design targeted capacity development programmes that align with technological advancement and digitalisation goals within the built environment. Importantly, the book fosters a culture of innovation by showing that blockchain implementation is not solely a technological issue but also one of leadership, change management, and stakeholder alignment. It emphasises the need for strong governance mechanisms and regulatory clarity to support sustained adoption. These insights are valuable for both private and public sector actors involved in infrastructure delivery and digital transformation initiatives.

Through its rich practical orientation, the book offers an indispensable guide for industry actors seeking to harness blockchain to solve real challenges in construction information management. It empowers practitioners to make evidence-based decisions, promote technological inclusivity, and build resilient, data-driven ecosystems that enhance productivity, accountability, and sustainability in construction projects.

9.3.2 Theoretical Contribution

The book makes a significant theoretical contribution to the evolving discourse on digital transformation, technology adoption, and information systems in the construction industry by developing an integrated and empirically validated conceptual framework for blockchain technology adoption. This contribution is distinguished by its ability to synthesise and extend existing theories in a way that addresses the unique complexities of the construction sector. It brings theoretical clarity to a field that is still in the early stages of engaging with blockchain and offers a structured foundation upon which future academic inquiry can be built.

Drawing from a wide range of established theoretical models such as the Technology Acceptance Model, Diffusion of Innovation Theory, Adaptive Structuration Theory, Knowledge-Based View of the Firm, and the Information System Success Model, the book does not merely adopt existing theories in their original forms. Instead, it critically evaluates them, identifies their limitations within the context of construction, and extends their application by integrating relevant constructs into a new, cohesive framework. This blending of theories results in a hybrid model that captures the interplay between technological, organisational, environmental, regulatory, and governance-related factors that shape blockchain adoption in information management systems.

One of the most profound theoretical contributions is the detailed mapping of latent variables that underpin each construct within the proposed framework. These variables, drawn from both literature and qualitative expert input, add empirical depth to theoretical abstractions. This dual approach strengthens the framework's theoretical robustness and ensures that it is grounded in both academic knowledge and practitioner insight. It also provides a replicable model that can be tested, modified, and extended by other researchers in related fields or geographical contexts. The framework challenges traditional technology adoption models that often treat implementation as a linear or individual-focused process. By incorporating organisational culture, governance mechanisms, and policy and regulatory environments, the book presents a systemic view of technology adoption that is particularly suited to complex and multi-stakeholder industries like construction. This theoretical repositioning enhances the academic understanding of how disruptive technologies like blockchain can be adopted in practice and sheds light on the social, institutional, and technical interdependencies that influence innovation.

Furthermore, the book contributes to theory by introducing the dimension of outcomes specific to blockchain-based information management, such as enhanced traceability, improved information efficiency, and decentralised collaboration. These outcomes offer a new vocabulary for evaluating the success of blockchain implementation beyond traditional metrics of cost or time, thus enriching the theoretical discourse on performance and value generation in information systems.

9.4 Recommendations

To advance the adoption of blockchain technology for information management in the construction industry, several recommendations emerge from the insights, findings, and reflections shared throughout this book. First and foremost, there is an urgent need for heightened awareness and education about blockchain's capabilities among construction professionals. Despite its immense potential to address long-standing inefficiencies in information handling, many stakeholders remain unaware or unsure of how to incorporate blockchain into their operations. Institutions responsible for training, certification, and professional development must therefore prioritise the inclusion of blockchain literacy in their programmes. Universities, training centres, and professional bodies should develop specialised modules, workshops, and continuous professional development initiatives to ensure the workforce is equipped with both conceptual and practical knowledge of this disruptive technology.

Organisations within the construction ecosystem are encouraged to carry out strategic readiness assessments to identify the gaps in infrastructure, culture, and digital capabilities that may hinder blockchain implementation. These assessments should lead to phased digital transformation roadmaps that align with the firm's long-term goals while embedding blockchain into core operational processes. Investment in digital infrastructure particularly in secure networks, cloud computing, and data storage must be treated as essential, not optional. Alongside this, organisations must embrace a culture that values innovation, encourages experimentation, and fosters collaboration between departments and stakeholders. Leadership commitment to change, openness to new business models, and employee engagement are critical to successful adoption.

Governments and regulatory agencies are called upon to create enabling environments that support innovation without compromising accountability and compliance. Clear regulatory frameworks, data governance policies, and standards for digital construction technologies are crucial. Public-private partnerships should be fostered to pilot blockchain-based systems on public infrastructure projects, thereby creating demonstrable case studies that could inspire private sector adoption. Financial incentives, such as tax rebates or grant funding for technology implementation, could accelerate uptake among small- and medium-sized enterprises, which often face the highest barriers to entry.

Industry stakeholders should embrace multi-stakeholder platforms for collaboration, where construction professionals, IT experts, policymakers, and researchers come together to share knowledge, align standards, and promote interoperable solutions. These platforms should be used to develop shared protocols, address cybersecurity concerns, and ensure that blockchain solutions are not implemented in silos but are instead integrated across the value chain. Joint research and pilot projects, coordinated through professional councils or sector clusters, can help de-risk adoption and offer validated models for replication.

Finally, further research is recommended to evaluate blockchain adoption outcomes using measurable performance indicators, particularly in the context of information traceability, data integrity, project delivery time, and stakeholder trust. Such studies would not only reinforce the theoretical framework proposed in this book but also guide practitioners with evidence-based insights. Cross-national studies comparing blockchain implementation across different regulatory and cultural contexts could enrich the global understanding of adoption enablers and constraints.

Bibliography

Aarons, G. A., M. Hurlburt, and S. M. Horwitz. 2011. Advancing a conceptual model of evidence-based practice implementation in public service sectors. *Administration and Policy in Mental Health and Mental Health Services Research* 38 (1): 4–23.

Abad-Segura, E., A. Infante-Moro, M. D. González-Zamar, and E. López-Meneses. 2024. Influential factors for a secure perception of accounting management with blockchain technology. *Journal of Open Innovation: Technology, Market, and Complexity* 10 (2): https://doi.org/10.1016/J.JOITMC.2024.100264.

Abdel-Maksoud, A. B. 2004. Manufacturing in the UK: Contemporary characteristics and performance indicators. *Journal of Manufacturing Technology Management* 15 (2): 155–171.

Abdin, Z. 2024. Empowering the hydrogen economy: The transformative potential of blockchain technology. *Renewable and Sustainable Energy Reviews* 200. https://doi.org/10.1016/J.RSER.2024.114572.

Abdulai, R. T. 2007. The operation of urban traditional landholding institutions in sub-Saharan Africa: A Ghana study. Unpublished PhD thesis, School of Engineering and Built Environment, University of Wolverhampton.

Abeyratne, S.A. and Monfared, R.P. (2016). Blockchain ready manufacturing supply chain using distributed ledger," International Journal of Research in Engineering and Technology., 5(9), pp. 1–10.

Ablyazov, T., and I. Petrov. 2019. Influence of blockchain on development of interaction system of investment and construction activity participants. *IOP Conference Series: Materials Science and Engineering* 497 (1): https://doi.org/10.1088/1757-899X497/1/012001.

Abrell, C., J. Rowold, J. Weibler, and M. Moenninghoff. 2011. Evaluation of a long-term transformational leadership development program. *German Journal of Human Resource Management* 25 (3): 205–224.

Abunadi, I., M. M. Althobaiti, F. N. Al-Wesabi, A. M. Hilal, M. Medani, M. A. Hamza, M. Rizwanullah, and A. S. Zamani. 2022. Federated learning with blockchain assisted image classification for clustered UAV networks. *Computers, Materials and Continua* 72 (1): 1195–1212. https://doi.org/10.32604/CMC.2022.025473.

Accenture. 2017. Blockchain banking for investment banks. Accenture. https://www.accenture.com/lv-en/insight-banking-on-blockchain. Accessed 1 January 2020.

Adamska, B. A., D. Blahak, and F. H. Abanda. 2021. Blockchain in construction practice. In *Collaboration and integration in construction, engineering, management and technology: Proceedings of the 11th international conference on construction in the 21st century, London 2019*, 339–343. Springer International Publishing.

O. I. Akinradewo et al., *Blockchain Technology for Information Management: A New Era for Sustainable Construction Practices*, Artificial Intelligence and Sustainable Development, https://doi.org/10.1007/978-981-95-2664-2

Adekunle, P., C. Aigbavboa, D. Thwala, A. Oke, and O. Akinradewo. 2022. Construction information management: The role of fourth industrial revolution tools. *Human Factors Architecture: Sustainable Urban Planning for Infrastructure* 58:254–261.

Adeleke, A. Q., A. Y. Bahaudin, A. M. Kamaruddeen, J. A. Bamgbade, M. G. Salimon, M. W. A. Khan, and S. Sorooshoian. 2018. The influence of organizational external factors on construction risk management among Nigerian construction companies. *Safety and Health at Work.* 9:115–124.

Afuah, A. 2002. Mapping technological capabilities into product markets and competitive advantage: The case of cholesterol drugs. *Strategic Management Journal* 23 (2): 171–179.

Agibalova, E. N., I. B. Ilovaysky, Y. Y. Kayl, and V. A. Usanova. 2020. Use of letter of credit form of payment in the implementation of smart contracts and blockchain technology. In *Lecture notes in networks and systems*, 160–170. Springer. https://doi.org/10.1007/978-3-030-47945-9_18.

Agumba, J. N. 2013. A construction health and safety performance improvement model for South African small and medium enterprises. Doctoral dissertation submitted to University of Johannesburg, South Africa.

Ahmad, R. W., K. Salah, R. Jayaraman, I. Yaqoob, and M. Omar. 2022. Blockchain in oil and gas industry: Applications, challenges, and future trends. *Technology in Society* 68. https://doi.org/10.1016/J.TECHSOC.2022.101941.

Ahmadisheykhsarmast, S., and R. Sonmez. 2020. A smart contract system for security of payment of construction contracts. *Automation in Construction* 120. https://doi.org/10.1016/J.AUTCON.2020.103401.

Ahmed, I. U., J. S. Russell, and A. Abou-Zeid. 1995. Information technology and integration in the construction industry. *Construction Management Economics* 13 (2): 163–171.

Aigbavboa, C. O. 2014. An integrated beneficiary centered satisfaction model for publicly funded housing schemes in South Africa. Doctorate Thesis submitted to University of Johannesburg, South Africa.

Aigbavboa, C., and E. Kissi. 2025a. Digital construction project cost management. *Digital Management of Construction Costs*39–58. https://doi.org/10.1016/B978-0-443-23715-7.00004-4.

Aigbavboa, C., and E. Kissi. 2025b. Digital construction project cost management—An Industry 4.0 framework. *Digital Management of Construction Costs*147–158. https://doi.org/10.1016/B978-0-443-23715-7.00009-3.

Aigbavboa, C., and E. Kissi. 2025c. Digital construction project cost management—Practical steps. *Digital Management of Construction Costs*117–145. https://doi.org/10.1016/B978-0-443-23715-7.00008-1.

Aigbavboa, C., and E. Kissi. 2025d. Digitalization and cost dynamics of construction projects. *Digital Management of Construction Costs*75–92. https://doi.org/10.1016/B978-0-443-23715-7.00006-8.

Aigbavboa, C., and E. Kissi. 2025e. Understanding digital construction management. *Digital Management of Construction Costs*27–38. https://doi.org/10.1016/B978-0-443-23715-7.00003-2.

Akadiri, O. P. 2011. Development of a multi-criteria approach for the selection of sustainable materials for building projects. Doctoral dissertation submitted to University of Wolverhampton, UK.

Akanfe, O., D. Lawong, and H. R. Rao. 2024. Blockchain technology and privacy regulation: Reviewing frictions and synthesizing opportunities. *International Journal of Information Management* 76. https://doi.org/10.1016/J.IJINFOMGT.2024.102753.

Akanni, P. O., A. E. Oke, and O. A. Akpomiemie. 2015. Impact of environmental factors on building project performance in Delta State, Nigeria. *HBRC Journal* 11 (1): 91–97.

Akinradewo, O., C. Aigbavboa, A. Oke, and H. Coffie. 2021. Modelling a cost profile for road projects. *Canadian Journal of Civil Engineering* 48 (4): 366–376. https://doi.org/10.1139/cjce-2019-0739.

Akinsola, A., N. Dawood, and B. Hobbs. 2000. Construction planning process improvement using information technology tool. In Proceedings of CIT 2000-Taking. The Construction Industry into the 21st Century, pp. 40–51.

Al Shaar, E. M., S. A. Khattab, R. N. Alkaied, and A. Q. Manna. 2015. The effect of top management support on innovation: The mediating role of synergy between organizational structure and information technology. *International Review of Management and Business Research* 4 (2): 499–513.

Alavi, M. D., and D. E. Leider. 2001. Knowledge management and knowledge management systems: Conceptual foundations and research issue. *MIS Quarterly* 25 (1): 107–113.

Alcazar, V. 2017. Data you can trust: Blockchain technology. *Air and Space Power Journal*91–101.

Aldag, R. J., and T. M. Stearns. 1991. *Management*. 2nd ed. Cincinnati: South-Western.

Al-Dmour, A., R. Al-Dmour, H. Al-Dmour, and A. Al-Adwan. 2024. Blockchain applications and commercial bank performance: The mediating role of AIS quality. *Journal of Open Innovation: Technology, Market, and Complexity* 10 (2): https://doi.org/10.1016/J.JOITMC.2024.100302.

Alemeye, F., and F. Getahun. 2015. Cloud readiness assessment framework and recommendation system. In *AFRICON 2015*, 1–5. IEEE.

Alhadi, A., B. Tom, and R. Yacine. 2025. Enhancing asset management: Integrating digital twins for continuous permitting and compliance—A systematic literature review. *Journal of Building Engineering* 99. https://doi.org/10.1016/J.JOBE.2024.111515.

Ali, O., P. A. Murray, S. Muhammed, Y. K. Dwivedi, and S. Rashiti. 2022a. Evaluating organizational level IT innovation adoption factors among global firms. *Journal of Innovation & Knowledge* 7 (3): 1–14.

Ali, O., A. Shrestha, A. Jaradat, and A. Al-Ahmad. 2022b. An evaluation of key adoption factors towards using the fog technology. *Big Data and Cognitive Computing* 6 (3): 1–35.

Aliza, A. H., K. Stephen, and T. Bambang. 2011. The importance of project governance framework in project procurement planning. Paper presented at the 12th East AsiaPacific conference on structural engineering and construction. August 23, 2011.

Allen, B. 1995. Qualitative enquiry for rural development: A review. *Journal of Rural Studies* 11 (1): 110–111. https://doi.org/10.1016/0743-0167(95)90023-3.

Alnagrat, A., R. C. Ismail, S. Z. S. Idrus, and R. M. A. Alfaqi. 2022. A review of extended reality (XR) technologies in the future of human education: Current trend and future opportunity. *Journal of Human Centered Technology* 1 (2): 81–96.

Alotaibi, E. M., H. Issa, and M. Codesso. 2025. Blockchain-based conceptual model for enhanced transparency in government records: A design science research approach. *International Journal of Information Management Data Insights* 5 (1): https://doi.org/10.1016/J.JJIMEI.2024.100304.

Alqahtani, S., and S. F. Wamba. 2012. Determine of RFID technology adoption intention in the Saudi retail industry: An empirical study. In IEEE 45th Hawaii International Conference on System Science, pp. 4720–4729.

Altamimi, F., W. Asif, and M. Rajarajan. 2020. DADS: Decentralized (mobile) applications deployment system using blockchain: Secured decentralized applications store. In *Proceedings of the 2020 international conference on computer, information and telecommunication systems, CITS 2020*, 1–8. Institute of Electrical and Electronics Engineers Inc. https://doi.org/10.1109/CITS49457.2020.9232506.

Amadu, L., S. S. Muhammad, A. S. Mohammed, G. Owusu, and S. Lukman. 2018. Using technology acceptance model to measure the use of social media for collaborative learning in Ghana. *Journal of Technology and Science Education* 8 (4): 321–336. https://doi.org/10.3926/jotse.383.

Aman, A. H. M., N. Shaari, Z. S. Attar Bashi, S. Iftikhar, S. Bawazeer, S. H. Osman, and N. S. Hasan. 2024. A review of residential blockchain internet of things energy systems: Resources, storage and challenges. *Energy Reports* 11:1225–1241. https://doi.org/10.1016/J.EGYR.2023.12.062.

Amaratuga, D., D. Baldry, M. Sarshar, and R. Newton. 2002. Quantitative qualitative research in the environment. *Work study* 51 (1): 17–31.

Amaratunga, D., D. Baldry, and M. Sarshar. 2001. Process improvement through performance measurement: The balanced scorecard methodology. *Work Study* 50 (5): 179–188.

Amor, R., B. Kumar, and R. Watson. 2024. Digital regulatory compliance checking for the construction industry. *Advanced Engineering Informatics* 61. https://doi.org/10.1016/J.AEI.2024.102764.

Amsah, S. K. 2011. Causes and effects of delayed payments by clients on construction projects in Ghana. *Journal of Construction Project Management and Innovation* 1:27–45.

Amusan, L. M., L. I. Oloniju, M. Akomolafe, A. Makinde, P. Nkolika-Peter, H. Farayola, and O. Faith. 2018. Adopting Information and Communication Technology in Construction Industry. *International Journal of Mechanical Engineering and Technology* 9 (1): 739–746. http://www.iaeme.com/IJMET/issues.asp?jType=IJMET&Vtype=9&iType=1.

Anderson, R. 2007. *Thematic content analysis (TCA) - Descriptive presentation of qualitative data*, 1–4. Palo Alto: Institute of Transpersonal Psychology.

Andoni, M., V. Robu, D. Flynn, S. Abram, D. Geach, D. Jenkins, P. McCallum, and A. Peacock. 2019. Blockchain technology in the energy sector: A systematic review of challenges and opportunities. *Renewable and Sustainable Energy Reviews* 100:143–174. https://doi.org/10.1016/j.rser.2018.10.014.

Angraal, S., H. M. Krumholz, and W. L. Schulz. 2017. Blockchain technology: Applications in health care. *Circulation: Cardiovascular Quality and Outcomes* 10 (9): https://doi.org/10.1161/CIRCOUTCOMES.117.003800.

Anik, F. I., N. Sakib, and S. I. Ahamed. 2025. Integration of blockchain technology into telehealth framework. *Digital Twin, Blockchain, and Sensor Networks in the Healthy and Mobile City* 59–76. https://doi.org/10.1016/B978-0-443-34174-8.00006-5.

Anjum, A., M. Sporny, and A. Sill. 2017. Blockchain standards for compliance and trust. *IEEE Cloud Computing* 4:84–90.

Anokye, K., O. B. Apea, A. O. Darko, and L. A. Kwabi. 2024. The future of waste management in Ghana: Assessing the feasibility and scalability of smart waste solutions amidst key adoption challenges. *Cleaner Waste Systems* 9. https://doi.org/10.1016/J.CLWAS.2024.100183.

Anumba, C. J., J. Pan, R. R. A. Issa, and I. Mutis. 2008. Collaborative project information management in a semantic web environment. *Engineering, Construction and Architectural Management* 15 (1): 7894. https://doi.org/10.1108/09699980810842089.

Apeh, O. O., and N. I. Nwulu. 2025. Improving traceability and sustainability in the agri-food industry through blockchain technology: A bibliometric approach, benefits and challenges. *Energy Nexus* 17. https://doi.org/10.1016/J.NEXUS.2025.100388.

Apte, S., and N. Petrovsky. 2016. Will blockchain technology revolutionize excipient supply chain management. *Journal of Excipients and Food Chemicals* 7 (3): 76–78.

Arifin, Z. 2015. The effect of dynamic capability to technology adoption and its determinant factors for improving firm's performance; Toward a conceptual model. *Procedia—Social and Behavioral Sciences* 207:786–796.

Arner, D. W., J. Barberis, and R. P. Buckley. 2017. FinTech, RegTech, and the reconceptualization of financial regulation. *Northwestern Journal of International Law & Business* 37 (3): 371–413.

Aronson, J. 1995. A pragmatic view of thematic analysis. *The Qualitative Report* 2 (1): 1–3.

Arora, S., S. Oberoi, T. Nabi, and B. Verma. 2024. How does blockchain impact sustainable food security? Insights from literature review. *International Journal of Information Management Data Insights* 4 (2): https://doi.org/10.1016/J.JJIMEI.2024.100276.

Arsecularatne, B. P., N. Rodrigo, and R. Chang. 2024. Review of reducing energy consumption and carbon emissions through digital twin in built environment. *Journal of Building Engineering* 98. https://doi.org/10.1016/J.JOBE.2024.111150.

Asamoah, M. K. 2013. Penteco/charismatic worldview of prosperity theology. *African Educational Research Journal* 1 (3): 198–208.

Asamoah, K. O., A. P. Darko, C. O. Antwi, C. Sey, A. H. Osei, X. Ma, and J. Zhu. 2024. A probabilistic reliable linguistic model for blockchain-based student information management system assessment. *Applied Soft Computing* 159. https://doi.org/10.1016/J.ASOC.2024.111645.

Ashworth, A., and S. Perera. 2018. *Contractual procedures in the construction industry*. London: Routledge.

Aste, T., P. Tasca, and T. Di Matteo. 2017. Blockchain technologies: The foreseeable impact on society and industry. *IEEE Computer Society*18–28.

Atkin, B., and A. Brooks. 2009. *Total facilities management*. 3rd ed. Chichester, UK: Wiley-Blackwell.

Atzei, N., M. Bartoletti, and T. Cimoli. 2017. A survey of attacks on Ethereum smart contracts (SoK). In *Lecture notes in computer science*, 164–186. Berlin, Heidelberg: Springer. https://doi.org/10.1007/978-3-662-54455-6_8.

Awal, M. R., and M. S. Chowdhury. 2024. Threat or prospect? Exploring the impact of digital entrepreneurs' artificial intelligence perception and intention to adopt blockchain technology on the achievement of SDGs. *Heliyon* 10 (13): https://doi.org/10.1016/J.HELIYON.2024.E33853.

Awodele, I. A., E. C. Eze, A. M. G. Municio, M. S. Ramabodu, and N. A. Olatunde. 2025. Advancing circular economy transition in the Nigeria construction industry through digital twin technology adoption. *Green Technologies and Sustainability* 100201. https://doi.org/10.1016/J.GRETS.2025.100201.

Axon, D. R. 2023. Book review. *Currents in Pharmacy Teaching and Learning* 15 (5): 541–542. https://doi.org/10.1016/J.CPTL.2023.04.021.

Aydin, F., and C. H. Başaran. 2025. Blockchain revolution: Transforming digital health for a secure future. In *Digital healthcare, digital transformation and citizen empowerment in in Asia-Pacific and Europe for a healthier society*, ed. Patricia Ordóñez De Pablos, Mohammad Nabil Almunawar, and Muhammad Anshari, 475–502. Academic Press. https://doi.org/10.1016/B978-0-443-30168-1.00017-7.

Ayeboafo, B., S. Anomah, and K. Amofah. 2025. Leveraging blockchain technology adoption in the fight against corruption: An evaluation of Ghana's readiness. *Journal of Economic Criminology* 100158. https://doi.org/10.1016/J.JECONC.2025.100158.

Aytekin, A., S. Korucuk, H. Akyurt, H. Doğan, Ž. Stević, and E. K. Zavadskas. 2025. Evaluation of metaverse-based digital transformation strategies via an interval-valued q-rung orthopair fuzzy methodology. *Applied Soft Computing* 169. https://doi.org/10.1016/J.ASOC.2024.112566.

Babaei, A., E. Babaee Tirkolaee, and S. S. Ali. 2025. Assessing the viability of blockchain technology in renewable energy supply chains: A consolidation framework. *Renewable and Sustainable Energy Reviews* 212. https://doi.org/10.1016/J.RSER.2025.115444.

Babanagar, N., B. Sheil, J. Ninić, Q. Zhang, and S. Hardy. 2025. Digital twins for urban underground space. *Tunnelling and Underground Space Technology* 155. https://doi.org/10.1016/J.TUST.2024.106140.

Backblom, M., A. Ruohtula, and B. C. Bjork. 2003. Use of document management systems—A case study of the Finnish construction industry. *Electronic Journal of Information Technology in Construction* 8:367–380.

Bagozzi, R. P., and Y. Yi. 2012. Specification, evaluation, and interpretation of structural equation models. *Journal of the Academy of Marketing Science* 40 (1): 8–34.

Bahnas, N., K. Adel, R. Khallaf, and A. Elhakeem. 2024. Monitoring and controlling engineering projects with blockchain-based critical chain project management. *Automation in Construction* 165. https://doi.org/10.1016/J.AUTCON.2024.105484.

Bailey, J. S., and M. R. Burch. 2017. *Research methods in applied behaviour analysis*. UK: Routledge.

Balasubramanian, S., V. Jagannathan, and T. Natarajan. 2018. An extension to the Delone and Mclean information systems success model and validation in the internet banking context. In *Encyclopedia of Information Science and Technology*, ed. M. Khosrow-Puour, 4th ed., 49–60. USA: Information Science Reference.

Bamberger, K. A. 2010. Technologies of compliance: Risk and regulation in a digital age. *Texas Law Review* 88 (4): 669–739.

Banaeian Far, S., and S. M. Hosseini Bamakan. 2025. Third layer blockchains are being rapidly developed: Addressing state-of-the-art paradigms and future horizons. *Journal of Network and Computer Applications* 233. https://doi.org/10.1016/J.JNCA.2024.104044.

Banegas, D. L. 2020. Book review. *Journal of English for Academic Purposes* 43:100826. https://doi.org/10.1016/J.JEAP.2019.100826.

Bao, C. 2025. Book review. *System* 129:103593. https://doi.org/10.1016/J.SYSTEM.2025.103593.

Barima, O. 2017. Leveraging the blockchain technology to improve construction value delivery: The opportunities, benefits and challenges. *Construction Projects*93–112.

Basit, T. 2003. Manual or electronic? The role of coding in qualitative data analysis. *Educational Research* 45 (2): 143–154.

Bateman, T. S., S. Snell, and R. Konopaske. 2018. *Management*. 5th ed. New York: McGraw-Hill Education.

Bates, T. 2001. *Cómo gestionar el cambio tecnológico: Estrategias para los responsables de centros universitarios (6)*. Barcelona: Gedisa.

Bauerle, N. 2017. What is the difference between public and permissioned blockchains?. https://www.coindesk.com/information/what-is-the-difference-betweenopen-and-permissioned-blockchains/. Accessed 15 March 2018.

Beaudry, J. S. 1991. Qualitative research: Analysis types and software tools. *Evaluation Practice* 12 (1): 79–82. https://doi.org/10.1016/0886-1633(91)90027-U.

Becker, M. S. 2009. Project governance: Definition and framework. *Journal of Contemporary Management* 6:214–228.

Bedeian, A. 1993. *Management*. 3rd ed. Orlando: The Dryden Press.

Beikverdi, A., and J. Song. 2015. Trend of centralization in Bitcoin's distributed network. In *2015 IEEE/ACIS 16th international conference on software engineering, artificial intelligence, networking and parallel/distributed computing, SNPD 2015—Proceedings*, 1–6. Institute of Electrical and Electronics Engineers Inc. https://doi.org/10.1109/SNPD.2015.7176229.

Bell, D. S. 2009. *The SAGE encyclopedia of qualitative research methods. Reference reviews*. Sage.

Bellini Machado, L., and M. Massao Futai. 2024. Tunnel performance prediction through degradation inspection and digital twin construction. *Tunnelling and Underground Space Technology* 144. https://doi.org/10.1016/J.TUST.2023.105544.

Bennett, J. 1991. *International construction project management: General theory and practice*. 2nd ed. Oxford: Butterworths Heinemann.

Bennouri, M., T. Chtioui, H. Nagati, and M. Nekhili. 2018. Female board directorship and firm performance: What really matters? *Journal of Banking & Finance* 88:267–291.

Bentler, P. M., and D. G. Bonett. 1980. Significance tests and goodness of fit in the analysis of covariance structures. *Psychological Bulletin* 88 (3): 564–588.

Bentler, P. M., and D. G. Weeks. 1980. Linear structural equations with latent variables. *Psychometrika* 45 (3): 289–308.

Best, D. P. 1996. *The Fourth Resource—Information and its Management*. Aldershot, England: Aslib/Gower.

Bharadwaj, A., O. A. El Sawy, P. A. Pavlou, and N. V. Venkatraman. 2013. Digital business strategy: Toward a next generation of insights. *MIS Quarterly*471–482.

Bhaskaran, K., P. Ilfrich, D. Liffman, C. Vecchiola, P. Jayachandran, A. Kumar, F. Lim, K. Nandakumar, Z. Qin, V. Ramakrishna, and E. G. Teo. 2018. Double-blind consent-driven data sharing on blockchain. In *Proceedings—2018 IEEE international conference on cloud engineering, IC2E 2018*, 385–391. Institute of Electrical and Electronics Engineers Inc. https://doi.org/10.1109/IC2E.2018.00073.

Bilal, M., L. O. Oyedele, J. Qadir, K. Munir, O. O. Akinade, S. O. Ajayi, H. A. Alaka, and H. A. Owolabi. 2015. Analysis of critical features and evaluation of BIM software: Towards a plug-in for construction waste minimization using big data. *International Journal of*

Sustainable Building Technology and Urban Development 6 (4): 211–228. https://doi.org/10.1080/2093761X.2015.1116415.

Bin-Nashwan, S. A., J. Z. Li, H. C. Jiang, A. R. Bajary, and Ma'aji, M. M. 2025. Does AI adoption redefine financial reporting accuracy, auditing efficiency, and information asymmetry? An integrated model of TOE-TAM-RDT and big data governance. *Computers in Human Behavior Reports* 17. https://doi.org/10.1016/J.CHBR.2024.100572.

Biswas, K., and V. Muthukkumarasamy. 2017. Securing smart cities using blockchain technology. In *18th IEEE international conference on high performance computing and communications, 14th IEEE international conference on smart city and 2nd IEEE international conference on data science and systems, HPCC/SmartCity/DSS 2016*, 1392–1393. https://doi.org/10.1109/HPCC-SmartCity-DSS.2016.0198.

Bitmessage. 2019. Bitmessage. https://bitmessage.org/. Accessed 15 January 2022.

Bittorrent. 2019. BitTorrent. https://www.bittorrent.com/. Accessed 15 January 2022.

Bjork, B. C. 1999. Information technology in construction: Domain definition and research issues. *International Journal of Computer Integrated Design and Construction* 1 (1): 3–16.

Bjork, B.-C. 2003. Electronic document management in construction—Research issues and results. *Journal of Information Technology in Construction.* 8:105–117.

Blanco-González-Tejero, C., E. Cano-Marin, K. Ulrich, and S. Giralt-Escobar. 2024. Leveraging blockchain for industry funding: A social media analysis. *Sustainable Technology and Entrepreneurship* 3 (3): https://doi.org/10.1016/J.STAE.2024.100071.

Boddy, D. 2017. *Management—An Introduction*. 7th ed. Harlow: Pearson Education.

Böhmecke-Schwafert, M. 2024. The role of blockchain for trade in global value chains: A systematic literature review and guidance for future research. *Telecommunications Policy* 48 (9): https://doi.org/10.1016/J.TELPOL.2024.102835.

Bohner, E., T. Vehmas, A. Laikari, M. Okkonen, M. Kiviniemi, P. Lahdenperä, and M. Ferreira. 2019. Digitalisation of the quality control of concrete manufacturing and construction. In *Proceedings of the fib symposium 2019: Concrete—Innovations in materials, design and structures*, vol. 900, 1435–1442.

Bolpagni, M., A. Boutle, P. Dodd, J. Dearlove, E. Hooper, J. Ford, D. Rossiter, R. Tennyson, N. Thompson, M. Winfield, and S. Zahiroddiny. 2020. Information management according to BSENISO 19650 guidance Part 2: Processes for project delivery.

Bond, S. 1986. Nursing research—The application of qualitative approaches. *International Journal of Nursing Studies* 23 (4): 366–367. https://doi.org/10.1016/0020-7489(86)90062-3.

Boomsma, A. 2000. Reporting analyses of covariance structures. *Structural Equation Modeling* 7 (3): 461–483.

Boon, W. P., E. Aarden, and J. E. Broerse. 2015. Path creation by public agencies—The case of desirable futures of genomics. *Technological Forecasting and Social Change* 99:67–76.

Boote, D. N., and P. Beile. 2005. Scholars before researchers: On the centrality of the dissertation literature review in research preparation. *Educational Researcher* 34 (6): 3–15.

Boucher, P., S. Nascimento, and M. Kritikos. 2017. *How blockchain technology could change our lives*. European Parliament.

Bougie, R., and U. Sekaran. 2019. *Research methods for business: A skill building approach*. New York: Wiley.

Boumaiza, A., and K. Maher. 2024. Leveraging blockchain technology to enhance transparency and efficiency in carbon trading markets. *International Journal of Electrical Power and Energy Systems* 162. https://doi.org/10.1016/J.IJEPES.2024.110225.

Bourdakis, V. 1997. The future of VRM on Large Urban models. In *Proceedings of UKVRSIG'97*, ed. R. Bowden, 32–40.

Bovée, C. L., J. V. Thill, M. B. Wood, and G. P. Dovel. 1993. *Management*. 11th ed. New York: McGraw-Hill.

Bowden, S. 2005. Application of mobile IT in construction. PhD dissertation, University of Loughborough, Department of Civil and Building Engineering. https://dspace.lboro.ac.uk/dspace-jspui/bitstream/2134/794/3/SarahBowden.pdf. Accessed 22 August 2021.

Bowden, S., A. Dorr, T. Thorpe, and C. Anumba. 2006. Mobile ICT support for construction process improvement. *Automation in Construction* 15 (5): 664–676.

Bower, J., and C. Christensen. 1996. Disruptive technologies: Catching the wave. *The Journal of Product Innovation Management* 1 (13): 75–76.

Boyatzis, R. E. 1998. *Transforming qualitative information: Thematic analysis and code development*. Thousand Oaks: Sage.

Braman, S. 2010. The interpretation of technical and legal decision-making for the internet. *Information, Communication & Society* 13 (3): 309–324.

Brand, V. 2009. Empirical business ethics research and paradigm analysis. *Journal of Business Ethics* 86 (4): 429–449.

Brandín, R., and S. Abrishami. 2024. IoT-BIM and blockchain integration for enhanced data traceability in offsite manufacturing. *Automation in Construction* 159. https://doi.org/10.1016/J.AUTCON.2024.105266.

Braun, V., and V. Clarke. 2006. Using thematic analysis in psychology. *Qualitative Research in Psychology* 3 (2): 77–101.

Bremser, W. G., and N. P. Barsky. 2004. Utilizing the balanced scorecard for R&D performance measurement. *R&D Management* 34 (3): 229–238.

Brickschain. 2018. Brickschain. https://www.brickschain.com/. Accessed 16 July 2021.

Brieschke, P. A. 1992. Reparative praxis: Rethinking the catastrophe that is social science. *Theory into Practice* 31 (2): 173–180.

Briq. 2019. BRIQ: A modern construction data analytics platform. https://www.br.iq/. Accessed 3 Jan 2020.

Brown, A. E., and G. G. Grant. 2005. Framing the frameworks: A review of IT governance research. *Communications of the Association for Information Systems* 15 (1): 38–52.

Brown, C. V., and S. L. Magill. 1994. Alignment of the IS functions with the enterprise: Toward a model of antecedents. *MIS Quarterly*371–403.

Brozovsky, J., N. Labonnote, and O. Vigren. 2024. Digital technologies in architecture, engineering, and construction. *Automation in Construction* 158. https://doi.org/10.1016/J.AUTCON.2023.105212.

Bryman, A. 2009. *Social research methods*. 4th ed. Oxford: Oxford University Press.

Bryman, A., and E. Bell. 2007. *Business research methods*. 2nd ed. UK: Oxford University Press.

Buhalis, D., and E. Marinakou. 2017. Book review. *Tourism Management* 63:12–13. https://doi.org/10.1016/J.TOURMAN.2017.05.010.

Burns, E., and W. Groove. 2014. Research method. *Ergonomics* 32 (3): 237–248.

Burns, A. C., R. F. Bush, and N. Sinha. 2014. *Marketing research*. Vol. 7. Harlow: Pearson.

Burton-Jones, A., and G. S. Hubona. 2005. Individual differences and usage behavior: Revisiting a technology acceptance model assumption. *ACM SIGMIS Database: The Database for Advances in Information Systems* 36 (2): 58–77.

Busby, M. 2018. Blockchain is this year's buzzword—But can it outlive the hype? *The Guardian*.

Buterin, V. 2014. A next-generation smart contract and decentralized application platform. *WhitePaper* 3 (37): 2–10.

Byrd, T. A., and D. E. Turner. 2001. An exploratory examination of the relationship between flexible IT infrastructure and competitive advantage. *Information & Management* 39 (1): 41–52.

Byrne, B. M. 2013. *Structural equation modeling with Mplus: Basic concepts, applications, and programming*. New York: Routledge.

C.P.S. 1991. £13.95 Basis of Qualitative Research: Grounded Theory Procedures and Techniques, A. Strauss, J. Corbin, Sage, New York and Berlin (1990), ISBN: 0-8039-3251-0. *Journal of Environmental Psychology* 11 (4): 387–388. https://doi.org/10.1016/S0272-4944(05)80117-3.

C.P.S. 1992. 77 pp. £6.50 Michael S. Ball, Gregory W.M. Smith, Analyzing Visual Data: Sage Qualitative Research Methods Series No. 24, Sage, New York (1992), ISBN 0 8039 3435. *Journal of Environmental Psychology* 12 (4): 361. https://doi.org/10.1016/S0272-4944(05)80089-1.

Caerteling, J. S., C. A. Di Benedetto, A. G. Dorée, J. I. Halman, and M. Song. 2011. Technology development projects in road infrastructure: The relevance of government championing behaviour. *Technovation* 31 (5–6): 270–283. https://doi.org/10.1016/j.technovation.2011.02.001.

Cai, W., Z. Wang, J. B. Ernst, Z. Hong, C. Feng, and V. C. Leung. 2018. Decentralized applications: The blockchain-empowered software system. *IEEE Access* 6:53019–53033. https://doi.org/10.1109/ACCESS.2018.2870644.

Calvetti, D., P. Mêda, E. Hjelseth, and H. de Sousa. 2025. Incremental digital twin framework: A design science research approach for practical deployment. *Automation in Construction* 170. https://doi.org/10.1016/J.AUTCON.2024.105954.

Campo Gay, I., L. Hvam, A. Haug, G. Q. Huang, and R. Larsson. 2024. A digital tool for life cycle assessment in construction projects. *Developments in the Built Environment* 20. https://doi.org/10.1016/J.DIBE.2024.100535.

Campos, J. 2016. Managing the information systems in the industrial domain. *Cogent Business and Management* 3 (1): 1–33. https://doi.org/10.1080/23311975.2016.1180967.

Capurro, R. 1996. On the genealogy of information. In *New questions to a multidisciplinary concept*, 259–270. Berlin: Akademie Verlag.

Cardeira, H. 2015. Smart contracts and their applications in the construction industry. *Romanian Construction Law Review* 1 (1): 1–6.

Castro, C., V. Leiva, D. Garrido, M. Huerta, and V. Minatogawa. 2024. Blockchain in clinical trials: Bibliometric and network studies of applications, challenges, and future prospects based on data analytics. *Computer Methods and Programs in Biomedicine* 255. https://doi.org/10.1016/J.CMPB.2024.108321.

Catalini, C., and J. S. Gans. 2018. Initial coin offerings and the value of crypto tokens. *National Bureau of Economic Research*. https://www.nber.org/system/files/working_papers/w24418/w24418.pdf. Accessed 14 March 2022.

Çekin, E., and S. Seyis. 2020. BIM execution plan based on BS EN ISO 19650-1 and BS EN ISO 19650-2 standards. In *6th international project and construction management conference, Istanbul*, 1–9.

Celik, Y., I. Petri, and Y. Rezgui. 2023. Integrating BIM and blockchain across construction lifecycle and supply chains. *Computers in Industry* 148. https://doi.org/10.1016/J.COMPIND.2023.103886.

Celoza, A. 2024. Information management for digital asset development and delivery. *Automation in Construction* 165. https://doi.org/10.1016/J.AUTCON.2024.105518.

Certo, S. C., and S. T. Certo. 2016. *Modern management—Concepts and skills (14th global edition)*. Essex: Pearson Education.

Chafiq, T., R. Azmi, A. Fadil, and O. Mohammed. 2024. Investigating the potential of blockchain technology for geospatial data sharing: Opportunities, challenges, and solutions. *Geomatica* 76 (2): https://doi.org/10.1016/J.GEOMAT.2024.100026.

Chakrabarti, A., A. K. Chaudhuri, and W. Bengal. 2017. Blockchain and its Scope in retail. *International Research Journal of Engineering and Technology (IRJET)* 4 (7): 30533056.

Chalmers, M. 2008. *Re-architecting an information/technology literacy course: Breaking new ground and laying foundational pedagogies LOEX conference proceedings* 2008:11. https://commons.emich.edu/loexconf2008/11.

Chan, D. S. 2001. Combining qualitative and quantitative methods in assessing hospital learning environments. *International Journal of Nursing Studies* 38 (4): 447–459.

Chan, F. T., and A. Y. L. Chong. 2013. Determinants of mobile supply chain management system diffusion: A structural equation analysis of manufacturing firms. *International Journal of Production Research* 51 (4): 1196–1213.

Chan, S. L., and N. N. Leung. 2004. Prototype web-based construction project management system. *Journal of Construction Engineering and Management* 130 (6): 935–943. https://doi.org/10.1061/(ASCE)0733-9364(2004)130:6(935).

Chang, J. 2021. Book review. *System* 99:102504. https://doi.org/10.1016/J.SYSTEM.2021.102504.

Chapman-Novakofski, K. 1998. Qualitative Media Analysis David L. Altheide. Newbury Park, CA: Sage, 1996, 88 pp. *The American Journal of Evaluation* 19 (2): 271–272. https://doi.org/10.1016/S1098-2140(99)80209-4.

Charles, D. H., and J. Chris. 2004. *Visualization handbook*. Academic.

Chen, W., and K. Liu. 2023. Book review. *Applied Corpus Linguistics* 3 (1): 100045. https://doi.org/10.1016/J.ACORP.2023.100045.

Chen, Y., X. Qin, and H. Huang. 2024a. Book review. *System* 125:103432. https://doi.org/10.1016/J.SYSTEM.2024.103432.

Chen, Z. S., C. Z. Liang, Y. Q. Xu, W. Pedrycz, and M. J. Skibniewski. 2024b. Dynamic collective opinion generation framework for digital transformation barrier analysis in the construction industry. *Information Fusion* 103. https://doi.org/10.1016/J.INFFUS.2023.102096.

Chen, Z., Y. Liu, E. Wang, H. You, Q. Gao, F. D. Yeung, and J. Li. 2024c. Advancing the deployment and information management of direct air capture: A solution enabled by integrating consortium blockchain system. *Carbon Capture Science and Technology* 13. https://doi.org/10.1016/J.CCST.2024.100300.

Chen, Z., Y. Zhu, F. Pu, and W. Tian. 2024d. A study on basic research priorities and development suggestions for the digital transformation of air traffic management. *Aerospace Traffic and Safety* 1 (1): 1–9. https://doi.org/10.1016/J.AETS.2024.06.004.

Chen, C., K. Zhao, J. Leng, C. Liu, J. Fan, and P. Zheng. 2025a. Integrating large language model and digital twins in the context of industry 5.0: Framework, challenges and opportunities. *Robotics and Computer-Integrated Manufacturing* 94. https://doi.org/10.1016/J.RCIM.2025.102982.

Chen, S., Y. Zheng, F. Wang, E. Cai, Y. Zhang, H. Liu, and Z. Qu. 2025b. Computer vision-based reliability analysis in digital twinning for structural dynamic safety assessment. *Engineering Structures* 326. https://doi.org/10.1016/J.ENGSTRUCT.2024.119532.

Cheng, W. 2011. Exploring problems, controversies and debates: Multiple research methods and analytical approaches in linguistics. *Linguistics and Education* 22 (3): 302–303. https://doi.org/10.1016/J.LINGED.2011.03.003.

Cheng, J. C. P., H. Liu, V. J. L. Gan, M. Das, X. Tao, and S. Zhou. 2023. Construction cost management using blockchain and encryption. *Automation in Construction* 152. https://doi.org/10.1016/J.AUTCON.2023.104841.

Chinda, T., and M. Sherif. 2008. Structural equation model of construction safety culture. *Engineering, Construction and Architectural Management* 15 (2): 98–114.

Cho, S., M. Khan, J. Pyeon, and C. Park. 2021. Blockchain-based network concept model for reliable and accessible fine dust management system at construction sites. *Applied Sciences (Switzerland)* 11 (18): https://doi.org/10.3390/app11188686.

Cho, J., J. Shin, J. Jang, and T. W. Kim. 2025. Automated identification of hazardous zones on construction sites using a 2D digital information model. *Automation in Construction* 170. https://doi.org/10.1016/J.AUTCON.2024.105922.

Chong, H. Y., and A. Diamantopoulos. 2020. Integrating advanced technologies to uphold security of payment: Data flow diagram. *Automation in Construction* 114:103158. https://doi.org/10.1016/j.autcon.2020.103158.

Chowdhury, S., P. Ranaweera, and A. D. Jurcut. 2025. Blockchain for security and privacy in the smart healthcare. *Blockchain and Digital Twin for Smart Healthcare*453–502. https://doi.org/10.1016/B978-0-443-30300-5.00025-7.

Chuen, D. L. K. 2015. *Handbook of digital currency: Bitcoin, innovation, financial instruments, and big data*. Elsevier. https://doi.org/10.1016/C2014-0-01905-3.

Clack, C. D., V. A. Bakshi, and L. Braine. 2016. Smart contract templates: Foundations, design landscape and research directions. arXiv preprint arXiv:1608.00771.

Clarke, M. 1987. From practice to grounded theory: Qualitative research in nursing. *International Journal of Nursing Studies* 24 (3): 271–272. https://doi.org/10.1016/0020-7489(87)90009-5.

Clarke, A., and R. Dawson. 1999. Methods of data collection. *Evaluation Research*c65–c93.

Clayton, D. 2017a. Book review. *Tourism Management* 60:3–4. https://doi.org/10.1016/J.TOURMAN.2016.10.023.

Clayton, D. 2017b. Book review. *Tourism Management* 60:79–80. https://doi.org/10.1016/J.TOURMAN.2016.11.015.

Cleveland, J. A. B. 1997. Computers in construction: What's next? In *Proceedings of the 5th construction congress, Minneapolis, Minnesota.*

Cohen, D. A., R. A. Scribner, and T. A. Farley. 2000. A structural model of health behaviour: A pragmatic approach to explain and influence health behaviours at the population level. *Preventive Medicine* 30 (2): 146–154.

Cohn, A., T. West, and C. Parker. 2017. Smart after all: Blockchain, smart contracts, parametric insurance, and smart energy grids. *Georgetown Law Technology Review* 1:273–304.

Cole, G. A., and P. Kelly. 2015. *Management—Theory and practice*. 8th ed. Andover: Cengage Learning EMEA.

Collins, K. M., A. J. Onwuegbuzie, and I. L. Sutton. 2006. A model incorporating the rationale and purpose for conducting mixed-methods research in special education and beyond. *Learning Disabilities: A Contemporary Journal* 4 (1): 67–100.

Collis, J., and R. Hussey. 2013. *Business research: A practical guide for undergraduate and postgraduate students*. London: Macmillan International Higher Education.

Comer, J. S., and P. C. Kendall. 2013. *The Oxford handbook of research strategies for clinical psychology*. London, UK: Oxford University Press.

Computer Mediated Communication. 2003. Adaptive structuration theory. http://www.uky.edu/~rhuma0/cmc/ast.htm. Accessed 7 Sept 2020.

Condos, J., W. H. Sorrell, and S. L. Donegan. 2016. Blockchain technology: Opportunities and risks. https://legislature.vermont.gov/assets/Legislative-Reports/blockchain-technology-report-fi-nal.pdf. Accessed 15 March 2018.

Conner, D. R. 1993. *Managing at the speed of change: How resilient managers succeed and prosper where others fail*. New York: Random House.

Conway, J. M., and A. I. Huffcutt. 2003. A review and evaluation of exploratory factor analysis practices in organizational research. *Organizational Research Methods* 6 (2): 147–168.

Cooper, D. R., P. S. Schindler, and J. Sun. 2006. *Business research methods*. New York: McGraw-Hill.

Cornick, T. 1990. *Quality management for building design*. London: Butterworth Architecture Management Guides.

Craig, N., and J. Sommerville. 2007. Records management and information processing on construction sites using digital pen and paper. *Records Management Journal* 17 (3): 201–215. https://doi.org/10.1108/09565690710833107.

Cresswell, J. W., and V. L. Plano-Clark. 2011. *Designing and conducting mixed method research*. 2nd ed. Thousand Oaks: SAGE.

Creswell, J. W., and J. D. Creswell. 2017. *Research design: Qualitative, quantitative, and mixed methods approaches*. Thousand Oaks: Sage.

Creswell, J. W., and A. Tashakkori. 2007. Differing perspectives on mixed methods research. *Journal of Mixed Methods Research* 1 (4): 303–308.

Creswell, J. W., V. L. Plano Clark, M. L. Gutmann, and W. E. Hanson. 2003. Advanced mixed methods research designs. In *Handbook of mixed methods in social and behavioural research*, ed. A. Tashakkori and C. Teddlie, 209–240. Thousand Oaks, CA: Sage.

Crosby, M., P. Pattanayak, S. Verma, and V. Kalyanaraman. 2016. Blockchain technology: Beyond bitcoin. *Applied Innoovation* 2:6–10.

Crotty, M. 1998. *The foundations of social research: Meaning and perspective in the research process*. London: Sage Publishing.

Cui, Y. 2025. Book review. *System* 129:103567. https://doi.org/10.1016/J.SYSTEM.2024.103567.

Cunningham, J., N. Davies, S. Devaney, M. Harding, S. Holm, V. Neumann, and J. Ainsworth. 2025. The development of a blockchain-based business model simulator with an application to civic medical data management. *Digital Business* 100112. https://doi.org/10.1016/J.DIGBUS.2025.100112.

Curado, C., and N. Bontis. 2006. The knowledge-based view of the firm and its theoretical precursor. *International Journal of Learning and Intellectual Capital* 3 (4): 367–381.

D4H. 2021. Information management: Challenges in an emergency response. D4H Technologies. www.d4htechnologies.com/blog/6-informationmanagement-challenges-in-an-emergency-response. Accessed 6 September 2021.

Daah, C., A. Qureshi, I. Awan, and S. Konur. 2025. Simulation-based evaluation of advanced threat detection and response in financial industry networks using zero trust and blockchain technology. *Simulation Modelling Practice and Theory* 138. https://doi.org/10.1016/J.SIMPAT.2024.103027.

Dai, H., H. P. Young, T. J. Durant, G. Gong, M. Kang, H. M. Krumholz, W. L. Schulz, and L. Jiang. 2018. TrialChain: A blockchain-based platform to validate data integrity in large, biomedical research studies. *Biomedical Research Studies*1–7.

Dai, Y., J. Wu, S. Mao, X. Rao, B. Gu, Y. Qu, and Y. Lu. 2024. Blockchain empowered access control for digital twin system with attribute-based encryption. *Future Generation Computer Systems* 160:564–576. https://doi.org/10.1016/J.FUTURE.2024.06.037.

Dakhli, Z., Z. Lafhaj, and A. Mossman. 2019. The potential of blockchain in building construction. *Buildings* 9 (4): https://doi.org/10.3390/buildings9040077.

Dalkir, K. 2013. *Knowledge management in theory and practice*. Oxfordshire: Routledge.

Damodaran, A. 2009. *Gestão estratégica do risco*. Porto Alegre: Bookman.

Danuri, M. M., M. C. Munaaim, H. A. Rahman, and M. Hanid. 2006. Late and non-payment issues in the Malaysian construction industry—Contractor's perspective. In *International conference on construction, culture, innovation and management (CCIM)*.

Dapp.com. 2018. 2018 Dapp market report. https://www.dapp.com/article/annual-dapp-market-report-2018. Accessed 15 January 2022.

Das, U. C., and A. K. Mishra. 2019. *Management concepts and practices*. New Delhi: Excel Books Private.

Das, M., X. Tao, and J. C. Cheng. 2021. BIM security: A critical review and recommendations using encryption strategy and blockchain. *Automation in Construction* 126:103682.

Das, M., X. Tao, Y. Liu, and J. C. Cheng. 2022. A blockchain-based integrated document management framework for construction applications. *Automation in Construction* 133:104001.

Dasgupta, S., and B. Gupta. 2010. Organizational culture and technology use in a developing country: An empirical study. In *Proceeding of the SIG global development third annual workshop, Saint Louis, USA, 12 December 2020*, 1–16.

Datta, S., S. K. Jauhar, and S. K. Paul. 2023. Leveraging blockchain to improve nutraceutical supply chain resilience under post-pandemic disruptions. *Computers and Industrial Engineering* 183. https://doi.org/10.1016/J.CIE.2023.109475.

Datti, Y. U. 2017. Appraisal of information technology requirements in quantity surveying firms in Northern Nigeria. *Arid Zone Journal of Engineering, Technology and Environment (AZOJETE)* 13 (3): 24–229.

Davidson, K. 2009. *Monitoring systems for sustainability: What are they measuring?*. Doctoral dissertation submitted to. Australia: University of Adelaide.

Davis, F. D. 1986. A technology acceptance model for empirically testing new end-user information systems: Theory and results. PhD thesis.

Davis, F. D. 1989. Perceived usefulness, perceived ease of use, and user acceptance of information technology. *MIS Quarterly* 13 (3): 319–340.

Davis, F. D., and V. Venkatesh. 1996. A critical assessment of potential measurement biases in the technology acceptance model: Three experiments. *International Journal of Human Computer Studies* 45 (1): 19–45. https://doi.org/10.1006/ijhc.1996.0040.

Davis, F. D., R. P. Bagozzi, and P. R. Warshaw. 1989. User acceptance of computer technology: A comparison of two theoretical models. *Management Science* 35 (8): 982–1003. https://doi.org/10.1287/mnsc.35.8.982.

Davletshina, D., V. K. Reja, and I. Brilakis. 2024. Automating construction of road digital twin geometry using context and location aware segmentation. *Automation in Construction* 168. https://doi.org/10.1016/J.AUTCON.2024.105795.

De Vaus, D. 2013. *Surveys in social research*. Oxfordshire: Routledge.

DeCarlo, L. T. 1997. On the meaning and use of kurtosis. *Psychological Methods* 2 (3): 280–292.

Decker, C., and R. Wattenhofer. 2013. Information propagation in the Bitcoin network. In *13th IEEE international conference on peer-to-peer computing, IEEE P2P 2013—Proceedings*. https://doi.org/10.1109/P2P.2013.6688704.

Dehghani, M., R. William Kennedy, A. Mashatan, A. Rese, and D. Karavidas. 2022. High interest, low adoption. A mixed-method investigation into the factors influencing organisational adoption of blockchain technology. *Journal of Business Research* 149:393–411. https://doi.org/10.1016/J.JBUSRES.2022.05.015.

Deloitte Insights. 2019. The symphonic enterprise Tech Trends 2018. https://www2.deloitte.com/us/en/insights/multimedia/podcasts/tech-trends-2018.html. Accessed 18 December 2019.

DeLone, W. H., and E. R. McLean. 1992. Information systems success: The quest for the dependent variable. *Information Systems Research* 3 (1): 60–95. https://doi.org/10.1287/ISRE.3.1.60.

Demian, P., and D. Walters. 2014. The advantages of information management through building information modelling. *Construction Management and Economics* 32 (12): 1153–1165. https://doi.org/10.1080/01446193.2013.777754.

Denscombe, M. 2008. Communities of practice: A research paradigm for the mixed methods approach. *Journal of Mixed Methods Research* 2 (3): 270–283.

Denzin, N. K., and Y. S. Lincoln. 2011. *Handbook of qualitative research*. London: Sage.

Derakhshan, A., and Javad Zare. 2023. Book review. *Journal of English for Academic Purposes* 66:101312. https://doi.org/10.1016/J.JEAP.2023.101312.

Derenskaya, Y. 2018. Project scope management process. *Baltic Journal of Economic Studies* 4 (1): 118–125.

DeSanctis, G., and M. S. Poole. 1994. Capturing the complexity in advanced technology use: Adaptive structuration theory. *Organization Science* 5 (2): 121–147.

DeSanctis, G., and M. S. Poole. 2004. Structuration theory in information systems research: Methods and controversies. In *Handbook of information systems research*, ed. M. E. Whitman and A. B. Woszczynski, 206–249. Hershey, PA: Idea Group.

Designing Buildings. 2020. Information management. https://www.designingbuildings.co.uk/wiki/Information_management. Accessed 14 April 2021.

Detlor, B. 2010. Information management. *International Journal of Information Management* 30 (2): 103–108. https://doi.org/10.1016/j.ijinfomgt.2009.12.001.

Devitt, P. 2003. Qualitative research and evaluation methods (third edition). *Nurse Education Today* 23 (6): 467. https://doi.org/10.1016/S0260-6917(03)00079-0.

Dhaliwal, A., and S. Malik. 2021. Acceptance and adoption of blockchain technology: An examination of the security & privacy challenges. In *Blockchain for business: How it works and creates value*, 231–249.

Dikbas, A., B. Morten, S. Bayramoglu, and İ. Yitmen. 1999. An automated decision support system model for construction management. In *Proceedings of international conference on durability of building materials and components 8—Service life and asset management, information technology in construction, CIB W78 Workshop, Vancouver, Canada*, 2452–2464.

Dikbas, A., E. Ergen, and H. Giritli. 2009. *Managing IT in construction/managing construction for tomorrow*. London: CRC Press. https://doi.org/10.1201/9781482266665.

Ding, H., H. Huang, Z. Liu, and F. Wang. 2025. Digital aggregate for concrete smart management and lifecycle traceability from gamma-dicalcium silicate carbonation. *Construction and Building Materials* 472:140869. https://doi.org/10.1016/J.CONBUILDMAT.2025.140869.

Dingfelder, H. E., and D. S. Mandell. 2011. Bridging the research-to-practice gap in autism intervention: An application of diffusion of innovation theory. *Journal of Autism and Developmental Disorders* 41 (5): 597–609.

Dixit, S., S. N. Mandal, J. V. Thanikal, and K. Saurabh. 2019. Evolution of studies in construction productivity: A systematic literature review (2006–2017). *Ain Shams Engineering Journal* 10 (3): 555–564.

Dong, Y. 2023. Book review. *Journal of Second Language Writing* 62:101044. https://doi.org/10.1016/J.JSLW.2023.101044.

Dong, J., Y. Jing, Z. He, and C. Dong. 2024. How to empower commercial satellite supply chain: Insurance, government subsidy or blockchain adoption? *Omega (United Kingdom)* 127. https://doi.org/10.1016/J.OMEGA.2024.103083.

Dorri, A., S. S. Kanhere, and R. Jurdak. 2017. Towards an optimized blockchain for IoT. In *2017 IEEE/ACM 2nd international conference on internet-of-things design and implementation, IoTDI 2017 (part of CPS Week)*, 173–178. https://doi.org/10.1145/3054977.3055003.

Drescher, D. 2017. *Blockchain basics—A non-technical introduction in 25 steps*, 81–92. New York: Springer Science and Business Media.

Dressen-Hammouda, D. 2022. Book review. *Journal of English for Academic Purposes* 60:101185. https://doi.org/10.1016/J.JEAP.2022.101185.

Drucker, P. F. 1954. *The practice of management*. New York: Harper Collins.

Drucker, P. (2012). Management challenges for the 21st century., Google eBook.

Du, Y., T. Fujiwara, Habuer, Y. Zhou, and J. Wang. 2025. Optimizing cell phone recycling process: A design science approach integrating blockchain framework, SWOT-AHP strategy, and NFT incentives. *Process Safety and Environmental Protection* 197. https://doi.org/10.1016/J.PSEP.2025.107004.

Duan, K., H. Onyeaka, G. Pang, and Z. Meng. 2024. Pioneering food safety: Blockchain's integration in supply chain surveillance. *Journal of Agriculture and Food Research* 18. https://doi.org/10.1016/J.JAFR.2024.101281.

Ducas, E., and A. Wilner. 2017. The security and financial implications of blockchain technologies: Regulating emerging technologies in Canada. *International Journal* 72 (4): 538–562.

Duffy, A. 2012. Qualitative research methods. *Nurse Education in Practice* 12 (2): e13. https://doi.org/10.1016/J.NEPR.2011.09.003.

Dunham, R. B., and J. L. Pierce. 1989. *Management*. 6th ed. Jon Lepley.

Duo. 2019. State of the Dapps. https://www.stateofthedapps.com/. Accessed 15 January 2022.

Durán, C., C. Fernández-Campusano, R. Carrasco, and E. Carrillo. 2024. DMLBC: Dependable machine learning for seaports using blockchain technology. *Journal of King Saud University—Computer and Information Sciences* 36 (1): https://doi.org/10.1016/J.JKSUCI.2024.101918.

Duyshart, B. H. 1997. *The digital document*. Architectural Press, Reed Educational and Professional Publishing.

Earl, M. J. 1989. *Management strategies for information technology*. Prentice Hall, University Press Cambridge.

Easterby-Smith, M., L. J. Jaspersen, R. Thorpe, and D. Valizade. 2021. *Management and business research*. Thousand Oaks: Sage.

Economist. 2018. The Facebook scandal could change politics as well as the internet. Economist (United Kingdom), 5 February 2018.

Egbu, C., M. P. Vines, and J. Tookey. 2003. The role of knowledge management in e-procurement initiatives for construction organizations. In *19th annual ARCOM conference, 3–5 September 2003*, ed. D. J. Greenwood, 661–669. University of Brighton. Association of Researchers in Construction Management.

Ejiaku, S. A. 2014. Technology adoption: Issues and challenges in information technology adoption in emerging economies. *Journal of International Technology and Information Management* 23 (2): 59–68.

Ekung, S., L. Agu, and N. Iheama. 2017. Influence of project governance on project performance. *PM World Journal*. VI (VIII): 1–18.

Electric. 2017. Blockchain technology: Will it make a difference? *The Electricity Journal* 30 (3): 86–87. https://doi.org/10.1016/jztej.2017.04.007.

Elghaish, F., M. R. Hosseini, S. Matarneh, S. Talebi, S. Wu, I. Martek, M. Poshdar, and N. Ghodrati. 2021. Blockchain and the 'Internet of Things' for the construction industry: Research trends and opportunities. *Automation in Construction* 132. https://doi.org/10.1016/J.AUTCON.2021.103942.

Elghamrawy, T., and F. Boukamp. 2010. Managing construction information using RFID-based semantic contexts. *Automation in Construction* 19 (8): 1056–1066. https://doi.org/10.1016/j.autcon.2010.07.015.

Ellis, D. 1990. Qualitative evaluation and research methods. *International Journal of Information Management* 10 (4): 323. https://doi.org/10.1016/0268-4012(90)90041-P.

Ellis, D. 1998. *Progress and problems in information retrieval*. 2nd ed. London: L.A. Publishing.

Elrom, E. 2019. NEO blockchain and smart contracts, The Blockchain Developer. *Apress*257–298. https://doi.org/10.1007/978-1-4842-4847-8_7.

Enakrire, T. R., and O. G. Onyenania. 2007. Factors affecting the development of information infrastructure in Africa. *Library Hi Tech News* 2:15–20.

Enare Abang, J., H. Takruri, R. Al-Zaidi, and M. Al-Khalidi. 2024. Latency performance modelling in hyperledger fabric blockchain: Challenges and directions with an IoT perspective. *Internet of Things (Netherlands)* 26. https://doi.org/10.1016/J.IOT.2024.101217.

Engle, M. 1999. Qualitative data analysis: An expanded sourcebook (2nd Ed.) Matthew B. Miles and A. Michael Huberman. Thousand Oaks, CA: Sage publications, 1994, 336 pp. *The American Journal of Evaluation* 20 (1): 159–160. https://doi.org/10.1016/S1098-2140(99)80125-8.

Erhan, M., A. Tarhan, and A. Ozsoy. 2019. A conceptual model for blockchain-based software project information sharing. *CEUR Workshop Proceedings* 2476:1–14.

Eriksson, P., and A. Kovalainen. 2008. Case study research. *Qualitative methods in business research*115–136.

Ertz, M., C. Ouerghemmi, and Y. N. Njika. 2024. Impact of the metaverse on sustainability in the construction industry. *Sustainable Futures* 8. https://doi.org/10.1016/J.SFTR.2024.100335.

Estaji, M., and F. Ghiasvand. 2022. Book review. *Journal of English for Academic Purposes* 60:101174. https://doi.org/10.1016/J.JEAP.2022.101174.

Estélyiová, K. 2012. Governance structure of strategic alliances-evidences from the South Moravian Region. *Journal of Competitiveness* 4 (2):

Estélyiová, K., and V. Koráb. 2011. Conditions for making strategic alliances: The case of two enterprises from the South Moravian Region. *Acta Universitatis Agriculturae et Silviculturae Mendelianae Brunensis* 59 (4): 71–78.

Etges, A. P. B. D. S., J. S. D. Souza, and F. J. Kliemann. 2017. Risk management for companies focused on innovation processes. *Production* 27:1–15.

Ethereum. 2018. Ethereum project. https://www.ethereum.org/. Accessed 14 August 2021.

Fan, J. S., M. N. Xu, Y. C. Li, Y. F. Ding, Y. F. Liu, B. Geng, and X. J. Liao. 2025. Mechanics-based digital twin model for structural construction using 3D scanning and FE model updating. *Automation in Construction* 173. https://doi.org/10.1016/J.AUTCON.2025.106109.

Fang, W., W. Chen, P. E. D. Love, H. Luo, H. Zhu, and J. Liu. 2024. A status digital twin approach for physically monitoring over-and-under excavation in large tunnels. *Advanced Engineering Informatics* 62. https://doi.org/10.1016/J.AEI.2024.102648.

Farah, M. B., Y. Ahmed, H. Mahmoud, S. A. Shah, M. O. Al-kadri, S. Taramonli, X. Bellekens, R. Abozariba, M. Idrissi, and A. Aneiba. 2024. A survey on blockchain technology in the maritime industry: Challenges and future perspectives. *Future Generation Computer Systems* 157:618–637. https://doi.org/10.1016/J.FUTURE.2024.03.046.

Faria, F. L. F., A. K. V. de Oliveira, and R. Rüther. 2025. A sustainable blockchain-based framework to develop the Li-ion second-life batteries market. *Energy* 316. https://doi.org/10.1016/J.ENERGY.2025.134603.

Fathi, M. S., M. Abedi, S. Rambat, S. Rawai, and M. Z. Zakiyudin. 2012. Context-aware cloud computing for construction collaboration. *Journal of Cloud Computing* 20:1–15.

Fayol, H. 1916. *Administration industrielle et générale; Prévoyance, organisation, commandement, coordination, controle*. Paris: H. Dunod & E. Pinat.

Feilzer, Y. M. 2010. Doing mixed methods research pragmatically: Implications for the rediscovery of pragmatism as a research paradigm. *Journal of Mixed Methods Research* 4 (1): 6–16.

Fellows, R., and A. Liu. 2008. *Research methods for construction.* 3rd ed. Oxford, UK: Blackwell Science.

Feng, Y. P. 2006. Application of information technology in construction management. In *The CRIOCM 2006 international symposium on "Advancement of Construction Management and Real Estate" Beijing, China, 3rd–5th November*, 46–67.

Feng, H. 2020. Book review. *System* 93:102293. https://doi.org/10.1016/J.SYSTEM.2020.102293.

Ferdous, O., S. Yousefi, and B. M. Tosarkani. 2024. Implications of blockchain technology to sustainable supply chain management. *Encyclopedia of Sustainable Technologies*861–875. https://doi.org/10.1016/B978-0-323-90386-8.00089-9.

Field, A. 2013. *Discovering statistics using IBM SPSS statistics*. Thousand Oaks: Sage.

Figueiredo, K., A. W. A. Hammad, A. Haddad, and V. W. Y. Tam. 2022. Assessing the usability of blockchain for sustainability: Extending key themes to the construction industry. *Journal of Cleaner Production* 343. https://doi.org/10.1016/J.JCLEPRO.2022.131047.

Filecoin. 2021. A decentralized storage network for humanity's most important information | Filecoin. https://filecoin.io/. Accessed 15 January 2022.

Fink, L. 2011. How do IT capabilities create strategic value? Toward greater integration of insights from reductionistic and holistic approaches. *European Journal of Information Systems* 20 (1): 16–33.

Fink, L., and S. Neumann. 2009. Exploring the perceived business value of the flexibility enabled by information technology infrastructure. *Information & Management* 46 (2): 90–99.

FIPS. 1999. *Federal Information Processing Standards Publication: Data encryption standard (DES)*. National Institute of Standards and Technology (NIST), USA.

Flick, U. 2009. *An introduction to qualitative research.* Thousand Oaks, CA: Sage Publications.

Forcada, N. 2005. *Life cycle document management system for construction*. Universitat Politecnica De Catalunya.

Franco, C. W., G. B. Benitez, P. R. de Sousa, F. J. Kliemann Neto, and A. G. Frank. 2024. Managing resources for digital transformation in supply chain integration: The role of hybrid governance structures. *International Journal of Production Economics* 278. https://doi.org/10.1016/J.IJPE.2024.109428.

Fratesi, U. 2018. Handbook of research methods and applications in economic geography. *Papers in Regional Science* 97 (2): 461–462. https://doi.org/10.1111/PIRS.12363.

Frazier, E. 2021. Book review. *Emotion, Space and Society* 40:100820. https://doi.org/10.1016/J.EMOSPA.2021.100820.

Frechtling, D. C. 2012. Research methods for leisure, recreation and tourism. *Tourism Management* 33 (6): 1606–1607. https://doi.org/10.1016/J.TOURMAN.2012.01.009.

Frigo, M. L., and R. J. Anderson. 2011. Strategic risk management: A foundation for improving enterprise risk management and governance. *Journal of Corporate Accounting & Finance* 22 (3): 81–88.

Fu, H. P., and T. S. Chang. 2016. An analysis of the factors affecting the adoption of cloud consumer relationship management in the machinery industry in Taiwan. *Information Development* 32 (5): 1741–1756.

Gaith, F. H., A. R. Khalim, and I. Amiruddin. 2012. Application and efficacy of information technology in construction industry. *Scientific Research and Essays* 7 (38): 3223–3242.

Gálvez-Martos, J. L., D. Styles, H. Schoenberger, and B. Zeschmar-Lahl. 2018. Construction and demolition waste best management practice in Europe. *Resources, Conservation and Recycling* 136:166–178. https://doi.org/10.1016/j.resconrec.2018.04.016.

Gao, L., and R. Huang. 2024. Digital transformation and green total factor productivity in the semiconductor industry: The role of supply chain integration and economic policy uncertainty. *International Journal of Production Economics* 274. https://doi.org/10.1016/J.IJPE.2024.109313.

Garcia, R. D., J. C. Ferreira, L. Zanotti, G. Ramachandran, J. C. Estrella, and J. Ueyama. 2024. An automated decision-making system employing complex networks and blockchain for the decentralized stock market. *Expert Systems with Applications* 257. https://doi.org/10.1016/J.ESWA.2024.125131.

Gaur, A. S., H. O. Sharan, and C. Dudhagara. 2024. Research trends in blockchain and digital twins. *Digital Twins for Smart Cities and Villages*561–580. https://doi.org/10.1016/B978-0-443-28884-5.00024-5.

Georgiev, G. 2018. Russia moves to regulate crypto, issues first commercial bonds via blockchain, bitcoinist. http://bitcoinist.com/russia-moves-to-regulate-crypto-issues-firstcommercial-bonds-transaction-via-blockchain/. Accessed 8 June 2021.

Gervais, A., G. O. Karame, K. Wüst, V. Glykantzis, H. Ritzdorf, and S. Capkun. 2016. On the security and performance of proof of work blockchains. In *Proceedings of the ACM conference on computer and communications security*, 316. https://doi.org/10.1145/2976749.2978341.

Ghaffar, S. H., J. Corker, and M. Fan. 2018. Additive manufacturing technology and its implementation in construction as an eco-innovative solution. *Automation in Construction* 93:1–11. https://doi.org/10.1016/j.autcon.2018.05.005.

Ghobakhloo, M., J. Benitez-Amado, and D. Arias-Aranda. 2011. Reasons for information technology adoption and sophistication within manufacturing SMEs. In *POMS 22nd annual conference: Operations management: The enabling link. Reno, USA, April (29)*, 87–98.

Ghobakhloo, M., T. S. Hong, M. S. Sabouri, and N. Zulkifli. 2012. Strategies for successful information technology adoption in small and medium-sized enterprises. *Information* 3 (1): 36–67.

Giaglis, G. M., and K. N. Kypriotaki. 2014. Towards an agenda for information systems research on digital currencies and bitcoin. *Lecture Notes in Business Information Processing* 183:3–13. https://doi.org/10.1007/978-3-319-11460-6_1.

Giddens, A. 1979. *Central problems in social theory: Action, structure, and contradictions in social analysis*. London, UK: Macmillan.

Gilmour, P., D. Pandey, and D. Goldbarsht. 2025. Registers of beneficial owners based on blockchain technology: Implications for the accounting profession. *Technological Forecasting and Social Change* 214. https://doi.org/10.1016/J.TECHFORE.2025.124051.

Giugliani, E. A. 2012. *Governance model for science and technology parks: What are the STP's evolving into*. Tallin: International Association of Science Parks.

Glasgow, R. E. 2013. What does it mean to be pragmatic? Pragmatic methods, measures, and models to facilitate research translation. *Health Education & Behavior* 40 (3): 257–265.

Global Industry Council. 2018. Five Keys to Unlocking Digital Transformation in Engineering & Construction. Australia.

Goldsby, C. M., and M. Hanisch. 2023. Agency in the algorithmic age: The mechanisms and structures of blockchain-based organizing. *Journal of Business Research* 168. https://doi.org/10.1016/J.JBUSRES.2023.114195.

Golosova, J., and A. Romanovs. 2018. The Advantages and disadvantages of the blockchain technology. https://doi.org/10.1109/AIEEE.2018.8592253.

Gong, H., D. Su, S. Zeng, and X. Chen. 2024a. Advancements in digital twin modeling for underground spaces and lightweight geometric modeling technologies. *Automation in Construction* 165. https://doi.org/10.1016/J.AUTCON.2024.105578.

Gong, Y., B. Yu, L. Yang, F. Meng, L. Liu, X. Hu, and Z. Xu. 2024b. Toward next-generation networks: A blockchain-based approach for core network architecture and roaming identity verification. *Digital Communications and Networks*. https://doi.org/10.1016/J.DCAN.2024.08.008.

Goodman, J. 2009. Thomson Financial's Comms resources for managers. *Strategic Communication Management* 13 (4): 12.

Goosen, R., and R. Rudman. 2013. An integrated framework to implement IT governance principles at a strategic and operational level for medium-to large-sized South African businesses. *International Business and Economics Research Journal* 12 (7): 835–854.

Görçün, Ö. F., D. Pamucar, and S. Biswas. 2023. The blockchain technology selection in the logistics industry using a novel MCDM framework based on Fermatean fuzzy sets and Dombi aggregation. *Information Sciences* 635:345–374. https://doi.org/10.1016/J.INS.2023.03.113.

Govindan, K., P. Jain, R. Kr. Singh, and R. Mishra. 2024. Blockchain technology as a strategic weapon to bring procurement 4.0 truly alive: Literature review and future research agenda. *Transportation Research Part E: Logistics and Transportation Review* 181. https://doi.org/10.1016/J.TRE.2023.103352.

Govindarajan, U. H., G. Narang, D. K. Singh, and V. S. Yadav. 2025. Blockchain technologies adoption in healthcare: Overcoming barriers amid the hype cycle to enhance patient care. *Technological Forecasting and Social Change* 213. https://doi.org/10.1016/J.TECHFORE.2025.124031.

Goyal, N., M. Howlett, and A. Taeihagh. 2021. Why and how does the regulation of emerging technologies occur? Explaining the adoption of the EU General Data Protection Regulation using the multiple streams framework. *Regulation & Governance* 15 (4): 1020–1034.

Graf-Vlachy, L., K. Buhtz, and A. König. 2018. Social influence in technology adoption: Taking stock and moving forward. *Management Review Quarterly* 68 (1): 37–76.

Grant, R. 1996. Towards a knowledge-based view of the firm. *Strategic Management Journal* 17:109–122.

Greene, J. C., and V. J. Caracelli. 1997. *Advances in mixed-method evaluation: The challenges and benefits of integrating diverse paradigms*. San Francisco: Jossey.

Griffin, R. W. 2013. *Management—Principles and practices (11th international edition)*. Boston: Cengage Learning South-Western.

Griffis, M. 2013. Book Review. *Library & Information Science Research* 35 (3): 252–253. https://doi.org/10.1016/J.LISR.2013.05.001.

Griffith, A. 2000. Integrated management systems: A single management system for project control? *Engineering, Construction and Architectural Management* 7 (3): 232–240.

Grover, V., and T. H. Davenport. 2001. General perspectives on knowledge management: Fostering a research agenda. *Journal of Management Information Systems* 18 (1): 5–21.

Grubesic, T. H., and A. T. Murray. 2004. Waiting for broadband: Local competition and the spatial distribution of advanced telecommunication services in the United States. *Growth and Change* 35 (2): 139–165.

Guan, Z., and L. J. Zhang. 2024. Book review. *System* 125:103421. https://doi.org/10.1016/J.SYSTEM.2024.103421.

Gulati, R., A. J. Mayo, and N. Nohrian. 2017. *Management—An integrated approach*. Boston: Cengage Learning.

Guldentops, E., S. De Haes, G. Hardy, J. Ormsby, D. F. Ramos, J. Singleton, and P. A. Williams. 2011. *Board briefing on IT governance*. Rolling Meadows, IL: IT Governance Institute.

Gulen, M. F., and O. Arslan. 2025. Holistic risk assessment approach for seafarers' adaptation to digital transformation. *Ocean Engineering* 328:121024. https://doi.org/10.1016/J.OCEANENG.2025.121024.

Gulen, M. F., E. Uflaz, F. Gumus, M. Orhan, and O. Arslan. 2025. An integrated SWOT-based interval type-2 fuzzy AHP and TOPSIS methodology for digital transformation strategy selection in maritime safety. *Ocean Engineering* 323. https://doi.org/10.1016/J.OCEANENG.2025.120518.

Guo, Y., and C. Liang. 2016. *Blockchain application and outlook in the banking industry, financial innovation*. SpringerOpen. https://doi.org/10.1186/s40854-016-0034-9.

Guo, Y., and W. Ren. 2022. Book review. *Journal of Pragmatics* 200:191–193. https://doi.org/10.1016/J.PRAGMA.2022.09.002.

Guo, F., C. T. Jahren, and Y. Turkan. 2021. Electronic document management systems for the transportation construction industry. *International Journal of Construction Education and Research* 17 (1): 52–67.

Guo, Y., J. Ren, Y. Liang, and Y. Ding. 2023. Construction of digital twin for clamped near-net-shape blade in adaptive manufacturing. *Journal of Manufacturing Processes* 108:12–25. https://doi.org/10.1016/J.JMAPRO.2023.10.055.

Guo, C., R. Li, and B. Yuan. 2025. Mathematical models of digital transformation asymmetric information game in energy enterprises. *Alexandria Engineering Journal* 113:584–592. https://doi.org/10.1016/J.AEJ.2024.11.047.

Gutek, B. A., T. K. Bikson, and D. Mankin. 1984. Individual and organizational consequences of computer-based office information technology. *Applied Social Psychology Annual: Applications in Organizational Settings* 5:231–254.

Guz, A. N., and J. J. Rushchitsky. 2009. Scopus: A system for the evaluation of scientific journals. *International Applied Mechanics* 45 (4): 351–362. https://doi.org/10.1007/s10778-009-0189-4.

Hair, J. F., W. C. Black, B. J. Babin, and R. E. Anderson. 2010. *Multivariate data analysis. A global perspective*. Upper Saddle River: Pearson.

Halawi, L. and Mccarthy, R. (2006) Which Theory Applies:An analysis of information Systems Research Issues in Information Systems, 7(2), pp. 252–256.

Hall, G. 2004. Book review. *System* 32 (4): 605–608. https://doi.org/10.1016/J.SYSTEM.2004.09.004.

Hameed, M. A., S. Counsell, and S. Swift. 2012a. A conceptual model for the process of IT innovation adoption in organizations. *Journal of Engineering and Technology Management* 29 (3): 358–390. https://doi.org/10.1016/jjengtecman.2012.03.007.

Hameed, M. A., S. Counsell, and S. Swift. 2012b. A meta-analysis of relationships between organizational characteristics and IT innovation adoption in organizations. *Information & Management* 49 (5): 218–232.

Hamida, E. B., K. L. Brousmiche, H. Levard, and E. Thea. 2017. Blockchain for enterprise: Overview, opportunities and challenges. In *ICWMC 2017: The thirteenth international conference on wireless and mobile communications*, vol. 3, 83–88.

Hamidi, S. M. M., S. F. Hoseini, H. Gholami, and M. Kananizadeh-Bahmani. 2024. A three-stage digital maturity model to assess readiness for blockchain implementation in the maritime logistics industry. *Journal of Industrial Information Integration* 41. https://doi.org/10.1016/J.JII.2024.100643.

Hamidoğlu, A., Ö. M. Gül, and S. N. Kadry. 2024. A game-theoretical approach for the adoption of government-supported blockchain application in the IoT-enabled agricultural supply chain. *Internet of Things (Netherlands)* 26. https://doi.org/10.1016/J.IOT.2024.101163.

Hamledari, H., and M. Fischer. 2021. The application of blockchain-based crypto assets for integrating the physical and financial supply chains in the construction & engineering industry. *Automation in Construction* 127. https://doi.org/10.1016/J.AUTCON.2021.103711.

Hammoud, O., I. Tarkhanov, and A. Kosmarski. 2021. An architecture for distributed electronic documents storage in decentralized blockchain B2B applications. *Computers* 10 (11): 1–14. https://doi.org/10.3390/computers10110142.

Han, M., J. Zhang, Y. Huang, J. Xu, X. Chen, and B. M. Chen. 2025. Enhancing worker monitoring and management on large-scale construction sites with UAVs and digital twin modeling. *Automation in Construction* 174. https://doi.org/10.1016/J.AUTCON.2025.106108.

Hanafizadeh, P., and M. Alipour. 2024. Taxonomy of theories for blockchain applications in business and management. Digital. *Business* 4 (2): https://doi.org/10.1016/J.DIGBUS.2024.100080.

Hanson, W. E., J. W. Creswell, V. P. Clark, K. S. Petska, and J. D. Creswell. 2005. Mixed methods research designs in counseling psychology. *Journal of Counseling Psychology* 52 (2): 224–235.

Harber, C. 1991. Doing educational research in developing countries: Qualitative strategies. *International Journal of Educational Development* 11 (1): 85–86. https://doi.org/10.1016/0738-0593(91)90013-X.

Hargaden, V., N. Papakostas, A. Newell, A. Khavia, and A. Scanlon. 2019. The role of blockchain technologies in construction engineering project management. In *Proceedings—2019 IEEE international conference on engineering, technology and innovation, ICE/ITMC 2019*. https://doi.org/10.1109/ICE.2019.8792582.

Hariyani, D., P. Hariyani, S. Mishra, and M. K. Sharma. 2025. A literature review on transformative impacts of blockchain technology on manufacturing management and industrial engineering practices. *Green Technologies and Sustainability* 3 (3): https://doi.org/10.1016/J.GRETS.2025.100169.

Harris, M. M., and J. Schaubroeck. 1990. Confirmatory modeling in organizational behavior/human resource management: Issues and applications. *Journal of Management* 16 (2): 337–360.

Hasan, H., E. AlHadhrami, A. AlDhaheri, K. Salah, and R. Jayaraman. 2019. Smart contract-based approach for efficient shipment management. *Computers and Industrial Engineering* 136:149–159. https://doi.org/10.1016/j.cie.2019.07.022.

Hassan, M., S. S. A. S. Kazmi, and S. F. Padlee. 2019. Technology acceptance model (TAM) and dynamics of online purchase adaptability. *International Journal of Recent Technology and Engineering* 8 (1): 390–402.

Hassan, A. M., Y. T. Negash, and F. Hanum. 2024. An assessment of barriers to digital transformation in circular construction: An application of stakeholder theory. *Ain Shams Engineering Journal* 15 (7): https://doi.org/10.1016/J.ASEJ.2024.102787.

Hassani, H., and S. MacFeely. 2025. Integration of digital twin and blockchain for smart hospitals. *Sensor Networks for Smart Hospitals* 603–616. https://doi.org/10.1016/B978-0-443-36370-2.00030-X.

Hasson, F., S. Keeney, and H. McKenna. 2000. Research guidelines for the Delphi survey technique. *Journal of Advanced Nursing* 32 (4): 1008–1015.

Hauser, J., G. J. Tellis, and A. Griffin. 2006. Research on innovation: A review and agenda for marketing science. *Marketing Science* 25 (6): 687–717.

Hawashin, D., M. Nemer, S. A. Gebreab, K. Salah, R. Jayaraman, M. K. Khan, and E. Damiani. 2024. Blockchain applications in UAV industry: Review, opportunities, and challenges. *Journal of Network and Computer Applications* 230. https://doi.org/10.1016/J.JNCA.2024.103932.

Hazarika, N., and X. Zhang. 2019. Factors that drive and sustain eco-innovation in the construction industry: The case of Hong Kong. *Journal of Cleaner Production* 238:117816. https://doi.org/10.1016/jjdepro.2019.117816.

He, Y., Z. Zhou, Y. Pan, F. Chong, B. Wu, K. Xiao, and H. Li. 2024. Review of data security within energy blockchain: A comprehensive analysis of storage, management, and utilization. *High-Confidence Computing* 4 (3): https://doi.org/10.1016/J.HCC.2024.100233.

Heap, I. 2017. Blockchain could help musicians make money again, Harvard Business Review. *Harvard Business School Publishing Corporation*2–7.

Heather, N. 1996. The public health and brief interventions for excessive alcohol consumption: The British experience. *Addictive Behaviours* 21 (6): 857–868.

Heiskanen, A. 2017. The technology of trust: How the Internet of Things and blockchain could usher in a new era of construction productivity. *Construction Research and Innovation* 8 (2): 66–70. https://doi.org/10.1080/20450249.2017.1337349.

Hennink, M. M., B. N. Kaiser, and V. C. Marconi. 2017. Code saturation versus meaning saturation: How many interviews are enough? *Qualitative Health Research* 27 (4): 591–608.

Heppner, P.P., Witty, T.E. and Dixon, W.A. (2004). Problem-solving appraisal and human adjustment: A review of 20 years of research using the problem-solving \inventory. The Counseling Psychologist, 32(3), pp. 344–428.

Heron, J. 1996. *Co-operative inquiry: Research into the human condition*. Sage.

Herrera, D. I. 2023. Book review. *System* 114:103026. https://doi.org/10.1016/J.SYSTEM.2023.103026.

Heydari, M., and A. Shojaei. 2025. Blockchain applications in the construction supply chain. *Automation in Construction* 171. https://doi.org/10.1016/J.AUTCON.2025.105998.

Hitt, M. A., J. S. Black, and L. W. Porter. 2012. *Management*. 3rd ed. Hoboken, NJ: Pearson.

Hjelt, M., and B.-C. Bjork. 2006. Experiences of EDM usage in construction projects. *Journal of Information Technology in Construction: Itcon* 11:113–125.

Holden, H., and R. Rada. 2011. Understanding the influence of perceived usability and technology self-efficacy on teachers' technology acceptance. *Journal of Research on Technology in Education* 43 (4): 343–367.

Hollander, A., E. Denna, and J. O. Cherrington. 1999. *Accounting, information technology, and business solutions*. McGraw-Hill Higher Education.

Holotiuk, F., and J. Moormann. 2018. Organizational adoption of digital innovation: The case of blockchain technology. In *26th European conference on information systems: Beyond digitization—Facets of socio-technical change, ECIS 2018*.

Holt, G. D. 2013. Asking questions, analysing answers: Relative importance revisited. *Construction Innovation* 14 (1): 2–16.

Hong, W., J. Y. L. Thong, W. Wong, and K. Tam. 2002. Determinants of user acceptance of digital libraries: An empirical examination of individual differences and system characteristics. *Journal of Management Information Systems/Winter 2001–2002* 18 (3): 97–124.

Hong, W., F. K. Chan, J. Y. Thong, L. C. Chasalow, and G. Dhillon. 2014. A framework and guidelines for context-specific theorizing in information systems research. *Information Systems Research* 25 (1): 111–136.

Honghong, S., Y. Gang, L. Haijiang, Z. Tian, and J. Annan. 2023. Digital twin enhanced BIM to shape full life cycle digital transformation for bridge engineering. *Automation in Construction* 147. https://doi.org/10.1016/J.AUTCON.2022.104736.

Hooper, D., J. Coughlan, and M. Mullen. 2008. Evaluating model fit: A synthesis of the structural equation modelling literature. In *7th European Conference on research methodology for business and management studies*, 195–200.

Hsu, C. W., and C. C. Yeh. 2017. Understanding the factors affecting the adoption of the Internet of Things. *Technology Analysis & Strategic Management* 29 (9): 1089–1102.

Hsu, I. Y., T. S. Su, C. S. Kao, Y. L. Shu, P. R. Lin, and J. M. Tseng. 2012. Analysis of business safety performance by structural equation models. *Safety Science* 50 (1): 1–11.

Hu, L. T., and P. M. Bentler. 1999. Cut-off criteria for fit indexes in covariance structure analysis: Conventional criteria versus new alternatives. *Structural Equation Modeling: A Multidisciplinary Journal* 6 (1): 1–55.

Hu, X., B. Xia, M. Skitmore, and Q. Chen. 2016. The application of case-based reasoning in construction management research: An overview. *Automation in Construction*65–74. https://doi.org/10.1016/j.autcon.2016.08.023.

Huang, L., and L. Chen. 2024. Book review. *Journal of Second Language Writing* 65:101133. https://doi.org/10.1016/J.JSLW.2024.101133.

Huang, W., Y. Han, Q. Gu, X. Han, and T. Gao. 2025. Smart blockchain-powered natural resource asset management and ecological governance countermeasures. *Heliyon* 11 (2): https://doi.org/10.1016/J.HELIYON.2024.E41475.

Huckle, S., R. Bhattacharya, M. White, and N. Beloff. 2016. Internet of things, blockchain and shared economy applications. *Procedia Computer Science*461–466. https://doi.org/10.1016/j.procs.2016.09.074.

Hughes, W. P. 1989. Identifying environment of construction projects. *Construction Management Economics* 5 (2): 7–29.

Hughes, D. 2017. The impact of blockchain technology on the construction industry. https://medium.com/the-basics-of-blockchain/the-impact-ofblockchain-technology-on-the-construction-industry-85ab78c4aba6. Accessed 30 July 2021.

Hultgren, M., and F. Pajala. 2018. *Blockchain technology in construction industry*. Transparency and Traceability in Supply Chain.

Hussey, L. K. 2010. Qualitative methods in business research. By Päivi Eriksson and Anne Kovalainen. Los Angeles: SAGE, 2008. (Introducing Qualitative Methods Series). 352pp. $99.95 (cloth), $49.95 (pbk). ISBN978-1412903165 (cloth), 978-1412903172 (pbk). *Library & Information Science Research* 32 (1): 92–93. https://doi.org/10.1016/J.LISR.2009.09.001.

Hussey, S. R. 2012. BOOK REVIEW. *The Journal of Academic Librarianship* 38 (3): 186. https://doi.org/10.1016/J.ACALIB.2012.03.002.

Iacobucci, D. 2010. Structural equations modeling: Fit indices, sample size, and advanced topics. *Journal of Consumer Psychology* 20 (1): 90–98.

Ibrahim, H. S., N. Hashim, and K. A. A. Jamal. 2019. The potential benefits of building information modelling (BIM) in construction industry. In *IOP conference series: Earth and environmental science*, vol. 385, 012047. IOP Publishing.

Idol, C. 2018. China to establish blockchain national standards, coin idol. https://coinidol.com/china-to-establish-blockchain-national-standards/. Accessed 8 June 2021.

Idrissi Gartoumi, K. 2024. Five-year review of blockchain in construction management: Scientometric and thematic analysis (2017–2023). *Automation in Construction* 168. https://doi.org/10.1016/J.AUTCON.2024.105773.

Ikpe, E. O. 2009. Development of cost benefit analysis model of accident prevention on construction projects. Doctoral dissertation, University of Wolverhampton.

Ikudayisi, A. E., A. P. C. Chan, A. Darko, and Y. M. D. Adedeji. 2023. Integrated practices in the architecture, engineering, and construction industry: Current scope and pathway towards Industry 5.0. *Journal of Building Engineering* 73. https://doi.org/10.1016/J.JOBE.2023.106788.

Imbambi, R. M., M. Oloko, and C. M. Rambo. 2017. Influence of technology capability on competitive advantage of sugar companies in Western Kenya. *International Journal of Academic Research in Business and Social Sciences* 7 (2): 178–192.

Information Technology Association of America (ITAA). 2010. Information Technology (p. 30). http://www.itaa.org/es/docs/Information%20Technology%20Definitions.pdf. Accessed August 3, 2021.

Institution of Civil Engineers. 2018. Shaping a Digital World POST EVENT REPORT Harnessing digitally enabled innovation.

International Organisation for Standardisation (ISO). 2018a. ISO 19650-1:2018(en), Organization and digitization of information about buildings and civil engineering works, including building information modelling (BIM)—Information management using building information modelling—Part 1: Concepts and principles. https://www.iso.Org/obp/ui/#iso:std:iso:19650:-1:ed-1:v1:en. Accessed 4 January 2022.

International Organisation for Standardisation (ISO). 2018b. ISO 19650-2:2018(en), Organization and digitization of information about buildings and civil engineering works, including building information modelling (BIM)—Information management using building information modelling—Part 2: Delivery phase of the assets. https://www.iso.org/obp/ui/#iso:std:iso:19650:-2:ed-1:v1:en. Accessed 4 January 2022.

InterPlanetary File System. 2021. IPFS powers the distributed web. https://ipfs.io/. Accessed 15 January 2022.

Iorio, E. D. D. 2017. Blockchain applications that are transforming society. Blockgeeks. https://blockgeeks.com/guides/blockchain-applications/. Accessed 07 July 2021.

Isiaku, L., and A. Adalier. 2024. Analyzing the barriers to blockchain adoption in educational sectors: A comprehensive literature review using the Technology-Organizational-Environment (TOE) framework. On the Horizon. https://doi.org/10.1108/OTH-05-2024-0029.

Jack, E. P., and A. S. Raturi. 2006. Lessons learned from methodological triangulation in management research. *Management Research News* 29 (6): 345–357.

Jallow, A. K., P. Demian, C. J. Anumba, and A. N. Baldwin. 2017. An enterprise architecture framework for electronic requirements information management. *International Journal of Information Management* 37 (5): 455–472.

Jaskyte, K. 2011. Predictors of administrative and technological innovations in non-profit organizations. *Public Administration Review* 71 (1): 77–86.

Jasrotia, S. S., S. S. Rai, S. Rai, and S. Giri. 2024. Stage-wise green supply chain management and environmental performance: Impact of blockchain technology. *International Journal of Information Management Data Insights* 4 (2): https://doi.org/10.1016/J.JJIMEI.2024.100241.

Jean, K. 1992. *Livelihood strategies among farm youth in Rwanda*. Michigan: Michigan State University.

Jessop, B. 1997. The governance of complexity and the complexity of governance: Preliminary remarks on some problems and limits of economic guidance. In *Beyond market and hierarchy: Interactive governance and social complexity*, 111–147. London: Edward Elgar.

Jha, A. K., C. M. DesRoches, E. G. Campbell, K. Donelan, S. R. Rao, T. G. Ferris, A. Shields, S. Rosenbaum, and D. Blumenthal. 2009. Use of electronic health records in US hospitals. *New England Journal of Medicine* 360 (16): 1628–1638.

Jia, X., J. Xu, M. Han, Q. Zhang, L. Zhang, and X. Chen. 2023. International standardization of blockchain and distributed ledger technology: Overlaps, gaps and challenges. *CMES—Computer Modeling in Engineering and Sciences* 137 (2): 1491–1523. https://doi.org/10.32604/CMES.2023.026357.

Jiang, P., Zhang, L., You, S., Fan, Y. van, Tan, R. R., Klemeš, J. J., & You, F. (2023). Blockchain technology applications in waste management: Overview, challenges and opportunities. Journal of Cleaner Production, 421. doi:https://doi.org/10.1016/J.JCLEPRO.2023.138466.

Jiang, L., A. Yao, W. Li, and Q. Wei. 2024a. Blockchain technology empowers the cross-border dual-channel supply chain: Introduction strategy, tax differences, optimal decisions. *Computers and Industrial Engineering* 195. https://doi.org/10.1016/J.CIE.2024.110431.

Jiang, Y., S. Su, S. Zhao, R. Y. Zhong, W. Qiu, M. J. Skibniewski, I. Brilakis, and G. Q. Huang. 2024b. Digital twin-enabled synchronized construction management: A roadmap from construction 4.0 towards future prospect. *Developments in the Built Environment* 19. https://doi.org/10.1016/J.DIBE.2024.100512.

Jiang, T., H. Luo, K. Yang, G. Sun, H. Yu, Q. Huang, A. Vasilakos, and v. 2025. Blockchain for energy market: A comprehensive survey. *Sustainable Energy, Grids and Networks* 41. https://doi.org/10.1016/J.SEGAN.2024.101614.

Jin, S., and B. Karki. 2024. Integrating IoT and blockchain for intelligent inventory management in supply chains: A multi-objective optimization approach for the insurance industry. *Journal of Engineering Research (Kuwait)*. https://doi.org/10.1016/J.JER.2024.04.021.

JNT Association. 2007. Introduction to video conferencing. http://www.ja.net/vtas © The JNT Association.

Johnman, C. 2010. Research methods in health—Investigating health and health services. *Public Health* 124 (2): 122. https://doi.org/10.1016/J.PUHE.2010.01.006.

Johnson, R. 2015. Book review. *Journal of Transport Geography* 44:89. https://doi.org/10.1016/J.JTRANGEO.2015.03.003.

Johnson, B., and L. A. Turner. 2003. Data collection strategies in mixed methods research. In *Handbook of mixed methods in social and behavioral research*, 297–319.

Johnston, D., S. O. Yilmaz, J. Kandah, N. Bentenitis, F. Hashemi, R. Gross, and S. Mason. 2014. *The general theory of decentralized applications*. Haettu osoitteesta. http://cryptochainuni.com/wpcontent/uploads/The-General-Theory-of-Decentralized-Applications-DApps.pdf.

Jokonya, O. 2014. A framework to assist organisations with information technology adoption governance. Doctoral dissertation, University of South Africa.

Jones, G. R., and J. M. George. 2018. *Contemporary management*. 10th ed. New York: McGraw-Hill Education.

Jonker, J., and B. W. Pennink. 2010. *The essence of research methodology*. Heidelberg, Germany: Springer. https://doi.org/10.1159/000046658.

Joshi, R., S. Kumari, and K. Pandey. 2024. Rise of blockchain based digital twin: A transformative tool for new research trends. In *Digital twins for smart cities and villages*, 601–630. https://doi.org/10.1016/B978-0-443-28884-5.00026-9.

Jung, Y., and S. Woo. 2004. Flexible work breakdown structure for integrated cost and schedule control. *Journal of Construction Engineering and Management* 130 (5): 616–625. https://doi.org/10.1061/(ASCE)0733-9364(2004)130:5(616).

Jüttner, U. 2005. Supply chain risk management: Understanding the business requirements from a practitioner perspective. *The International Journal of Logistics Management*.

Jwaifell, M., and A. Gasaymeh. 2013. Using the diffusion of innovation theory to explain the degree of English teachers' adoption of interactive whiteboards in the modern systems school in Jordan: A case study. *Contemporary Educational Technology* 4 (2): 138–149.

Kagioglou, M., R. Cooper, G. Aouad, and M. Sexton. 2000. Rethinking construction: The generic design and construction process protocol. *Engineering, Construction and Architectural Management* 7 (2): 141–153.

Kaiser, F. H. 1970. A second-generation little jiffy. *Psychometrika* 35 (4): 401–415.

Kakavand, H., N. Kost De Sevres, and B. Chilton. 2017. The blockchain revolution: An analysis of regulation and technology related to distributed ledger technologies. *Social Science Research Network (SSRN)*. https://doi.org/10.2139/ssrn.2849251.

Kaladharan, S., D. Manayath, and R. Patri. 2024. Barriers to blockchain-enabled drug recycling: A TISM-MICMAC approach. *Sustainable Chemistry and Pharmacy* 41. https://doi.org/10.1016/J.SCP.2024.101737.

Kang, T. W. 2018. Blockchain-based BIM, smart contract and trend. In *Proceedings of communications of the Korean institute of information scientists and engineers, December 12–23, Seoul, Korea*.

Kang, J., R. Yu, X. Huang, S. Maharjan, Y. Zhang, and E. Hossain. 2017. Enabling localized peer-to-peer electricity trading among plug-in hybrid electric vehicles using consortium blockchains. *IEEE Transactions on Industrial Informatics* 13 (6): 3154–3164. https://doi.org/10.1109/TII.2017.2709784.

Kaplan, D. 2008. *Structural equation modeling: Foundations and extensions*. Vol. 10. California: SAGE Publishing.

Karafiloski, E., and A. Mishev. 2017. Blockchain solutions for big data challenges: A literature review. In *IEEE international conference on smart technologies, EUROCON 2017 conference proceedings*, 763–768. https://doi.org/10.1109/EUROCON.2017.8011213.

Karahanna, E., J. R. Evaristo, and M. Srite. 2005. Levels of culture and individual behavior: An investigative perspective. *Journal of Global Information Management (JGIM)* 13 (2): 1–20.

Karapetrovic, S., and W. Willborn. 2000. Quality assurance and effectiveness of audit systems. *International Journal of Quality & Reliability Management* 17:679–703.

Karisma, K., and P. M. Tehrani. 2022. Data protection governance framework: A silver bullet for blockchain-enabled applications. *Procedia Computer Science* 218:2480–2493. https://doi.org/10.1016/J.PROCS.2023.01.223.

Kaufhold, K. 2022. Book review. *System* 110:102904. https://doi.org/10.1016/J.SYSTEM.2022.102904.

Kaupa, S., and K. Chisa. 2020. Adoption of the electronic document records management system within the public sector in Namibia: Exploring the challenges and opportunities. *International Journal of Operations Management* 1 (1): 7–18.

Ke, W., H. Liu, K. K. Wei, J. Gu, and H. Chen. 2009. How do mediated and non-mediated power affect electronic supply chain management system adoption? The mediating effects of trust and institutional pressures. *Decision Support Systems* 46 (4): 839–851.

Kelly, A. G. 1984. Varieties of qualitative research. *Social Science Information Studies* 4 (1): 69–70. https://doi.org/10.1016/0143-6236(84)90059-0.

Kelly, T. 2016. 5 Major benefits to using a bim execution plan. https://assemblesystems.com/blog/benefits-of-bim-execution-plan/. Accessed 4 January 2022.

Kemp, R. 2000. Technology and environmental policy—Innovation effects of past policies and suggestions for improvement. *Innovation and the Environment* 1:35–61.

Kemp, B., and J. Olivan. 2003. European data format "plus" (EDF+), an EDF alike standard format for the exchange of physiological data. *Clinical Neurophysiology* 114 (9): 1755–1761. https://doi.org/10.1016/S1388-2457(03)00123-8.

Kenny, C. 2004. Playin' in the band: A qualitative study of popular music styles as clinical improvisation. *The Arts in Psychotherapy* 31 (2): 106–109. https://doi.org/10.1016/J.AIP.2004.01.003.

Kenny, D. A., and D. B. McCoach. 2003. Effect of the number of variables on measures of fit in structural equation modeling. *Structural Equation Modeling* 10 (3): 333–351.

Kerlinger, F., and H. Lee. 2000. *Foundations of behavioural research*. Fort Worth, TX: Harcourt.

Kerry, C. F., and P. D. Gallagher. 2013. Digital signature standard (DSS). In *FIPs PUB?* 186–194.

Khaqqi, K. N., J. J. Sikorski, K. Hadinoto, and M. Kraft. 2018. Incorporating seller/buyer reputation-based system in blockchain-enabled emission trading application. *Applied Energy* 209:8–19. https://doi.org/10.1016/j.apenergy.2017.10.070.

Kholaif, M. M. N. H. K., W. Gu, X. Tang, and W. H. Salama. 2024. Post-emergencies opportunities for green supply chain management and urban supply chains' robustness; the moderating influence of blockchains as a sustainable urban resources management technique. *Journal of Cleaner Production* 475. https://doi.org/10.1016/J.JCLEPRO.2024.143646.

Kilström, T. 2016. Factors limiting adoption of new technology: A study of drawbacks affecting transition from on-premise systems to cloud computing. Master of Science Thesis submitted to KTH Royal Institute of Technology, Stockholm, Sweden.

Kim, J. K. 2018. *Effects and implications of block chain on industry and international trade*. Seoul, Korea: Institute for International Trade Publication.

Kim, M., and Y. W. Kim. 2024. Applications of blockchain for construction project procurement. *Automation in Construction* 165. https://doi.org/10.1016/J.AUTCON.2024.105550.

Kim, H. W., Y. Xu, and S. Gupta. 2012. Which is more important in Internet shopping, perceived price or trust? *Electronic Commerce Research and Applications* 11 (3): 241–252. https://doi.org/10.1016/j.elerap.2011.06.003.

Kim, N. H., S. M. Kang, and C. S. Hong. 2017. Mobile charger billing system using lightweight Blockchain. In *19th Asia-Pacific network operations and management symposium: Managing a world of things, APNOMS 2017*, 374–377. https://doi.org/10.1109/APNOMS.2017.8094151.

Kim, K., S. H. Son, and S. K. Kim. 2019. *A basic study of construction procurement management using block chain & big data technology*. Seoul, Korea: The Korea Institute of Building Construction Publication.

Kim, K., G. Lee, and S. Kim. 2020. A study on the application of blockchain technology in the construction industry. *KSCE Journal of Civil Engineering*1–11.

Kinicki, Angelo, and Brian K. Williams. 2018. *Management—A practical introduction*. 8th ed. New York: McGraw-Hill.

Kinnaird, C., and M. Geipel. 2017. *Blockchain technology—How the inventions behind bitcoin are enabling a network of trust for the built environment*. London: ARUP. https://doi.org/10.4018/978-1-5225-9257-0.ch005.

Kipkebut, D. J. 2010. Organisational commitment and job satisfaction in higher educational institutions: The Kenyan case. Doctoral dissertation, Middlesex University.

Kiran Sankar, M. S., S. Gupta, and S. Luthra. 2025. Unlocking digitalization in the spool fabrication industry: Analysis of roadblocks using the IMF-SWARA integrated TFBM. *Procedia CIRP* 132:171–177. https://doi.org/10.1016/J.PROCIR.2025.01.029.

Kiu, M. S., F. C. Chia, and P. F. Wong. 2019. The potentials and impacts of blockchain technology in construction industry: A literature review. In *IOP conf. series: Materials science and engineering*, 1–9.

Klakegg, O. J., T. Williams, O. M. Magnussen, and H. Glasspool. 2008. *Governance. Journal* 39:S27–S42.

Kliemann, N. J. F. 2010. A gestão de riscos como ferramenta para aumento da competitividade das empresas. *Encontro Nacional De Engenharia De Produção* 30:1–15.

Kline, R. B. 2012. Assumptions in structural equation modeling. *Handbook of Structural Equation Modeling* 111:125.

Ko, H., and M. R. Ogiela. 2025. Security strategy of digital medical contents based on blockchain in generative AI model. *Computers, Materials and Continua* 82 (1): 259–278. https://doi.org/10.32604/CMC.2024.057257.

Kock, F. 2020. Book review. *Tourism Management* 78:104063. https://doi.org/10.1016/J.TOURMAN.2019.104063.

Kodikara, J., A. Sounthararajah, and L. Chen. 2024. Reimagining unbound road pavement technology: Integrating testing, design, construction and performance in the post-digital era. *Transportation Geotechnics* 47. https://doi.org/10.1016/J.TRGEO.2024.101274.

Kolade, O., V. Odumuyiwa, S. Abolfathi, P. Schröder, K. Wakunuma, I. Akanmu, T. Whitehead, B. Tijani, and M. Oyinlola. 2022. Technology acceptance and readiness of stakeholders for transitioning to a circular plastic economy in Africa. *Technological Forecasting and Social Change* 183:1–13.

Konashevych, O. I. 2016. Advantages and current issues of blockchain use in microgrids. *Elektronnoe Modelirovanie* 38 (2): 93–104. https://doi.org/10.15407/emodel.38.02.093.

Koontz, H. 1961. The management theory jungle. *The Journal of the Academy of Management*174–188. https://doi.org/10.2307/254541.

Korea Institute of Science and Technology Information. 2018. *Blockchain technology development strategy*. Seoul: KISTI Publication.

Kosba, A., A. Miller, E. Shi, Z. Wen, and C. Papamanthou. 2016. Hawk: The blockchain model of cryptography and privacypreserving smart contracts. In *Proceedings—2016 IEEE symposium on security and privacy, SP 2016*, 839–858. Institute of Electrical and Electronics Engineers Inc. https://doi.org/10.1109/SP.2016.55.

Kothari, C. C. R. 2004. *Research methodology: Methods and techniques*. 2nd ed. New Delhi: New Age International.

Koutsogiannis, A., and N. Berntsen. 2017a. *Blockchain and construction: The how, why and when*. Chartered Institute of Building.

Koutsogiannis, A., and N. Berntsen. 2017b. Blockchain and construction: The how, why and when | BIM+X Chartered Institute of Building. http://www.bimplus.co.uk/people/blockchain-and-construction-how-why-and-when/. Accessed 30 July 2021.

Krasonikolakis, I., A. Vrechopoulos, and A. Pouloudi. 2014. Store selection criteria and sales prediction in virtual worlds. *Information & Management* 51 (6): 641–652.

Krug, S. 2008. An introduction to qualitative research, third edition, Uwe Flick (Ed.), SAGE Publications, Thousand Oaks, CA (2006), 443 pp., $44.95, ISBN 1-4129-1146-X, $120.00, ISBN1-4129-1145-1Designing Qualitative Research, Fourth edition, Catherine Marshall, Gretchen B. Rossman (Eds.), SAGE Publications, Thousand Oaks, CA (2006), 262 pp. $_*$$44.95 (paperback). ISBN 1-4129-2489-8. $_*$$79.95 (hardcover). ISBN 1-4129-2488-8-X. *Library & Information Science Research* 30 (1): 77–78. https://doi.org/10.1016/J.LISR.2007.08.003.

Kumar Singh, A., V. R. P. Kumar, G. Dehdasht, S. R. Mohandes, P. Manu, and F. Pour Rahimian. 2023. Investigating the barriers to the adoption of blockchain technology in sustainable construction projects. *Journal of Cleaner Production* 403. https://doi.org/10.1016/J.JCLEPRO.2023.136840.

Kumari, S., A. K. Tyagi, Richa, and S. S. Ahmad. 2025. Blockchain technology in AI-powered smart hospital. *Blockchain and Digital Twin for Smart Hospitals* 109–132. https://doi.org/10.1016/B978-0-443-34226-4.00007-1.

Kuraesin, A. D. 2017. The influence of organizational culture on management information system. *International Journal of Scientific & Technology Research* 6:140–141.

Kushwaha, P., N. Srivastava, and S. P. Kushwaha. 2024. Enhancing clinical drug trial monitoring with blockchain technology. *Contemporary Clinical Trials* 146. https://doi.org/10.1016/J.CCT.2024.107684.

Kuzminykh, A., J. Granja, M. Parente, and M. Azenha. 2024. Promoting circularity of construction materials through demolition digitalisation at the preparation stage: Information requirements and openBIM-based technological implementation. *Advanced Engineering Informatics* 62. https://doi.org/10.1016/J.AEI.2024.102755.

Kyle, K. 2013. Research methods in second language acquisition: A practical guide. *System* 41 (2): 491–493. https://doi.org/10.1016/J.SYSTEM.2013.04.009.

Lahdenperä, P. 2012. Making sense of the multi-party contractual arrangements of project partnering, project alliancing and integrated project delivery. *Construction Management and Economics* 30 (1): 57–79.

Langendorf, R. 1992. Information systems and computer visualization for urban design, planning and management. *Environment and Planning* 19:723–738.

Lanko, A., N. Vatin, and A. Kaklauskas. 2018. Application of RFID combined with blockchain technology in logistics of construction materials. *MATEC Web of Conferences* 170:1–6. https://doi.org/10.1051/matecconf/201817003032.

Lanzillo, J. D., E. Sirakaya-Turk, M. Uysal, W. Hammitt, and J. J. Vaske. 2012. Research methods for leisure, recreation and tourism. *Sport Management Review* 15 (3): 385–386. https://doi.org/10.1016/J.SMR.2012.02.006.

Laryea, E. T. 1999. The technology challenges facing developing countries in the move to paperless international trade. *Bond Law Review* 11:1–10.

Laudon, K., and J. Laudon. 1995. *Management information systems: Organization and technology*. Upper Saddle River, NJ: Prentice-Hall, Inc.

Laudon, K., and J. P. Laudon. 2000. *Management information systems: Organization and technology in the networked enterprise*. Upper Saddle River, NJ: Prentice Hall.

Lawrence, B. F. 2007. *The management of construction: A project life cycle approach*. Boston: Routledge.

Lazaroiu, C., and M. Roscia. 2017. Smart district through IoT and blockchain. In *6th international conference on renewable energy research and applications*, 454–461. https://doi.org/10.1109/icrera.2017.8191102.

Lee, Y., K. A. Kozar, and K. R. T. Larsen. 2003. The technology acceptance model: Past, present, and future. *Communications of the Association for Information Systems* 12 (50): 751–781. https://doi.org/10.17705/1cais.01250.

Lei, P. W., and Q. Wu. 2008. Introduction to structural equation modeling: Issues and practical considerations. *Educational Measurement: Issues and Practice* 26 (3): 33–43.

Leible, S., S. Schlager, M. Schubotz, and B. Gipp. 2019. A review on blockchain technology and blockchain projects fostering open science. *Frontiers in Blockchain* 2:1–28. https://doi.org/10.3389/fbloc.2019.00016.

Leibson, S. 2018. Blockchain is not bitcoin—Bitcoin is not blockchain, EEJournal. https://www.eejournal.com/article/blockchain-is-not-bitcoin-bitcoin-is-not-blockchain/. Accessed 1 January 2020.

Lemieux, L. V. 2015. Trusting records: Is Blockchain technology the answer? *Records Management Journal*. 26 (2): 110–139.

Lessing, N., and C. Scheepers. 2001. *Information is a management issue*. 5th ed. Johannesburg: CSIC.

Lethbridge, N. 2003. Adaptive structuration theory: Relevant structures for web technologies. In 14th Australasian Conference on Information Systems, pp. 1–8.

Li, H. 2025. The effect of digital technology innovation on low carbon investment in renewable energy enterprises. *Renewable Energy* 239. https://doi.org/10.1016/J.RENENE.2024.121991.

Li, Z., & Xu, Z. (2025). Digital technology and innovation:The impact of blockchain application on enterprise innovation. Technovation, 139. doi:https://doi.org/10.1016/J.TECHNOVATION.2024.103136.

Li, T., and L. J. Zhang. 2024. Review of "Conducting genre-based research in applied linguistics: A methodological guide". *English for Specific Purposes* 74:82–84. https://doi.org/10.1016/J.ESP.2024.01.004.

Li, H., Z. Irani, and P. E. D. Love. 2000. The IT performance evaluation in the construction industry. In *Paper read at 33rd annual Hawaii international conference on system sciences*, 4–7.

Li, J., D. Greenwood, and M. Kassem. 2019a. Blockchain in the built environment and construction industry: A systematic review, conceptual models and practical use case. *Automation in Construction* 102 (2): 288–307.

Li, J., D. Greenwood, and M. Kassem. 2019b. Blockchain in the built environment and construction industry: A systematic review, conceptual models and practical use cases. *Automation in Construction* 102:288–307. https://doi.org/10.1016/J.AUTCON.2019.02.005.

Li, C. Z., Z. Chen, F. Xue, X. T. R. Kong, B. Xiao, X. Lai, and Y. Zhao. 2021. A blockchain- and IoT-based smart product-service system for the sustainability of prefabricated housing construction. *Journal of Cleaner Production* 286. https://doi.org/10.1016/J.JCLEPRO.2020.125391.

Li, L., Z. Yi, F. Jiang, S. Zhang, and J. Zhou. 2023a. Exploring the mechanism of digital transformation empowering green innovation in construction enterprises. *Developments in the Built Environment* 15. https://doi.org/10.1016/J.DIBE.2023.100199.

Li, L., Z. Yi, S. Zhang, and Z. Shao. 2023b. Competitive threat or win-win cooperation? Evolutionary analysis of digital alliances in construction. *Developments in the Built Environment* 15. https://doi.org/10.1016/J.DIBE.2023.100182.

Li, T., X. Li, Y. Rui, J. Ling, S. Zhao, and H. Zhu. 2024a. Digital twin for intelligent tunnel construction. *Automation in Construction* 158. https://doi.org/10.1016/J.AUTCON.2023.105210.

Li, T., Y. Shen, Y. Li, Y. Zhang, and S. Wu. 2024b. The status quo and future prospects of digital twins for healthcare. *EngMedicine* 1 (3): 100042. https://doi.org/10.1016/J.ENGMED.2024.100042.

Li, C., W. He, and E. Cao. 2025a. Impact of green data center pilots on the digital economy development: An empirical study based on dual machine learning methods. *Computers and Industrial Engineering* 201. https://doi.org/10.1016/J.CIE.2025.110914.

Li, J., Z. Wang, S. Zhang, J. Ji, Y. Xiang, D. Wang, and J. Tan. 2025b. Digital-Twin virtual model real-time construction via spatio-temporal cascade reconstruction for full-field plastic deformation monitoring in metal tube bending manufacturing. *Robotics and Computer-Integrated Manufacturing* 91. https://doi.org/10.1016/J.RCIM.2024.102860.

Liang, X., N. Alam, T. Sultana, E. Bandara, and S. Shetty. 2023. Designing A Blockchain Empowered Telehealth Artifact for Decentralized Identity Management and Trustworthy Communication: An Interdisciplinary Approach (Preprint). *Journal of Medical Internet Research*. https://doi.org/10.2196/46556.

Liao, K., L. Lin, and Y. Sun. 2025. Blockchain adoption and corporate financial reporting quality. *Journal of Accounting and Public Policy* 49. https://doi.org/10.1016/J.JACCPUBPOL.2024.107265.

Liebeskind, J. 1996. Knowledge, strategy, and the theory of the firm. *Southern Medical Journal* 17:93–107.

Lim, A., and E. Pan. 2021. 'Toward a Global Social Contract for Trade'—A Rawlsian approach to Blockchain Systems Design and Responsible Trade Facilitation in the New Bretton Woods era. *Journal of Responsible Technology* 6. https://doi.org/10.1016/J.JRT.2021.100011.

Lim, H. S. M., and A. Taeihagh. 2019. Algorithmic decision-making in AVs: Understanding ethical and technical concerns for smart cities. *Sustainability* 11 (20): 77–91.

Lin, B. W. 2007. Information technology capability and value creation: Evidence from the US banking industry. *Technology in Society* 29 (1): 93–106.

Lin, H. F. 2014. Understanding the determinants of electronic supply chain management system adoption: Using the technology–organization–environment framework. *Technological Forecasting and Social Change* 86:80–92.

Lin, A., and N. C. Chen. 2012. Cloud computing as an innovation: Perception, attitude, and adoption. *International Journal of Information Management* 32 (6): 533–540.

Lin, Y. H., S. P. Ho, H. K. Wang, and W. C. Hsu. 2021. Application of blockchain in construction inspection activities. In *ACM international conference proceeding series, PartF168982*.

Lin, X., Z. Guo, X. Jin, and H. Guo. 2025. Digital twin-enabled safety monitoring system for seamless worker-robot collaboration in construction. *Automation in Construction* 174:106147. https://doi.org/10.1016/J.AUTCON.2025.106147.

Lindahl, K. 2019. Exploring the mixed methods research paradigm in language teaching and learning. *Linguistics and Education* 49:100–101. https://doi.org/10.1016/J.LINGED.2018.01.005.

Ling, J., Z. Li, F. Yang, L. Han, and J. Zhang. 2025. Construction of airport digital runway based on in-situ sensing data. *International Journal of Transportation Science and Technology*. https://doi.org/10.1016/J.IJTST.2025.01.010.

Liu, A., and C. Chen. 2025. From real estate financialization to decentralization: A comparative review of REITs and blockchain-based tokenization. *Geoforum* 159. https://doi.org/10.1016/J.GEOFORUM.2024.104193.

Liu, Y., and J. Huang. 2019. Data circulation blockchain model construction and data access management. *Journal of Physics: Conference Series* 1345 (2): https://doi.org/10.1088/1742-6596/1345/2Z022048.

Liu, X., and J. Wen. 2020. Book review. *Tourism Management* 81:104174. https://doi.org/10.1016/J.TOURMAN.2020.104174.

Liu, B., T. Huo, X. Wang, Q. Shen, and Y. Chen. 2013. The decision model of the intuitionistic fuzzy group bid evaluation for urban infrastructure projects considering social costs. *Canadian Journal of Civil Engineering* 40 (3): 263–273. https://doi.org/10.1139/cjce-2012-0283.

Liu, B., B. Xue, T. Huo, G. Shen, and M. Fu. 2018. Project external environmental factors affecting project delivery systems selection. *Journal of Civil Engineering and Management* 25 (3): 276–286.

Liu, H., J. Zhang, Y. Cheng, F. Tao, and Q. Qi. 2023a. Digital Twin shop-floor: A Complex System-oriented Construction Method and Operation Mechanism. *Procedia CIRP* 119:52–57. https://doi.org/10.1016/J.PROCIR.2023.03.083.

Liu, X., Y. Yang, Y. Jiang, Y. Fu, R. Y. Zhong, M. Li, and G. Q. Huang. 2023b. Data-driven ESG assessment for blockchain services: A comparative study in textiles and apparel industry. *Resources, Conservation and Recycling* 190. https://doi.org/10.1016/J.RESCONREC.2022.106837.

Liu, C., V. Muravskyi, and W. Wei. 2024a. Evolution of blockchain accounting literature from the perspective of CiteSpace (2013–2023). *Heliyon* 10 (11): https://doi.org/10.1016/J.HELIYON.2024.E32097.

Liu, Q., Y. Ma, L. Chen, W. Pedrycz, M. J. Skibniewski, and Z. S. Chen. 2024b. Artificial intelligence for production, operations and logistics management in modular construction industry: A systematic literature review. *Information Fusion* 109. https://doi.org/10.1016/J.INFFUS.2024.102423.

Liu, Y., J. He, X. Li, J. Chen, X. Liu, S. Peng, H. Cao, and Y. Wang. 2024c. An overview of blockchain smart contract execution mechanism. *Journal of Industrial Information Integration* 41. https://doi.org/10.1016/J.JII.2024.100674.

Liu, Y., X. Tao, M. Das, X. Gong, H. Liu, Y. Xu, A. Xie, and J. C. P. Cheng. 2024d. Blockchain-enabled platform-as-a-service for production management in off-site construction design using openBIM standards. *Automation in Construction* 164. https://doi.org/10.1016/J.AUTCON.2024.105447.

Liu, L., Z. Liu, A. Hou, and X. Qian. 2025a. Research on key technologies of digital twin cloud platform: A case study of rebar thread production line. *Transactions of the Canadian Society for Mechanical Engineering* 49 (1): 157–174. https://doi.org/10.1139/TCSME-2024-0061.

Liu, M., X. Xin, X. Wang, T. Zhang, and K. Chen. 2025b. Dual-channel slot sales strategy for container liner shipping companies with blockchain technology adoption. *Transport Policy* 162:200–220. https://doi.org/10.1016/J.TRANPOL.2024.12.006.

Liu, X., C. Wang, F. Wang, X. Qiu, F. Feng, and Y. Sun. 2025c. A generic digital twin model construction strategy for cross-field implementations with comprehensiveness, operability and scalability. *Journal of Manufacturing Systems* 80:366–379. https://doi.org/10.1016/J.JMSY.2025.02.020.

Lohry, M., and B. Bodell. 2015. Blockchain enabled co-housing. https://medium.com/@MatthewLohry/blockchain-enabled-co-housing-de48e4f2b441. Accessed 06 August 2021.

Long, W., Z. Bao, K. Chen, S. Thomas Ng, and I. Yahaya Wuni. 2024. Developing an integrative framework for digital twin applications in the building construction industry: A systematic literature review. *Advanced Engineering Informatics* 59. https://doi.org/10.1016/J.AEI.2023.102346.

Lorences, P. P., and L. F. G. Ávila. 2013. The evaluation and improvement of IT governance. *Journal of Information Systems and Technology Management* 10:219–234.

Low, C., Y. Chen, and M. Wu. 2011. Understanding the determinants of cloud computing adoption. *Industrial management & data* systems,111(7):1006–1023.

Lu, W., X. Li, F. Xue, R. Zhao, L. Wu, and A. G. O. Yeh. 2021. Exploring smart construction objects as blockchain oracles in construction supply chain management. *Automation in Construction* 129. https://doi.org/10.1016/J.AUTCON.2021.103816.

Lui, A. K., E. W. Ngai, and C. K. Lo. 2016. Disruptive information technology innovations and the cost of equity capital: The moderating effect of CEO incentives and institutional pressures. *Information & Management* 53 (3): 345–354.

Luiten, G. T., and F. P. Tolman. 1997. Automating communication in civil engineering. *Journal of Construction Engineering and Management* 123 (2): 113–120. https://doi.org/10.1061/(ASCE)0733-9364(1997)123:2(113).

Luiten, G. T., F. P. Tolman, and M. A. Fischer. 1998. Project modelling to integrate design and construction. *Computers in Industry* 35 (1): 13–29.

Luu, L., D. H. Chu, H. Olickel, P. Saxena, and A. Hobor. 2016. Making smart contracts smarter. In *Proceedings of the ACM conference on computer and communications security*, 254–269. https://doi.org/10.1145/2976749.2978309.

Ma, L., J. Zhang, K. Deng, P. Xue, Z. Cui, Y. Fang, M. Tan, Y. Zhao, M. Zhu, Z. Ding, and D. Shen. 2024. Construction of unbiased dental template and parametric dental model for precision digital dentistry. *Biomedical Signal Processing and Control* 95. https://doi.org/10.1016/J.BSPC.2024.106458.

Mabope, N. 2018. Strategies and practices for effective talent management in the Mangaung Metropolitan Municipality.

Macieira, B., E. Mota, and L. Ferreira. 2025. Unleashing DeFi's potential with dharma network: Fusion of functional programming and Algorand blockchain. *Procedia Computer Science* 256:649–656. https://doi.org/10.1016/J.PROCS.2025.02.163.

Mackenzie, M. L. 2010. Creative methods in organizational research, M.P. Broussine (Ed.), SAGE, Los Angeles (2008), (SAGE Series in Management Research). 184 pp. $99.95 (cloth), $42.95 (pbk). ISBN 978-141-290-133-8, 978-141-290-134-5 (pbk). *Library & Information Science Research* 32 (1): 91–92. https://doi.org/10.1016/J.LISR.2009.08.003.

MacLeod, M. L. P. 1992. Qualitative nursing research: A contemporary dialogue. *International Journal of Nursing Studies* 29 (3): 330–332. https://doi.org/10.1016/0020-7489(92)90037-H.

MacRae, E. 2002. Understanding and responding to drug use: The role of qualitative research, European Monitoring Centre for Drugs and Drug Addiction, Scientific Monograph Series No. 4. *International Journal of Drug Policy* 13 (4): 334–335. https://doi.org/10.1016/S0955-3959(02)00032-4.

Madden, A. D. 2000. A definition of information. *ASLIB Proceedings* 52 (9): 343–349. https://doi.org/10.1108/EUM0000000007027.

Madumali, S., A. Thibbotuwawa, S. Saniuk, and P. Nielsen. 2024. Evaluating barriers to the adoption of blockchain for enhancing transparency in the procurement process within apparel supply chains. *IFAC-PapersOnLine* 58 (19): 807–812. https://doi.org/10.1016/J.IFACOL.2024.09.196.

Mafakheri, F., L. Dai, D. Slezak, and F. Nasiri. 2007. Project delivery system selection under uncertainty: Multicriteria multilevel decision aid model. *Journal of Management in Engineering* 23 (4): 200–206. https://doi.org/10.1061/(ASCE)0742-597X(2007)23:4(200).

Maguire, M. 1987. *Doing participatory research: A feminist approach*. Amherst, MA: The Center of International Education, University of Massachusetts.

Mahalingam, A., R. Kashyap, and C. Mahajan. 2010. An evaluation of the applicability of 4D CAD on construction projects. *Automation in Construction* 19 (2): 148–159. https://doi.org/10.1016/j.autcon.2009.11.015.

Mahdaly, K., and I. Adeinat. 2022. Factors that affect the adoption of RFID in the Saudi logistics industry: An empirical investigation. *The International Journal of Logistics Management*.

Mahdi, I. M., and K. Alreshaid. 2005. Decision support system for selecting the proper project delivery method using analytical hierarchy process (AHP). *International Journal of Project Management* 23 (7): 564–572. https://doi.org/10.1016/j.ijproman.2005.05.007.

Mai, T. G., M. Nguyen, A. Ghobakhlou, W. Q. Yan, B. Chhun, and H. Nguyen. 2024. Decoding a decade: The evolution of artificial intelligence in security, communication, and maintenance within the construction industry. *Automation in Construction* 165. https://doi.org/10.1016/J.AUTCON.2024.105522.

Makhdoom, I., I. Zhou, M. Abolhasan, J. Lipman, and W. Ni. 2020. Privy sharing: A blockchain-based framework for privacy preserving and secure data sharing in smart cities. *Computers and Security* 88:101653. https://doi.org/10.1016/j.cose.2019.101653.

Makovhololo, P., N. Batyashe, T. Sekgweleo, and T. Iyamu. 2017. Diffusion of innovations theory for information technology decision making in organisational strategy. *Journal of Contemporary Management* 14:461–481.

Malhotra, N., J. Hall, M. Shaw, and P. Oppenheim. 2006. *Marketing research: An applied orientation*. Pearson Education Australia.

Malik, F. 2000. *Managing performing living: Effective management for a new era (English edition 2006)*. Frankfurt am Main: Campus.

Mamun, Q. 2025. Sensor networks and blockchain platforms for the future healthcare. *Sensor Networks for Smart Hospitals* 155–216. https://doi.org/10.1016/B978-0-443-36370-2.00010-4.

Mao, S., and W. J. Cao. 2025. Evaluating material passports for circularity in the construction industry. *Sustainable Production and Consumption* 54:88–101. https://doi.org/10.1016/J.SPC.2024.12.021.

Marczyk, G. R., D. DeMatteo, and D. Festinger. 2010. *Essentials of research design and methodology (2)*. Ontario: Wiley.

Maritz, S. G. 2003. Data management: Managing data as an organisational resource. *Acta Commercii* 3 (1): 75–84. https://doi.org/10.4102/ac.v3i1.44.

Marqués Graells, P. 2001. Algunas notas sobre el impacto de las TIC en la universidad. *Educar* 28:83–98.

Martinez, E., and L. Pfister. 2023. Benefits and limitations of using low-code development to support digitalization in the construction industry. *Automation in Construction* 152. https://doi.org/10.1016/J.AUTCON.2023.104909.

Martinez-Roman, J. A., J. A. Tamayo, and J. Gamero. 2017. Innovativeness and its influence on growth and market extension in construction firms in the Andalusian region. *Journal of Engineering and Technology Management* 43:19–33. https://doi.org/10.1016/jjengtecman.2016.11.002.

Maruti Techlabs. 2017. Blockchain—Benefits, drawbacks and everything you need to know—Maruti techlabs, maruti techlabs. https://marutitech.com/benefits-of-blockchain/. Accessed 5 January 2020.

Maskuriy, R., A. Selamat, P. Maresova, O. Krejcar, and O. O. David. 2019. Industry 4.0 for the construction industry: Review of management perspective. *Economies* 7 (3): 51–68. https://doi.org/10.3390/economies7030068.

Mason, J. 2017. Intelligent contracts and the construction industry. *Journal of Legal Affairs and Dispute Resolution in Engineering and Construction* 9 (3): 04517012. https://doi.org/10.1061/(asce)la.1943-4170.000023_3.

Matarneh, R., and B. M. Mohsen. 2024. Exploring the implementation of digital technologies in supply chain management within the Jordanian Construction Industry. *Procedia Computer Science* 238:519–527. https://doi.org/10.1016/J.PROCS.2024.06.055.

Mathews, M., D. Robles, and B. Bowe. 2017. BIM+ blockchain: A solution to the trust problem in collaboration? In *CITA BIMGathering 2017*, 1–11.

Matz, R., B. Smith, and A. C. Sparkes. 2019. Routledge Handbook of Qualitative Research in Sport and Exercise, 1st Edn. *Sport Management Review* 22 (4): 566–567. https://doi.org/10.1016/J.SMR.2019.01.003.

Maxcy, S. J. 2003. Pragmatic threads in mixed methods research in the social sciences: The search for multiple modes of inquiry and the end of the philosophy of formalism. In *Handbook of mixed methods in social and behavioral research*, 51–89.

May, T. 2001. *Social research—Issues and process*. 3rd ed. Buckingham & Philadelphia: Open University Press.

Mayouf, M., F. Afsar, A. Iqbal, V. Javidroozi, and S. R. Mohandes. 2024. Synergies between digital construction technologies in smart buildings and smart city development to meet building users' expectations. *Heliyon* 10 (8): https://doi.org/10.1016/J.HELIYON.2024.E28585.

McConnell, W. S. 2009. *Technology adoption: Influence of availability and accessibility*. University of Phoenix.

Mccoy, S., D. F. Galletta, and W. R. King. 2007. Applying TAM across cultures: The need for caution. *European Journal of Information Systems* 16:81–90.

McCreadie, M., and R. E. Rice. 1997. Trends in analysing access to information. *Journal of Documentation* 53 (4): 457–476.

McCreadie, M. M., and R. Rice. 1999. Trends in analyzing access to information. Part I: Cross-disciplinary conceptualizations of access. *Information Process and Management* 35:45–76.

McDonald, R. P., and M. H. R. Ho. 2002. Principles and practice in reporting structural equation analyses. *Psychological Methods* 7 (1): 64.

McDowell, N. 2005. Qualitative research for the information professional: A practical handbook. 2nd ed. *Library Collections, Acquisitions, and Technical Services* 29 (3): 338–339. https://doi.org/10.1016/J.LCATS.2005.10.003.

McGeorge, D., and P. Zou. 2012. *Construction management: New directions*. Ontario: Wiley.

McKenna, H. P. 1994. The Delphi technique: A worthwhile research approach for nursing? *Journal of Advanced Nursing* 19 (6): 1221–1225.

McQueen, R. A., and C. Knussen. 2002. *Research methods for social science: A practical introduction*. London: Pearson Education.

Mêda, P., J. Fauth, C. Schranz, H. Sousa, and H. Urban. 2024. Developments in the Built Environment Twinning the path of digital building permits and digital building logbooks—Diagnosis and challenges. *Developments in the Built Environment* 20:16. https://doi.org/10.1016/J.DIBE.2024.100573.

Mehta, P., R. Gupta, and S. Tanwar. 2020. Blockchain envisioned UAV networks: Challenges, solutions, and comparisons. *Computer Communications* 151:518–538. https://doi.org/10.1016/j.comcom.2020.01.023.

Mendel, P., L. S. Meredith, M. Schoenbaum, C. D. Sherbourne, and K. B. Wells. 2008. Interventions in organizational and community context: A framework for building evidence on dissemination and implementation in health services research. *Administration and Policy in Mental Health and Mental Health Services Research* 35 (1): 21–37.

Meng, Y., S. Nazir, J. Guo, and I. Uddin. 2021. A decision support system for the uses of lightweight blockchain designs for P2P computing. *Peer-to-Peer Networking and Applications* 14 (5): 27082718. https://doi.org/10.1007/S12083-021-01083-9/FIGURES/9.

Mengelkamp, E., B. Notheisen, and C. Beer. 2018. A blockchain-based smart grid: Towards sustainable local energy markets. *Computer Science—Research and Development* 33:207–214. https://doi.org/10.1007/s00450-017-0360-9.

Menny, T., S. le Guirriec, and C. de Wolf. 2024. The butterfly matchmaking model for circular construction: Towards a digital matchmaking platform tailored to French policy. *Sustainable Production and Consumption* 49:130–143. https://doi.org/10.1016/J.SPC.2024.06.011.

Merschbrock, C. 2012. Unorchestrated symphony: The case of inter-organizational collaboration in digital construction design. *Electronic Journal of Information Technology in Construction* 17:333–350.

Mertens, D. M. 2003. Mixed methods and the politics of human research: The transformative-emancipatory perspective. In *Handbook of mixed methods in social and behavioral research*, ed. A. Tashakkori and C. Teddlie, 135–164. Thousand Oaks, CA: Sage.

Michel, C., J. Mieaust Ali, and M. Fieaust. 2000. Collaboration and integration of project life cycle design information using IT system. In *International conference on construction information technology (INCITE), Hong Kong*.

Miglani, A., K. Patel, M. Modi, Y. Gadhvi, and M. Shah. 2025. A comprehensive study on energy trading and finance using blockchain technology. *Unconventional Resources* 6:100160. https://doi.org/10.1016/J.UNCRES.2025.100160.

Mik, E. 2017. Smart contracts: Terminology, technical limitations and real-world complexity. *Law, Innovation and Technology* 9 (2): 269–300. https://doi.org/10.1080/17579961.2017.1378468.
Miller, D. 2018. Vocabulary and English for specific purposes: Quantitative and qualitative perspectives. *English for Specific Purposes* 51:124–125. https://doi.org/10.1016/J.ESP.2018.04.002.
Miller, R., and D. R. Lessard. 2000. *The strategic management of large engineering projects: Shaping institutions, risk and governance*. Cambridge: MIT Press.
Min, H. 2019. Blockchain technology for enhancing supply chain resilience. *Business Horizons* 62 (1): 35–45. https://doi.org/10.1016/j.bushor.2018.08.012.
Mintzberg, H. 2009. What managers really do. *Wall Street Journal*, August 17. http://www.mintzberg.org/sites/default/files/article/download/mgrsreallydo.pdf. Accessed 12 August 2021.
Miraz, M. H., and M. Ali. 2018. Applications of blockchain technology beyond cryptocurrency. *Annals of Emerging Technologies in Computing* 2 (1): 1–6. https://doi.org/10.33166/aetic.2018.01.001.
Mirhosseini, S.-A. 2019. Book review. *Tourism Management* 74:408–409. https://doi.org/10.1016/J.TOURMAN.2019.04.027.
Mishra, R., R. Kr Singh, T. U. Daim, S. Fosso Wamba, and M. Song. 2024. Integrated usage of artificial intelligence, blockchain and the internet of things in logistics for decarbonization through paradox lens. *Transportation Research Part E: Logistics and Transportation Review* 189. https://doi.org/10.1016/J.TRE.2024.103684.
Mitchell, J. C. 1983. Case and situation analysis. *The Sociological Review* 31 (2): 187–211.
Miyatake, Y., and R. Kangari. 1993. Experiencing computer integrated construction. *Journal of Construction Engineering and Management* 119 (2): 307–322.
Modares, A., V. Bafandegan Emroozi, H. Gholinezhad, and A. Modares. 2024. An integrated Cognitive Reliability and Error Analysis Method (CREAM) and optimization for enhancing human reliability in blockchain. *Decision Analytics Journal* 12. https://doi.org/10.1016/J.DAJOUR.2024.100506.
Modares, A., V. B. Emroozi, P. Roozkhosh, and A. Modares. 2025. A Bayesian best-worst approach with blockchain integration for optimizing supply chain efficiency through supplier selection. *Supply Chain Analytics* 9. https://doi.org/10.1016/J.SCA.2024.100100.
Mohammed, A. L., and I. N. Yakubu. 2024. Revolutionizing energy systems: The impact of blockchain on renewable energy integration. *The Intersection of Blockchain and Energy Trading: Exploring Decentralized Solutions for Next-Generation Energy Markets* 143–170. https://doi.org/10.1016/B978-0-443-23627-3.00007-7.
Mohammed, A., A. Almousa, A. Ghaithan, and L. A. Hadidi. 2021. The role of blockchain in improving the processes and workflows in construction projects. *Applied Sciences (Switzerland)* 11 (19): https://doi.org/10.3390/APP11198835.
Mohebbi, H., and E. Park. 2025. Book Review. *Journal of Second Language Writing* 67:101177. https://doi.org/10.1016/J.JSLW.2025.101177.
Montana, P. J., and B. H. Charnov. 2008. *Management*. 4th ed. New York: Barron's Educational Series.
Moodie, I. 2020. Book review. *System* 90:102239. https://doi.org/10.1016/J.SYSTEM.2020.102239.
Moody, P. W. 2007. Interpretation of a single-point P buffering index for adjusting critical levels of the Colwell soil P test. *Soil Research* 45 (1): 55–62.
Moore, A. C. 2009. Basics of qualitative research: Techniques and procedures for developing grounded theory. By Juliet Corbin and Anselm Strauss. 3rd ed. Los Angeles: Sage Publications, 2008. 379 pp. $96.95. ISBN 9781412906432 (hardback); $55.95. ISBN 9781412906449 (paperback). *Library & Information Science Research* 31 (4): 267–268. https://doi.org/10.1016/J.LISR.2009.06.003.
Moosavi, N., H. Taherdoost, N. Mohamed, M. Madanchian, Y. Farhaoui, and I. U. Khan. 2024. Blockchain technology, structure, and applications: A survey. *Procedia Computer Science* 237:645–658. https://doi.org/10.1016/J.PROCS.2024.05.150.
Moran, B. B., and C. J. Morner. 2017. *Library and information center management*. ABC-CLIO.

Morgan, M. 2003. Meta-study of qualitative health research: A practical guide to meta-analysis and meta-synthesis. *International Journal of Nursing Studies* 40 (2): 217. https://doi.org/10.1016/S0020-7489(02)00059-7.

Morgan, B. 2019. Organizing for digitalization through mutual constitution: The case of a design firm. *Construction Management and Economics* 37 (7): 400–417. https://doi.org/10.1080/01446193.2018.1538560.

Moshood, T. D., J. O. Rotimi, W. Shahzad, and J. A. Bamgbade. 2024. Infrastructure digital twin technology: A new paradigm for future construction industry. *Technology in Society* 77. https://doi.org/10.1016/J.TECHSOC.2024.102519.

Mothafar, N. A., J. Zhang, A. Alsoffary, M. A. Aslam, A. Al-Barakani, O. S. Alhady, C. O. Esangbedo, and S. D. Kone. 2024. Effecting the adoption of blockchain technology enablers in supply chain sustainability with green hydrogen acceptance role as a mediator: Evidence from complex decarbonization industries in the United Arab Emirates. *International Journal of Hydrogen Energy* 84:1085–1100. https://doi.org/10.1016/J.IJHYDENE.2024.08.243.

Mott-Smith, J. A. 2019. Book review. *Journal of Second Language Writing* 45:73–75. https://doi.org/10.1016/J.JSLW.2019.05.002.

Müller, R. 2017. Organizational project governance. In *Governance and governmentality for projects: Enablers, practices and consequences*, ed. R. Müller, 11–24. New York: Routledge.

Muller, R. 2019. Governance, governmentality and project performance: The role of sovereignty. *International Journal of Information Systems and Project Management* 7 (2): 5–17. https://doi.org/10.12821/ijispm070201.

Müller, R., S. Pemsel, and J. Shao. 2014. Organizational enablers for governance and governmentality of projects: A literature review. *International Journal of Project Management* 32 (8): 1309–1320.

Müller, R., L. Zhai, A. Wang, and J. Shao. 2016. A framework for governance of projects: Governmentality, governance structure and projectification. *International Journal of Project Management* 34 (6): 957–969.

Müller, R., N. Drouin, and S. Sankaran. 2019. Modeling organizational project management. *Project Management. Journal* 50 (4): 1–15.

Mulligan, C., S. Morsfield, and E. Cheikosman. 2024. Blockchain for sustainability: A systematic literature review for policy impact. *Telecommunications Policy* 48 (2): https://doi.org/10.1016/J.TELPOL.2023.102676.

Murkin, J., R. Chitchyan, and A. Byrne. 2016. Enabling peer-to-peer electricity trading. In *4th international conference on ICT for sustainability*.

Musa, P. F. 2006. Making a case for modifying the technology acceptance model to account for limited accessibility in developing countries. *Information Technology for Development* 12 (3): 213–224.

Musarat, M. A., W. S. Alaloul, A. M. Khan, S. Ayub, and N. Jousseaume. 2024. A survey-based approach of framework development for improving the application of internet of things in the construction industry of Malaysia. *Results in Engineering* 21. https://doi.org/10.1016/J.RINENG.2024.101823.

Musonda, I. 2012. Construction health and safety (H&S) performance improvement—A client-centred model. Doctoral dissertation submitted to University of Johannesburg, South Africa.

Mutimba, C. J. 2014. Implementation of electronic document and records management system in the public sector: A case study of the Ministry of Higher Education Science and Technology. Doctoral dissertation, University of Nairobi.

Nanayakkara, S., S. Perera, and S. Senaratne. 2019a. Stakeholders' perspective on blockchain and smart contracts solutions for construction supply chains, CIB World Building Congress 2019. https://doi.org/10.6084/m9.figshare.8868386.

Nanayakkara, S., S. Perera, D. Bandara, G. T. Weerasuriya, and J. Ayoub. 2019b. Blockchain technology and its potential for the construction industry. In *AUBEA conference 2019*, 662–672.

Naoum, S. G. 2012. *Dissertation research and writing for construction students*. Boston: Routledge.

Narayan, K. L. 2008. *Computer aided design and manufacturing*. New Delhi: Prentice Hall.

Narayanamurthy, G., R. S. S. Jayanth, R. Moser, T. Schaefers, and N. P. Nagendra. 2025. Data-driven digital transformation for uncertainty reduction—Application of satellite imagery analytics in institutional crop credit management. *International Journal of Production Economics* 280. https://doi.org/10.1016/J.IJPE.2024.109498.

Narayanan, A. 2012. A review of eight software packages for structural equation modeling. *The American Statistician* 66 (2): 129–138.

Natoli, C., and V. Gramoli. 2016. *The blockchain anomaly in proceedings—2016 IEEE 15th international symposium on network computing and applications, NCA 2016*, 310–317. Institute of Electrical and Electronics Engineers Inc. https://doi.org/10.1109/NCA.2016.7778635.

Nawari, N. O., and S. Ravindran. 2019. Blockchain technology and BIM process: Review and potential applications. *Journal of Information Technology in Construction* 24:209238.

Nawari, N. O., and S. Ravindran. 2019a. Blockchain and building information modeling (BIM). *Review and applications in post-disaster recovery Buildings*. https://doi.org/10.3390/BUILDINGS9060149.

Nawari, N. O., and S. Ravindran. 2019b. Blockchain and the built environment: Potentials and limitations. *Journal of Building Engineering* 25. https://doi.org/10.1016/JJOBE.2019.100832.

Nawari, N. O., and S. Ravindran. 2019c. *Blockchain technology and BIM process: Review and potential applications Journal of Information Technology in Construction* 24:209–238.

Naylor, J. 2004. *Management*. 2nd ed. Essex: Pearson Education/Prentice Hall.

Neely, A., M. Gregory, and K. Platts. 2005. Performance measurement system design: A literature review and research agenda. *International Journal of Operations and Production Management* 25 (12): 1228–1263.

Nemutanzhela, P., and T. Iyamu. 2015. Theory of diffusion of innovation for analysis in information systems studies. In Science and Information Conference (SAI), pp. 603–608.

Neuman, W. L. 2006. *Social research methods qualitative and quantitative approaches*. 6th ed. Boston: Pearson.

Newman, I., C. R. Benz, and C. S. Ridenour. 1998. *Qualitative-quantitative research methodology: Exploring the interactive continuum*. Illinois: SIU Press.

Nguyen, L. H., and T. Watanabe. 2017. The impact of project organizational culture on the performance of construction projects. *Sustainability* 9:78–91. https://doi.org/10.3390/su9050781.

Nguyen, S., P. S. L. Chen, and Y. Du. 2023. Blockchain adoption in container shipping: An empirical study on barriers, approaches, and recommendations. *Marine Policy* 155. https://doi.org/10.1016/J.MARPOL.2023.105724.

Nik-Bakht, M., and T. Zayed. 2023. Automation and digital transformation, a road to the next-generation construction. *Canadian Journal of Civil Engineering* 50 (3): i–iii. https://doi.org/10.1139/CJCE-2022-0504.

Nikseresht, A., S. Shokouhyar, E. B. Tirkolaee, and N. Pishva. 2024. Applications and emerging trends of blockchain technology in marketing to develop Industry 5.0 businesses: A comprehensive survey and network analysis. *Internet of Things (The Netherlands)* 28. https://doi.org/10.1016/J.IOT.2024.101401.

Nitecki, D. A. 2010. Qualitative research in the study of leadership, by Karin Klenke. *Library & Information Science Research* 32 (1): 93–94. https://doi.org/10.1016/J.LISR.2009.09.002.

Nitithamyong, P., and M. J. Skibniewski. 2004. Web-based construction project management systems: How to make them successful? *Automation in Construction* 13 (4): 491506. https://doi.org/10.1016/j.autcon.2004.02.003.

Niu, Y. 2008. The performance and problems of affordable housing policy in Chana: The estimations of benefits, costs and affordability. *International Journal of Housing Market Analysis* 12:125–146.

Nnaji, C., and A. A. Karakhan. 2020. Technologies for safety and health management in construction: Current use, implementation benefits and limitations, and adoption barriers. *Journal of Building Engineering* 29 (12): 10–21. https://doi.org/10.1016/jjobe.2020.101212.

Nofer, M., P. Gomber, O. Hinz, and D. Schiereck. 2017. Blockchain, business and information. *Systems Engineering* 59 (3): 183–187. https://doi.org/10.1007/s12599-017-0467-3.

Nonaka, I., and H. Takeuchi. 1995. *The knowledge creating company: How Japanese companies create the dynamics of innovation*. New York: Oxford University Press.

Nonaka, I., and R. Toyama. 2005. The theory of the knowledge-creating firm: Subjectivity, objectivity and synthesis. *Industrial and Corporate Change* 14:419–436.

Nuryanto, U. W., Basrowi, I. Quraysin, and I. Pratiwi. 2024. Environmental management control system, blockchain adoption, cleaner production, and product efficiency on environmental reputation and performance: Empirical evidence from Indonesia. *Sustainable Futures* 7. https://doi.org/10.1016/J.SFTR.2024.100190.

Nwaiwu, F., M. A. Kwarteng, A. B. Jibril, L. Buřita, and M. Pilik. 2020. Impact of security and trust as factors that influence the adoption and use of digital technologies that generate, collect and transmit user data. In *International conference on cyber warfare and security*, 363–378.

O'Boyle, R. 2017. Block capital: How blockchain could change planning, The Planner. https://www.theplanner.co.uk/features/block-capital-how-blockchain-could-change-planning. Accessed 1 January 2020.

O'Hara, K. 2017. Smart contracts—Dumb idea. *IEEE Internet Computing* 21 (2): 97101. https://doi.org/10.1109/MIC.2017.48.

Odeh, A. 2025. Healthcare data management using blockchain-enabled sensor networks. In *Sensor networks for smart hospitals*, 139–154. https://doi.org/10.1016/B978-0-443-36370-2.00009-8.

Oesterreich, T. D., and F. Teuteberg. 2016. Understanding the implications of digitisation and automation in the context of Industry 4.0: A triangulation approach and elements of a research agenda for the construction industry. *Computers in Industry* 83:121–139. https://doi.org/10.1016/j.compind.2016.09.006.

Oguz, F. 2016. Organizational influences in technology adoption decisions: A case study of digital libraries. *College & Research Libraries* 77 (3): 314–334.

Oguz, F., C. V. Marsh, and C. Landis. 2010. Collaboration through communities of practice in the digital age. In *International symposium on information management in a changing world*, 18–30. Berlin, Heidelberg: Springer.

Okada, H. 2024. Book review. *Journal of Second Language Writing* 63:101089. https://doi.org/10.1016/J.JSLW.2023.101089.

Oke, A. E., J. Aliu, P. Oluwasefunmi Fadamiro, P. O. Akanni, and S. S. Stephen. 2023. Attaining digital transformation in construction: An appraisal of the awareness and usage of automation techniques. *Journal of Building Engineering* 67. https://doi.org/10.1016/J.JOBE.2023.105968.

Okello-Obura, C. 2012. Records and information management practices among SMEs in Tororo district, Uganda. *Library Review*447–469.

Oladapo, A. A. 2007. An Investigation into the use of ICT in the Nigerian Construction Industry. *Journal of Information Technology in Construction* 12:20–23.

Olawumi, T. O., D. W. M. Chan, S. Ojo, and M. C. H. Yam. 2022. Automating the modular construction process: A review of digital technologies and future directions with blockchain technology. *Journal of Building Engineering* 46. https://doi.org/10.1016/J.JOBE.2021.103720.

Oldenburg, B., and K. Glanz. 2008. Diffusion of innovations. *Health Behavior and Health Education: Theory, Research, and Practice* 4:313–333.

Oliveira, T., and M. F. Martins. 2010. Information technology adoption models at firm level: Review of literature. In European Conference on Information Management and Evaluation, pp. 312–324.

Onwuegbuzie, A. J., and N. L. Leech. 2005. On becoming a pragmatic researcher: The importance of combining quantitative and qualitative research methodologies. *International Journal of Social Research Methodology* 8 (5): 375–387.

Organization for Economic Cooperation and Development. 2004. *OECD principles of corporate governance*. Paris: OECD Publications.

Orlikowski, W. J. 1992. The duality of technology: Rethinking the concept of technology in organizations. *Organization Science* 3:398–427. https://doi.org/10.1287/orsc.3.3.398.

Orlikowski, W. J., and D. Robey. 1991. Information technology and the structuring of organizations. *Information Systems Research* 2 (2): 143–169. https://doi.org/10.1287/isre.2.2.143.

Oruwari, Y., M. Jev, and O. Owei. 2002. Acquisition of technological capability in Africa: A case study of indigenous building materials firms in Nigeria. ATPS working paper series/African Technology Policy Studies Network; no. 33.

Osama, Z. 2024. The digital twin framework: A roadmap to the development of user-centred digital twin in the built environment. *Journal of Building Engineering* 98. https://doi.org/10.1016/J.JOBE.2024.111081.

Osorio-Gómez, C. C., R. F. Herrera, J. M. Prieto-Osorio, and E. Pellicer. 2024. Conceptual model for implementation of digital transformation and organizational structure in the construction sector. *Ain Shams Engineering Journal* 15 (7): https://doi.org/10.1016/J.ASEJ.2024.102749.

Ou, C., X. Chen, K. Hu, Y. Cao, and Y. Shao. 2024. Factors influencing the digital intelligence transformation of offshore wind power enterprise. *Ocean and Coastal Management* 259. https://doi.org/10.1016/J.OCECOAMAN.2024.107463.

Pacheco-Torgal, F., and S. Jalali. 2012. Earth construction: Lessons from the past for future eco-efficient construction. *Construction and Building Materials* 29:512–519.

Padma, A., and M. Ramaiah. 2024. Blockchain based solution for secure information sharing in pharma supply chain management. *Heliyon* 10 (22): https://doi.org/10.1016/J.HELIYON.2024.E40273.

Paik, H. Y., X. Xu, H. D. Bandara, S. U. Lee, and S. K. Lo. 2019. Analysis of data management in blockchain-based systems: From architecture to governance. *IEEE Access* 7:186091–186107. https://doi.org/10.1109/ACCESS.2019.2961404.

Paiz, J. M. 2016. Book Review. *Journal of Second Language Writing* 34:28–30. https://doi.org/10.1016/J.JSLW.2016.09.002.

Pal, A., J. J. Lin, S. H. Hsieh, and M. Golparvar-Fard. 2023. Automated vision-based construction progress monitoring in built environment through digital twin. *Developments in the Built Environment* 16. https://doi.org/10.1016/J.DIBE.2023.100247.

Park, L. W., S. Lee, and H. Chang. 2018. *A sustainable home energy prosumer-chain methodology with energy tags over the blockchain Sustainability (Switzerland)* 10 (3): https://doi.org/10.3390/su10030658.

Pärn, E., N. Ghadiminia, B. García de Soto, and K. Oti-Sarpong. 2024. A perfect storm: Digital twins, cybersecurity, and general contracting firms. *Developments in the Built Environment* 18. https://doi.org/10.1016/J.DIBE.2024.100466.

Patel, H., and R. Connolly. 2007. Factors influencing technology adoption: A review. In *Information management in the networked economy: Issues and solutions*, 416–431.

Patil, S. S., and P. Y. L. Puranik. 2019. Blockchain technology. *International Journal of Trend in Scientific Research and Development* 3 (4): 573–574. https://doi.org/10.31142/ijtsrd23774.

Patton, M. Q. 2002. *Qualitative research & evaluation methods*. Oxford: Sage.

Pazaitis, A., P. De Filippi, and V. Kostakis. 2017. Blockchain and value systems in the sharing economy: The illustrative case of Backfeed. *Technological Forecasting and Social Change* 125:105–115. https://doi.org/10.1016/j.techfore.2017.05.025.

Peansupap, V., and D. Walker. 2005. Factors affecting ICT diffusion: A case study of three large Australian construction contractors. *Engineering, Construction and Architectural Management* 12 (1): 21–37.

Peck, M. E. 2017. Blockchain world—Do you need a blockchain? This chart will tell you if the technology can solve your problem. *IEEE Spectrum* 54 (10): 38–60. https://doi.org/10.1109/MSPEC.2017.8048838.

Penrose, E. T. 1959. The theory of the growth of the firm. https://doi.org/10.4324/9781315257068-16.

Pentury, C., R. H. Karsaman, H. Rahman, and Y. Rosmansyah. 2025. Application of digitalization and computerization technology in road construction. *Automation in Construction* 171. https://doi.org/10.1016/J.AUTCON.2025.106018.

Penzes, B. 2018. *Blockchain technology in the construction industry*. Westminster, London: Institution of Civil Engineers.

Pereira, C. S., B. Veloso, N. Durão, and F. Moreira. 2022. The influence of technological innovations on international business strategy before and during COVID-19 pandemic. *Procedia Computer Science* 196:44–51.

Perera, S., Senaratne, S. and Xiaohua, J. (2019) Conceptual model on estimating embodied carbon in construction supply chains using value chain and blockchain (November).

Perera, S., S. Nanayakkara, M. N. N. Rodrigo, S. Senaratne, and R. Weinand. 2020. Blockchain technology: Is it hype or real in the construction industry? *Journal of Industrial Information Integration* 17. https://doi.org/10.1016/J.JII.2020.100125.

Phua, F., and S. Rowlinson. 2003. Cultural differences as an explanatory variable for adversarial attitudes in the construction industry: The case of Hong Kong. *Construction Management and Economics* 21:777–785.

Pillay, J. 2019. Effectiveness of technology adoption for strategy implementation. Doctoral dissertation, University of Pretoria.

Pinto, J. K. 2016. *Project management: Achieving competitive advantage*. 4th ed. Harlow: Pearson Education.

Pinto Lopes, D., P. Rita, and H. Treiblmaier. 2021. The impact of blockchain on the aviation industry: Findings from a qualitative study. *Research in Transportation Business and Management* 41. https://doi.org/10.1016/J.RTBM.2021.100669.

Pischke, E. 2016. Methods of sustainability research in the social sciences. *The Social Science Journal* 53 (4): 583–584. https://doi.org/10.1016/J.SOSCIJ.2016.10.003.

Pitt, M., M. Tucker, M. Riley, and J. Longden. 2009. Towards sustainable construction: Promotion and best practices. *Construction Innovation* 9:201–224.

Plumridge, L. 2005. Qualitative methods and health policy research, Elizabeth Murphy, Robert Dingwall, Aldine de Gruyter, New York (2003), (320pp., Cost $49.95 (cloth), $29.95 (paper)), ISBN: 0-202-30710-7. *Social Science & Medicine* 61 (10): 2265. https://doi.org/10.1016/J.SOCSCIMED.2005.03.005.

Podsakoff, P. M., S. B. MacKenzie, and N. P. Podsakoff. 2012. Sources of method bias in social science research and recommendations on how to control it. *Annual Review of Psychology* 63 (1): 539–569.

Ponomarev, E. 2019. DApp survey results 2019. Current state and the future of DApps. https://medium.com/fluence-network/dapp-survey-results-2019-a04373db6452. Accessed 15 January 2022.

Ponomarev, E. 2020. DApp developers survey results. https://hackernoon.com/dapp-developers-survey-results-1c763901e756. Accessed 15 January 2022.

Poole, M. S. 2008. Adaptive structuration in a first look at communication theory.

Popper, N. 2018. What is the blockchain? Explaining the tech behind cryptocurrencies, *The New York Times*, 1 June 2018.

Pradeep, A. S. E., T. W. Yiu, Y. Zou, and R. Amor. 2021. Blockchain-aided information exchange records for design liability control and improved security. *Automation in Construction* 126:103667.

Prasad, V., and J. Koner. 2019. Using blockchain enabled smart contracts in Indian Crip sector: A literature review. In *International conference on construction real-estate infrastructure and project, Pune, Maharashtra, India*, 1–13.

Qiu, C., and X. Li. 2022. Blended analysis of occupational safety hazards and digital transformation of risk assessment in construction industries. *Canadian Journal of Civil Engineering* 50 (3): 184–196. https://doi.org/10.1139/CJCE-2022-0036.

Quattrone, P. 2000. Constructivism and accounting research: Towards a trans-disciplinary perspective. *Accounting, Auditing and Accountability Journal* 13 (2): 130–155.

Quinn Patoon, M. 2002. Learning in the field: An introduction to qualitative research, edited by Gretchen B. Rossman and Sharon F. Rallis. Sage, Beverly Hills, 1998. *American Journal of Evaluation* 23 (1): 115–116. https://doi.org/10.1016/S1098-2140(01)00162-X.

Radford, M. L. 2008. Constructing grounded theory: A practical guide through qualitative analysis. By Kathy Charmaz. London: Sage Publications, 2006. 224 pp. $34.95. ISBN

0761973532 (paperback). *Library & Information Science Research* 30 (2): 158–159. https://doi.org/10.1016/J.LISR.2007.11.003.

Rafique, W., and J. Qadir. 2024. Internet of everything meets the metaverse: Bridging physical and virtual worlds with blockchain. *Computer Science Review* 54. https://doi.org/10.1016/J.COSREV.2024.100678.

Rai, H. M., K. K. Shukla, L. Tightiz, and S. Padmanaban. 2024. Enhancing data security and privacy in energy applications: Integrating IoT and blockchain technologies. *Heliyon* 10 (19): https://doi.org/10.1016/J.HELIYON.2024.E38917.

Raitoharju, R. 2007. *Information technology acceptance in the Finnish social and healthcare sector: Exploring the effects of cultural factors*. Publications of the Turku School of Economics. www.tukkk.fi/julkaisut/vk/Ae4_2007.pdf. Accessed 3 July 2021.

Raja, U., R. A. Sheikh, M. Abbas, and D. Bouckenooghe. 2018. Do procedures really matter when rewards are more important? A Pakistani perspective on the effects of distributive and procedural justice on employee behaviors. *European Review of Applied Psychology* 68 (2): 79–88.

Ramachandra, T., and J. O. Rotimi. 2011. The nature of payment problems in the New Zealand construction industry. *Construction Economics and Building* 11:22–33.

Ramage, M. 2018. From BIM to blockchain in construction: What you need to know, constructible. https://constructible.trimble.com/construction-industry/from-bim-to-blockchain-in-construction-what-you-need-to-know. Accessed 3 January 2020.

Ramalingam, S., M. Subramanian, B. S. Kumar, S. Rushma, N. Tarakaramu, A. Trigui, F. Yuldashev, T. Saidani, and M. I. Khan. 2025. Blockchain-enhanced optimization for a secure and transparent global energy supply chain with reduced environmental impact and cost. *Egyptian Informatics Journal* 30:100647. https://doi.org/10.1016/J.EIJ.2025.100647.

Rame, R., P. Purwanto, and S. Sudarno. 2024. Industry 5.0 and sustainability: An overview of emerging trends and challenges for a green future. *Innovation and Green Development* 3 (4): https://doi.org/10.1016/J.IGD.2024.100173.

Ramey, M. 1995. Writing up qualitative research. *Evaluation Practice* 16 (3): 299–301. https://doi.org/10.1016/0886-1633(95)90047-0.

Rana, M. T., M. Numan, M. Yousif, T. Hussain, A. Z. Khan, and X. Zhao. 2024. Enhancing sustainability in electric mobility: Exploring blockchain applications for secure EV charging and energy management. *Computers and Electrical Engineering* 119. https://doi.org/10.1016/J.COMPELECENG.2024.109503.

Rashid, M. R. A., A. Al Rafi, M. A. Islam, S. U. Sharkar, Z. H. Rafi, M. Hasan, M. S. Ali, and M. S. H. Khan. 2025. Enhancing land management policy in Bangladesh: A blockchain-based framework for transparent and efficient land management. *Land Use Policy* 150. https://doi.org/10.1016/J.LANDUSEPOL.2024.107436.

Rasoloharijaona, S., B. Rakotosamimanana, B. Randrianambinina, and E. Zimmermann. 2003. Pair-specific usage of sleeping sites and their implications for social organization in a Nocturnal Malagasy Primate, the Milne Edwards' Sportive Lemur (Lepilemur edwardsi). *American Journal of Physical Anthropology* 122 (3): 251–258. https://doi.org/10.1002/ajpa.10281.

Ratnasabapathy, S., R. Rameezdeen, and N. A. Lebbe. 2008. Exploratory study of external environmental factors influencing the procurement selection in construction. In Proceedings of the CIB International Conference on Building Education and Research, 10–15 February 2008, Kandalama.

Redfern, S. J. 1986. Nursing research: The application of qualitative approaches. *Nurse Education Today* 6 (4): 186–187. https://doi.org/10.1016/0260-6917(86)90011-0.

Regona, M., T. Yigitcanlar, C. Hon, and M. Teo. 2024. Artificial intelligence and sustainable development goals: Systematic literature review of the construction industry. *Sustainable Cities and Society* 108. https://doi.org/10.1016/J.SCS.2024.105499.

Reyna, A., C. Martín, J. Chen, E. Soler, and M. Díaz. 2018. On blockchain and its integration with IoT. Challenges and opportunities. *Future Generation Computer Systems* 88:173–190.

Riaz, M., R. Kausar, T. Jameel, and D. Pamucar. 2024. Cubic picture fuzzy topological data analysis with integrating blockchain and the metaverse for uncertain supply chain management. *Engineering Applications of Artificial Intelligence* 131. https://doi.org/10.1016/J.ENGAPPAI.2023.107827.

Richards, J. D. 1994. Qualitative health research special issue. *Evaluation Practice* 15 (1): 107–108. https://doi.org/10.1016/0886-1633(94)90070-1.

Richards, G., and W. Munsters. 2010. Cultural tourism research methods. In *Cultural tourism research methods*, 1–228. https://doi.org/10.1016/J.ANNALS.2011.07.014.

Říhová, Z. 2015. Influence of organization management on systems of performance measurement and management control. *Acta Informatica Pragensia* 4 (1): 80–89.

Risius, M., and K. Spohrer. 2017. A blockchain research framework: What we (don't) know, where we go from here, and how we will get there. *Business and Information Systems Engineering* 59 (6): 385–409. https://doi.org/10.1007/s12599-017-0506-0.

Rivard, H., T. Froese, L. M. Waugh, T. El-Diraby, R. Mora, H. Torres, S. M. Gill, and T. O'Reilly. 2004. Case studies on the use of information technology in the Canadian construction industry. *Journal of Information Technology in Construction* 9 (2): 19–34.

Rob, P., C. Coronel, and K. Crockett. 2000. *Database systems: Design implementation & management*. 4th ed. Cambridge: Course.

Robbins, S. P., and M. Coulter. 2005. *Management*. 8th ed. Upper Saddle River, NJ: Pearson Prentice Hall.

Robson, C. 2002. *Real world research: A resource for social scientists and practitioner-researchers*. London: Wiley-Blackwell.

Rodrigo, M. N. N., S. Perera, S. Senaratne, and X. Jin. 2018. Blockchain for construction supply chains: A literature synthesis. In *Proceedings of ICEC-PAQS conference, Sydney, Australia*.

Rodrigo, M. N. N., S. Perera, S. Senaratne, and X. Jin. 2019. Embodied carbon mitigation strategies in the construction industry. In *CIB world building congress, Hong Kong*.

Rogers, E. M. 1995. Diffusion of innovations: Modifications of a model for telecommunications. In *Die Diffusion von Innovationen in der Telekommunikation*, ed. M. W. Stoetzer and A. Mahler, 25–38. Heidelberg: Springer. https://doi.org/10.1007/978-3-642-79868-9_2.

Rogers, E. M. 2003. *Diffusion of innovation*. 5th ed. New York, NY: Free Press.

Rogers, M. R., and E. C. Lopez. 2002. Identifying critical cross-cultural school psychology competencies. *Journal of School Psychology* 40 (2): 115–141.

Rosic, A. 2017. Blockchain applications that are transforming society Blockgeeks. https://blockgeeks.com/guides/blockchain-applications/. Accessed 07 July 2021.

Rowley, J. E. 2008. *Organizing knowledge: An introduction to managing access to information*. Farnham: Ashgate Publishing.

Rudden, K. 2019. *BIM and ISO 19650from a project management perspective*. Bern: EFCA.

Russell, D. M., and A. M. Hoag. 2004. People and information technology in the supply chain: Social and organizational influences on adoption. *International Journal of Physical Distribution & Logistics Management* 34 (2): 102–122.

Rutten, M. E. J., A. G. Doree, and J. I. M. Halman. 2009. Innovation and interorganizational cooperation: A synthesis of literature. *Construction Innovation*285–297. https://doi.org/10.1108/14714170910973501.

Ryan, J. C., and S. A. Tipu. 2013. Leadership effects on innovation propensity: A two-factor full range leadership model. *Journal of Business Research* 66 (10): 2116–2129.

Sabharwal, M. 2007. Foundations of qualitative research: Interpretive and critical approaches. *The Social Science Journal* 44 (3): 582–584. https://doi.org/10.1016/J.SOSCIJ.2007.07.007.

Sadeghi, M., A. Mahmoudi, and X. Deng. 2021. Adopting distributed ledger technology for the sustainable construction industry: Evaluating the barriers using ordinal priority approach. *Environmental Science and Pollution Research*1–26. https://doi.org/10.1007/s11356-021-16376-y.

Sadeghi, M., A. Mahmoudi, X. Deng, and M. Luo. 2024. A novel performance measurement of innovation and R&D projects for driving digital transformation in construction using ordinal priority approach. *KSCE Journal of Civil Engineering*. https://doi.org/10.1007/S12205-024-1437-1.

Sadri, H. 2025. AI-driven integration of digital twins and blockchain for smart building management systems: A multi-stage empirical study. *Journal of Building Engineering* 105:112439. https://doi.org/10.1016/J.JOBE.2025.112439.

Saheb, T., and F. H. Mamaghani. 2021. Exploring the barriers and organizational values of blockchain adoption in the banking industry. *Journal of High Technology Management Research* 32 (2): 100417. https://doi.org/10.1016/J.HITECH.2021.100417.

Sajn, N. 2016. European parliament, electricity 'prosumers'.

Sakib Sizan, N., D. Dey, Md. Abu Layek, M. A. Uddin, and E.-N. Huh. 2025. Evaluating blockchain platforms for IoT applications in Industry 5.0: A comprehensive review. *Blockchain: Research and Applications* 100276. https://doi.org/10.1016/J.BCRA.2025.100276.

Saleh, A. M. 2004. *Adoção de tecnologia: Um estudo sobre a adoção de software livre nas empresas*. São Paulo: USP, 149 f. Dissertação (Mestrado em Administração)—Faculdade de Economia, Administração e Contabilidade, Universidade de São Paulo, São Paulo.

Salykov, A., U. Shalbolova, and A. Junusova. 2024. Transformation in Kazakhstan's construction industry amidst digitalisation of the economy. *Infrastructure Asset Management*. https://doi.org/10.1680/JINAM.24.00037.

Salzano, F., L. Marchesi, R. Pareschi, and R. Tonelli. 2024. Integrating Blockchain technology within an Information Ecosystem. *Blockchain: Research and Applications* 100225. https://doi.org/10.1016/J.BCRA.2024.100225.

Samaha, P., F. el Kalach, and R. Harik. 2024. Leveraging the usage of blockchain toward trust-dominated manufacturing systems. *Journal of Manufacturing Systems* 77:612–638. https://doi.org/10.1016/J.JMSY.2024.10.010.

Sampaio, L., J. Varjao, E. J. S. Pires, and P. B. Oliveira. 2012. Diffusion of innovation in organizations: Simulation using evolutionary computation. In *IEEE fourth world congress on nature and biologically inspired computing (NaBIC)*, 25–30.

Samset, K., and G. H. Volden. 2016. Front-end definition of projects: Ten paradoxes and some reflections regarding project management and project governance. *International Journal of Project Management* 34 (2): 297–313.

San, K. M., C. F. Choy, and W. P. Fung. 2019. The potentials and impacts of blockchain technology in construction industry: A literature review IOP Conference Series. *Materials Science and Engineering* 495 (1): https://doi.org/10.1088/1757-899X/495/1/012005.

Sánchez, B. N., E. Budtz-Jørgensen, L. M. Ryan, and H. Hu. 2005. Structural equation models: A review with applications to environmental epidemiology. *Journal of the American Statistical Association* 100 (472): 1443–1455.

Sandanayake, M. S. 2022. Environmental Impacts of Construction in Building Industry—A Review of Knowledge Advances. *Gaps and Future Directions. Knowledge* 2 (1): 139–156.

Saradara, S. M., M. M. A. Khalfan, S. V. Jaya, V. Swarnakar, A. Rauf, and M. el Fadel. 2024. Advancing building construction: A novel conceptual framework integrating circularity with modified lean project delivery systems. *Developments in the Built Environment* 20. https://doi.org/10.1016/J.DIBE.2024.100531.

Sarantakos, S. 2005. *Social research*. 3rd ed. Basingstoke: Palgrave Macmillan.

Sargent, K., P. Hyland, and S. Sawang. 2012. Factors influencing the adoption of information technology in a construction business. *Australasian Journal of Construction Economics and Building* 12 (2): 72–86.

Saunders, L. 2008. Qualitative research for the information professional: A practical handbook, 2nd edition, G.E. Gorman, Peter Clayton (Eds.), Facet Publishing, London (2005), (distributed by Neal-Schuman), $95.00., ISBN: 1-85604-472-6. *Library & Information Science Research* 30 (1): 78. https://doi.org/10.1016/J.LISR.2007.10.001.

Saunders, L. 2014. Book review. *Library & Information Science Research* 36 (2): 131. https://doi.org/10.1016/J.LISR.2014.04.002.

Saunders, M., P. Lewis, and A. Thornhill. 2012. *Research methods for business students*. 5th ed. Harlow: Prentice Hall.

Savioz, P., and M. Blum. 2002. Strategic forecast tool for SMEs: How the opportunity landscape interacts with business strategy to anticipate technological trends. *Technovation* 22 (2): 91–100.

Sawang, S. 2011. Key performance indicators for innovation implementation: Perception vs. actual usage. *Asia Pacific Management Review* 16 (1): 23–29.

Sayrs, L. 1998. InterViews: An Introduction to Qualitative Research Interviewing Steinar Kvale. Thousand Oaks, CA: Sage, 1996. 326 pp. *The American Journal of Evaluation* 19 (2): 267–270. https://doi.org/10.1016/S1098-2140(99)80208-2.

Scharpf, F. W. 1994. Games real actors could play positive and negative coordination in embedded negotiations. *Journal of Theoretical Politics* 6 (1): 27–53.

Scheffe, H. 1999. *The analysis of variance*. Ontario: Wiley.

Schermerhorn, J. R., Jr. 2005. *Management*. 8th ed. Hoboken: Wiley.

Schlenger, J., K. Pluta, A. Mathew, T. Yeung, R. Sacks, and A. Borrmann. 2025. Reference architecture and ontology framework for digital twin construction. *Automation in Construction* 174. https://doi.org/10.1016/J.AUTCON.2025.106111.

Schreiber, J. B., A. Nora, F. K. Stage, E. A. Barlow, and J. King. 2006. Reporting structural equation modeling and confirmatory factor analysis results: A review. *The Journal of Educational Research* 99 (6): 323–338.

Serpell, A., S. Barai, and A. Oladapo. 2005. An investigation into the use of ICT in the Nigerian construction industry.

Sestino, A., M. I. Prete, L. Piper, and G. Guido. 2020. Internet of Things and Big Data as enablers for business digitalization strategies. *Technovation* 98:102173.

Sexton, M., and P. Barrett. 2003. A literature synthesis of innovation in small construction firms: Insights, ambiquities and questions. *Construction Management and Economics* 21 (6): 613–622. https://doi.org/10.1080/0144619032000134147.

Shafique, F., and K. Mahmood. 2010. The role of educational information systems for survival in information society and the case of Pakistan. *International Information and Library Review* 42 (3): 164–173. https://doi.org/10.1016/j.iilr.2010.07.007.

Shah, M. A., and N. Raj. 2025. Examining the role of blockchain and public-private partnerships in design and deployment of blockchain-enabled CBDC. *Digital Business* 5 (1): https://doi.org/10.1016/J.DIGBUS.2025.100111.

Shahrasbi, N., and G. Paré. 2014. Rethinking the concept of organizational readiness: What can is researchers learn from the change management field? In *Proceedings of twentieth Americas conference on information systems, Savannah*, 1–16.

Shahrubudin, N., T. C. Lee, and R. Ramlan. 2019. An overview on 3D printing technology: Technological, materials, and applications. *Procedia Manufacturing* 35:1286–1296. https://doi.org/10.1016/j.promfg.2019.06.089.

Sharmila, K., S. Kamalakkannan, M. R. Devi, and M. C. Shanthi. 2019. A comprehensive study on blockchain with its components, taxonomy and consensus. *International Journal of Management, Technology and Engineering* 9 (1): 971–975.

Shepherd, M. 1997a. Making sense of qualitative data. *Applied Geography* 17 (3): 252–253. https://doi.org/10.1016/S0143-6228(97)87233-5.

Shepherd, M. 1997b. Qualitative researching. *Applied Geography* 17 (3): 252. https://doi.org/10.1016/S0143-6228(97)90005-9.

Shi, H. 2024. Book review. *Journal of Pragmatics* 225:66–68. https://doi.org/10.1016/J.PRAGMA.2024.03.011.

Shi, M., A. Hoffmann, A. Wagner, T. Huyeng, C. D. Thiele, and U. Rüppel. 2021. Using blockchain technology to implement peer-to-peer network in construction industry. In *Lecture notes in civil engineering*, 839–849. Springer. https://doi.org/10.1007/978-3-030-51295-8_58.

Shibeika, A., and C. Harty. 2015. Diffusion of digital innovation in construction: A case study of a UK engineering firm. *Construction Management and Economics* 33 (5–6): 453466. https://doi.org/10.1080/01446193.2015.1077982.

Shillcock, P. 2019. ISO 19650: When you should adopt it and why. https://www.bimplus.co.uk/iso-19650-timetable-implementation/. Accessed 4 January 2022.

Shin, I. 2006. Adoption of enterprise application software and firm performance. *Small Business Economics* 26 (3): 241–256.

Shirwa, A. M., A. M. Hassan, A. Q. Hassan, and M. Kilinc. 2025. A cooperative governance framework for sustainable digital transformation in construction: The role of digital enablement and digital strategy. *Results in Engineering* 25. https://doi.org/10.1016/J.RINENG.2025.104139.

Shojaei, A. 2019. Exploring applications of blockchain technology in the construction industry. In *10th international structural engineering and construction conference*. https://doi.org/10.14455/isec.res.2019.78.

Shook, C. L., D. J. Ketchen Jr., G. T. M. Hult, and K. M. Kacmar. 2004. An assessment of the use of structural equation modeling in strategic management research. *Strategic Management Journal* 25 (4): 397–404.

Showkat, N., and H. Parveen. 2017. In-depth interview. Quadrant-I (e-Text).

Shukla, A., P. Jirli, A. Mishra, and A. K. Singh. 2024. An overview of blockchain research and future agenda: Insights from structural topic modeling. *Journal of Innovation and Knowledge* 9 (4): https://doi.org/10.1016/J.JIK.2024.100605.

Silva, A. L. M. R. 2005. *A influência do treinamento de usuários na aceitação de sistemas ERP em empresas no Brasil*. Rio de Janeiro: UFRJ., 118f. Dissertação (Mestrado em Administração)—Instituto COPPEAD de Administração, Universidade Federal do Rio de Janeiro, Rio de Janeiro.

Silva, L. 2006. Post-positivist review of technology acceptance model. *Journal of the Association for Information Systems* 8 (4): 256–266.

Silva, P. M., and G. A. Dias. 2007. Theories about technology acceptance: Why the users accept or reject the information technology? *Brazilian Journal of Information Science* 1 (2): 69–86.

Silva, F. C., A. Ahmed, J. M. Martínez, and Y. C. Kim. 2019. Design and implementation of a blockchain-based energy trading platform for electric vehicles in smart campus parking lots. *Energies* 12 (24): https://doi.org/10.3390/en12244814.

Silverman, K. 2013. *The interaction of emotion and reasoning in contemporary talking therapy*. The University of Manchester.

Silvestri, R., E. Carloni, D. Morrone, and S. Santovito. 2024. The role of blockchain technology in supply chain relationships: Balancing efficiency and relational dynamics. *Journal of Purchasing and Supply Management*. https://doi.org/10.1016/J.PURSUP.2024.100967.

Simões, A., L. Oliveira, J. C. Rodrigues, O. Simas, G. Dalmarco, and A. C. Barros. 2019. Environmental factors influencing the adoption of digitalization technologies in automotive supply chains. In *2019 IEEE international conference on engineering, technology and innovation (ICE/ITMC)*, 1–7.

Singh, Y. K. 2006. *Fundamental of research methodology and statistics*. New Delhi, India: New Age International.

Singh, A. K., and V. R. P. Kumar. 2024. Integrating blockchain technology success factors in the supply chain of circular economy-driven construction materials: An environmentally sustainable paradigm. *Journal of Cleaner Production* 460. https://doi.org/10.1016/J.JCLEPRO.2024.142577.

Singh, A. K., V. R. P. Kumar, G. Dehdasht, S. R. Mohandes, P. Manu, and F. Pour Rahimian. 2023a. Investigating barriers to blockchain adoption in construction supply chain management: A fuzzy-based MCDM approach. *Technological Forecasting and Social Change* 196. https://doi.org/10.1016/J.TECHFORE.2023.122849.

Singh, A. K., V. R. P. Kumar, M. Shoaib, T. S. Adebayo, and M. Irfan. 2023b. A strategic roadmap to overcome blockchain technology barriers for sustainable construction: A deep learning-based dual-stage SEM-ANN approach. *Technological Forecasting and Social Change* 194. https://doi.org/10.1016/J.TECHFORE.2023.122716.

Siraparapu, S. R., and S. M. A. K. Azad. 2024. Securing the IoT landscape: A comprehensive review of secure systems in the digital era. *E-Prime—Advances in Electrical Engineering, Electronics and Energy* 10. https://doi.org/10.1016/J.PRIME.2024.100798.

Smeijsters, H. 1996. Music Therapy Research: Quantitative and Qualitative Perspectives. *The Arts in Psychotherapy* 23 (3): 277–280. https://doi.org/10.1016/0197-4556(96)00019-6.

Smith, K. 1985. Implications of value-added network services. *Data Processing* 27 (6): 41–45. https://doi.org/10.1016/0011-684X(85)90272-2.

Smith, P. 2003. Trend in the Australian quantity surveying 1995–2003. *The Australian Journal of Construction Economics and Building* 1 (1): 1–15.

Smith, A. M. 2013. Research methods in education. *Nurse Education in Practice* 13 (3): e3. https://doi.org/10.1016/J.NEPR.2012.06.001.

Smith, D., and K. Langfield-Smith. 2004. Structural equation modeling in management accounting research: Critical analysis and opportunities. *Journal of Accounting Literature* 23:49.

Smith, S., and L. O'rourke. 2019. Exploring the potential of blockchain technology for the UK construction industry. *Sustainability* 1:1–53.

Smith, M. E., R. Thorpe, and P. Jackson. 2008. *Management research: Theory and research*. Los Angeles: SAGE.

Smithies, G., G. Papi, E. McGillycuddy, and E. McGillycuddy. 2025. The blueprint of digital advancement: A study of construction technology implementation. *Proceedings of the Institution of Civil Engineers: Civil Engineering*. https://doi.org/10.1680/JCIEN.24.01004.

Snieder, R., and K. Larner. 2009. *The art of being a scientist: A guide for graduate students and their mentors*. Cambridge: Cambridge University Press.

Snyder, H. 1996. Qualitative interviewing: The art of hearing data. *Library & Information Science Research* 18 (2): 194–195. https://doi.org/10.1016/S0740-8188(96)90024-9.

Snyder, R. A., and W. L. Fields. 2006. Measuring hospital readiness for information technology (IT) innovation: A multisite study of the organizational information technology innovation readiness scale. *Journal of Nursing Measurement* 14 (1): 45–55.

Söhne, J. 2015. The Blockchain—Can it change the world? http://www.the-blockchain.com/2015/11/04/the-blockchain-can-it-change-the-world/. Accessed 14 July 2021.

Solahudeen Tando, M., S. Gawusu, S. Yakubu, O. S. Kwabena, D. Donatus, and S. Raqib Abu. 2024. Decentralized energy trading with blockchain technology. In *The intersection of blockchain and energy trading: Exploring decentralized solutions for next-generation energy markets*, 75–101. https://doi.org/10.1016/B978-0-443-23627-3.00004-1.

Sommerville, J., N. Craig, and J. Hendry. 2010. The role of the project manager: All things to all people? *Structural Survey*.

Sompolgrunk, A., S. Banihashemi, H. Golzad, and K. le Nguyen. 2024. Strategic alignment of BIM and big data through systematic analysis and model development. *Automation in Construction* 168. https://doi.org/10.1016/J.AUTCON.2024.105801.

Soori, M., R. Dastres, and B. Arezoo. 2023. AI-powered blockchain technology in industry 4.0, a review. *Journal of Economy and Technology* 1:222–241. https://doi.org/10.1016/J.JECT.2024.01.001.

Soori, M., F. K. G. Jough, R. Dastres, and B. Arezoo. 2024. Blockchains for industrial Internet of Things in sustainable supply chain management of industry 4.0, a review. *Sustainable Manufacturing and Service Economics* 3:100026. https://doi.org/10.1016/J.SMSE.2024.100026.

Spanaki, K., D. Dennehy, T. Papadopoulos, and R. Dubey. 2025. Data-driven digital transformation in operations and supply chain management. *International Journal of Production Economics* 284:109599. https://doi.org/10.1016/J.IJPE.2025.109599.

Staszczak, J., P. Mikalef, and S. Angelopoulos. 2025. Navigating blockchain assimilation in private institutions: A multi-level perspective analysis. *Procedia Computer Science* 256:36–46. https://doi.org/10.1016/J.PROCS.2025.02.093.

Stephens, D. 2011. Review essay: Narrative and biographical methods in education and social sciences research. *International Journal of Educational Development* 31 (3): 326–327. https://doi.org/10.1016/J.IJEDUDEV.2010.11.009.

Stoner, J. A. F., R. F. Edward, and Gilbert. Jr.D. R. 1995. *Management*. 6th ed. Englewood Cliffs, NJ: Prentice Hall.

Straub, E. T. 2009. Understanding technology adoption: Theory and future directions for informal learning. *Review of Educational Research* 79 (2): 625–649.

Sturgill, R. E., C. Van Dyke, S. McCormack, and S. D. Kreis. 2015. Case analysis of inherent programmatic sustainability resulting from application of context sensitive design principles. In *Paper presented at the 94th annual meeting of the Transportation Research Board, Washington, DC.*

Su, S., R. Y. Zhong, Y. Jiang, J. Song, Y. Fu, and H. Cao. 2023. Digital twin and its potential applications in construction industry: State-of-art review and a conceptual framework. *Advanced Engineering Informatics* 57. https://doi.org/10.1016/J.AEI.2023.102030.

Subramani, T., A. Sarkunam, and J. Jayalakshmi. 2014. Planning and scheduling of high-rise building using primavera. *International Journal of Engineering Research and Applications* 4 (6): 134–144.

Succar, B. 2009. Building information modelling framework: A research and delivery foundation for industry stakeholders. *Automation in Construction* 18 (3): 357–375. https://doi.org/10.1016/j.autcon.2008.10.003.

Sun, M., and R. Howard. 2003. *Understanding IT in construction*. London: Spon Press. https://doi.org/10.4324/9780203645239.

Sun, J., J. Yan, and K. Z. K. Zhang. 2016. Blockchain-based sharing services: What blockchain technology can contribute to smart cities Financial. *Innovation* 2 (1): https://doi.org/10.1186/s40854-016-0040-y.

Sung, C. S., and J. Y. Park. 2021. Understanding of blockchain-based identity management system adoption in the public sector. *Journal of Enterprise Information Management* 34 (5): 1481–1505.

Swam, M. 2015. *Blockchain blueprint for a new economy*. O'Reilly Media.

Swan, M. 2015. Blockchain: Blueprint for a new economy, Climate Change 2013—The Physical Science Basis. https://doi.org/10.1017/CBO9781107415324.004.

Szabo, N. 1994. Smart contracts. https://www.fon.hum.uva.nl/rob/Courses/InformationInSpeech/CDROM/Literature/LOTwinterschool2006/szabo.best.vwh.net/smart.contracts.html. Accessed 1 January 2020.

Tabachnick, B. G., and L. S. Fidell. 2007. *Experimental designs using ANOVA*. Belmont, CA: Thomson/Brooks/Cole.

Taherdoost, H. 2018. Development of an adoption model to assess user acceptance of e-service technology: E-service technology acceptance model. *Behaviour & Information Technology* 37 (2): 173–197.

Taherdoost, H. 2022. A critical review of blockchain acceptance models—Blockchain technology adoption frameworks and applications. *Computers* 11 (2): 1–31.

Taherdoost, H., and M. Madanchian. 2020. Developing and validating a theoretical model to evaluate customer satisfaction of e-services. In *Digital innovations for customer engagement, management, and organizational improvement*, 46–65. IGI Global.

Takahashi, B. R.. 2017. *How can creative industries benefit from blockchain?* McKinsey & Company. https://www.mckinsey.com/industries/technology-media-and-telecommunications/our-insights/how-can-creative-industries-benefit-from-blockchain. Accessed 5 January 2020.

Tan, K. 2008. A guide to qualitative field research. *The Social Science Journal* 45 (4): 703–705. https://doi.org/10.1016/J.SOSCIJ.2008.09.002.

Tang, A., E. T. Tchao, A. S. Agbemenu, E. Keelson, G. S. Klogo, and J. J. Kponyo. 2024. Assessing blockchain and IoT technologies for agricultural food supply chains in Africa: A feasibility analysis. *Heliyon* 10 (15): https://doi.org/10.1016/J.HELIYON.2024.E34584.

Tangsakul, M., and P. Sureeyatanapas. 2024. Understanding critical barriers to the adoption of blockchain technology in the logistics context: An interpretive structural modelling approach. *Journal of Open Innovation: Technology, Market, and Complexity* 10 (3): https://doi.org/10.1016/J.JOITMC.2024.100355.

Tao, Z., X. Liu, Y. Li, P. Hu, W. Tang, N. Luo, J. Wu, and R. Yang. 2024. Intelligent emergency assisted decision-making method based on standard digitalization: Hazardous chemical accidents in industrial parks. *Journal of Safety Science and Resilience*. https://doi.org/10.1016/J.JNLSSR.2024.06.009.

Tapscott, D., and A. Tapscott. 2017. How blockchain will change organizations. *MIT Sloan Management Review* 58 (2): 10–13. https://doi.org/10.7551/mitpress/11645.003.0010.

Tashakkori, A., and C. Teddlie. 2003. *Handbook of mixed methods in social and behavioral research*. Thousand Oaks, CA: Sage.

Taylor, F. W. 1911. *Shop management (new edition 2008)*. Nu Vision Publications.

Taylor, R. S. 1966. *Information management in engineering education*. Bethlehem, PA: Lehigh University Press.

Technopedia. 2017). Electronic customer relationship management (E-CRM). https://www.techopedia.com/definition/30914/electronic-customer-relationship-management-e-crm. Accessed 16 February 2017.

Terra, J., and T. Angeloni. 2003. Understanding the difference between information management and knowledge management. In *KM advantage*, 1–9.

Thomson Reuters. 2018. Blockchain for construction/real estate.

Thorpe, D., N. Ryan, and M. B. Charles. 2009. Innovation and small residential builders: An Australian study. *Construction Innovation* 9 (2): 184–200. https://doi.org/10.1108/14714170910950821.

Tian, M. H., and Y. Chen. 2025. Book review. *System* 130:103628. https://doi.org/10.1016/J.SYSTEM.2025.103628.

Tilson, D., Lyytinen, K. and Sorensen, C. (2010) Digital infrastructures: The missing IS research agenda Information Systems Research, 21(4), pp. 748–759. adoi:10.1287/isre.1100.0318.

Toderean, L., T. Cioara, I. Anghel, E. Sarmas, V. Michalakopoulos, and V. Marinakis. 2025. Demand response optimization for smart grid integrated buildings: Review of technology enablers landscape and innovation challenges. *Energy and Buildings* 326. https://doi.org/10.1016/J.ENBUILD.2024.115067.

Tong, A., P. Sainsbury, and J. Craig. 2007. Consolidated criteria for reporting qualitative research (COREQ): A 32-item checklist for interviews and focus groups. *International Journal for Quality in Health Care* 19 (6): 349–357.

Truong, N. B., K. Sun, G. M. Lee, and Y. Guo. 2020. GDPR-compliant personal data management: A blockchain-based solution. *IEEE Transactions on Information Forensics and Security* 15:1746–1761. https://doi.org/10.1109/TIFS.2019.2948287.

Tuan, L. T., and S. Venkatesh. 2010. Organizational culture and technological innovation adoption in private hospitals. *International Business Research* 3 (3): 144–153.

Tuman, J. J. 1998. Shaping corporate strategy with internet-based project management. In *Paper read at Proceedings of the 14th world congress on project management, Where? When?* 599–607.

Turban, E., E. McLean, J. Wetherbe, and D. Leidner. 2004. *Information technology for management: Transforming organizations in the digital economy place?* Wiley.

Turban, E., D. Leidner, E. McLean, and J. Wetherbe. 2007. *Information technology for management: Transforming organizations in the digital economy*. Ontario: Wiley.

Turk, Z., and R. Klinc. 2017. Potentials of blockchain technology for construction management. *Procedia Engineering* 196 (6): 638–645. https://doi.org/10.1016/_j.proeng.2017.08.052.

Turner, J. R. 2004. Farsighted project contract management: Incomplete in its entirety. *Construction Management and Economics* 22 (1): 75–83.

Turner, J. R. 2006. Towards a theory of project management: The nature of the functions of project management. *International Journal of Project Management* 24 (4): 277–279.

Turner, J. R. 2009. *The handbook of project-based management*. London, UK: McGraw-Hill.

Turner, J. R., and A. Keegan. 2001. Mechanisms of governance in the project-based organization: Roles of the broker and steward. *European Management Journal* 19 (3): 254–267.

Turner, J. R., and R. Müller. 2003. On the nature of the project as a temporary organization. *International Journal of Project Management* 21 (1): 1–8.

Turner, J. R., M. Morris, and I. Atamenwan. 2019. A Theoretical literature review on adaptive structuration theory as its relevance to human resource development. *Advances in Developing Human Resources* 21 (3): 289–302. https://doi.org/10.1177/1523422319851275.

Udokwu, C., A. Norta, and C. Wenna. 2021. Designing a collaborative construction-project platform on blockchain technology for transparency, traceability, and information symmetry. In *ACM international conference proceeding series*, 1–9. https://doi.org/10.1145/3456126.3456134.

Ullah, Z., M. Naeem, A. Coronato, P. Ribino, and G. de Pietro. 2023. Blockchain applications in sustainable smart cities. *Sustainable Cities and Society* 97. https://doi.org/10.1016/J.SCS.2023.104697.

Ullah, N., W. M. Al-Rahmi, F. Alblehai, Y. Fernando, Z. H. Alharbi, R. Zhanbayev, A. S. Al-Adwan, and M. Habes. 2024. Blockchain-powered grids: Paving the way for a sustainable and efficient future. *Heliyon* 10 (10): https://doi.org/10.1016/J.HELIYON.2024.E31592.

Underwood, S. 2016. Blockchain beyond bitcoin. *Communications of the ACM* 59 (11): 15–17. https://doi.org/10.1145/2994581.

Urbach, N., and B. Muller. 2012. The updated DeLone and McLean model of information system success. In *Information systems theory: Explaining and predicting*, Integrated series in information systems, vol. 28. New York, NY: Springer. https://doi.org/10.1007/978-1-4419-6108-2_1.

Valsan, V., N. S. K. Vuppala, S. S. H. Koganti, L. S. E. Kalla, K. A. Pappala, and M. V. Ramesh. 2025. Conceptual study—Artificial intelligence-integrated blockchain micromarkets for sustainable energy. *Renewable and Sustainable Energy Reviews* 214. https://doi.org/10.1016/J.RSER.2025.115482.

van Arsdale, P. W. 1996. Research methods in Anthropology: Qualitative and quantitative approaches. *Evaluation Practice* 17 (1): 91–92. https://doi.org/10.1016/S0886-1633(96)90044-6.

Vanderstoep, S. W., and D. D. Johnston. 2009. *Research methods for everyday life: Blending qualitative and quantitative approaches*. San Francisco, CA: Jossey-Bass.

Vanson, S. 2014. What on earth are ontology and epistemology? www.theperformancesolution.com/earth-ontology-epistemology/. Accessed 24 March 2017.

Velastegui, R., R. Poler, and M. Díaz-Madroñero. 2025. Revolutionising industrial operations: The synergy of multiagent robotic systems and blockchain technology in operations planning and control. *Expert Systems with Applications* 269. https://doi.org/10.1016/J.ESWA.2025.126460.

Veliquette, A. J. 2013. Structuration theory's relevance to HRD: A review and application. *Human Resource Development Review* 12:200–220. https://doi.org/10.1177/1534484312461636.

Venkatesh, V., and F. D. Davis. 2000. Theoretical extension of the Technology Acceptance Model: Four longitudinal field studies. *Management Science* 46 (2): 186–204. https://doi.org/10.1287/mnsc.46.2.186.11926.

Venkatesh, V., M. Morris, G. Davis, and F. Davis. 2003. User acceptance of information technology: Towards a unified view. *MIS Quarterly* 27 (3): 479–501.

Verma, G., and S. Yadav. 2025. Blockchain for management of healthcare data. In *Blockchain and digital twin for smart healthcare*, 419–437. https://doi.org/10.1016/B978-0-443-30300-5.00023-3.

Vieira, E. S., and J. A. N. F. Gomes. 2009. A comparison of Scopus and Web of science for a typical university. *Scientometrics* 81 (2): 587–600. Available at:. https://doi.org/10.1007/s11192009-2178-0.

Vinther Daugaard, T., J. Bisgaard Jensen, R. J. Kauffman, and K. Kim. 2024. Blockchain solutions with consensus algorithms and immediate finality: Toward Panopticon-style monitoring to enhance anti-money laundering. *Electronic Commerce Research and Applications* 65. https://doi.org/10.1016/J.ELERAP.2024.101386.

Vodáček, L., and O. Vodáčková. 1996. Management—Theory and practices for the 1990s.

Voshmgir, S. 2020. What is a dApp? Decentralized application on the blockchain. https://blockchainhub.net/decentralized-applications-dapps/. Accessed 15 January 2022.

Vranken, H. 2017. Sustainability of bitcoin and blockchains. *Current Opinion in Environmental Sustainability* 28:1–9.

Walker, A. 1989. *Project management in construction*. 2nd ed. Oxford: BSP Professional Books.

Walker, J. 2004. Qualitative research in nursing, 2nd edition. *Nurse Education Today* 24 (2): 155–156. https://doi.org/10.1016/J.NEDT.2003.12.006.

Walport. 2015. *Distributed ledger technology: Beyond blockchain*. Government Office for Science. http://www.ameda.org.eg/files/gs-16-1-distributed-ledger-technology.pdf. Accessed 18 December 2019.

Walster, D. 2011. Applications of social research methods to questions in library and information science, Barbara M. Wildemuth (Ed.), Westport, CT, Libraries Unlimited (2009), 421 pp. $50 (pbk), ISBN: 978-1591585039. *Library & Information Science Research* 33 (1): 98–99. https://doi.org/10.1016/J.LISR.2010.09.001.

Wang, C. C., and P. Jim. 2012. A review on document and information management in the construction industry: From paper-based documents to BIM-based approach. In *Proceedings of 2012 international conference on construction & real estate management, October 2012*, 369–373.

Wang, R., and Y. Tai. 2025. How does blockchain mitigate false advertising in live streaming E-commerce? A tripartite stochastic evolutionary game approach. *Journal of Retailing and Consumer Services* 85:104287. https://doi.org/10.1016/J.JRETCONSER.2025.104287.

Wang, J., and H. Wang. 2019. Monoxide: Scale out blockchain with asynchronous consensus zones. In *Proceedings of the 16th USENIX symposium on networked systems design and implementation, NSDI2019*, 95–112.

Wang, Y. (Yoka), and W. Wang. 2023. Book review. *System* 112: 102968. https://doi.org/10.1016/J.SYSTEM.2022.102968.

Wang, M., and X. Yin. 2022. Construction and maintenance of urban underground infrastructure with digital technologies. *Automation in Construction* 141. https://doi.org/10.1016/J.AUTCON.2022.104464.

Wang, H., K. Chen, and D. Xu. 2016. A maturity model for blockchain adoption. *Financial Innovation* 2 (1): https://doi.org/10.1186/s40854-016-0031-z.

Wang, J., P. Wu, X. Wang, and W. Shou. 2017. The outlook of blockchain technology for construction engineering management Frontiers of. *Engineering Management* 4 (1): 67. https://doi.org/10.15302/j-fem-2017006.

Wang, T., P. Cheng, and L. Zhen. 2023. Green development of the maritime industry: Overview, perspectives, and future research opportunities. *Transportation Research Part E: Logistics and Transportation Review* 179. https://doi.org/10.1016/J.TRE.2023.103322.

Wang, Q., Y. Ding, J. Liu, and Y. Huang. 2024a. Blockchain mania: A perspective on corporate executive opportunism. *Borsa Istanbul Review* 24 (2): 424–434. https://doi.org/10.1016/J.BIR.2024.02.003.

Wang, X., Y. Pan, and J. Chen. 2024b. Digital twin with data-mechanism-fused model for smart excavation management. *Automation in Construction* 168. https://doi.org/10.1016/J.AUTCON.2024.105749.

Wang, X., H. Yu, W. McGee, C. C. Menassa, and V. R. Kamat. 2024c. Enabling Building Information Model-driven human-robot collaborative construction workflows with closed-loop digital twins. *Computers in Industry* 161. https://doi.org/10.1016/J.COMPIND.2024.104112.

Wang, F., Q. Ye, J. Li, and W. Shi. 2025a. Blockchain adoption and analyst forecast accuracy. *Research in International Business and Finance* 73:102593. https://doi.org/10.1016/J.RIBAF.2024.102593.

Wang, T., Z. Liu, L. Wang, M. Li, and X. V. Wang. 2025b. A design framework for high-fidelity human-centric digital twin of collaborative work cell in Industry 5.0. *Journal of Manufacturing Systems* 80:140–156. https://doi.org/10.1016/J.JMSY.2025.02.018.

Wanjau, K. N., B. W. Muiruri, and E. Ayodo. 2012. Factors affecting provision of service quality in the public health sector: A case of Kenyatta national hospital. *International Journal of Humanities and Social Science* 2 (13): 14–29.

Waqar, A., Andri, A. H. Qureshi, H. R. Almujibah, L. E. Tanjung, and C. Utami. 2023. Evaluation of success factors of utilizing AI in digital transformation of health and safety management systems in modern construction projects. *Ain Shams Engineering Journal* 14 (11): https://doi.org/10.1016/J.ASEJ.2023.102551.

Waqar, A., A. Mateen Khan, and I. Othman. 2024. Blockchain empowerment in construction supply chains: Enhancing efficiency and sustainability for an infrastructure development. *Journal of Infrastructure Intelligence and Resilience* 3 (1): https://doi.org/10.1016/J.IINTEL.2023.100065.

Watanabe, H., S. Fujimura, A. Nakadaira, Y. Miyazaki, A. Akutsu, and J. J. Kishigami. 2016. Blockchain contract: A complete consensus using blockchain. In *2015 IEEE 4th global conference on consumer electronics, GCCE 2015, (July 2018)*, 577–578. https://doi.org/10.1109/GCCE.2015.7398721.

Watson, K. 1997. Qualitative educational research in developing countries. Current perspectives. *International Journal of Educational Development* 17 (4): 474–475. https://doi.org/10.1016/S0738-0593(97)82320-6.

Webb, C. 1992. Qualitative nursing research. *Nurse Education Today* 12 (2): 158–159. https://doi.org/10.1016/0260-6917(92)90052-P.

Weill, P., and J. W. Ross. 2004. *IT governance: How top performers manage IT decision rights for superior results*. Harvard Business Press.

White, G. 2013. A survival guide for health research methods. *Nurse Education in Practice* 13 (6): e30. https://doi.org/10.1016/J.NEPR.2013.04.002.

Wiener, J. B. 2004. The regulation of technology, and the technology of regulation. *Technology in Society* 26 (2–3): 483–500.

Wiles, J. 2011. Reasoning, robots, and navigation: Dual roles for deductive and abductive reasoning. *Behavioral and Brain Sciences* 34 (2): 45–92.

Williams, C. 2018. *Principles of management*. 10th ed. Boston: Cengage Learning.

Williamson, K. 2006. The Sage handbook of qualitative research, 2nd ed. Edited by Norman K. Denzin, and Yvonna S. Lincoln. Thousands Oaks, CA: Sage, 2005. 1210 pp. 130.00 (hardcover). ISBN 0-7619-2757-3. *Library* 28 (3): 467–468. https://doi.org/10.1016/J.LISR.2006.05.004.

Winch, G. M. 2010. *Managing construction projects*. 2nd ed. London: Wiley-Blackwell.

Winkler, T.J., 2012. Information technology governance and innovation adoption in varying organizational contexts: Mobile government and software as a service. Doctoral dissertation submitted to Humboldt Universität zu Berlin, Wirtschaftswissenschaftliche Fakultät.

Wirth, S., and J. Markard. 2011. Context matters: How existing sectors and competing technologies affect the prospects of the Swiss Bio-SNG innovation system. *Technological Forecasting and Social Change* 78 (4): 635–649.

Wisdom, J. P., K. H. B. Chor, K. E. Hoagwood, and S. M. Horwitz. 2014. Innovation adoption: A review of theories and constructs. *Administration and Policy in Mental Health and Mental Health Services Research* 41 (4): 480–502.

Wohrer, M., and U. Zdun. 2018. Smart contracts: Security patterns in the ethereum ecosystem and solidity. In *2018 IEEE 1st international workshop on blockchain oriented software engineering, IWBOSE 2018—Proceedings*, 2–8. Institute of Electrical and Electronics Engineers. https://doi.org/10.1109/IWBOSE.2018.8327565.

Wong, P. S. P. 2011. Structural equation modelling of trust and patterning successes. *Journal of Management in Engineering* 21 (2): 70–80.

Wood, G. 2014. Ethereum: A secure decentralised generalised transaction ledger, Ethereum project yellow paper.

Wörner, D., T. Von Bomhard, Y. P. Schreier, and D. Bilgeri. 2016. The bitcoin ecosystem: Disruption beyond financial services? In *24th European conference on information systems, ECIS 2016*.

Wu, A. 2023. A comprehensive approach for the evaluation of the impact of blockchain on photovoltaic supply chain using hybrid data analytic method. *Optik* 291. https://doi.org/10.1016/J.IJLEO.2023.171361.

Wu, L., and C. H. Chuang. 2009. Analyzing contextual antecedents for the stage-based diffusion of electronic supply chain management. *Electronic Commerce Research and Applications* 8 (6): 302–314.

Wu, J., and N. Tran. 2018. Application of blockchain technology in sustainable energy systems: An overview. *Sustainability* 10 (9): 30–67.

Wu, L., X. Du, W. Wang, and B. Lin. 2017. An out-of-band authentication scheme for Internet of Things using blockchain technology. In *Proceeding of international conference of computing, networking and communication (ICNC)*, 769–773.

Wu, K., Y. Ma, G. Huang, and X. Liu. 2021. A first look at blockchain-based decentralized applications. *Software—Practice and Experience* 51 (10): 2033–2050. https://doi.org/10.1002/spe.2751.

Wuni, I. Y., D. A. Abankwa, K. Koc, S. E. Adukpo, and M. F. Antwi-Afari. 2024. Critical barriers to the adoption of integrated digital delivery in the construction industry. *Journal of Building Engineering* 83. https://doi.org/10.1016/J.JOBE.2024.108474.

Xia, J. 2014. Book review. *Telecommunications Policy* 38 (7): 653–657. https://doi.org/10.1016/J.TELPOL.2013.08.002.

Xiao, J., S. Ma, S. Wang, and G. Q. Huang. 2024. Fine-grained digital twin sharing framework for smart construction through an incentive mechanism. *International Journal of Production Economics* 276. https://doi.org/10.1016/J.IJPE.2024.109382.

Xie, J. 2020. Book review. *System* 89:102217. https://doi.org/10.1016/J.SYSTEM.2020.102217.

Xing, P., and M. Wang. 2025. The interplay of recycling channel selection and blockchain adoption in the new energy vehicle supply chain under the government reward-penalty scheme. *Journal of Cleaner Production* 487. https://doi.org/10.1016/J.JCLEPRO.2024.144384.

Xu, Y., H. Y. Chong, and M. Chi. 2022. Blockchain in the AECO industry: Current status, key topics, and future research agenda. *Automation in Construction* 134. https://doi.org/10.1016/J.AUTCON.2021.104101.

Xu, L., Y. Zou, Y. Lu, and A. Chang-Richards. 2025a. Automation in manufacturing and assembly of industrialised construction. *Automation in Construction* 170. https://doi.org/10.1016/J.AUTCON.2024.105945.

Xu, Q., Z. Lei, S. Gu, G. Wen, Y. Su, Z. Zhang, J. Huang, and R. Qin. 2025b. Digital twin-driven operational CycleGAN-based multiple virtual-physical mappings for remaining useful life prediction under limited life cycle data. *Journal of Advanced Research*. https://doi.org/10.1016/J.JARE.2025.02.029.

Xue, X., R. Zhang, R. Yang, and J. Dai. 2014. Innovation in construction: A critical review and future research. *International Journal of Innovation Science* 6 (2): 111–125. https://doi.org/10.1260/1757-2223.6.2.111.

Xue, J., G. Li, and D. Ivanov. 2025. Digital transformation in the blockchain era: Balancing efficiency and resilience in operations management. *International Journal of Production Economics* 282. https://doi.org/10.1016/J.IJPE.2025.109525.

Yakubu, M. N., and S. I. Dasuki. 2018. Assessing eLearning systems success in Nigeria: An application of the DeLone and McLean information systems success model. *Journal of Information Technology Education Research* 17:182–202. https://doi.org/10.28945/4077.

Yan, H., M. Ma, Y. Wu, H. Fan, and C. Dong. 2022. Overview and analysis of the text mining applications in the construction industry. *Heliyon* 8 (12): https://doi.org/10.1016/J.HELIYON.2022.E12088.

Yan, Z., X. Zhao, Y. Liu (Alison), and X. Luo (Robert). 2024. Blockchain-driven decentralized identity management: An interdisciplinary review and research agenda. *Information and Management* 61(7). https://doi.org/10.1016/J.IM.2024.104026.

Yan, J., Q. Gui, S. Jiang, Z. Yu, K. Fernandes, K. Tian, S. Xia, and Y. Gong. 2025. How does blockchain application impact on supply chain alliance? *Technovation* 143. https://doi.org/10.1016/J.TECHNOVATION.2025.103199.

Yang, L. 2023. Manuscript title: Digital management method of municipal infrastructure engineering construction. In *Proceedings of the institution of civil engineers: Smart infrastructure and construction*. https://doi.org/10.1680/JSMIC.22.00038.

Yang, Z., and Q. Liu. 2007. Research and development of web-based virtual online classroom. *Computers & Education* 48 (2): 171–184.

Yang, R., R. Wakefield, S. Lyu, S. Jayasuriya, F. Han, X. Yi, X. Yang, G. Amarasinghe, and S. Chen. 2020. Public and private blockchain in construction business process and information integration. *Automation in Construction* 118:103276. https://doi.org/10.1016/j.autcon.2020.103276.

Yang, Y., S. Zhang, Y. Hua, and H. Wang. 2025. Mapping the digital transformation of AEC industry: Content analysis of digital public policy in China. *Developments in the Built Environment* 21. https://doi.org/10.1016/J.DIBE.2025.100621.

Yao, D., and B. García de Soto. 2024. Enhancing cyber risk identification in the construction industry using language models. *Automation in Construction* 165. https://doi.org/10.1016/J.AUTCON.2024.105565.

Ye, X., and M. Konig. 2021. Framework for automated billing in the construction industry using BIM and smart contracts. *Lecture Notes in Civil Engineering* 98:824–838. https://doi.org/10.1007/978-3-030-51295-8_57.

Ye, Z., M. Yin, L. Tang, and H. Jiang. 2018. Cup-of-water theory: A review on the interaction of BIM, IoT and blockchain during the whole building lifecycle. In *ISARC 2018—35th international symposium on automation and robotics in construction and international AEC/FM Hackathon: The future of building things (ISARC)*. https://doi.org/10.22260/isarc2018/0066.

Yermack, D. 2017. *Corporate governance and blockchains review of finance* 21 (1): 7–31. https://doi.org/10.1093/rof/rfw074.

Yi, K., Z. Zhou, Y. Wu, Q. Zhang, and X. Li. 2023. Empathic connectivity of exhibition technology and users in the digital Transformation: An integrated method of social network analysis and LDA model. *Advanced Engineering Informatics* 56. https://doi.org/10.1016/J.AEI.2023.102019.

Yilmaz, G., L. Salter, D. McFarlane, and B. Schönfuß. 2023. Low-cost (Shoestring) digital solution areas for enabling digitalisation in construction SMEs. *Computers in Industry* 150. https://doi.org/10.1016/J.COMPIND.2023.103941.

Yin, R. 2009. *Case study research: Design and methods*. Thousand Oaks, CA: Sage Publications.

Yli-Huumo, J., D. Ko, S. Choi, S. Park, and K. Smolander. 2016. Where is current research on blockchain technology?—A systematic review. *PLoS One* 11 (10): 1–27.

Yoo, G. S., and K. H. Kim. 2018. *Blockchain*. Seoul, Korea: Korea Institute of S&T Evaluation and Planning.

Yoo, Y., R. J. Boland Jr., K. Lyytinen, and A. Majchrzak. 2012. Organizing for innovation in the digitized world. *Organization Science* 23 (5): 1398–1408. https://doi.org/10.1287/orsc.1120.0771.

Yousefi, S., M. R. Khodoomi, and B. M. Tosarkani. 2025. Data-driven robust strategic sourcing considering supply-side competition: Insights into blockchain adoption for coordination. *Transportation Research Part E: Logistics and Transportation Review* 197. https://doi.org/10.1016/J.TRE.2025.103977.

Yu, H., B. Wen, I. Zahidi, C. M. Fai, and D. Ø. Madsen. 2024. Constructing the future: Policy-driven digital fabrication in China's urban development. *Results in Engineering* 22. https://doi.org/10.1016/J.RINENG.2024.102096.

Yuan, M., A. Ekici, Z. Lu, and R. Monteiro. 2007. Dimension reduction and coefficient estimation in multivariate linear regression. *Journal of the Royal Statistical Society: Series B (Statistical Methodology)* 69 (3): 329–346.

Yun, J., G. Li, D. Jiang, M. Xu, F. Xiang, L. Huang, G. Jiang, X. Liu, Y. Xie, B. Tao, and Z. Fang. 2023. Digital twin model construction of robot and multi-object under stacking environment for grasping planning. *Applied Soft Computing* 149. https://doi.org/10.1016/J.ASOC.2023.111005.

Zachariah, M., N. M. Avanesh, and K. Raghupathi. 2025. Application of blockchain technology in disaster risk management. In *The role of blockchain in disaster management*, 87–110. https://doi.org/10.1016/B978-0-443-13472-2.00004-8.

Zack, M. 1999. Managing codified knowledge. *Sloan Management Review* 40:45–58.

Zafir, E. I., A. Akter, M. N. Islam, S. A. Hasib, T. Islam, S. K. Sarker, and S. M. Muyeen. 2024. Enhancing security of Internet of Robotic Things: A review of recent trends, practices, and recommendations with encryption and blockchain techniques. *Internet of Things (Netherlands)* 28. https://doi.org/10.1016/J.IOT.2024.101357.

Zarbà, C., G. Chinnici, A. Matarazzo, D. Privitera, and A. Scuderi. 2024. The innovative role of blockchain in agri-food systems: A literature analysis. *Food Control* 164. https://doi.org/10.1016/J.FOODCONT.2024.110603.

Zavery, A. 2020. *Digital transformation isn't a project, it's a way of operating*. Forbes. https://www.forbes.com/sites/googlecloud/2020/01/22/digital-transformation-isnt-a-project-its-a-way-of-operating. Accessed 11 February 2022.

Zboinska, M. A., and F. Göbel. 2025. Digital tool integrations for architectural reuse of salvaged building materials. *Automation in Construction* 170. https://doi.org/10.1016/J.AUTCON.2024.105947.

Zech, P., S. Hammes, E. Goldin, D. Geisler-Moroder, R. Breu, and R. Pfluger. 2025. From BIM to Digital Twin: A transformation process through advanced control modeling and automated commissioning using daylight and artificial lighting as examples. *Energy and Buildings* 329. https://doi.org/10.1016/J.ENBUILD.2024.115184.

Zeng, C., T. Hartmann, and L. Ma. 2024. ConSE: An ontology for visual representation and semantic enrichment of digital images in construction sites. *Advanced Engineering Informatics* 60. https://doi.org/10.1016/J.AEI.2024.102446.

Zhang, L. 2022. Book review. *System* 110:102903. https://doi.org/10.1016/J.SYSTEM.2022.102903.

Zhang, Y. 2023. Book Review. *English for Specific Purposes* 69:48–50. https://doi.org/10.1016/J.ESP.2022.09.004.

Zhang, X., P. Yu, J. Yan, and I. A. M. Spil. 2015. Using diffusion of innovation theory to understand the factors impacting patient acceptance and use of consumer e-health innovations: A case study in a primary care clinic. *BMC Health Services Research* 15:71–84.

Zhang, D., Z. Liu, F. Li, Y. Zhao, C. Zhang, X. Li, and Y. Zhang. 2023a. The rapid construction method of the digital twin polymorphic model for discrete manufacturing workshop. *Robotics and Computer-Integrated Manufacturing* 84. https://doi.org/10.1016/J.RCIM.2023.102600.

Zhang, J., M. Chen, P. Ballesteros-Pérez, Y. Ke, Z. Gong, and Q. Ni. 2023b. A new framework to evaluate and optimize digital transformation policies in the construction industry: A China case study. *Journal of Building Engineering* 70. https://doi.org/10.1016/J.JOBE.2023.106388.

Zhang, J., M. Zhang, P. Ballesteros-Pérez, and S. P. Philbin. 2023c. A new perspective to evaluate the antecedent path of adoption of digital technologies in major projects of construction industry: A case study in China. *Developments in the Built Environment* 14. https://doi.org/10.1016/J.DIBE.2023.100160.

Zhang, A., J. Wang, Y. Zhang, and G. Shangguan. 2024a. Joint detection PCD-based method for automatic construction of geometric digital twin in cable dome structure. *Engineering Structures* 320. https://doi.org/10.1016/J.ENGSTRUCT.2024.118908.

Zhang, X., Y. Yang, X. Zhang, Y. Hu, H. Wu, M. Li, H. Handroos, H. Wang, and B. Wu. 2024b. A multi-level digital twin construction method of assembly line based on hybrid worker digital twin models. *Advanced Engineering Informatics* 62. https://doi.org/10.1016/J.AEI.2024.102597.

Zhang, Y., M. M. Tavalaei, G. Parry, and P. Zhou. 2024c. Evolution or involution? A systematic literature review of organisations' blockchain adoption factors. *Technological Forecasting and Social Change* 208. https://doi.org/10.1016/J.TECHFORE.2024.123710.

Zhang, Y., V. K. Gupta, K. Karimi, Y. Wang, M. A. Yusoff, H. Vatanparast, J. Pan, M. Aghbashlo, M. Tabatabaei, and A. Rajaei. 2025. Synergizing blockchain and internet of things for enhancing efficiency and waste reduction in sustainable food management. *Trends in Food Science and Technology* 156: 104873. https://doi.org/10.1016/J.TIFS.2025.104873.

Zhao, G., S. Liu, C. Lopez, H. Lu, S. Elgueta, H. Chen, and B. M. Boshkoska. 2019. Blockchain technology in agri-food value chain management: A synthesis of applications, challenges and future research directions. *Computers in Industry* 109:83–99. https://doi.org/10.1016/j.compind.2019.04.002.

Zhao, R., Z. Chen, and F. Xue. 2023. A blockchain 3.0 paradigm for digital twins in construction project management. *Automation in Construction* 145. https://doi.org/10.1016/J.AUTCON.2022.104645.

Zheng, S., and C. Jiang. 2024. Consortium blockchain in Shipping: Impacts on industry and social welfare. *Transportation Research Part A: Policy and Practice* 183. https://doi.org/10.1016/J.TRA.2024.104071.

Zheng, Z., S. Xie, H. Dai, X. Chen, and H. Wang. 2017. An overview of blockchain technology: Architecture, consensus, and future trends. In *Proceedings of the 2017 IEEE big data congress, Honolulu, Hawaii, USA*, 557–564.

Zhou, K. Z., and F. Wu. 2010. Technological capability, strategic flexibility, and product innovation. *Strategic Management Journal* 31 (5): 547–561.

Zhou, X., X. Li, Y. Zhu, and C. Ma. 2025. Towards building digital twin: A computer vision enabled approach jointly using multi-camera and building information model. *Energy and Buildings* 335. https://doi.org/10.1016/J.ENBUILD.2025.115523.

Zhu, Y., and R. R. A. Issa. 2003. Viewer controllable visualization for construction document processing. *Automation in Construction* 12 (3): 255–269. https://doi.org/10.1016/S0926-5805(02)00089-4.

Zhu, X., Y. Badr, J. Pacheco, and S. Hariri. 2017. Autonomic identity framework for the internet of things. In *Proceedings—2017 IEEE international conference on cloud and autonomic computing, ICCAC 2017*, 69–79. https://doi.org/10.1109/ICCAC.2017.14.

Zhuang, Y. 2025. Blockchain technology in clinical trials. In *Blockchain and digital twin for smart healthcare*, 229–249. https://doi.org/10.1016/B978-0-443-30300-5.00015-4.

Zineb, K. I., L. Mohamed, H. Hamid, Y. Meryem, L. Ghita, and H. Hanae. 2024. BlockSupply: Blockchain-based logistics traceability solution. *Software Impacts* 21. https://doi.org/10.1016/J.SIMPA.2024.100666.

Zou, Y. 2024. Book review. *English for Specific Purposes* 76:136–138. https://doi.org/10.1016/J.ESP.2024.08.003.

MIX
Papier aus verantwortungsvollen Quellen
Paper from responsible sources
FSC® C105338

If you have any concerns about our products,
you can contact us on
ProductSafety@springernature.com

In case Publisher is established outside the EU,
the EU authorized representative is:
Springer Nature Customer Service Center GmbH
Europaplatz 3, 69115 Heidelberg, Germany

Printed by Libri Plureos GmbH
in Hamburg, Germany